READINGS IN
SOCIOLOGY

ABOUT THE EDITOR

Alfred McClung Lee received his B.A. and M.A. degrees from the University of Pittsburgh and his Ph.D. degree from Yale University. He has been on the faculties of Yale University, the University of Kansas, New York University, Wayne University, the University of Michigan, and Brooklyn College, where he has been Chairman of the Department of Sociology and Anthropology since 1950. Professor Lee organized and served as second president of the Society for the Study of Social Problems. He has also been president of the Michigan and the Eastern Sociological Societies. He is regarded as a leading national authority on public opinion, propaganda analysis, and mass communications. In addition to numerous articles in professional journals here and abroad, his published works include *The Daily Newspaper in America, The Fine Art of Propaganda* (coauthor), *Race Riot* (coauthor), *Social Problems in America* (coauthor), *How to Understand Propaganda, Public Opinion and Propaganda* (coeditor, coauthor), *Fraternities Without Brotherhood,* and a companion College Outline, *Principles of Sociology* (editor, coauthor).

COLLEGE OUTLINE SERIES

READINGS IN SOCIOLOGY

EDITED BY
ALFRED McCLUNG LEE

BARNES & NOBLE, INC.   NEW YORK

Publishers · Booksellers · Since 1873

ACKNOWLEDGMENTS

FIFTY-SIX social scientists—almost all sociologists—wrote the fifty selections in this book. I am therefore primarily indebted to the co-authors in this venture and to the editors and publishers who granted permission to reprint these materials.

In selecting readings for this volume, I have been guided in part by recollections of students' reactions to these and other assigned writings. Consequently, to students in my introductory sociology classes since 1935 I wish to express special gratitude.

Colleagues in the Department of Sociology and Anthropology at Brooklyn College contributed many helpful suggestions.

Dr. Samuel Smith, Editor, and Mrs. Carol Ann Luten, of the Editorial Department, Barnes and Noble, Inc., have done much to encourage me in this project and to help bring it to completion.

As always, my wife, Dr. Elizabeth Briant Lee, of the Hartford Seminary Foundation, has aided generously, especially with her sympathetic understanding.

A. McC. L.

CONTENTS

Section Three

HUMAN ECOLOGY

Section Four

RACE

Section Five

INTERGROUP RELATIONS

Section Eight

INSTITUTIONS

Section Nine

SOCIOLOGY IN SOCIAL POLICY

INTRODUCTION

CHARACTERIZATIONS of science emphasize many aspects of the work of scientists. Some stress measurement, semantics, teamwork, contributions to a theoretical system, or logic. Others speak of special training, discipline, or physical equipment. In their own statements about their work, many outstanding scientists subordinate such specifics to what might be called the scientific mood or attitude. This is an attitude dominated by curiosity and patient observation, efforts at conceptualization, and then re-observation.

When Albert Einstein viewed from the perspective of seventy years his own early struggles to become a productive physical scientist, he observed, "It is, in fact, nothing short of a miracle that the modern methods of instruction have not yet entirely strangled the holy curiosity of inquiry; for this delicate little plant, aside from stimulation, stands mainly in need of freedom; without this it goes to wrack and ruin without fail."[1]

The curiosity of a scientist places him in a position marginal to or even outside of established views concerning his specialty. If his specialty is the study of a geological formation, for example, his deviance from prevailing beliefs on that subject is no longer fraught with much personal danger. If his specialty is the study of some aspect of human relationships, however, his deviance may place him at odds with powerful vested authorities—political, economic, ecclesiastical, and familial. In view of Einstein's testimony concerning the inhibition of curiosity in physical science, a relatively secure field, it is little wonder that curiosity in social science constantly confronts suspicion and suppression from representatives of societal interests. One can still say about our knowledge of human relationships what Francis Bacon concluded about all human knowledge more than three centuries ago in his *Novum Organum* (1620): "No one has yet been found so firm of mind and purpose as resolutely to compel himself to sweep away all theories and common notions, and to apply the understanding, thus made fair and even, to a fresh examination of

[1] "Notes for an Autobiography," *Saturday Review of Literature*, XXXII, No. 48 (November 26, 1949), 9–12, 36, 38–44; p. 11 quoted.

particulars. Thus it happens that human knowledge, as we have it, is a mere medley and ill-digested mass, made up of much credulity and much accident, and also of the childish notions which we at first imbibed." [2]

The sociologist is thus in a very tenuous position. On his subject, honored traditions have much to say, cast in the hallowed generalities of a given culture. He is constantly tempted to abandon his individualistic course of observing and reporting conceptually various characteristics of society and of human relationships complacently ignored by his less observant and less inquisitive fellows. He is offered many rewards to forget about scientific inquiry and to become a plausible rationalizer of the status quo. He would then be in demand as an after-dinner speaker or as an adviser to managerial manipulators of personnel or of publics. For all the American delight in the mechanical novelties made possible by "science," the sociologist is still assured of a stunted career, if not disgrace or the social label of failure, should he succeed too well in replacing folklore with more accurate descriptions of human relationships and behavior. This is especially true in the areas touching most significantly the control and manipulation of social power. It is thus easy to understand why we still, as a wise sociologist has pointed out, "depend upon three sorts of lying prophets for our interpretations of social institutions: upon men of affairs, who lie like Ananias in their own interest, or lie as advocates do to prove their cases; upon literary men, who lie like Baron Munchausen, primarily to amuse, or from sheer lack of mental discipline; and upon scholars, who lie at second hand by quoting something somebody else has said that is not so." [3] The scientific attitude can produce through sociology and the more specialized social sciences the satisfactory alternative to these three kinds of perennial lying, but, as Einstein has insisted, it "stands mainly in need of freedom." This freedom must be fought for. It cannot be bought with careerist compromises and ideological oversimplifications.

In the selections of this volume, an effort is made to present something of the drama of the scientific sociologist at work and to indicate some of the major problems of observation and of conceptualization

---

[2] *The Works of Francis Bacon,* col., ed., and transl. by J. Spedding, R. L. Ellis, and D. D. Heath (Boston, 1863), VIII, Sec. xcvii.

[3] Willard Waller, "Insight and Scientific Method," *The American Journal of Sociology,* XL (1934–35), 285–297; p. 297 quoted.

with which he is attempting to cope. These nine groups of papers might be called episodes from sociology; they provide stimulating and challenging supplements to any standard introductory text in the field or to the present editor's companion book in the "College Outline Series": *New Outline of the Principles of Sociology*. Many of the readings have been drawn from reports on field studies. Some present statements by certain "old masters" on controversial aspects of sociological theory; they also furnish contrasting interpretations, in a number of cases, of fundamental issues as to the values which a scientist should seek to maintain and serve. A few deal, either specifically or generally, with problems and techniques in the application of sociological knowledge.

Let us look briefly at the contents of the nine sections of the text to see how the readings fit together.

Section I (Readings 1–7)—The Scientific Study of Human Relations. Auguste Comte (1798–1857) introduced the term "sociology," but Herbert Spencer published in 1873 the book first used as a college text in the subject, and William Graham Sumner organized the first class in sociology in the world at Yale University to study that text as it appeared in installment form. Our opening selection, Sumner's trenchant outline of the main purpose of sociological study, applies as well to the mid-twentieth century as to 1882. It is followed by Spencer's warning against the subtleties of class-bias in distorting thought—a warning just as appropriate today as in 1873. Robert E. Park and Ernest W. Burgess, in the next selection (taken from their very influential text), offer a classification of the types of problems sociologists should attempt to study.

In Readings 4–7, Willard Waller, William F. Ogburn, F. Stuart Chapin, and Robert K. Merton bring us face to face with theoretical and practical problems in the investigation of contemporary human relationships. Both Waller and Ogburn urge the goals of broadening our knowledge about society and making such knowledge more precise. Both relegate methodological devices—whether statistical or other types—to a significant, useful, but secondary role in sociology. Chapin discusses the kinds of experimental method available to sociologists. Merton analyzes the relations between fact-gathering and the modification of sociological theory.

Sections II–VIII (Readings 8–46) deal with five major perspectives upon society. These perspectives, which overlap somewhat in the various selections, are as follows:

1. The socialization of the individual (Section II).
2. The distribution and redistribution of human beings over the world—the ecological point of view (Section III).
3. Man as a biological creature (Section IV).
4. Group behavior (Sections V, VI, VII).
5. Societal structure (Sections VI, VII, VIII).

Each Section differs from the others in its emphasis on a particular perspective which, however, also appears to a lesser degree in other Sections. The Readings in all nine Sections are, in fact, closely inter-related.

Section II (Readings 8–17)—Socialization of the Individual. In the first Reading, which emphasizes stages in the physiological maturation of the child, Gesell summarizes aspects of his famous studies and attempts to relate them to societal factors. The discussion by Cooley, Angell, and Carr amplifies the primary-group conception which is associated with the name of the senior author, Cooley. Thomas then describes how group dynamics define the situation for group members and hence influence individual thought and behavior. Loomis translates and interprets Tönnies' distinction between community (*Gemeinschaft*) and society (*Gesellschaft*) in terms that can be related to Thomas' "definition of the situation."

In Readings 12–17, Mead, Parsons, Waller, and Folsom concern themselves especially with the relations of the individual to culture and to specific institutional controls. Mead theorizes about the internalization of traditional patterns of usage and morality in the minds of individuals. Parsons, in the manner of a student of a primitive tribe, sets forth the structure of the American family as he has observed it. Waller carefully reports and analyzes, with many keen and wise insights, the general characteristics of that most important socializing agency outside of the home, the school. Folsom considers the impacts upon American sex patterns of the notable Kinsey report on male sexual behavior. Elliott and Dollard treat behavior which is ordinarily thought to be deviant, to be that of biologically different or inadequately socialized people. Elliott does this through a critical reconsideration of theories of delinquency and crime. Dollard does it through the presentation of certain hypotheses based upon his first-hand studies of patients in psychiatric hospitals. From these Readings by Elliott and Dollard, one gathers that there are no categories of people clearly labeled criminal and neurotic or even psychotic.

Section III (Readings 18–21)—Human Ecology. In this Section, Wirth analyzes the contributions of human ecology to sociology and the limitations of this approach. Davie and Koenig outline problems in one ecological area, those of the refugees to the United States. Whelpton recounts briefly the characteristics of past and present internal migrations in this country. Finally, Odum interprets the significance of his theory of a regional balance of man and culture.

Section IV (Readings 22, 23)—Race. Foreign and domestic bigots and unscrupulous power-seekers have seized upon misconceptions of race as a means of glorifying some groups and of scapegoating or even destroying others. Reuter's essay shows how the perspective on racial differences has gradually changed and how the emphasis has turned more and more away from the biological and toward the cultural in the understanding of intergroup differences. Haring's discussion brings together what is known scientifically about contemporary human racial types and explains why we can speak accurately of only one human race.

Section V (Readings 24–28)—Intergroup Relations. Even though human beings are recognized as ranging biologically through many mixed types within one human race, with quite a few examples to meet the hypothetical criteria of "pure" types, tensions between ethnic and "racial" groups continue as one of our most serious social problems. To begin this Section, Aginsky reports the reaction of an American Indian to the acceptance of European-American culture traits in his tribe. Levinson, upon the basis of detailed personality studies, formulates a more precise and useful theory of ethnocentrism than the theories which have been current. Frazier sketches the changing character of Negro life in the United States. Handlin discusses the organization-making proclivities of various ethnic groups and the social significance of such tendencies. Young, upon the basis of sociological studies extending over two decades, diagnoses the problems of intergroup tension and prescribes techniques for coping with them.

Section VI (Readings 29–31)—Social Class. Despite traditional claims of the United States and the Soviet Union to classlessness, sociologists cannot take either claim seriously. Determined by access or lack of access to the control of social power, techniques, and resources, more or less well-defined social classes exist in all societies of any appreciable size. Warner and his associates describe the pattern of social class in the United States as they have observed it in a number of American communities. Mosca, upon the basis of historical evidence, offers theories about class circulation in changing societies. Sorokin discusses the nature and causes of vertical mobility, the movement of individuals up or down in the class hierarchy.

Section VII (Readings 32–39)—Collective Behavior. The dynamics of group and mass behavior emerge as a more and more significant area for scientific study. In this Section, Park and Burgess set forth their impressive analysis of social process in terms of four major types. Lowenthal and Guterman conclude from their study of American agitators that such potentially dangerous persons exploit social malaise. Heberle makes a contribution toward an integration of the sociology of social movements. Weber suggests reasons for the ineffectuality of efforts to forestall wars through the stimulation of mass support for pacifism.

Social surveys have become an increasingly significant tool in sociological research as the decades of the twentieth century have passed. Studies of public opinion and propaganda have made them of especial importance in the development of a knowledge of collective behavior and particularly of interpersonal- and mass-communication. Parten notes briefly the variety of surveys and polls now undertaken and then adds, in a second selection, a cogent discussion of the sources of error in one type of survey, the pre-election poll. Lee brings together a compact outline of five interrelated ways of analyzing propaganda and its contexts and its effects. Dodson summarizes his wealth of experience with the application of a knowledge of collective behavior to education and social action.

Section VIII (Readings 40–46)—Institutions. In the early development of sociology, special emphasis was given to the evolution of social institutions, a conception eventually stripped of connotations of a mandate of progress "upward and onward." Sumner and Keller, as a result of their vast cross-cultural study of institutions, state the significance of a societal perspective upon such phenomena. MacIver and Page, on the other hand, relate associations—the specific manifestations of institutions—to human groups and personal interests. Von Wiese and Becker theorize about the processes through which behavior becomes institutionalized.

Bendix, Hart, and Lynd discuss aspects of institutional manipulation and of personal relationships within institutional contexts, with special reference to the industrial and business institutions of society. Bendix analyzes critically the literature of industrial sociology. Hart describes the changing institutional situation he found in Windsor, Ontario, and analyzes how the growth of trade unionism there has affected the relative balance of personal and organizational power. Lynd conceptualizes some basic characteristics of power systems.

Hertzler's essay, in contrast to the selections on business and industry, digests research into the nature of religious institutions.

Section IX (Readings 47–50)—Sociology Applied to Social Problems. For whom shall sociologists work? For whom *can* they work and remain scientific? To what extent can and should sociology and sociologists attempt to achieve intellectual autonomy? The clashing views in this Section attempt to pose such questions as these and to suggest some of the possible answers. Lundberg believes that science must be free of value judgments, and he sets forth what he regards as the strengths and weaknesses of a value-free social science in the solution of social problems. Lee points to the dangers inherent in the acceptance of subsidies for research from special interests. Simpson looks upon Lundberg as the champion of the "behaviorist, neo-positivist school of sociology in America" which he calls "deceptive and laden with false promises." Finally, Riemer interprets the relation of sociology to social planning and of social planning to the organization of society.

This book, then, gives the introductory student vivid glimpses of what people can do in sociology when they are under the influence of the scientific mood. The collected papers focus attention upon major problems and controversies. They include samples of field reports. They picture the ambitions and aspirations of sociologists. They provide background to understand the late Russell Gordon Smith's comment to his introductory sociology students in Columbia College: "The scientific seeker after truth realizes that his greatest contribution is not in absolutes but in relatives, that all his skill lies in enlightening the darkness of the path that others after him will tread. We must acquire the intellectual and moral courage to face a world in which nothing is final; in which everything is relative." [4]

Out of such labors are evolving new and more tenable conceptions of man in society. If the possessors of power in our society can be patient with the individualistic and incautious sociologists, the gains to human welfare from sociological research can be thought of as having scarcely started.

[4] *Fugitive Papers of Russell Gordon Smith* (New York: Columbia University Press, 1930), p. 16.

SECTION ONE
The Scientific Study of Human Relations

1 THE SCIENCE OF SOCIOLOGY *

BY WILLIAM GRAHAM SUMNER (1840–1910)
YALE UNIVERSITY

WE HAVE now acquired the method of studying sociology scientifically so as to attain to assured results. We have acquired it none too soon. The need for a science of life in society is urgent, and it is increasing every year. It is a fact which is generally overlooked that the great advance in the sciences and the arts which has taken place during the last century is producing social consequences and giving rise to social problems. We are accustomed to dwell upon the discoveries of science and the development of the arts as simple incidents, complete in themselves, which offer only grounds for congratulation. But the steps which have been won are by no means simple events. Each one has consequences which reach beyond the domain of physical power into social and moral relations, and these effects are multiplied and reproduced by combination with each other. The great discoveries and inventions redistribute population. They reconstruct industries and force new organization of commerce and finance. They bring new employments into existence and render other employments obsolete, while they change the relative value of many others. They overthrow the old order of society, impoverishing some classes and enriching others. They render old political traditions grotesque and ridiculous, and make old maxims of statecraft null and empty. They give old vices of human nature a chance to parade in new masks, so that it demands new skill to detect the same old foes. They produce a kind of social chaos in which contradictory social and economic phenomena appear side by side to bewilder and deceive the student who is not fully armed to deal with them. New interests are brought into existence, and new faiths, ideas, and hopes are engendered in the minds of men. Some of these are doubtless good and sound; others are delusive; in every case a competent criticism is of the first necessity. In the up-

* From a speech at the farewell banquet to Herbert Spencer, held November 9, 1882. Reprinted from *Herbert Spencer on the Americans and the Americans on Herbert Spencer* (New York: D. Appleton & Company, 1883), pp. 35–40; shortened to pp. 36–39.

heaval of society which is going on, classes and groups are thrown against each other in such a way as to produce class hatreds and hostilities. As the old national jealousies, which used to be the lines on which war was waged, lose their distinctness, class jealousies threaten to take their place. Political and social events which occur on one side of the globe now affect the interests of population on the other side of the globe. Forces which come into action in one part of human society rest not until they have reached all human society. The brotherhood of man is coming to be a reality of such distinct and positive character that we find it a practical question of the greatest moment what kind of creatures some of these hitherto neglected brethren are. Secondary and remoter effects of industrial changes, which were formerly dissipated and lost in the delay and friction of communication, are now, by our prompt and delicate mechanism of communication, caught up and transmitted through society.

It is plain that our social science is not on the level of the tasks which are thrown upon it by the vast and sudden changes in the whole mechanism by which man makes the resources of the globe available to satisfy his needs, and by the new ideas which are born of the new aspects which human life bears to our eyes in consequence of the development of science and the arts. Our traditions about the science and art of living are plainly inadequate. They break to pieces in our hands when we try to apply them to the new cases. A man of good faith may come to the conviction sadly, but he must come to the conviction honestly, that the traditional doctrines and explanations of human life are worthless.

A progress which is not symmetrical is not true; that is to say, every branch of human interest must be developed proportionately to all the other branches, else the one which remains in arrears will measure the advance which may be won by the whole. If, then, we cannot produce a science of life in society which is broad enough to solve all the new social problems which are now forced upon us by the development of science and art, we shall find that the achievements of science and art will be overwhelmed by social reactions and convulsions.

We do not lack for attempts of one kind and another to satisfy the need which I have described. Our discussion is in excess of our deliberation, and our deliberation is in excess of our information. Our journals, platforms, pulpits, and parliaments are full of talking and writing about topics of sociology. The only result, however, of all this discussion is to show that there are half a dozen arbitrary codes of morals, a heterogeneous tangle of economic doctrines, a score of religious creeds and ecclesiastical traditions, and a confused jumble of humanitarian and sentimental notions which jostle each other in the brains of the men of this generation. It is astonishing to watch a discussion and to see how a disputant, starting from a given point of view, will run along on one line of thought until he encounters some fragment of another code or doctrine, which he has derived from some other source of education; whereupon he turns at an angle, and goes on in a new course until he finds himself face to face with another of his old prepossessions. What we need are adequate criteria by which to make the necessary tests and classifications, and appropriate canons of procedure, or the adaptation of universal canons to the special tasks of sociology.

Unquestionably it is to the great philosophy which has now been established by such ample induction in the experimental sciences, and which offers to man such new command of all the relations of life, that we must look for the establishment of the guiding lines in the study of sociology. I can see no boundaries to the scope of the philosophy of evolution. That philosophy is sure to embrace all the interests of man on this earth. It will be one of its crowning triumphs to bring light and order into the social problems which are of universal bearing on all mankind.

2 CLASS–BIAS IN THE STUDY OF SOCIOLOGY *

BY HERBERT SPENCER (1820–1903)

M ANY years ago a solicitor, sitting by me at dinner, complained bitterly of the injury which the then lately-established County Courts were doing his profession. He enlarged on the topic in a way implying that he expected me to agree with him in therefore con-

* Reprinted from chap. x, "The Class-Bias," in his *The Study of Sociology* (New York: D. Appleton and Company, 1873), pp. 241–246.

demning them. So incapable was he of going beyond the professional point of view that what he regarded as a grievance he thought I also ought to regard as a grievance—oblivious of the fact that the more economical administration of justice of which his lamentation gave me proof, was to me, not being a lawyer, matter of rejoicing.

The bias thus exemplified is a bias by which nearly all have their opinions warped. Naval officers disclose their unhesitating belief that we are in imminent danger because the cry for more fighting ships and more sailors has not been met to their satisfaction. The debates on the purchase-system proved how strong was the conviction of military men that our national safety depended on the maintenance of an army-organization like that in which they were brought up and had attained their respective ranks. Clerical opposition to the Corn-Laws showed how completely that view which Christian ministers might have been expected to take was shut out by a view more congruous with their interests and alliances. In all class and sub-classes it is the same. Hear the murmurs uttered when, because of the Queen's absence, there is less expenditure in entertainments and the so-called gaieties of the season, and you perceive that London traders think the nation suffers if the consumption of superfluities is checked. Study the pending controversy about co-operative stores *versus* retail shops, and you find the shop-keeping mind possessed by the idea that Society commits a wrong if it deserts shops and goes to stores—is quite unconscious that the present distributing system rightly exists only as a means of economically and conveniently supplying consumers, and must yield to another system if that should prove more economical and convenient. Similarly with other trading bodies, general and special . . .

The class-bias, like the bias of patriotism, is a reflex egoism; and like it has its uses and abuses. As the strong attachments citizens feel for their nation cause that enthusiastic co-operation by which its integrity is maintained in presence of other nations, severally tending to spread and subjugate their neighbours, so the *esprit de corps* more or less manifest in each specialized part of the body politic prompts measures to preserve the integrity of that part in opposition to other parts, all somewhat antagonistic. The egoism of individuals leads to an egoism of the class they form; and besides the separate efforts, generates a joint effort to get an undue share of the aggregate proceeds of social activity. The aggressive tendency of each class, thus produced, has to be balanced by like aggressive tendencies of other classes. The implied feelings do, in short, develop one another; and the respective organizations in which they embody themselves develop one another. Large classes of the community marked-off by rank, and sub-classes marked-off by special occupations, severally combine, and severally set up organs advocating their interests: the reason assigned being in all cases the same—the need for self-defence.

Along with the good which a society derives from this self-asserting and self-preserving action, by which each division and sub-division keeps itself strong enough for its functions, there goes, among other evils, this which we are considering—the aptness to contemplate all social arrangements in their bearings on class-interests, and the resulting inability to estimate rightly their effects on Society as a whole. The habit of thought produced perverts not merely the judgments on questions which directly touch class-welfare, but it perverts the judgments on questions which touch class-welfare very indirectly, if at all. It fosters an adapted theory of social relations of every kind, with sentiments to fit the theory; and a characteristic stamp is given to the beliefs on public matters in general. . . .

More recently, this same class-bias has been shown by the protest made when Mr. Cowan was dismissed for executing the Kooka rioters who had surrendered. The Indian Government, having inquired into the particulars, found that this killing of many men without form of law and contrary to orders, could not be defended on the plea of pressing danger; and finding this, it ceased to employ the officer who had committed so astounding a deed, and removed to another province the superior officer who had approved of the deed. Not excessive punishment, one would say. Some might contend that extreme mildness was shown in thus inflicting no greater evil than is inflicted on a labourer when he does not execute his work properly. But now mark what is thought by one who displays in words the bias of the governing classes, intensified by life in India. In a letter published in the *Times* of May 15, 1872, the late Sir Donald M'Leod writes concerning this dismissal and removal:—

> All the information that reaches me tends to prove that a severe blow has been given to all chance of vigorous or independent action in future, when emergencies may arise. The whole service appears to have been astonished and appalled by the mode in which the officers have been dealt with.

That we may see clearly what amazing perversions of sentiment and idea are caused by contemplating actions from class points of view, let us turn from this feeling of sympathy with Mr. Cowan, to the feeling of detestation shown by members of the same class in England towards a man who kills a fox that destroys his poultry. Here is a paragraph from a recent paper:—

> Five poisoned foxes have been found in the neighbourhood of Penzance, and there is consequently great indignation among the western sportsmen. A reward of 20*l*. has been offered for information that shall lead to the conviction of the poisoner.

So that wholesale homicide, condemned alike by religion, by equity, by law, is approved, and the mildest punishment of it blamed; while vulpicide, committed in defence of property, and condemned neither by religion, nor by equity, nor by any law save that of sportsmen, excites an anger that cries aloud for positive penalties!

I need not further illustrate the more special distortions of sociological belief which result from the class-bias. They may be detected in the conversations over every table, and in the articles appearing in every party-journal or professional publication. The effects here most worthy of our attention are the general effects—the effects produced on the minds of the upper and lower classes.

3 CLASSIFICATION OF SOCIAL PROBLEMS *

BY ROBERT E. PARK (1864–1944) AND
ERNEST W. BURGESS (1886–   )
UNIVERSITY OF CHICAGO

EVERY society and every social group, *capable of consistent action,* may be regarded as an organization of the wishes of its members. This means that society rests on, and embodies, the appetites and natural desires of the individual man; but it implies, also, that wishes,

* Reprinted by permission of the publisher and Ernest W. Burgess from Robert E. Park and Ernest W. Burgess, *Introduction to the Science of Sociology* (2d ed.; Chicago: University of Chicago Press, 1924), pp. 45–47.

in becoming *organized,* are necessarily disciplined and controlled in the interest of the group as a whole.

Every such society or social group, even the most ephemeral, will ordinarily have (*a*) some relatively formal method of defining its aim and formulating its policies, making them explicit, and (*b*) some machinery, functionary, or other arrangement for realizing its aim and carrying its policies into effect. Even in the family there is government, and this involves something that corresponds to legislation, adjudication, and administration.

Social groups, however, maintain their organizations, agencies, and all formal methods of behavior on a basis and in a setting of instinct, of habit, and of tradition which we call human nature. Every social group has, or tends to have, its own culture, what Sumner calls "folkways," and this culture, imposing its patterns upon the natural man, gives him that particular individuality which characterizes the members of groups. Not races merely but nationalities and classes have marks, manners, and patterns of life by which we infallibly recognize and classify them.

Social problems may be conveniently classified with reference to these three aspects of group life, that is to say, problems of (*a*) organization and administration, (*b*) policy and polity (legislation), and (*c*) human nature (culture).

(*a*) Administrative problems are mainly practical and technical. Most problems of government, of business and social welfare, are technical. The investigations, i.e., social surveys, made in different parts of the country by the Bureau of Municipal Research of New York City, are studies of local administration made primarily for the purpose of improving the efficiency of an existing administrative machine and its personnel rather than of changing the policy or purpose of the administration itself.

(*b*) Problems of policy, in the sense in which that term is used here, are political and legislative. Most social investigations in recent years have been made in the interest of some legislative program or for the purpose of creating a more intelligent public opinion in regard to certain local problems. The social surveys conducted by the Sage Foundation, as distinguished from those carried out by the New York Bureau of Municipal Research, have been concerned with problems of policy, i.e., with changing the character and policy of social institutions rather than improving their efficiency. This distinction between administration and policy is not always clear, but it is always important. Attempts at reform usually begin with an effort to correct administrative abuses, but eventually it turns out that reforms must go deeper and change the character of the institutions themselves.

(c) Problems of human nature are naturally fundamental to all other social problems. Human nature, as we have begun to conceive it in recent years, is largely a product of social intercourse; it is, therefore, quite as much as society itself, a subject for sociological investigation. Until recent years, what we are now calling the human factor has been notoriously neglected in most social experiments. We have been seeking to reform human nature while at the same time we refused to reckon with it. It has been assumed that we could bring about social changes by merely formulating our wishes, that is, by "arousing" public opinion and formulating legislation. This is the "democratic" method of effecting reforms. The older "autocratic" method merely decreed social changes upon the authority of the monarch or the ruling class. What reconciled men to it was that, like Christian Science, it frequently worked.

The oldest but most persistent form of social technique is that of "ordering-and-forbidding"—that is, meeting a crisis by an arbitrary act of will decreeing the disappearance of the undesirable or the appearance of the desirable phenomena, and the using arbitrary physical action to enforce the decree. This method corresponds exactly to the magical phase of natural technique. In both, the essential means of bringing a determined effect is more or less consciously thought to reside in the act of will itself by which the effect is decreed as desirable and of which the action is merely an indispensable vehicle or instrument; in both, the process by which the cause (act of will and physical action) is supposed to bring its effect to realization remains out of reach of investigation; in both, finally, if the result is not attained, some new act of will with new material accessories is introduced, instead of trying to find and remove the perturbing causes. A good instance of this in the social field is the typical legislative procedure of today.[1]

[1] [W. I.] Thomas and [Florian] Znaniecki, *The Polish Peasant in Europe and America* (Boston, 1918), I, 3. [Reprinted by permission of Alfred A. Knopf, Inc., New York, the copyright owners.—*Ed.*]

4 INSIGHT AND SCIENTIFIC METHOD *

BY WILLARD WALLER (1899–1945)

BARNARD COLLEGE, COLUMBIA UNIVERSITY

SCIENCE is man's attempt to understand his universe. One focuses his attention upon various aspects of phenomena, attempting to perceive with insight. The advancement of science depends upon the search for insight. The mind of man is a tiny pencil of light exploring the illimitable dark. Causal relations are an inseparable part of experience, to be treated as real because experience must be treated as real; we may seek to refine our perceptions of cause, but we cannot reject them without rejecting our whole world of experiential reality.

If cause is an elementary datum of experience, then the thing to do is to experience it. The essence of scientific method, quite simply, is to try to see how data arrange themselves into causal configurations.[1] Scientific problems are solved by collecting data and by "thinking about them all the time." We need to look at strange things until, by the appearance of known configurations, they seem familiar, and to look at familiar things until we see novel configurations which make them appear strange. We must look at events until they become luminous. That is scientific method. Quantification is not the touchstone of scientific method. Insight is the touchstone.

In the social sciences, we may proceed to obtain insight in three distinct ways:

1. By direct study of human and interhuman behavior in order to perceive with insight. It is difficult to maintain this objective and external approach to human behavior because of the ease with which

---

* Reprinted by permission of Mrs. T. H. Brady and of the editor from *The American Journal of Sociology*, XL (1934–35), 285–297; pp. 287–293 reproduced in this Reading.

[1] Herbert Blumer seems to be very close to this point of view in the following passage: "What is needed is observation freely redirective and flexible in perspective. Scientific observation, as I understand it, is just this. It places emphasis on exploration, turning over and around, looking intently here and there, now focusing attention on this, now on that. It is flexible scrutiny guided by sensitized imagination. One sees it clearly in the work of Darwin who, incidentally, used neither instruments nor mathematics." (Herbert Blumer, review of Lundberg's *Social Research*, *American Journal of Sociology*, XXXV, No. 6 [1930], 1102.)

interpretations based upon sympathetic insight (Type 3) creep in.

2. We may obtain insight by studying certain symbols abstracted from reality and supposed to stand in a constant relation to it. These symbols are usually numerical.

3. We may obtain insight through sympathetic penetration. This insight is based upon the fact that the behavior of others, either directly perceived or mediated to us through language or mathematical symbols, starts certain mental processes in ourselves. This kind of insight is peculiarly liable to error, but of all kinds of insight it is the most significant.

These methods of obtaining insight are of course only analytically separable. All three are used at different stages of every research procedure. The behaviorist cannot dispense with sympathetic insight. Introspection, properly a method of studying phenomena directly, is most useful as an approach to the minds of others. The statistician must usually draw more or less upon sympathetic insight for the interpretation of his phenomena.

Apparently it is possible to offer a valid explanation of the principal methods of science in terms of the search for insight, and to subsume each of these methods under one of our three headings.

In studying any set of phenomena directly, we pass them before our eyes in the attempt to discover recurrent patterns and, if possible, to make out the entire configuration of events. Sumner's study of customs may be taken as a good example of the use of this method. These recurrent patterns gradually crystallize into concepts. Concepts result from the capacity of the mind to perceive the similarity of configurations perceived in succession.[2] Concepts may be defined as transposable perceptual patterns to which we have given names. Imagination is often called into play to fit together pieces of configurations, to perceive with insight configurations of events which have

[2] Herbert Blumer ("Science without Concepts," *American Journal of Sociology,* XXXVI, No. 4, 515–33) has defined the concept in terms of the assistance which it renders in filling in the gaps and open spaces of perception. It is true that the concept does this, but this aspect of the concept should be interpreted rather as imagination, which is the tendency of the mind to complete a configuration when only its rudiments are presented to consciousness. Blumer's view apparently bears the earmarks of sensationalistic psychology, as do most other interpretations of concepts. A concept is not necessarily a construct, and not even scientific concepts are always and necessarily constructs; although the physiologist would have occasion to frame a number of constructs in order to understand the physiological processes of a dog, yet it is likely that the physiologist's concept of a dog as a dog is not much further removed from sensory data than the layman's concept of a dog. The scientific con-

not actually been present to the senses. A high degree of insight into causal relations is implicit in the scientific concept. A concept must be transposable not only from one set of phenomena to another but also from one mind to another. The most effective way to communicate concepts is always to describe or to point to phenomena and to give to each configuration of events its name. All directed thought is conceptualizing activity. An unfortunate circumstance is that communication often breaks down, so that one acquires names without their attendant perceptual patterns. There is abundant evidence in sociological literature that many of our colleagues have learned words without perceiving processes, so that they literally do not know what they are talking about.

Experimentation may be classified as a mode of getting insight through the direct study of phenomena. Experimentation is not a method of establishing causal relations by mechanical manipulation or numerical criteria, for experimentation grows out of pre-existing insight and is useful only in so far as it leads to the acquisition, refinement, or verification of insight. The experimental procedure enables us to isolate one causal mechanism and to observe it in standardized form, to repeat it over and over, or to repeat it with variations until we obtain insight. Any other trained observer may repeat the experiment and get the same result, and the same insight; the ultimate test of the experiment is the ability of different observers to obtain the same insight. Experiments are meant to be repeated. Also, it is pre-existing grasp of causal processes and functional connections which makes an experiment critical or significant. Further, an experiment always flows out of empirical insight as to suspected causal relations and relevant variables; the experiment succeeds if it is based upon good insight, and it usually fails if it is based upon false insight. No virtuosity of technique can compensate for want of understanding.

The application of insight as the touchstone of method enables us to evaluate properly the rôle of imagination in scientific method. The scientific process is akin to the artistic process; it is a process of selecting out those elements of experience which fit together and recombining them in the mind. Much of this kind of research is simply a ceaseless mulling over, and even the physical scientist has

cept often is a construct, a configuration whose rudiments are present to the senses, whose totality is the work of the imagination. Blumer's discussion of this type of concept is particularly enlightening.

considerable need of an armchair. Constructs so formed must be conformable to reality, must be internally consistent, and as far as possible consistent with other members of the same system.

A second method by which insight may be derived is that of the study of symbols derived from phenomena. We shall consider particularly quantitative symbols, although all reports furnished by others would strictly come under this heading. We have ruled out the justification of statistical method which makes counting of cases a condition precedent to establishing a causal relationship; with this must go the belief that what is not quantified is not science. But statistical method remains immensely important in any system of methodology. We do not deny the validity of statistical method, nor contemplate a limitation of its field, but the rationale of statistics which we here present may strike some as strange.

It is submitted that statistical method is successful as a means of discovering truth when it is used to subserve insight, and that it fails when it is used without insight or in such a manner as to obstruct insight. Statistical enterprises depart from pre-existing insight, and are only worth while if they lead to further or more accurate insight. The valid uses of statistics seem to be: (1) to treat mass phenomena. (2) to give objectivity to social investigations by substituting the study of quantitative symbols for the direct study of social phenomena, (3) to sum up and to check partial insights, and (4) to determine the relative numerical importance of known causal configurations.

1. Probably the best use of statistics is for the study of various kinds of mass phenomena. In certain classes of phenomena, the important facts are numerical relations; this is the case with the unemployment problem. Sometimes, too, social facts are so widespread that they cannot be directly studied but must be converted into figures and studied in this symbolic form. As social centralization increases this will be increasingly important. But mass phenomena must be studied until they are seen to fall into a pattern, and until one glimpses, at least, the causal interdependence of parts; they must be studied, in short, with a view to obtaining insight. It is noteworthy that some of the most illuminating studies of mass phenomena would not pass the Pearsonian tests of scientific truth; the parts are quantitative and to some extent repetitive, but the whole is a single case study. Much of what we know about human ecology is as yet generalization from a single case. In the study of mass phenomena, it is

well to insist that there can be no talk of a causal relation unless a definite causal pattern appears.

2. Statistics may give added objectivity to social investigations by substituting the study of quantitative symbols for the direct study of social phenomena. If we are to have an objective social science, we must utilize statistics in this manner wherever it is possible to do so. Social phenomena are so emotionally toned that even the most impartial observer may well doubt whether he has interpreted them without bias. Perhaps this is how it comes about that even those researchers who say the most unkind things about statistics are overjoyed when the turn of events makes it possible for them to quantify their results. It is clear, however, that the use of quantitative symbols by no means guarantees objectivity, for faulty insight underlying the investigation or prejudice in the interpretation may vitiate the entire research. And if symbols are substituted for reality, it is well to remember that a generalization tends to be significant only as an interpretation of that order of phenomena from the study of which it emerges. A study of marriage statistics is not a study of marriage, and all too commonly fails to reveal anything concerning marriage.

3. There is also partial insight which reveals causal processes inconclusively; this appears where we are not able to analyze or control our phenomena properly, and must therefore deal with a nucleus of interlocking and perhaps interfering causal processes. Statistics may be used to refine such fragmentary insight, as a means of gaining control over phenomena of multiple causation. Psychologists, when they are not able to set up their experiments in such a way as to control all the variables, attempt to gain additional control through statistical technique. Statistics may also be used as simple statements of fragmentary insight, or as signposts pointing to undiscovered causal processes.

4. A most important use of statistics is in determining the relative numerical importance of known causal configurations. It would be interesting, and possibly of some importance, to know how many small men have developed the state of mind known as the inferiority complex; only statistics can tell us. The questionnaire, for all the absurdities that unintelligent persons have committed in its name, has served the social sciences well, and its principal utility comes under this heading. The questionnaire is oriented by the empirical insight of the person who frames the questions, and it can

seldom reveal anything that was not implicit in those questions; it can rarely, therefore, discover anything new, although it has considerable value in the testing of hypotheses. The greater the quantitative value of the questionnaire, the more nearly defined and interchangeable its units, the more completely it must fail to reveal previously unsuspected connections of cause and effect. However, it is of great practical and administrative importance to know which causal relations are most frequent, for in administration we must always play the main chance; statistics can help us to find the main chance.

It is insight, then, that makes the statistical method work.

5   LIMITATIONS OF STATISTICS *

BY WILLIAM FIELDING OGBURN (1886–   )
UNIVERSITY OF CHICAGO

THE increasing usefulness of statistics has brought it devotees. But devotion is unreasoning, and loyalties are more appropriate to group action than to clear thinking. Schools of thought based on loyalty to authority or emotional attachments should be more frequent among scholars and artists than among scientists. For these reasons a discussion of some of the limitations of statistics seems appropriate. These limitations contemplated are not, however, territorial, but rather methodological. Statistics, like science, began in a small way with certain types of problems, and from such a center of dispersal the expansion movement has swept into a great variety of fields, one after another. Each new conquest, like each new wave of immigrants to our country, is looked down upon by the established. Of course, there is no special reason for building a fence around a preserve for statistics. The only fence should be that one inherent in the method, for which many devotees claim too much. Science, for instance, cannot be all things to all men. Its place is quite limited in scholarship, in intellectuality, in the control of human affairs, in

* Reprinted by permission of the author and of the editor from *The American Journal of Sociology*, XL (1934–35), 12–20.

leadership, in the determination of values, and in furnishing human happiness. Similarly limited is the place of statistics in science.

DISCOVERY

The word "science" is used by different readers with different meanings. As here used it means the discovery of reliable and precise knowledge. Usage in the physical and biological sciences has given it this meaning. As the word is taken over by the social sciences, its content may undergo some change. At least the question may very well be asked whether discovery will be emphasized as much in the social sciences as it has been in the natural sciences. There, out of the unknown, have come such startling discoveries as that infinitesimal and invisible germs cause disease; that electrons travel at incredible rates of speed even through solid substances; that wood can be made into silken garments; that we can talk through the air for distances as far away as the poles. Is there an unknown in the social field that will yield any such unexpected discoveries? It has been said that the discovery of an "unconscious" that dominates much of our behavior is of that order of magnitude and of unexpectedness in the field of human relations—if, indeed, it has been discovered. There are also those claims that the causal rôle of technology in social change in general is of similar significance, if not perhaps as startling. But these are problematical.

There will, of course, be discovery of the new in social science, but these will be quite generally less dramatic than the most quoted ones. The vast number of discoveries in any science are quite minor. Science grows by the accumulation of small increments to the store of knowledge, and no doubt as the volume increases through the years there will be more of the big discoveries.

Whether the unknown in social science will have a small yield or not, statistics as one scientific method seems to have certain limitations as an agent of discovery. Some discoveries are made by statistics, of course. Thus our death-rate will rise; our population is approaching a stationary condition; oldest children are more often successes and more often failures; the sex ratio affects the marriageability of women much more than men; business depressions are more favorable to the increase in church membership than business prosperity. But the rôle of statistics is often that of making more exact something that is already known. Thus men are taller than women. Statistics only tells us with precision how much taller. The fact that such exactness is seldom needed often leads to the criticism that statistics proves the obvious. What is overlooked is that exactness is sometimes useful. In the familiar world of social relationships about us a good deal of observation is made about such matters as poverty, crime, conditions of the family, and this is called discovery; but in these cases statistics appears to be verifying what has already been discovered. It is in this sense that statistics is limited in discovery. There is probably more of this general observation in the social world than in the world of nature. It is seen that the analysis has led us into the question of what is a discovery, which cannot be answered until inquiry is made into what is knowledge.

KNOWLEDGE

Discovery usually proceeds from hunch to hypothesis to verification. The step from hypothesis to proof in social science is often in reality a series of steps, including the strengthening of the hypothesis and approximations. Undoubtedly many would claim knowledge before the final step is reached, which is the one where statistics is most often used. But the pressure is to reserve the seal of science until the last step is completed. Such seems appropriate in the case of the person who has a hunch or a hypothesis that he can send mail from New York to Paris by rocket, in the case of a discovery of a cure for cancer, or in the claim that acquired characteristics are inherited. But often in sociology observations are taken as proof when they are only approximations to certainty. Thus one is said to have discovered that the basis of neurosis is laid before a child is five years old. There is some evidence pointing that way; it is questioned whether this hypothesis has yet become knowledge. There is, no doubt, need for counting here. Often too readily accepted discoveries are found to be untrue when the verification process is carried far enough. Such is the case with the supposedly common knowledge that criminals are recruited more largely from the foreign-born; or that the villages have been decreasing, ruined by the automobile. Statistical verification is not always checking the obvious, or merely a useless compilation about what is already known. Still it seems to be true that the discipline of statistics helps little in the initial step of discovery, even though it be of importance in the final step.

There is another aspect of knowledge. Some is of the all or none type. Hydrogen and oxygen combine to produce water or they do not. But there is a knowledge of degree also which may be very important. It is not enough to know that when production and money do not increase at equal rates of speed there is fluctuation in business conditions. It is needed also to know how much. In the social sciences knowledge of the amount or degree may be as useful as the knowledge of the fact itself. Hence in social science there may come to be more emphasis on the adjective "precise" in the definition of science.

It still remains true, though, that a vast amount of the business of life is done on approximate information. We once got along very well without a thermometer, but the exact measurement it affords proves useful on occasion. One reason why we do not use more exact information is its costliness. Statistics is limited to the wealthy countries, or to those with dictators.

The Non-Quantitative

The greatest limitation of statistics is the one that needs to be stressed least, because it is obvious. It is that so much knowledge is either unique or the quantitative aspects are not sufficiently great to be called statistical. Such is the case in large part with history, political science, ethnology, law, ethics, religion, journalism, although there is some statistical measurement in each of these disciplines.

Another great area of non-statistical scientific work is in the general work preparatory to the task of deriving definitive conclusions. Concepts must be delineated, classifications and comparisons undertaken, rough observation must be made, preliminary surveys to get a perspective often need to be done. This kind of preliminary work is not always broken down into the hypothesis-verification pattern, but may go on for years over a large field, before the precise reliable knowledge is found. Statistics may help in this organizational work but is not always necessary. Indeed, most of it is undertaken without any reference to statistics. But the inapplicability of statistics to these non-quantitative fields is well known.

The Laboratory Method

The essence of the laboratory method is that one factor or combination of factors can be varied alone, to note the effect, while the others are held constant or eliminated. In this sense, so-called social experiments, such as the prohibition of the sale of liquor, are not experimental at all. In many of the natural and biological sciences, the laboratory has been the greatest source of advance. How will it be in the social sciences without a laboratory? Statistics has been looked upon as a substitute for the laboratory, because of its techniques for holding factors constant or eliminating them in measuring relationships. Statistics is, of course, not the only device for making comparisons between two factors when all the others are the same. Thus Professor Lowie compares the Chukchee culture with the Eskimo culture to note the influence of the change in the economic factor. However, the statistical technique is a little more facile in this regard than most other devices. Nevertheless, it is quite limited as compared with the laboratory, which is much more flexible and adaptable. One of the most beautiful devices is the control group to compare with the group being tested, say, for vaccination, as was done by Pasteur. All the factors, except the one under investigation, are readily held constant.

In statistics, with the device of partial correlation, it is quite a task to get a large-enough number of factors included, and the instrument becomes somewhat complicated when the relationships are not linear. For the device of subclassification a very large number of cases are necessary, if it is pushed through several factors. The method of standard population has only limited applicability. While statistics offers some facility, it seems very limited as compared with the simplicity, cheapness, and adaptability of the laboratory. This limitation of statistics is more apparent because of the much larger number of factors that are variable in social phenomena.

The difficulty due to these many varying factors is seen in the special situation when prediction is tried. In the case, for instance, of forecasting the future condition of business it is evident that many variable factors are involved. It so happens that under the present conditions not all these influences can be measured. The forecasting curves are based on a limited number of factors. Hence, predictions cannot be right all the time; and another limitation of statistics is chalked down. Certainly those forecasters who trust solely to their statistical measurements are to be blamed for their narrowness. It would probably be better if instead of relying wholly on the objective but incomplete measurements they drew on their best guesses, even though the subjective element entered, as to the influence of the unmeasured factors. Prediction is still largely an art and should be recognized as such, although naturally it should make use of such science as may be available. Prediction is a severe test of science. These same qualifications, discussed in regard to prediction, apply likewise to social or governmental control based on statistical information.

INTERPRETATION

The language of statistics is another limitation. Figures are necessarily very limited in conveying meanings as compared to the rich variety of nouns, adjectives, adverbs, and other words that make up the dictionary. Hence statistical tables are only a framework in which the data may be examined, and a coefficient or a curve is merely an abbreviation of the table. As to what the arrangement of figures means depends on what the author or reader brings to them in the way of associations—very much as one gets the meaning of a political cartoon in a newspaper. The process of deriving knowledge is one of explanation and interpretation. Thus if $r_{12} = -.14$, where the first variable is the birth-rate by cities and where the second is the percentage of young women married in the same cities, what is the meaning?

A certain amount of explanation is necessary to make the language of coefficients intelligible. In this case it means that on the average cities with a lower birth-rate have a larger percentage of young married women for a given number of cities at a certain time. But the meaning even after the terms are explained is still not clear. Hence an interpretation, in addition to explanation, is demanded. But interpretation nearly always calls for further scientific work and can hardly be done ex cathedra. Any such interpretation, in contrast to explanation, unsupported by evidence is merely a guess and hence not reliable knowledge and not science. Much looseness arises from a failure to distinguish between explanation and interpretation. In this particular case it is not the hypothesis that the marriage-rate affects the birth-rate. It is difficult to see how this could be. On the other hand, could the birth-rate affect the marriage-rate? Certainly the knowledge as to how the birth-rate may be lowered—that is, through birth-control information—might very well influence the marriage-rate. Young people might marry more readily if they knew that, for a time, there would not have to be babies to support. This hypothesis could be further checked if we had the information on the sale and use of contraceptive devices. There are, however, no statistical data available on this point.

A special type of interpretation is often demanded, namely, a statement of the significance of the implications of the statistics. But a reliable statement of the implications, like a reliable statement of other interpretations, cannot be made without evidence, and hence often without further research. Some implications are more or less obvious; others may be suggested as possible or probable. But interpretations, if reliable, require evidence and research as did the original statement. As a form of language, statistics has its limitations.

UNDERSTANDING

The aim of science is sometimes said to yield understanding rather than, or in addition to, discovering new knowledge. It is always desirable to understand new knowledge, but this further step is one for education or experience. The two terms "knowledge" and "understanding" may, at times, be used interchangeably. But there are also differences. Sometimes by knowledge is meant a clear and certain mental apprehension, while understanding by contrast implies the perception of a meaning in terms of a feeling tone on the level of sentiment or experience. Thus one may know that sacrifice is an element in many religions, but one may not understand it. One may know that the sun is ninety-three million miles away, but one may have little understanding of what this great distance means. It is often the interpretation that gives the meaning of knowledge. But since interpretation may be wrong, as is the case when unsupported by evidence, it is possible to understand something that is not true, and hence not knowledge. Poetry is probably a better medium for conveying understanding in this sense than statistics.

In the natural sciences it is possible that the divergence between knowledge and understanding may not be so great as in some of the social sciences. There is no particular demand in biology for understanding a zygote other than the knowledge conveyed by the objective scientific account. On the other hand, a neurosis needs to be understood more than in knowing objective equations showing its relationships. This demand for understanding is much greater in such social psychological phenomena as religion and crime than in, say, economics. The relation of the price level to the business cycle does not call for any great human understanding. The knowledge carries the meaning. In the study of symbols the search is for meanings. It is thus interesting to speculate on the possibility of a science of symbols. If it should be developed, the scientific test implied in the question "How do you know it?" will have to be applied to the meanings and understandings. If understanding is to be other than an artistic expression, we must ask the question, "How do we know that our understanding is correct?"

Equally as interesting as the symbol in science is the position of the proverb in knowledge. Is the proverb a scientific discovery? Much of the writings of sociologists is like the discussion of proverbs. The "consciousness of kind" is like the proverb "Birds of a feather flock together." The abstinence theory of interest suggests, "A bird in the hand is worth two in the bush." If "a stitch in time" were practiced, there would be no cultural lag. The "primary group" escapes the situation where "out of sight is out of mind." The proverb is a folk saying that is widely used with great applicability. Hence, any principle of social science that resembles a proverb is likely to be popular and widely used. But is it science? Certainly the discovery of a proverb is hardly the discovery of new knowledge, though it seems to be rich in its potentialities of conveying understanding, and it may be a scientific tool if it lends itself to measurement. Statistics certainly has a limited usefulness in bringing about understanding, particularly in social psychology.

THE COMPOSITE

A final limitation of statistics and of science in general remains to be mentioned. It is their lack of guaranty of a satisfactory composite picture, even when each element of the composite is scientifically accurate. The difficulty lies in selection and emphasis rather than in accuracy or exactness. For instance, in regard to an account of Soviet Russia, it is possible for a conservative and a radical to visit that country at the same time and write books so different that the time and place might not be recognizable as the same. Science has grown up in handling single relationships affected, perhaps, by a number of factors, or in describing a single phenomenon or a series of them, and in these cases has been able to eliminate the distorting influence of human bias. Such, for instance, is the relationship of temperature to crop production, or the account of a buried city. In such problems the question of a "fair picture" does not arise as it would if one were writing a book on, say, the influence of the machine. What goes into history is a matter of selection and values. Science does not tell us what to select for a general account of a large complex subject any more than it tells us what subject to choose for scientific investigation. What is a "fair" account is a matter of values, not of proof. One person thinks something should be included, another thinks it should not be emphasized so much, another may think it should be omitted. So we have different kinds of history—political, economic, social. History must be re-written every age, because the interest of each age selects different subjects for emphasis.

Indeed, statistics is not only not helpful in such a problem but is often an actual hindrance. For instance, if the purpose is to produce a well-balanced picture of the family as an institution, and if one relied solely on quantitative or factual records, the account would inevitably be one-sided. Because on certain aspects of the family we do not have adequate records. This is true, for instance, of the changes from one period of time to another in the personality influences of parents on children for the United States. If the purpose was to produce a "fair picture" of the family, it would be better to include non-quantitative material on these personality aspects, even if they were only estimates, than to omit them altogether. Perhaps it might be argued that one should not attempt a "fair picture," but general, well-balanced accounts are demanded; and they will be appraised as such. The purpose of science is to represent reality without distortion. The statistical method is undoubtedly limited in preventing a distortion or undue emphasis in a general picture, requiring omissions even when every part of the general picture consists of accurate reliable knowledge.

6 THE EXPERIMENTAL METHOD IN THE STUDY OF HUMAN RELATIONS *

BY F. STUART CHAPIN (1888–   )
UNIVERSITY OF MINNESOTA

THE experimental study of human relations in the free community can hardly be reduced to laboratory conditions of control. Hence the present article will exclude all experimental studies conducted in an artificial or classroom situation and confine attention

* Reprinted by permission of the author and of the editor from *The Scientific Monthly*, LXVIII (1949), 132–139.

to six illustrative studies that were made in the free community situation. This limitation has the advantages of distinguishing sharply, first, the fundamental principle that controlled observation relies on the matching of measurements rather than on physical manipulation; and, second, the kinds of practical obstacles encountered in all attempts at controlled observation in the free community situation. The six studies to be described are all published and show how . . . efforts were made to control variable factors by matching on measurements between an experimental group that received some social program and a control group denied this program.

In the interest of clear thinking about this problem it is helpful to distinguish, first, the trial-and-error "experiments" of social legislation as a means to achieve some desired end (public housing as a means to improve the adjustment of low-income families); second, the operations of natural social forces that produce an effect; and, third, the use of experimental designs as a method of study of the first two, in order to determine the degree of success in the attainment of a desired social end, or to measure the effect of some social force. Since a social reform program is a social force that operates according to some plan of action, our description will be confined to illustrations of this, the first of the foregoing distinctions, rather than illustrations of the use of experimental designs in the study of unplanned consequences of combinations of independently planned social actions, which is the second type distinguished above. This second type would take us too far afield, since it concerns the phenomena of conflict among the means-ends scheme of special interest groups, a resulting composition of social forces, and the emergence of unplanned consequences which plague the authors and the leaders of the component but independently planned programs. Business cycles, inflation, mass movements, etc., are examples of this second type. Such mass behavior can hardly be studied experimentally until we have solved some of the problems connected with experimental study of their simpler component means-ends relations. Hence the limitation noted above.

Five methods of observation and analysis are essential in studies of human relations by experimental designs: social measurements by use of standardized psychometric or sociometric scales; random samples or a stratified random sample; control of observations by matching on social measurements; use of the null hypothesis; and qualified application of the principle of probability.

Leaders of social reform have often found that the ends they desired to achieve by means of legislation are seldom fully attained, usually because there are unexpected results which flow from the unplanned combinations of other independently planned social actions. In the free community situation of a democratic social order, it is customary to protect the rights of minority groups (political, religious, and social) in freedom of assemblage, freedom of speech, freedom of religious worship, etc. The consequences of these democratic freedoms are that many special-interest groups in society set up their own means-ends schema and work at cross-purposes to other minorities to achieve their contradictory goals. These phenomena take the familiar forms of social tensions, group conflicts, achievement of one at the expense of the frustration of the other, etc., all of which appear to the foreign observer as evidences of internal confusion and mislead such observers about the existence of a deep current of agreement on essentials. This web of human relations fluctuates within certain limits of social elasticity, now seemingly stretched to the breaking point, and then contracting again to a more stable social structure. How can one ever untangle the separate strands of this complex social fabric? Although adequate answers to this question await the study by experimental designs, or by other methods of analysis, of the involved chain of causes and effects now hidden in the unplanned consequences that arise out of combinations of independently planned social actions, it can be shown that a real beginning has been made at a simpler level in the study of particular cause-and-effect sequences which are called the means-ends schema of social reform. The beginning is real because it is based upon concrete studies of social facts and not on armchair social philosophy; it is promising because the method of experimental design has now been used with moderate success in tests of such problems as direct relief versus work relief, public housing, and juvenile delinquency; it is objective because the method is susceptible of repetition by equally competent observers who use quantitative descriptions of human relations.

Despite some modest development in experimental designs, my present concern is with the still-unsolved problems of the method, so that the difficulties to be overcome may not be lost sight of in an account of some undoubted achievements.

There are three general patterns of experimental design in the study of human relations in the free community situation: first, a cross-sectional design in which comparison is made for a given date between an experimental group which receives a social program, and a matched control group denied this program; second, a projected design in which before and after measurements are made upon an experimental group which received a program over an interval of time, and a matched control group denied this program; and, third, what may be called the ex post facto design, in which a present situation is taken as an effect of some assumed and previously operating causal complex of factors, and, depending upon the adequacy of accessible records, an experimental group and a matched control group are traced back to an earlier date when the force to be measured began functioning upon the experimental group but not upon the control group.

Cross-sectional Experimental Design. Nathan Mandel used this method in a study of the Boy Scout program and the measured personal adjustment of boys. It is at once evident that some measures of personal adjustment that are reliable and valid will be required, and also some measures of other factors to be controlled, in order that the real association between the Scout program (the means, or causal variable) and the personal adjustment (the end, or effect variable) may be described. The three measures of adjustment used were the Bell *Adjustment Inventory,* Rundquist and Sletto's *Morale* and *General Adjustment* scales (all measures of how the individual feels), and the Chapin *Social Participation Scale* (a measure of overt activity in organized groups).

Choosing every tenth case in the file of 2,050 Boy Scouts in the 1934 "drop-out" file of the Minneapolis area yielded a total of 205 boys. Only 102 of these were found and interviewed in 1938. Since 103 had moved away, could not be located, would not cooperate, or were deceased, the residual sample ceased to be random. The remaining 102 cases were divided into two groups, an experimental group whose training had lasted 4 years on the average, and a control group with an average tenure of 1.3 years. When these were matched on four available traits in the record (birthplace, urban or rural, father's occupation, health rating, and school age-grade ratio), there was a further shrinkage of 22 cases, so that the final totals were 40 in each group.

It was found that the 4-year Scouts were slightly better adjusted on both the Bell and the Rundquist-Sletto scales than the control group of dropouts. Interpretation of these results as indicative of mere conformity and conventionality rather than of somewhat better integration of personality would then have to explain why it was that the drop-outs showed higher scores on the Chapin *Social Participation Scale* than did the 4-year Scouts, since a higher social participation score is evidence against the rejection from membership of the drop-outs by the organized groups in which they were active. All in all, this study was somewhat inconclusive, since the advantage evidenced by higher adjustment scores of the 4-year Scouts was too slight to provide local proof of the hypothesis upon which the Scout program is based; but the results were at least consistent with the expectations implicit in the Boy Scout program.

During the great depression of the 1930's it became evident that material relief alone was a mere stop-gap, and that self-respecting assistance [by the government] to the unemployed should take the form of a work-relief program. Hence the Works Progress Administration was undertaken. It was claimed that the WPA would develop morale and maintain it more effectively than a direct-relief program of material assistance.

To test the validity of this claim an experimental design study was made in St. Paul, Minnesota, in 1939. A total of 465 cases were on direct relief in March of that year, and 8,074 persons were on WPA. A 5 percent random sample of these WPA cases, or 412 persons, was taken as an experimental group to be compared with the 465 relief clients. To make these groups sufficiently homogeneous for valid comparison, seven conditions were set: living in St. Paul; working in Ramsey County; not previously on WPA; and not single, widowed, separated, or divorced. Meeting these conditions reduced the WPA experimental group to 324 cases, and the control group of relief clients to 198. These 522 cases were interviewed in April–May and the total still further reduced by 320 cases because of refusals, could not be located, had moved away, deceased, sickness, gainfully employed, changed status, etc. As a result there remained 130 cases in the experimental group of WPA and only 72 direct-relief clients. These two groups were then matched on seven factors: age, sex, race, nativity, years of formal education, usual occupation, and size of family. Had this matching on traits not been done the obtained variations in measured morale and adjustment might have been due to one or more of these factors, rather than associated with being on WPA or on direct relief, the association we set out to measure. Again, both groups lost cases because unable to match, so that the terminal groups consisted of an experimental group of 80 WPA matched on seven factors against a control group of 42 on direct relief.

During the interviews every individual was measured for his morale and his general adjustment score on the Rundquist-Sletto scales, and for social participation and social status on the Chapin scales. On each of these scales the WPA group showed better average measures of adjustment than did the relief group. Differences between these average group scores were, however, not statistically significant, so that chance could account for the differences. But the differences were in the expected direction, and a measure of all four in combination as a pattern of response to differential treatment by the two contrasting programs showed that these differences in pattern could occur by chance somewhere between 1 in 10 and 1 in 50. Again, our experimental design study failed to yield positive proof of a hypothesis of high association, although it did yield results not contrary to this hypothesis.

To summarize the most significant findings from these two examples of cross-sectional experimental design, it may be noted:

1. That no test of cause and effect or of concomitant variation is possible by this method; the only evidence obtained is that of an *association* at a given date between two factors (different programs of assistance on the one hand, and measured adjustment on the other), but this association was in the expected direction, if it is assumed that WPA is superior to direct relief in attaining better adjustment.

2. The enormous losses of cases owing to selective conditions in the natural community, plus losses from matching, destroyed any randomness of the original samples, and increased the magnitude of the standard errors, thus reducing the statistical significance of any differences obtained.

3. Since the residual groups departed from randomness, no generalization can be made from such studies to any larger universe or universes from which the groups were taken, although it remains true that conclusions for the limited groups studied do have a valid basis in fact.

Projected Experimental Design. Unless social cause and effect can be subsumed in the area of human relations, there is little hope of a rational explanation of the vexing problems of the social order. We have just shown that the cross-sectional experimental design, because it is limited to a controlled comparison of two groups at a given time, fails to disclose cause-and-effect relations, although it may be suggestive of hypotheses for study by more elaborate methods. Does the projected experimental design offer a more hopeful promise of discovery of social cause and effect? Two published studies will now be analyzed in an effort to answer this question.

The first study was an attempt to measure the effects of a public low-cost housing project upon the social adjustment of slum families in Minneapolis from 1939 to 1940. One year is admittedly too short an interval for any real test, but practical considerations set this time limit, and so we are obliged to make the best of it.

This study began in the spring of 1939 when 108 former slum families having low incomes had taken up residence in Sumner Field Homes, a PWA housing project planned in 1935. The control group consisted of 131 other families residing in the same slum dwelling during the period. Although these 131 families were initially so much like those eligible and admitted to residence in the project as to be borderline or deferred cases who might be admitted later, an attempt was made to make the experimental group of residents and the control group of slum dwellers still more alike by matching on ten control factors: race or cultural class of husband, of wife; occupational class of husband, of wife; employment status of husband, of wife; number of persons in the family; income of the family; and years of formal education of wife. As in the studies previously reported, many cases were lost by inability to match. In all, 59 cases dropped out for this reason—47 from the experimental group and 12 from the control group. Because of the lapse of time between initial and terminal measurements, various events intruded and 50 more cases dropped out for these reasons—12 from the experimental group, and 38 from the control group. Forty-eight more cases were lost before the initial interviews were completed, owing to mobility, refusals, and other reasons, of which 5 were from the experimental group and 43 from the control. Thus the final matched groups (frequency distributions equated) consisted of 82 persons, 44 in the experimental group and 38 in the control group.

This test of low-rent public housing as a means to achieve the end of improved adjustment of slum families, or as a measure of a program of social reform as a cause, to produce improved adjustment as the effect, as the case may be regarded, relied upon changes in measured social adjustment before (1939) and after (1940) the program had operated for one year, as evidence of proof. The measures of social adjustment used were the same as those applied in the WPA–

relief study described above. Since no changes in measured morale or in general adjustment were found statistically significant in a comparison of average scores of each group before and after, and also because each family had resided in the *same* dwelling unit for the period, there were in fact thus added three additional controls to the ten noted above, making in all, control on thirteen factors.

When, however, attention was directed to the changes that occurred in social activities (social participation scores), in the percentage use-crowded, and in the condition of the living room of each home (measured by the Chapin social status scale), it was found that a pattern of response consisting of these three factors in combination showed a difference between change in the experimental group and change in the control group that was of high statistical significance. Whereas the pattern of change on these three factors in the control group was not statistically significant (multiple critical ratio, 1.82), the corresponding change for the experimental group was highly significant (multiple critical ratio, 6.01); and the difference between the changes of the two groups on this measure was also highly significant (multiple critical ratio, 4.97). Such high critical ratios as these are so unlikely to occur in chance that a cause-and-effect relation may be inferred. In a certain sense this is a gratuitous conclusion because the public-housing program was intended to interfere with chance and to create for the project residents improved housing, so that it might be more surprising if it did not effect improved adjustment. This desired effect cannot be established by mere wishful thinking, however, but only by the evidence of measurements on scales that had been standardized to measure adjustment prior to the existence of the change they were used to test. Furthermore, although science often merely confirms the results of practices based on experience, it is by no means certain that a scientific test will not disprove the effectiveness of popular practices; hence the justification for the present study.

The real question that faces us in making inferences from the facts obtained by this experimental design is: Did housing per se cause these changes in pattern of response? Only a positive answer to this question, phrased in terms of a low probability of chance as an explanation, would prove the effectiveness of the public-housing program in this example, and then only if all unknown factors had been controlled. Although thirteen factors were controlled in rough degree, the remaining known but unmeasured factors (health, for example), and an undetermined number of unknown factors, were not controlled. Thus the results of this test by experimental design offer no final conclusion. Furthermore, since the groups compared were nonrandom samples, no reliance upon probability tests is permissible as a basis of generalization to any larger universe of similar "experiments" by public-housing authorities.

Where does this leave us? On the negative side we may offer the opinion that the results are sufficiently suggestive to urge repetition of this type of study on similar cases using like methods of research in the hope that replication will yield corroboration of the results. For only by replication in numerous similar studies may we escape from the dilemma of whether the obtained significant differences were due to the nonrandomness of the samples, or to the fact that they were drawn from different universes (i.e., universes that were made different by virtue of the public-housing program, the objective that was to be tested by the experimental design). Should the same results be found on many trials, then generalization from even nonrandom samples to a universe might be valid and justified. On the positive side we may say that the differences found were of an absolute magnitude which would be regarded as highly significant if they were found between two random samples.

Of the five principles enumerated as essential to study by experimental designs, three have been illustrated: social measurements by use of psychometric or sociometric scales; control by matching on measurements rather than by physical manipulation (the conventional and mistaken idea about control of variable factors); and qualified application of the principle of probability. But the housing study illustrates also the advantages to the research student that follow from the use of a null hypothesis in sociological research wherein the purpose is to test the results of a social reform program.

The conventional working hypothesis is a positive assertion: "Public housing improves the social adjustment of individuals and families living in a slum." There are at least two difficulties to be overcome in efforts to test such a hypothesis: first, the statement uses the normative term "improves," which implies the question "What is improvement?" Whose standards of what is improvement are to be taken? Shall we rely on the judgment of the housing manager, or on the opinions of those who promoted the project, or on the critics of all public housing? Obviously, any such definitions are open to subjective considerations which stem from different desires. This problem is simplified when standardized sociometric scales are used, since there was incorporated into the initial construction and testing of such scales elements of objectivity not present in individual opinions. Moreover, the norms of such scales were discovered in previous studies, so that the application of these scales in any present study is not affected by any desire to vindicate or to disprove the program being investigated. A second difficulty is more serious; it consists in the fact that "improvement" is an open-ended concept. How much change in the desired direction is improvement? When the positive hypothesis is replaced by a null hypothesis, this difficulty is avoided.

Three null hypotheses susceptible of proof or disproof by facts may be set up as follows:

1. When measures of adjustment are made upon an experimental group which receives a social program and an experimental group denied this program during an interval, and the two groups are matched on a number of factors, there are no changes in measured adjustment during the interval. Since the facts obtained in the housing study show the existence of changes, this null hypothesis is proved false.

2. If changes in measured adjustment are found in these groups, the changes are not statistically significant. Again this null hypothesis is proved false by the results found.

3. Although changes may be found, and these changes are statistically significant, the difference between changes of the two groups is not statistically significant. This null hypothesis is also proved false by the factual evidence.

It is evident that it is a much simpler task to prove that differences do exist, that these differences are statistically significant, and that the difference in changes is statistically significant as departures from zero than it is to prove that the changes are in the nature of improvement; and this is particularly the case in studies of problems of human relations, wherein bias is hard to avoid and the subject matter of study is emotionally disturbing to the observer because it involves his personal value systems.

A second study using the projected experimental design to test the effectiveness of a social program of differential treatment is that reported by Harry Shulman in New York City. This is a study of the effects of treatment to prevent juvenile delinquency by a controlled-activity program. The program consisted of workshop and game-room activities, classes in creative art, woodwork, leather, and metalworking, which met three sessions a week for two hours a session over a period of three successive school semesters. Groups of 50 problem boys and 80 normals were mingled naturally in these activities. The problem boys included chronic truants, incorrigibles, serious personality problem cases, and some charged with arson and theft. The normals were nonproblem cases obtained by serial selection from class-roll books of children who had never dropped below a B grade on their studies. The experimental group to receive the program consisted of 65 boys, including 25 of the problem cases and 40 normals. The control group was similarly constituted but denied the program. At the beginning there were 310 boys, 155 in each group, who were ten and one-half to fourteen and one-half years of age and in Grades 4–A to 8–A from four public schools in socially substandard areas of New York City.

The measure of community adjustment used consisted of 13 of the 66 Baker-Traphagen items which measured behavior status. Comparison of the results for the problem boys of the experimental group with the problem boys of the control showed that 72 percent of the problem boys in the experimental group which received the program improved, and only 33 percent of the problem boys in the control group gained. Meanwhile 28 percent of the former had lost, and 66 percent of the latter. In tests before and after in the classroom situation, all differences among the mild-to-medium conduct-disorder cases were statistically significant on scores of the Haggerty-Wickman-Olson behavior rating scale for the two problem children groups. Since these favorable results might have accrued from differential changes in home environment during the experimental period, a case study was made of factors of family disorganization (broken home, marital disharmony, public assistance, economic maladjustment, children's illness, mental deficiency and disease, unethical or antisocial example, etc.), of defective social relationships (between parents, parent-child, and community), and also of improper discipline. The results of this analysis showed no appreciable differences in changes for the problem children of the two contrasting groups. Thus the intrusion of environmental factors of the surrounding community had not operated to confuse the relationship between the treatment program as a cause and the diminution of behavior problems as an effect.

Although the two studies in projected experimental design just described illustrate some advance toward the scientific goal of discovery of social cause-and-effect relationships, each study stands by itself as a closed system, and no scientific generalization may be made from either to the larger universe of housing or juvenile delinquency. Again, repetition by similar studies on like subjects, using the same methods of research, is the only avenue of approach to a reliable basis of generalization.

Ex Post Facto Experimental Design. For many years students of human relations have sought a valid method to discover cause-and-effect relations which it is believed may be hidden in the records of past social events. The ex post facto experimental design was developed as one attempt to clarify this methodological problem.

A study that illustrates the use of this ex post facto method was made by Helen Christiansen under my direction in 1935–38. The positive hypothesis to be tested was the longer the period of high-school education before leaving school, the better the subsequent economic adjustment in the community. Here the formal high-school course of instruction is taken as the program variable, or the causal factor, and measured economic adjustment is taken as the effect variable. To test this hypothesis the records of 2,127 high-school students who left school nine years earlier (1926) were obtained and analyzed. In that year 1,130 had graduated from the 4-year course in all high schools of St. Paul, Minnesota, and 997 had dropped out of school, having been in 1926 at the end of their first, second, or third year of study. The graduates were taken as the experimental group and the drop-outs as the control group. The measure of economic adjustment in the community situation chosen as the dependent variable was the percentage of shifts on jobs from 1926 to 1935 which involved increase in salary, no change in salary, and decrease in salary. This is admittedly a crude measure, but the data could be obtained by interviews of all persons of the original 2,127 who could still be located in 1935.

Considering the relatively long experimental period of nine years, substantial losses of cases were to be expected. As a matter of fact, 933 individuals were lost for analysis, 459 of the graduates and 474 of the drop-outs, for reasons of death, moving away, not located, or incomplete records. After matching on six control factors, age, sex, father's occupation, parental nativity, neighborhood of residence, and average high-school marks (no I.Q. data were available in 1926), the two groups were reduced to 145 individuals each.

Analysis of economic adjustment to the community in 1935 showed a regular decline in percentage with decrease in salary or no change in salary, with each additional year of high-school education for drop-outs of 1, 2, and 3 years of study, and a regular increase in percentage with salary increases. The 4-year graduates attained the highest percentage with salary increase for 1926–35 of any group, and their percentages of cases with decline in salary or no change were approximately the same as those of the 3-year drop-outs. When the matching technique was made more precise—that is, by identical individual matching, instead of equating frequency distributions on each control factor—the two groups were reduced to 23 cases each. The trend in percentages on the salary criterion became even more pronounced, and the advantage of the graduates over the dropouts was much greater. All in all, the positive hypothesis seems to have been established for this study, provided the results can be explained as not due to health factors uncontrolled, the factor of persistence in school work, the existence in the group of 933 lost from study of trends contrary to those found in the groups that were analyzed, or unknown factors. Again no decisive proof has been achieved; only the probability of a cause-and-effect relation between length of school attendance and subsequent economic adjustment in the community.

But this matter of probability deserves further exploration. To test the statistical significance of the percentage differences found between the experimental and control groups, two random samples of 23 cases each were chosen from the larger experimental and control groups, but the individuals in these random samples were not matched (as were the individuals in the 23-case terminal experimental and control groups which showed the largest differentials). Analysis of the random samples showed indicia of differences in community adjustment occurring by chance as 1 in 14, as compared with 1 in 200 for the 23-case matched samples. Since the original 2,127 cases constituted the universe of all who left high school in 1926, and the remaining 1,194 cases composed the remainder after losses of 933 cases, both the random samples and the experimental groups were from a subuniverse, so that comparison of real random samples with nonrandom groups introduces in this experiment a more adequate basis for the use of probability tests than was the case in any of the other studies described in this article.

In summary, it may be said that the differentials in favor of the graduates seem too large to be explained as mere chance fluctuations,

nd of absolute magnitudes that cast some doubt upon the validity
of the four alternative explanations, which would set up the claim
hat it was not the length of high-school education that caused better
economic adjustment in the community of graduates. The comparison with the random samples yields results also consistent with
he foregoing inference.

But, again, we must caution against generalization to all high-
school programs of all areas of the United States. Perhaps the place
and time studied were unique. On the other hand, it may be pointed
out that the 1926–35 period included the depth of the great depression of the 1930s, so that the hypothesis was substantiated for an in-
erval of sharp testing by unemployment, and hence that our conclusions have a safety factor that makes them conservative.

A variation in the ex post facto design was made in a study of
public housing and juvenile delinquency in New Haven by Naomi
Barer from records of 1944 on 317 families traced back to 1924. She
made a self-comparison of a group of 649 children seven to seventeen years of age in these families, for the period 1940–44 to the
period 1924–40, when the same families and their children lived elsewhere. From 1924 to 1940 the rate of juvenile delinquency per 100
children per year was 3.18; when the same subjects were residents
of the housing project the rate had declined to 1.64. This is a statistically significant decline. During the years 1940–41 there was an
increase of 9.1 percent in total juvenile delinquency in the city of
New Haven over that of the period 1927–40, so that no general decline in juvenile delinquency occurred in the community at large,
which, if it had happened, might explain the decline of the experimental group of children in the housing project. No generalization
is justified from this study alone about housing and juvenile delinquency at large. Only corroboration from repetition of the experiment will furnish proof of a hypothesis that good housing operates
to reduce juvenile delinquency.

Two types of critics deplore the kind of studies herein described.
There are the "practical" reformers who have expressed the opinion
that this kind of detailed analysis is superfluous since it is mere
common sense to expect to find improvement following upon well-
matured plans for social betterment. But are desire and wishful
thinking the sort of support upon which to base and to justify expensive and elaborate social programs? Then there are sincere critics
who express the judgment that the time and expense of detailed

study by experimental designs might better have been applied to the investigation of problems wherein the expectation of significant results had a firmer basis in technical and precise research methods. No adequate answer can be made to this criticism. The reader will have to decide for himself whether exploration by these methods of experimental study, admittedly crude and lacking in precision, is worth the time and effort put forth. In any event, I have found these experimental designs interesting, and sometimes exciting, ventures. They are offered for what they may be worth, and their limitations have been stated and reiterated throughout this article.

Three closing comments may be made. First, objective evidence has been offered to show that experimental designs may be applied to the measurement of problems of human relations with some expectation of a partial clarification of social cause and effect in society. Second, the chief obstacle to the experimental method in the study of problems of human relations is removed, since it stemmed from a false analogy between "social experiments" that shove people around and laboratory experimentation that manipulates physical matter, whereas the fundamental principle involved is observation of social relations under conditions of control, which conditions are attained by matching on social measurements, and do not require interference with personal freedoms. Third, the methods of experimental design offer the promise of an objective procedure for evaluating the effects of some types of social reform programs. Such programs consist of the approved means chosen to attain some desired or valued end. This being the case, it seems possible that further extension of the methods described herein will lead to an experimental test of values, phenomena hitherto circumscribed by desire and wishful thinking and suffused with emotional attitudes.

If the first expectation is realized, we may have in it the beginnings of a rational basis for the amelioration and control of some of the problems of human relations. If the third is realized, we shall have a rational substitute for mere subjective opinions and sanctimonious or self-righteous judgments about what may be done by social action to achieve collective desires. Furthermore, through the replication of experimental design studies, which attempt to measure the effectiveness of specific means-ends schema planned to attain specific goals, it may be possible to develop a systematic mosaic of nonrandom samples that will possess a degree of representativeness to compensate for lack of randomization, and thus to supply a basic rep-

esentativeness upon which reliable scientific generalization may
est. Finally, if the foregoing development takes place, an approach
vill have been made to the solution of the most difficult methodologi-
al problem of all, to describe objectively the tortuous chain of social
:ause and effect that now lies hidden in the unplanned social consequences that seem to flow from the combinations of innumerable
ind independently planned social actions within a democratic society.

7 THE BEARING OF EMPIRICAL RE-SEARCH UPON THE DEVELOP-MENT OF SOCIAL THEORY *

BY ROBERT K. MERTON (1910–)
COLUMBIA UNIVERSITY

HISTORY has a certain gift for outmoding stereotypes. This can be
seen, for example, in the historical development of sociology.
The stereotype of the social theorist high in the empyrean of pure
ideas uncontaminated by mundane facts is fast becoming no less outmoded than the stereotype of the social researcher equipped with
questionnaire and pencil and hot on the chase of the isolated and
meaningless statistic. For in building the mansion of sociology during the last decades, theorist and empiricist have learned to work
together. What is more, they have learned to talk to one another in
the process. At times, this means only that a sociologist has learned
to talk to himself since increasingly the same man has taken up both
theory and research. Specialization and integration have developed
hand in hand. All this has led not only to the realization that theory
and empirical research *should* interact but to the result that they *do*
interact.

As a consequence, there is decreasing need for accounts of the re-

* Paper read before the annual meeting of the American Sociological Society,
Cleveland, Ohio, March 1–3, 1946. This may be identified as Publication No. A–89
of the Bureau of Applied Social Research, Columbia University. Reprinted by permission of the author and of the editor from the *American Sociological Review*, XIII
(1948), 505–515.

lations between theory and research to be wholly programmatic in character. A growing body of theoretically oriented research makes it progressively possible to discuss with profit the actual relations between the two. And, as we all know, there has been no scarcity of such discussions. Journals abound with them. They generally center on the role of theory in research, setting forth, often with admirable lucidity, the functions of theory in the initiation, design and prosecution of empirical inquiry. But since this is not a one-way relationship, since the two *inter*act, it may be useful to examine the other direction of the relationship: the role of empirical research in the development of social theory. That is the purpose of this paper.

THE THEORETIC FUNCTIONS OF RESEARCH

With a few conspicuous exceptions, recent sociological discussions have assigned but one major function to empirical research: "testing" or "verification" of hypotheses. The model for the proper way of performing this function is as familiar as it is clear. The investigator begins with a hunch or hypothesis, from this he draws various inferences and these, in turn, are subjected to empirical test which confirms or refutes the hypothesis.[1] But this is a logical model, and so fails, of course, to describe much of what actually occurs in fruitful investigation. It presents a set of logical norms, not a description of the research experience. And, as logicians are well aware, in purifying the experience, the logical model may also distort it. Like other such models, it abstracts from the temporal sequence of events. It exaggerates the creative role of explicit theory just as it minimizes the creative role of observation. For research is not merely logic tempered with observation. It has its psychological as well as its logical dimensions, although one would scarcely suspect this from the logically rigorous sequence in which research is usually reported.[2] It is both the psychological and logical pressures of research upon social theory which we seek to trace.

[1] See, for example, the procedural review of Stouffer's "Theory of intervening opportunities" by G. A. Lundberg, "What are Sociological Problems?", *American Sociological Review*, VI (1941), 357–359.

[2] See R. K. Merton, "Science, Population and Society," *Scientific Monthly*, XLIV (1937), 170–171; the apposite discussion by Jean Piaget, *Judgment and Reasoning in the Child* (London, 1929), chaps. v, ix, and the comment [on the methodological procedures of scientific research] by William H. George, *The Scientist in Action* (London, 1936), p. 153. "A piece of research does not progress in the way it is 'written up' for publication."

It is my central thesis that empirical research goes far beyond the passive role of verifying and testing theory: it does more than confirm or refute hypotheses. Research plays an active role: it performs at least four major functions which help shape the development of theory. It *initiates,* it *reformulates,* it *deflects* and *clarifies* theory.

1. THE SERENDIPITY PATTERN

(The unanticipated, anomalous and strategic datum exerts a pressure for initiating theory.)

Under certain conditions, a research finding gives rise to social theory. In a previous paper, this was all too briefly expressed as follows: "Fruitful empirical research not only tests theoretically derived hypotheses; it also originates new hypotheses. This might be termed the 'serendipity' component of research, *i.e.,* the discovery, by chance or sagacity, of valid results which were not sought for."[3]

The serendipity pattern refers to the fairly common experience of observing an *unanticipated, anomalous* and *strategic* datum which becomes the occasion for developing a new theory or for extending an existing theory. Each of these elements of the pattern can be readily described. The datum is, first of all, unanticipated. A research directed toward the test of one hypothesis yields a fortuitous by-product, an unexpected observation which bears upon theories not in question when the research was begun.

Secondly, the observation is anomalous, surprising,[4] either because it seems inconsistent with prevailing theory or with other established facts. In either case, the seeming inconsistency provokes curiosity; it stimulates the investigator to "make sense of the datum," to fit it into a broader frame of knowledge. He explores further. He makes fresh observations. He draws inferences from the observations, inferences depending largely, of course, upon his general

---

[3] R. K. Merton, "Sociological Theory," *American Journal of Sociology,* L (1945), 469n. Interestingly enough, the same outlandish term 'serendipity' which has had little currency since it was coined by Horace Walpole in 1754 has also been used to refer to this component of research by the physiologist Walter B. Cannon. See his *The Way of an Investigator* (New York: W. W. Norton, 1945), chap. vi, in which he sets forth numerous instances of serendipity in several fields of science.

[4] Charles Sanders Pierce had long before noticed the strategic role of the "surprising fact" in his account of what he called "abduction," that is, the initiation and entertaining of a hypothesis as a step in inference. See his *Collected Papers* (Harvard University Press, 1931–35), VI, 522–528.

theoretic orientation. The more he is steeped in the data, the greater the likelihood that he will hit upon a fruitful direction of inquiry. In the fortunate circumstance that his new hunch proves justified, the anomalous datum leads ultimately to a new or extended theory. The curiosity stimulated by the anomalous datum is temporarily appeased.

And thirdly, in noting that the unexpected fact must be "strategic," *i.e.,* that it must permit of implications which bear upon generalized theory, we are, of course, referring rather to what the observer brings to the datum than to the datum itself. For it obviously requires a theoretically sensitized observer to detect the universal in the particular. After all, men had for centuries noticed such "trivial" occurrences as slips of the tongue, slips of the pen, typographical errors, and lapses of memory, but it required the theoretic sensitivity of a Freud to see these as strategic data through which he could extend his theory of repression and symptomatic acts.

The serendipity pattern, then, involves the unanticipated, anomalous and strategic datum which exerts pressure upon the investigator for a new direction of inquiry which extends theory. Instances of serendipity have occurred in many disciplines, but I should like to draw upon a current sociological research for illustration. In the course of our research into the social organization of Craftown,[5] a suburban housing community of some 700 families, largely of working class status, we observed that a large proportion of residents were affiliated with more civic, political and other voluntary organizations than had been the case in their previous places of residence. Quite incidentally, we noted further that this increase in group participation had occurred also among the parents of infants and young children. This finding was rather inconsistent with commonsense knowledge. For it is well known that, particularly on the lower economic levels, youngsters usually tie parents down and preclude their taking active part in organized group life outside the home. But Craftown parents themselves readily explained their behavior. "Oh, there's no real problem about getting out in the evenings," said one mother who belonged to several organizations. "It's easy to find teen-agers around here to take care of the kids. There are so many more teen-agers around here than where I used to live."

The explanation appears adequate enough and would have quieted

[5] Drawn from continuing studies in the Sociology and Social Psychology of Housing, under a grant from the Lavanburg Foundation.

he investigator's curiosity, had it not been for one disturbing datum: like most new housing communities, Craftown actually has a very small proportion of adolescents—only 3.7%, for example, in the 15–19 year age group. What is more, the majority of the adults, 63%, are under 34 years of age, so that their children include an exceptionally large proportion of infants and youngsters. Thus, far from there being many adolescents to look after the younger children in Craftown, quite the contrary is true: the ratio of adolescents to children under ten years of age is 1:10, whereas in the communities of origin, the ratio hovers about 1:1.5.[6]

We were at once confronted, then, by an anomalous fact which was certainly no part of our original program of observation. This should be emphasized. . . . Here was an observation both unanticipated and anomalous. Was it also strategic? We did not prejudge its "intrinsic" importance. . . .

The clue was inadvertently provided by further interviews with residents. In the words of an active participant in Craftown affairs, herself the mother of two children under six years of age:

"My husband and I get out together much more. You see, there are more people around to mind the children. *You feel more confident about having some thirteen-or-fourteen-year-old in here when you know most of the people. If you're in a big city, you don't feel so easy about having someone who's almost a stranger come in.*"

This clearly suggests that the sociological roots of the "illusion" are to be found in the structure of community relations in which Craftown residents are enmeshed. The belief is an unwitting reflection, not of the statistical reality, but of the community cohesion. It is not that there are objectively more adolescents in Craftown, but more who are *intimately known* and who, therefore, *exist socially* for parents seeking aid in child supervision. Most Craftown residents having lately come from an urban setting now find themselves in a community in which proximity has developed into reciprocal intimacies. The illusion expresses the perspective of people for whom adolescents as potential child-care aides "exist" only if they are well-known and therefore merit confidence. In short, perception was a

---

[6] Essentially the same discrepancies in age distribution between Craftown and communities of origin are found if we compare proportions of children under ten with those between 10 and 19. If we make children under five the basis for comparison, the disproportions are even more marked.

function of confidence and confidence, in turn, was a function of social cohesion.[7]

From the sociological viewpoint, then, this unanticipated finding fits into and extends the theory that "social perception" is the product of a social framework. It develops further the "psychology of social norms,"[8] for it is not merely an instance of individuals assimilating particular norms, judgments, and standards from other members of the community. The social perception is, rather, a by-product, a derivative, of the structure of human relations.

This is perhaps sufficient to illustrate the operation of the serendipity pattern: an unexpected and anomalous finding elicited the investigator's curiosity, and conducted him along an unpremeditated by-path which led to a fresh hypothesis.

2. The Recasting of Theory

(New data exert pressure for the elaboration of a conceptual scheme.)

But it is not only through the anomalous fact that empirical research invites the extension of theory. It does so also through the repeated observation of hitherto neglected facts. When an existing conceptual scheme commonly applied to a given subject-matter does not adequtaely take these facts into account, research presses insistently for its reformulation. It leads to the introduction of variables which have not been systematically included in the scheme of analysis. Here, be it noted, it is not that the data are anomalous or unexpected or incompatible with existing theory; it is merely that they have not been considered pertinent. Whereas the serendipity pattern centers in an apparent inconsistency which presses for resolution, the

[7] Schedule data from the study provide corroborative evidence. In view of the exceptionally high proportion of young children, it is striking that 54 per cent of their parents affirm that it is "easier in Craftown to get people to look after our children when we want to go out" than it was in other places where they have lived; only 21 per cent say it is harder and the remaining 25 per cent feel there is no difference. Those who come from the larger urban communities are more likely to report greater ease in obtaining assistance in Craftown. Moreover, as we would expect from the hypothesis, those residents who are more closely geared in with Craftown, who identify themselves most fully with it, are more likely to believe it easier to find such aid; 61 per cent of these do so as against 50 per cent of those who identify with other communities, whereas only 12 per cent find it more difficult in comparison with 26 per cent of the latter group.

[8] Muzafer Sherif's book by this title should be cited as basic in the field, although it tends to have a somewhat limited conception of "social factors," *The Psychology of Social Norms* (New York, 1936).

reformulation pattern centers in the hitherto neglected but relevant fact which presses for an extension of the conceptual scheme.

Examples of this in the history of social science are far from limited. Thus it was a series of fresh empirical facts which led Malinowski to incorporate new elements into a theory of magic. It was his Trobrianders, of course, who gave him the clue to the distinctive feature of his theory. When these islanders fished in the inner lagoon by the reliable method of poisoning, an abundant catch was assured and danger was absent. Neither uncertainty nor uncontrollable hazards were involved. And here, Malinowski noted, magic was not practiced. But in the open-sea fishing, with the uncertain yield and its often grave dangers, the rituals of magic flourished. Stemming from these pregnant observations was his theory that magical belief arises to bridge the uncertainties in man's practical pursuits, to fortify confidence, to reduce anxieties, to open up avenues of escape from the seeming impasse. Magic was construed as a supplementary technique for reaching practical objectives. It was these empirical facts which suggested the incorporation of new dimensions into earlier theories of magic—particularly the relations of magic to the fortuitous, the dangerous and the uncontrollable. It was not that these facts were *inconsistent* with previous theories; it was simply that these conceptual schemes had not taken them adequately into account. Nor was Malinowski testing a preconceived hypothesis—he was developing an enlarged and improved theory on the basis of suggestive empirical data.

For another example of this pressure of empirical data for the recasting of a specific theory we turn closer home. The investigation dealt with a single dramatic instance of mass persuasion: broadcasting at repeated intervals over a span of eighteen hours, Kate Smith, a radio star, sold large quantities of war-bonds in the course of the day. It is not my intention to report fully on the dynamics of this case of mass persuasion; [9] for present purposes, we are concerned only with the implications of two facts which emerged from the study.

First of all, in the course of intensive interviews many of our informants—New Yorkers who had pledged a bond to Smith—expressed a thorough disenchantment with the world of advertising, commercials and propaganda. They felt themselves the object of

[9] R. K. Merton, M. Fiske and A. Curtis, *Mass Persuasion* (New York: Harper, 1946).

manipulation—and resented it. They objected to being the target for advertising which cajoles, insists and terrorizes. They objected to being engulfed in waves of propaganda proposing opinions and actions not in their own best interests. They expressed dismay over what is in effect a pattern of *pseudo-Gemeinschaft*—subtle methods of salesmanship in which there is the feigning of personal concern with the client in order to manipulate him the better. As one small businessman phrased it, "In my own business, I can see how a lot of people in their business deals will make some kind of gesture of friendliness, sincerity and so forth, most of which is phony." Drawn from a highly competitive, segmented metropolitan society, our informants were describing a climate of reciprocal distrust, of *anomie*, in which common values have been submerged in the welter of private interests. Society was experienced as an arena for rival frauds. There was small belief in the disinterestedness of conduct.

In contrast to all this was the second fact: we found that the persuasiveness of the Smith bond-drive among these same informants largely rested upon their firm belief in the integrity and sincerity of Smith. And much the same was found to be true in a polling interview with a larger cross-section sample of almost a thousand New Yorkers. Fully 80% asserted that in her all-day marathon drives, Smith was *exclusively* concerned with promoting the sale of war bonds, whereas only 17% felt that she was *also* interested in publicity for herself, and a negligible 3% believed she was *primarily* concerned with the resulting publicity. . . .

In short, it was not so much what Smith *said* as what she *did* which served to validate her sincerity. It was the presumed stress and strain of an eighteen-hour series of broadcasts, it was the deed not the word which furnished the indubitable proof. Listeners might question whether she were not unduly dramatizing herself, but they could not escape the incontrovertible evidence that she was devoting the entire day to the task. Appraising the direct testimony of Smith's behavior, another informant explains that "she was on all day and the others weren't. So it seemed that she was sacrificing more and was more sincere." Viewed as a process of persuasion, the marathon converted initial feelings of scepticism and distrust among listeners into at first a reluctant, and later, a full-fledged acceptance of Smith's integrity. The successive broadcasts served as a fulfillment in action of a promise in words. The words were reinforced by things she has actually done. The currency of talk was accepted because it is backed by the gold of conduct. The gold reserve, moreover, need not even approximate the amount of currency it can support.

This empirical study suggests that propaganda-of-the-deed may be effective among the very people who are distrustful of propaganda-of-the-word. Where there is social disorganization, *anomie,* conflicting values, we find propaganditis reaching epidemic proportions. Any statement of value is likely to be discounted as "mere propaganda." Exhortations are suspect. But the propaganda of the deed elicits more confidence. Members of the audience are largely permitted to draw their conclusions from the action—they are less likely to feel manipulated. When the propagandist's deed and his words symbolically coincide, it stimulates belief in his sincerity. Further research must determine whether this propaganda pattern is significantly more effective in societies suffering from *anomie* than in those which are more fully integrated. But not unlike the Malinowski case-in-point, this may illustrate the role of research in suggesting new variables to be incorporated into a specific theory.

3. THE RE-FOCUSSING OF THEORETIC INTEREST

(New methods of empirical research exert pressure
for new foci of theoretic interest.)

To this point we have considered the impact of research upon the development of particular theories. But empirical research also affects more general trends in the development of theory. This occurs chiefly through the invention of research procedures which tend to shift the foci of theoretic interest to the growing points of research.

The reasons for this are on the whole evident. After all, sound theory thrives only on a rich diet of pertinent facts and newly invented procedures help provide the ingredients of this diet. The new, and often previously unavailable, data stimulate fresh hypotheses. Moreover, theorists find that their hypotheses can be put to immediate test in those spheres where appropriate research techniques have been designed. It is no longer necessary for them to wait upon data as they happen to turn up—researches directed to the verification of hypotheses can be instituted at once. The flow of relevant data thus increases the tempo of advance in certain spheres of theory whereas in others, theory stagnates for want of adequate observations. Attention shifts accordingly.

In noting that new centers of theoretic interest have followed upon the invention of research procedures, we do not imply that these alone played a decisive role.[10] The growing interest in the theory of propaganda as an instrument of social control, for example, is in large part a response to the changing historical situation, with its conflict of major ideological systems; new technologies of mass communication which have opened up new avenues for propaganda; and the rich research treasuries provided by business and government interested in this new weapon of war, both declared and undeclared. But this shift is also a by-product of accumulated facts made available through such newly developed, and confessedly crude, procedures as content-analysis, the panel technique and the focussed interview.

Examples of this impact in the recent history of social theory are numerous but we have time to mention only a few. Thus, the increasing concern with the theory of character and personality formation in relation to social structure became marked after the introduction of new projective methods; the Rorschach test, the thematic apperception test, play techniques and story completions being among the most familiar. So, too, the sociometric techniques of Moreno and others, and fresh advances in the technique of the "passive interview" have revived interest in the theory of interpersonal relations. Stemming from such techniques as well is the trend toward what might be called the "rediscovery of the primary group," particularly in the shape of theoretic concern with informal social structures as mediating between the individual and large formal organizations. This interest has found expression in an entire literature on the role and structure of the informal group, for example, in factory social systems, bureaucracy and political organizations. Similarly, we may anticipate that the recent introduction of the panel technique—the repeated interviewing of the same group of informants—will in due course more sharply focus the attention of social psychologists upon the theory of attitude formation, decisions among alternative choices, factors in political participation and determinants of behavior in cases of conflicting role demands, to mention a few types of problems to which this technique is especially adapted.

Perhaps the most direct impact of research procedures upon theory has resulted from the *creation* of sociological statistics organized in

---

[10] It is perhaps needless to add that these procedures, instruments and apparatus are in turn dependent upon prior theory. But this does not alter their stimulating effect upon the further development of theory. *Cf.* Merton, "Sociological Theory," 463n.

terms of theoretically pertinent categories. Talcott Parsons has observed that numerical data are scientifically important only when they can be fitted into analytical categories and that "a great deal of current research is producing facts in a form which cannot be utilized by any current generalized analytical scheme." [11] These well-deserved strictures of a scant decade ago are proving progressively less applicable. In the past, the sociologist has largely had to deal with *pre-collected series* of statistics usually assembled for non-sociological purposes and, therefore, not set forth in categories directly pertinent to any given theoretical system. As a result, at least so far as quantitative facts are concerned, the theorist was compelled to work with makeshift data bearing only a tangential relevance to his problems. This not only left a wide margin for error—consider the crude indexes of social cohesion upon which Durkheim had to rely—but it also meant that theory had to wait upon the incidental and, at times, almost accidental availability of relevant data. It could not march rapidly ahead. This picture has now begun to change.

No longer does the theorist depend almost exclusively upon the consensus of administrative boards or social welfare agencies for his quantitative data. Tarde's programmatic sketch [12] a half century ago of the need for statistics in social psychology, particularly those dealing with attitudes, opinions and sentiments, has become a half-fulfilled promise. So, too, investigators of community organization are creating statistics on class structure, associational behavior, and clique formations, and this has left its mark on theoretic interests. Ethnic studies are beginning to provide quantitative data which are reorienting the theorist. It is safe to suppose that the enormous accumulation of sociological materials during the war—notably by the Research Branch of the Information and Education Division of the War Department—materials which are in part the result of new research techniques, will intensify interest in the theory of group morale, propaganda and leadership. But it is perhaps needless to multiply examples.

What we have said does not mean that the piling up of statistics of

[11] Talcott Parsons, "The Role of Theory in Social Research," *American Sociological Review,* III (1938), 19; *cf.* his *Structure of Social Action* (New York, 1937), pp. 328–329n. [Note his statement that] ". . . in the social field most available statistical information is on a level which cannot be made to fit directly into the categories of analytical theory."

[12] Gabriel Tarde, *Essais et mélanges sociologiques,* (Paris, 1895), pp. 230–270.

itself advances theory; it does mean that theoretic interest tends to shift to those areas in which there is an abundance of *pertinent* statistical data. Moreover, we are merely calling attention to this shift of focus, not evaluating it. It may very well be that it sometimes deflects attention to problems which, in a theoretic or humanistic sense, are "unimportant"; it may divert attention from problems with larger implications onto those for which there is the promise of immediate solutions. Failing a detailed study, it is difficult to come to any overall assessment of this point. But the pattern itself seems clear enough in sociology as in other disciplines: as new and previously unobtainable data become available through the use of new techniques, theorists turn their analytical eye upon the implications of these data and bring about new directions of inquiry.

4. THE CLARIFICATION OF CONCEPTS

(Empirical research exerts pressure for clear concepts.)

A good part of the work called "theorizing" is taken up with the clarification of concepts—and rightly so. It is in this matter of clearly defined concepts that social science research is not infrequently defective. Research activated by a major interest in methodology may be centered on the *design* of establishing causal relations without due regard for analyzing the variables involved in the inquiry. This methodological empiricism, as the design of inquiry without correlative concern with the clarification of substantive variables may be called, characterizes a large part of current research. Thus, in a series of effectively designed experiments, Chapin finds that "the rehousing of slum families in a public housing project results in improvement of the living conditions and the social life of these families."[13] Or through controlled experiments, psychologists search out the effects of foster home placement upon children's performances in intelligence tests.[14] Or, again through experimental inquiry, researchers seek to determine whether a propaganda film has achieved its purpose of improving attitudes toward the British. These several cases, and they are representative of a large amount of research which has

[13] F. S. Chapin, "The effects of slum clearance and rehousing on family and community relationships in Minneapolis," *American Journal of Sociology*, XLIII (1938), 744–763.
[14] R. R. Sears, "Child Psychology," in Wayne Dennis, ed., *Current Trends in Psychology* (University of Pittsburgh Press, 1947), pp. 55–56. Sears' comments on this type of research state the general problem admirably.

advanced social science method, have in common the fact that the empirical variables are not analyzed in terms of their conceptual elements.[15] As Rebecca West, with her characteristic lucidity, put this general problem of methodological empiricism, one might "know that A and B and C were linked by certain causal connexions, but he would never apprehend with any exactitude the nature of A or B or C." In consequences, these researches further the procedures of inquiry, but their findings do not enter into the repository of cumulative social science theory.

But in general, the clarification of concepts, commonly considered a province peculiar to the theorist, is a frequent result of empirical research. Research sensitive to its own needs cannot avoid this pressure for conceptual clarification. *For a basic requirement of research is that the concepts, the variables, be defined with sufficient clarity to enable the research to proceed,* a requirement easily and unwittingly not met in the kind of discursive exposition which is often miscalled "sociological theory."

The clarification of concepts ordinarily enters into empirical research in the shape of establishing *indices* of the variables under consideration. In non-research speculations, it is possible to talk loosely about "morale" or "social cohesion" without any clear conceptions of what is entailed by these terms, but they *must* be clarified if the researcher is to go about his business of systematically observing instances of low and high morale, of social cohesion or cleavage. If he is not to be blocked at the outset, he must devise indices which are observable, fairly precise and meticulously clear. The entire movement of thought which was christened "operationalism" is only one conspicuous case of the researcher demanding that concepts be defined clearly enough for him to go to work.

This has been typically recognized by those sociologists who combine a theoretic orientation with systematic empirical research. Durkheim, for example, despite the fact that his terminology and indices now appear crude and debatable, clearly perceived the need for devising indices of his concepts. Repeatedly, he asserted that "it is necessary . . . to substitute for the internal fact which escapes us an external fact that symbolizes it and to study the former through the

---

[15] However crude they may be, procedures such as the focused interview are expressly designed as aids for detecting possibly relevant variables in an initially undifferentiated situation. See R. K. Merton and P. L. Kendall, "The Focused Interview," *American Journal of Sociology,* LI (1946), 541–57.

latter." [16] The index, or sign of the conceptualized item, stands ideally in a one-to-one correlation with what it signifies (and the difficulty of establishing this relation is of course one of the critical problems of research). Since the index and its object are so related, one may ask for the grounds on which one is taken as the index and the other as the indexed variable. As Durkheim implied and as Suzanne Langer has indicated anew, the index is that one of the correlated pair which is perceptible and the other, harder or impossible to perceive, is theoretically relevant.[17] Thus, attitude scales make available indices of otherwise not discriminable attitudes, just as ecological statistics represent indices of diverse social structures in a given area.

What often appears as a tendency in research for quantification (through the development of scales) can thus be seen as a special case of attempting to clarify concepts sufficiently to permit the conduct of empirical investigation. The development of valid and observable indices becomes central to the use of concepts in the prosecution of research. A final illustration will indicate how research presses for the clarification of ancient sociological concepts which, on the plane of discursive exposition, have remained ill-defined and unclarified.

A conception basic to sociology holds that individuals have multiple social roles and tend to organize their behavior in terms of the structurally defined expectations assigned to each role. Further, it is said, the less integrated the society, the more often will individuals be subject to the strain of incompatible social roles. Type-cases are numerous and familiar: the Catholic Communist subjected to conflicting pressures from party and church, the marginal man suffering the pulls of conflicting societies, the professional woman torn between the demands of family and career. Every sociological textbook abounds with illustrations of incompatible demands made of the multiselved person.

Perhaps because it has been largely confined to discursive interpretations and has seldom been made the focus of systematic research, this central problem of conflicting roles has yet to be materially clarified and advanced beyond the point reached decades ago.

[16] Émile Durkheim, *Division of Labor in Society* (New York: Macmillan, 1933), p. 66; also his *Les règles de la méthode sociologique* (Paris, 1895), pp. 55–58; *Le Suicide* (Paris, 1930), pp. 356 and *passim. Cf.* R. K. Merton, "Durkheim's Division of Labor in Society," *American Journal of Sociology,* XL, 1934, esp. 326–7 which touches on the problem of indices.
[17] Suzanne K. Langer, *Philosophy in a New Key* (New York: Penguin Books, 1948), pp. 46–47.

Thomas and Znaniecki long since indicated that conflicts between social roles *can* be reduced by conventionalization and by role-segmentation (by assigning each set of role-demands to different situations).[18] And others have noted that frequent conflict between roles is dysfunctional for the society as well as for the individual. But all this leaves many salient problems untouched: on which grounds does one predict the behavior of persons subject to conflicting roles? And when a decision must be made, which role (or which group solidarity) takes precedence? Under which conditions does one or another prove controlling? On the plane of discursive thought, it has been suggested that the role with which the individual identifies most fully will prove dominant, thus banishing the problem through a tautological pseudo-solution. Or, the problem of seeking to predict behavior consequent to incompatibility of roles, a research problem requiring operational clarification of the concepts of solidarity, conflict, role-demands and situation, has been evaded by observing that conflicts of roles typically ensue in frustration.

More recently, empirical research has pressed for clarification of the key concepts involved in this problem. Indices of conflicting group pressures have been devised and the resultant behavior observed in specified situations. Thus, as a beginning in this direction, it has been shown that in a concrete decision-situation, such as voting, individuals subject to these cross-pressures respond by delaying their vote-decision. And, under conditions yet to be determined, they seek to reduce the conflict by escaping from the field of conflict: they "lose interest" in the political campaign. Finally, there is the intimation in these data that in cases of cross-pressures upon the voter, it is socio-economic position which is typically controlling.[19]

However this may be, the essential point is that, in this instance as in others, the very requirements of empirical research have been instrumental in clarifying received concepts. The process of empirical inquiry raises conceptual issues which may long go undetected in theoretic inquiry.

There remain, then, a few concluding remarks. My discussion has been devoted exclusively to four impacts of research upon the development of social theory: the initiation, reformulation, refocusing

[18] W. I. Thomas and F. Znaniecki, *The Polish Peasant* (New York: Knopf, 1927), pp. 1866–70, 1888, 1899 ff.

[19] P. F. Lazarsfeld, Bernard Berelson and Hazel Gaudet, *The People's Choice* (New York: Duell, Sloan & Pearce, 1944), chap. vi.

and clarification of theory. Doubtless there are others. Doubtless, too, the emphasis of this paper lends itself to misunderstanding. It may be inferred that some invidious distinction has been drawn at the expense of theory and the theorist. That has not been my intention. I have suggested only that an explicitly formulated theory does not invariably precede empirical inquiry, that as a matter of plain fact the theorist is not inevitably the lamp lighting the way to new observations. The sequence is often reversed. Nor is it enough to say that research and theory must be married if sociology is to bear legitimate fruit. They must not only exchange solemn vows—they must know how to carry on from there. Their reciprocal roles must be clearly defined. This paper is a brief essay toward that definition.

SECTION TWO
Socialization of the Individual

8 GROWTH POTENTIALS OF THE HUMAN INFANT *

BY ARNOLD GESELL (1880–   )
YALE UNIVERSITY

A LL educability is dependent upon innate capacities of growth. This intrinsic growth is a gift of nature. It can be guided, but it cannot be created; nor can it be transcended by any educational agency.

The problem of human educability therefore must reckon with two closely related concepts, namely, *learning* and *growth*. Darwin understood this when he suggested toward the end of his life that more accurate knowledge of the development of infants would probably give a foundation for some improvement in their education.

From the vantage point of post-Darwinian science, we begin to see each child as the focal end product of age-old processes of evolution. Biologically considered, infancy is a period of formative immaturity, which is most prolonged and most intensified in the very species which stands highest in the life scale—presumably in our own! Bernard Shaw rather deplores this circumstance. Accordingly, in his *Metabiological Pentateuch,* he arranges matters otherwise; and on a summer afternoon in the year A.D. 31,920, the Newly Born emerges from a fabulous eggshell (some "filaments of spare albumen clinging to her here and there")—an exquisite creature endowed with speech and the full-fledged intelligence of a seventeen-year-old youth. With such a precocious start and a Back-to-Methuselah life cycle, the race may indeed be in a better position to cope with its cultural problems.

The infant of today, nevertheless, is born with prodigious powers of psychological growth. Note how swiftly and progressively he gains command of his eyes and hands. Very soon after birth he is able to fixate an eye upon an object of interest; first he fixates with one eye, then with the other, later with each in rapid rhythmic alternation, and later conjointly and convergently. At four weeks he

---

* Reprinted by permission of the author and of the editor from *The Scientific Monthly,* LXVIII (1949), 252–253, 255–256.

gives sustained binocular regard to an object brought into his line of vision; at eight weeks he follows it with head rotation; at twelve weeks he looks regardfully at his own hand; at sixteen weeks, when seated in a supportive chair in front of a test table, he can focus eyes upon a tiny pellet 7 mm. in diameter. He takes hold of the world with his eyes before he does so with his hands. But at twenty-four weeks he can pick up a one-inch block on sight. His early manual grasp is pawlike, palmar and ulnar. Soon it becomes digital and radial. At forty weeks he picks up the pellet with fingertips by precise pincer prehension. At fifteen months he releases this same pellet into a bottle; he adaptively superimposes one block upon another. At eighteen months he builds a tower of three blocks; at two years, a wall; at three years, a bridge.

I rehearse this brief tale because it illustrates what the infant himself rehearses by way of his own ontogenetic development. The significant fact about these patterns of eye-hand behavior is that they are not products of formal instruction, training, nor of education in a narrow sense. They are self-taught, self-initiated. In sequence and form they represent a generic ground plan of child development. The ground plan is primarily determined by genes. Environmental factors support, inflect, and modify, but they do not generate, the basic progressions of development. When the infant enters the world, he is already in possession of fundamental growth potentials which are distinctively his own, though phyletic in their origin.

With the aid of motion-picture cameras at the Yale Clinic, we have documented thousands of behavior patterns and pattern phases at thirty-four progressive age levels, from the period of fetal infancy through the first ten years of life. Growth gradations were charted in four major fields of behavior: motor, language, adaptive, personal-social. These objective records show that, although no two individuals are exactly alike, all normal children tend to follow a general sequence of growth characteristic of the species and of a cultural group. Every child has a unique pattern of growth, but that pattern is a variant of a basic ground plan. The species sequences are part of an established order of nature. Accordingly, the eyes take the lead, the hands follow; palmar grasp comes before digital; creeping before walking; crying before laughing; towers before walls; vertical crayon strokes before horizontal, and horizontal before oblique. First the blade, then the ear.

Growth is a step-by-step process. Each step is made possible by the step that preceded. The mind thus grows by natural stages. Maximum educability is realized only when educational measures are attuned to the maturity status of the organism. We have demonstrated the significance of maturity factors by extensive use of the method of co-twin control. One of a pair of extremely similar, single-egg twins was intensively trained for periods of six to eight weeks in a specific activity; the other twin was reserved as a comparative control. Objective data supported by cinemanalysis were gathered for stair climbing, constructive play with blocks, vocabulary training, digit and object memory, and motor skills in ring tossing and paper cutting. In none of these activities was it possible to confer a permanent advantage of skill upon either twin. After a lapse of a few weeks or months, the performances of the twins on the various tests were as similar to each other as at the beginning of the given experiment. I hasten to say that this does not prove that twins (or singletons) should not be educated. We simply have demonstrated in quantitative terms that the efficacy of training varies enormously with the developmental readiness of the infant and child.

Maturation is the net sum of gene effects operating in a self-limited life cycle. If you are reluctant to acknowledge the educational importance of genes, you may say, "This is all very well for such physical reactions as walking, stair climbing, block building, writing, drawing, and motor skills. But does it apply to emotions, to morals, to personality, and to the spiritual aspects of childhood?"

Our studies show that the higher psychical manifestations of child life also are profoundly subject to laws of development. From the standpoint of development, body and mind are indivisible. The child comes by his mind as he comes by his body, through the organizing processes of growth. Psychically, he inherits nothing fully formed. Each and every part of his nature has to grow—and his sense of self, his fears, his affections and his curiosities, his feelings toward mother, father, playmates, and sex, his judgments of good and bad, of ugly and beautiful, his respect for truth and property, his sense of humor, his ideas about life and death, crime, war, nature, and deity. All his sentiments, concepts, and attitudes are products of growth and experience. For all these diverse areas of behavior it is possible to formulate gradations and gradients of growth which represent the natural maturational stages by which the child assimilates the complex culture into which he is born.

The culture also assimilates him through its "gigantic conditioning apparatus." But the process of acculturation is fundamentally delimited and pervasively patterned by the mechanisms of maturation inherent in the individual.

Educability is delimited and configured by the selfsame mechanisms; for educability does not depend upon a formless kind of plasticity. It depends upon the structured nascencies of the mind as a growing organism. The human mind is a minutely architectured action system which has an embryogenesis and a developmental morphology, manifested in patterns of behavior. The forms and lawful sequences of these patterns can be defined by scientific methods. This is the task of a genetic and clinical science of child development.

More knowledge needs to be applied at the beginnings of the life cycle to reduce the mounting tide of adolescent instability and of adult abnormalities of behavior. Through broadened methods of developmental diagnosis and supervision in infancy, through individualized growth guidance in nursery and elementary schools, we can strengthen the stamina of the child and of the family unit. We can foster basic virtues and discover distinctive gifts and talents—academic and nonacademic—in the early years of life. We cannot make democracy a genuine folkway, unless we bring into the homes of the people a *developmental philosophy* of child care that is rooted in scientific research.

No one has to teach a baby the elements of growing. He knows all that by heart, for nature drilled it into him through countless ages of evolution. What is more, nature compounded him so ingeniously that no one just like him will ever be born again. He is an individual. Under given environmental conditions, his inborn growth potentials will govern the extent and the modes of his maturing. His growth characteristics constitute the very core of his individuality, and by the same token his educability. To rear him aright, whether at home or at school, we must understand his individuality.

He manifests this individuality from the very beginning in his natural rhythms of feeding, sleep, and self-activity. Given wisely managed opportunity he seems to know when to sleep, when to be hungry, and how much to sleep and eat. His educability is not so bland and undifferentiated that he responds neatly to an iron-clad feeding schedule. Things work out better, if his own self-regulation mechanisms, which are really growth mechanisms, are given a reasonable scope. The discerning physician makes no arbitrary distinctions between physical and mental factors; he gives conjoint consideration to the infant's nutritional status, to his immunities, allergies, and behavior traits. The child grows as a unit.[1]

The task of the culture, likewise, is to watch for signs and symptoms of the child's total well-being with a special concern for psychological health. We must go along with the baby far enough to build up in him a sense of security. Step by step it is possible to build up his self-confidence through strengthening his confidence in his caretakers. Gradually he gains in morale and social insights, not through sheer indulgence, but through perceptive guidance on the part of his elders. And the more these elders know about the processes of growth, the more they will enjoy the truly remarkable progress which normal children make even in the first five years of life.

The intrinsic badness of children has, in my opinion, been vastly exaggerated by distorting interpretations. Well-constituted children with healthy inheritance have an intrinsic charm—a charm which betokens intrinsic goodness. The growth potentials for good far outweigh those for evil, unless the cultural odds are too heavily weighted against the child.

It is too freely said that science is indifferent to human values. I would say in this connection that science by implication is always concerned with values, and the life sciences which deal with the physiology and the pathologies of growth are coming profoundly to grips with the deepmost determiners of human values. The race evolved, the child grows. And we shall not have the requisite self-knowledge to manage our culture until we make a more sedulous effort to understand the ways of all growth and the potentials of child growth, which are the culminating evidences and products of organic evolution.

This evolution has not ceased; and to that degree man still remains educable. He seems to have reached the very acme of mass cruelty, confusion, conflict, and destructiveness. Therein lies a tithe of hope. It would seem that on sheer evolutional grounds of survival, man must and can shift to a higher cerebral plane of attitude and action. Among other things, he surely needs a science of behavior, a systematically prosecuted science, which will not only probe the lingering wickedness of old Adam, but which will explore with unrelenting penetration the rich repository of potentials for good, which are revealed with awesome mystery in the sequences of child development.

[1] [Cf. A. Gesell and F. L. Ilg, *Child Development* (New York: Harper, 1948. — Ed.]

9 PRIMARY AND NON-PRIMARY GROUPS *

BY CHARLES HORTON COOLEY (1864–1929),
ROBERT COOLEY ANGELL (1899–   ),
AND LOWELL JUILLIARD CARR (1885–   )
UNIVERSITY OF MICHIGAN

A GROUP is any two or more persons who are temporarily or permanently set off from others by differential association, *i.e.*, by closer association with one another than with others during the time in question. . . . Arranged in order of increasing size and decreasing intimacy, human groupings fall into four general classes:

I. *Intimate pair-groups* such as mother and child, husband and wife, lover and sweetheart. In a sense these are sub-primary groups.

II. *Primary groups* characterized by (1) face-to-face association, (2) small numbers, (3) unspecialized purpose, (4) comparative intimacy, (5) relative permanence. The home, the spontaneous play group, and the old-fashioned neighborhood are type examples.[1] . . .

III. *Quasi-primary groups.* These are organized face-to-face intimate groups, limited in some degree by special purpose and by the fact of organization. Boy Scout troops, college fraternities and sororities, luncheon clubs, etc., are examples. They have many of the characteristics of primary groups and may in fact perform many of the functions of primary groups, yet organization and the limitations of special purpose give them some of the characteristics of secondary groups.

IV. *Secondary groups.* These are groups wholly lacking in intimacy of association and usually in most of the other primary and quasi-primary characteristics. Crowds, communities, corporations, nations are among the examples. In general, secondary groups may be classified according as they are or are not basically organized around cultural elements. Six kinds of similarities seem to account for secondary groupings, as follows:

---

* Reprinted by permission of the authors and of the publisher from *Introductory Sociology* (New York: Charles Scribner's Sons, 1933), pp. 208, 210–211, 55–60, 211–215.

[1] [See *ibid.*, chap. iv.—*Ed.*]

1. Culturally organized groups:
   i. Status groups, *i.e.,* social classes.
   ii. Nationality groups—nations.
   iii. Residence groups—communities and regional groups.
   iv. Attention-, interest-, and purpose-groups—publics, institutional groups, corporations, etc.
2. Groups not basically organized by culture:
   v. Biological groups—age-groups, the sexes, races.
   vi. Casual groups—crowds and assemblages, such as audiences, mobs, etc. . . .

A primary group may be defined as a group of from two to possibly fifty or sixty people—*i.e.,* a small number—who are in relatively lasting face-to-face association for no single purpose, but merely as persons rather than as specialized functionaries, agents or employees of any organization. Type examples of the primary group are the family, or household group, the old-fashioned neighborhood, and the spontaneous play-group of children. In such groups all children everywhere participate, and the intimate association there realized works upon them everywhere in much the same way. It tends to develop sympathetic insight into the moods and states of mind of other people and this in turn underlies the development of both the flexible type of behavior and the common attitudes and sentiments which we have mentioned.

Human nature is, then, not something existing separately in the individual, but a *group nature or primary phase of society.* It is the nature which is developed and expressed in those simple face-to-face groups that are somewhat alike in all societies. Man does not have it at birth; he cannot acquire it except through fellowship; and it decays in isolation.

Characteristics of Primary Groups. The chief characteristics of a primary group are:

1. Face-to-face association.
2. The unspecialized character of that association.
3. Relative permanence.
4. The small number of persons involved.
5. The relative intimacy among the participants.

Such groups are primary in several senses, but chiefly in that they are fundamental in forming the social nature and ideals of the individual. The result of intimate association, psychologically, is a certain fusion of individualities in a common whole, so that one's very self, for many purposes at least, is the common life and purpose of the group. Perhaps the simplest way of describing this wholeness is by saying that it is a "we"; it involves the sort of sympathy and mutual identification for which "we" is the natural expression. One lives in the feeling of the whole and finds the chief aims of his will in that feeling.

It is not to be supposed that the unity of the primary group is one of mere harmony and love. It is always a differentiated and usually a competitive unity, admitting of self-assertion and various appropriative passions; but these passions are socialized by sympathy, and come, or tend to come, under the discipline of a common spirit. The individual will be ambitious, but the chief object of his ambition will be some desired place in the thought of the others, and he will feel allegiance to common standards of service and fair play. So the boy will dispute with his fellows a place on the team, but above such disputes will place the common glory of his class and school.

In primitive cultures, and even in advanced cultures before the growth of cities, the great bulk of human association occurs in primary groups. Probably the human race, all told, has lived more than 90 per cent of its total existence in such groups. That the home, the play-group and the neighborhood are relatively less prominent in modern American life than they were in Colonial days or among the original Americans themselves is not traceable to any decline in the absolute importance of the primary-group function itself but to the effects of modern communication, particularly the automobile, and to the resulting substitution of other less intimate forms of association.

It is well to remember, however, that no attempt to organize society on a non-primary basis has ever been permanently successful. Our own experiment in civilization is not escaping the difficulties that inevitably attend the effort to make large secondary groups such as corporations, cities, nations, satisfy the demands of human nature that issue from the primary group experience. As we shall see later, these difficulties are mainly difficulties of personality, of communication and of organization, but before attempting to analyze them more fully it is essential to understand more of the nature and functions of the groups themselves.

The Type Examples of the Primary Group. The most important spheres of this intimate association and co-operation, as we have said —though by no means the only ones—are the family, the spontane-

ous play-group of children, and the neighborhood, or "little community" of elders.[2] These are practically universal, belonging to all
times and all stages of development; and are accordingly a chief basis
of what is universal in human nature and human ideals. The best
comparative studies of the family, such as those of Westermarck,
Howard, or Briffault, show it to us as not only a universal institution, but as more alike the world over than the exaggeration of exceptional customs by an earlier school had led us to suppose.[3] Nor
can any one doubt the general prevalence of play-groups among
children or of informal assemblies of various kinds among their
elders. Such association is clearly the nursery of human nature in the
world about us, and there is no apparent reason to suppose that the
case has anywhere or at any time been essentially different.

As regards play, we might, were it not a matter of common observation, multiply illustrations of the universality and spontaneity
of the group discussion and co-operation to which it gives rise. The
general fact is that children, especially boys after about their twelfth
year, live in fellowships in which their sympathy, ambition, and
honor are engaged even more, often, than they are in the family. Most
of us can recall examples of the endurance by boys of injustice and
even cruelty, rather than appeal from their fellows to parents or
teachers—as for instance, in the hazing so prevalent at schools, and so
difficult, for that reason, to repress. And how elaborate the discussion,
how cogent the public opinion, how hot the ambitions in these fellowships!

Nor is this facility of juvenile association, as is sometimes supposed, a trait peculiar to English and American boys; since experience among our immigrant population, seems to show that the offspring of the more restrictive civilizations of the continent of Europe
form self-governing play-groups with almost equal readiness. Thus
Miss Jane Addams, after pointing out that the "gang" is almost universal, speaks of the interminable discussion which every detail of
the gang's activity receives, remarking that "in these social folk-

[2] The neighborhood is to be distinguished from the community proper by the
fact that within the neighborhood association is face to face while the community
may be made up of a number of such neighborhoods. Under primitive or rural
conditions the neighborhood may constitute the community, but in more advanced
cultures the two are seldom identical.

[3] Edward Westermarck, *The History of Human Marriage*, London, 1891.
G. E. Howard, *A History of Matrimonial Institutions*, Chicago, 1904. Robert Briffault,
The Mothers, New York, 1927.

moots, so to speak, the young citizen learns to act upon his own determination." [4]

Of the neighborhood group it may be said, in general, that from the time men formed permanent settlements upon the land, down, at least, to the rise of modern industrial cities, it has played a main part in the primary, heart-to-heart life of the people. Among our Teutonic forefathers the village community was apparently the chief sphere of sympathy and mutual aid for the commons all through the "dark" and middle ages, and for many purposes it remains so in rural districts at the present day. Terpenning's study of the neighborhood in America and in Europe, the open country neighborhood *vs.* the village neighborhood, is telling evidence of the importance of this form of association.[5] In America the intimacy of the neighborhood, which has never been that of the European village at best, has been further broken up by the growth of an intricate mesh of wider contacts which in cities at least often leaves us strangers to people who live in the same house. . . .

From Animal to Man.   In just what way is the primary group so powerful a humanizing agent? Biologically each of us is equipped with innate drives such as lust, greed, revenge, the thirst for power, and the like which are in their crudest forms not distinctively human drives at all but animal drives. The distinctively human level of behavior appears only when the raw instincts have been conditioned through sympathetic insight into *sentiments* such as love, ambition, and resentment. It is because we are always dealing with sentiments, *i.e., with instinctive emotions organized around ideas,* that attempts to explain human behavior by raw instinct are so hopelessly inadequate. *This humanizing of the animal drives is perhaps the greatest service performed by the primary group.* Other forms of association contribute in some degree to this same end, but the advantage of primary association is that it occurs spontaneously, over and over again, is not limited by conscious purpose, is accompanied by full and free play of pre-verbal as well as verbal communication with all that that implies for the emotional conditioning of personality, and finally, that it is a universal type of experience affecting the entire human race. For these reasons it produces as a matter of course

---

[4] *Newer Ideals of Peace,* p. 177. Thrasher, in *The Gang* (Chicago, 1926), presents much evidence of the same sort.

[5] Walter Terpenning, *Village and Open-Country Neighborhoods* (New York, 1931), p. 387.

a deeper psychological effect on more people per unit of time than society can manage to produce by elaborate social organization and deliberate effort.

Cyril Burt, for example, after a careful analysis of 200 juvenile delinquents, concluded that "Of environmental conditions, those obtaining outside the home are far less important than those obtaining within it; material conditions, such as poverty, are far less important than moral conditions, such as discipline, vice, and, most of all, the child's relation with his parents." [6]

Such evidence strongly suggests that *the primary group is a more efficient humanizer of animal drives per unit of time than any other form of association that man has been able to devise.* . . .

Decline of the Primary Group. To an extent unknown in any previous culture, modern civilization, in the United States at least, rests on non-primary forms of grouping. Other and more exciting forms of association are tending to crowd out the neighborhood, the home, and the spontaneous play-group. Thanks to electro-machine communication and to the automobile the great mass of Americans are no longer limited by vicinage in their associations: one's intimate friends need not and usually do not live near by. In our cities and in rural regions in which the old life has been disorganized by an influx of strangers, a neighborhood is no longer a distinguishable unit of social organization but a mere geographical expression. In Detroit, for example, the "neighborhood of the Dodge factory" is not a neighborhood at all, but a locality. Even under rural conditions neighborhoods are not all alike. [Dwight] Sanderson and [Warren S.] Thompson in a study of the group relationships of 5143 farm families in Otsego County, New York, found at least seven types of neighborhood, *i.e.,* the hamlet, the institutional neighborhood, the business neighborhood, the ethnic neighborhood, the kinship neighborhood, the topographic neighborhood, and the village neighborhood. The average number of homes per neighborhood in that county was 14, and in 150 neighborhoods which averaged 12.5 homes each the area averaged 2.25 square miles. [7]

Similar studies in Wisconsin, Minnesota, and elsewhere show that rural neighborhoods differ greatly; but they are at least alike in this

[6] *The Young Delinquent* (New York, 1925), p. 582.

[7] Dwight Sanderson and Warren S. Thompson, *The Social Areas of Otsego County* (Ithaca, N. Y.: Cornell University Agricultural Experiment Station, in cooperation with the U. S. Department of Agriculture, 1923).

—the people in them do know each other personally and have regard for one another's opinions. It is this psychological unity that modern communication is destroying. In cities people not only know little or nothing about their next-door "neighbors," but have no desire to and feel no interest in their opinions whatever. Thus, McKenzie in his study of the neighborhood in Columbus, Ohio, found little real neighboring going on and although kinship was still a factor in organizing association, it was distinctly less of a factor than in rural communities. People of like attitudes toward the *mores* do tend to segregate into territorial publics, in the city, but the mobility of modern life tends to destroy real neighborhood solidarity.[8] The Lynds in their study of Middletown, *i.e.,* Muncie, Ind., found similar tendencies at work: "Vicinage plays a part in the forming of friendships," but more of a part among the working class than among the well-to-do.[9] On the whole since 1890 in Middletown the neighborhood has declined as "a place of most constant association of friends." Correlative with this decline in the importance of place as determining association has come an increase in the rôle of occupational associations such as the service clubs and of casual and purpose associations based on the automobile, the motion picture theatre, the bridge club, the golf club,[10] and the like.

The decay of the neighborhood in cities is part and parcel of the transformation that modern communication is working in all the primary groups. The family and the play-group likewise are showing the effects of the increased mobility of their own members and of the community about them. In Middletown far more of the activities of the members of the average household are now spent away from home than was true in 1890 and there is a tendency for different members to do different things. More women now work outside the home and the agencies drawing children away from home have greatly multiplied. In the three upper years of the Middletown high school the number of times the young people go out at night and the hours at which they get in are the two leading sources of friction

[8] R. D. McKenzie, "The Neighborhood; A Study of Local Life in the City of Columbus, Ohio," *American Journal of Sociology*, XXVII (September, November, 1921, January, 1922). "Mutual aid has almost ceased to be a factor in the fragmentary and casual relations between neighbors in the city environment."—p. 503.

[9] Robert S. and Helen M. Lynd, *Middletown* (New York, 1929), p. 273.

[10] There were 458 active clubs in Middletown in the spring and summer of 1924, when Middletown's population was estimated at 38,000. Clubs were, however, largely business-class phenomena; the working-class home suffered from too much isolation rather than the reverse.

between parents and children.[11] Approximately half of the boys and girls who answered the question were home less than four nights a week. Athletics, dramatics, committee meetings, Y.M.C.A., Y.W.C.A., the movies, auto-riding—"all extra-neighborhood concerns unknown to his parents in their youth—are centres of interest; club meetings, parties, or dances, often held in public buildings, compete for his every evening." No wonder that Middletown parents complained of the early sophistication of their children. Mobility has destroyed the old neighborhood, and mobility plus the rest of modern invention is truncating the socializing function of the family. Likewise the whole juggernaut of modern culture drives the play-group from the streets to take refuge in the alleys and vacant lots whence Young America issues presently as the gang, intent on business of its own for whose control we must organize playground movements and Boy Scout troops and all the rest of the institutional paraphernalia of a society that does not know how to build cities for children as well as for grown-ups.

What all this means is that from childhood up the rôle of the primary group is changing. Facing the decline of the old spontaneous face-to-face associations, we have been driven to set up all sorts of quasi-primary organizations such as neighborhood clubs, Scout troops, Rotary clubs, and the like, to re-establish consciously and purposively the semblance at least of the primary group experience. But no matter how informally such organizations may be conducted and no matter how much familiarity may spring up between members, they are still *ad hoc* organizations, set up for a purpose, with rules and formal organization, to do more or less mechanically and at some cost for a few people some of the things that formerly were done for all the people incidentally, spontaneously, and without costing a penny.

What the Increase in Secondary Association Means. The decline of the primary group and the corresponding increase in secondary association has one very immediate consequence: because of the nature of secondary association we are now associating more as mere functionaries and less as whole persons. What does this mean?

In primary groups people meet as persons, *i.e.,* unconstrained by artificiality, special purpose, limited contact, and the like. In secondary groups, on the other hand, they are functioning units in an organization, or mere acquaintances at best. *Secondary association is*

[11] *Op. cit.,* p. 134.

partial association. It is association narrowed down by special purpose, by communication at a distance, by rules, by social barriers, or by the casual nature of contact. This means that under such conditions associating personalities present only special facets of themselves to one another. They cannot meet as whole persons.

Compare, for example, the degree of association that would exist between a student and a newsboy on the street and the same student and the newsboy if they were members of one family. As a seller of newspapers the newsboy is a mere functionary. The buyer knows nothing of his home background, his attitude toward his baby sister, his desire to be a football coach, his fear of the dark, and scores of other details of his personal life. As a mere newsboy, apart from the full context of his life, he is not a living personality at all; he is a specialized human atom, not a person.

Even those with whom we spend hours of our working lives each day seldom emerge as whole personalities. As students we listen to formal lectures from professors, and have no more conception of what the individual professors are like as persons than the professors have of what the individual students are like as persons. As business men we deal with customers and employees, but have neither time nor opportunity to go behind the specialized facet of his personality that each presents. As citizens and consumers we listen to political speeches and buy our household supplies from individuals who impinge upon us merely as functionaries, never as whole personalities.

10 GROUP DEFINITION OF THE SITUATION *

BY WILLIAM ISAAC THOMAS (1863-1947)

ONE of the most important powers gained during the evolution of animal life is the ability to make decisions from within instead of having them imposed from without. Very low forms of life do

* Reprinted by permission of the copyright owners, the Social Science Research Council, from *The Unadjusted Girl* (Boston: Little, Brown and Company, 1923), pp. 41-44.

not make decisions, as we understand this term, but are pushed and pulled by chemical substances, heat, light, etc., much as iron filings are attracted or repelled by a magnet. They do tend to behave properly in given conditions—a group of small crustaceans will flee as in a panic if a bit of strychnia is placed in the basin containing them and will rush toward a drop of beef juice like hogs crowding around swill—but they do this as an expression of organic affinity for the one substance and repugnance for the other, and not as an expression of choice or "free will." There are, so to speak, rules of behavior but these represent a sort of fortunate mechanistic adjustment of the organism to typically recurring situations, and the organism cannot change the rule.

On the other hand, the higher animals, and above all man, have the power of refusing to obey a stimulation which they followed at an earlier time. Response to the earlier stimulation may have had painful consequences and so the rule or habit in this situation is changed. We call this ability the power of inhibition, and it is dependent on the fact that the nervous system carries memories or records of past experiences. At this point the determination of action no longer comes exclusively from outside sources but is located within the organism itself.

Preliminary to any self-determined act of behavior there is always a stage of examination and deliberation which we may call *the definition of the situation*. And actually not only concrete acts are dependent on the definition of the situation, but gradually a whole life-policy and the personality of the individual himself follow from a series of such definitions.

But the child is always born into a group of people among whom all the general types of situation which may arise have already been defined and corresponding rules of conduct developed, and where he has not the slightest chance of making his definitions and following his wishes without interference. Men have always lived together in groups. Whether mankind has a true herd instinct or whether groups are held together because this has worked out to advantage is of no importance. Certainly the wishes in general . . . can be satisfied only in a society. But we have only to refer to the criminal code to appreciate the variety of ways in which the wishes of the individual may conflict with the wishes of society. And the criminal code takes no account of the many unsanctioned expressions of the wishes which society attempts to regulate by persuasion and gossip.

There is therefore always a rivalry between the spontaneous definitions of the situation made by the member of an organized society and the definitions which his society has provided for him. The individual tends to a hedonistic selection of activity, pleasure first; and society to a utilitarian selection, safety first. Society wishes its member to be laborious, dependable, regular, sober, orderly, self-sacrificing; while the individual wishes less of this and more of new experience. And organized society seeks also to regulate the conflict and competition inevitable between its members in the pursuit of their wishes. The desire to have wealth, for example, or any other socially sanctioned wish, may not be accomplished at the expense of another member of the society—by murder, theft, lying, swindling, blackmail, etc.

It is in this connection that a moral code arises, which is a set of rules or behavior norms, regulating the expression of the wishes, and which is built up by successive definitions of the situation. In practice the abuse arises first and the rule is made to prevent its recurrence. Morality is thus the generally accepted definition of the situation, whether expressed in public opinion and the unwritten law, in a formal legal code, or in religious commandments and prohibitions.

The family is the smallest social unit and the primary defining agency. As soon as the child has free motion and begins to pull, tear, pry, meddle, and prowl, the parents begin to define the situation through speech and other signs and pressures: "Be quiet," "Sit up straight," "Blow your nose," "Wash your face," "Mind your mother," "Be kind to sister," etc. This is the real significance of Wordsworth's phrase, "Shades of the prison house begin to close upon the growing child." His wishes and activities begin to be inhibited, and gradually, by definitions within the family, by playmates, in the school, in the Sunday school, in the community, through reading, by formal instruction, by informal signs of approval and disapproval, the growing member learns the code of his society.

In addition to the family we have the community as a defining agency. At present the community is so weak and vague that it gives us no idea of the former power of the local group in regulating behavior. Originally the community was practically the whole world of its members. It was composed of families related by blood and marriage and was not so large that all the members could not come together; it was a face-to-face group. I asked a Polish peasant what was the extent of an "*okolica*" or neighborhood—how far it reached.

"It reaches," he said, "as far as the report of a man reaches—as far as a man is talked about." And it was in communities of this kind that the moral code which we now recognize as valid originated. The customs of the community are "folkways," and both state and church have in their more formal codes mainly recognized and incorporated these folkways.

The typical community is vanishing and it would be neither possible nor desirable to restore it in its old form. It does not correspond with the present direction of social evolution and it would now be a distressing condition in which to live. But in the immediacy of relationships and the participation of everybody in everything, it represents an element which we have lost and which we shall probably have to restore in some form of coöperation in order to secure a balanced and normal society,—some arrangement corresponding with human nature.

11 GEMEINSCHAFT (COMMUNITY) AND GESELLSCHAFT (SOCIETY) *[1]

BY FERDINAND TÖNNIES (1855–1936)
UNIVERSITY OF KIEL
AND CHARLES P. LOOMIS (1905–   )
MICHIGAN STATE COLLEGE

HUMAN wills stand in manifold relations to one another. Every such relationship is a mutual action, inasmuch as one party is active or gives while the other party is passive or receives. These

* Reprinted by permission of Professor Loomis and of the publisher from a part entitled "Relations Between Human Wills—Gemeinschaft (Community) and Gesellschaft (Society) From a Linguistic Point of View," in Tönnies' *Fundamental Concepts of Sociology (Gemeinschaft und Gesellschaft)*, transl. and supplemented by Charles P. Loomis (New York: American Book Company, 1940), pp. 37–39. First edition published at Leipzig 1887, 8th German edition 1935.

[1] The parenthetical English renditions of the words *Gemeinschaft* and *Gesellschaft* found in this section indicate the difficulty which would be encountered if one attempted their translation by any one pair of terms. Elsewhere in the text these two substantives and their adjective forms are not translated when they are used in the ideal typological sense.

actions are of such a nature that they tend either towards preservation or towards destruction of the other will or life; that is, they are either positive or negative. This study will consider as its subject of investigation only the relationships of mutual affirmation. Every such relationship represents unity in plurality or plurality in unity. It consists of assistance, relief, services, which are transmitted back and forth from one party to another and are to be considered as expressions of wills and their forces. The group which is formed through this positive type of relationship is called an association (*Verbindung*) when conceived of as a thing or being which acts as a unit inwardly and outwardly. The relationship itself, and also the resulting association, is conceived of either as real and organic life—this is the essential characteristic of the *Gemeinschaft* (community),—or as imaginary and mechanical structure—this is the concept of *Gesellschaft* (society).

Through the application of these two terms we shall see that the chosen expressions are rooted in their synonymic use in the German language. But to date in scientific terminology they have been customarily confused and used at random without any distinction. For this reason, a few introductory remarks may explain the inherent contrast between these two concepts. All intimate, private, and exclusive living together, so we discover, is understood as life in Gemeinschaft (community). Gesellschaft (society) is public life— it is the world itself. In Gemeinschaft (community) with one's family, one lives from birth on bound to it in weal and woe. One goes into Gesellschaft (society) as one goes into a strange country. A young man is warned against bad Gesellschaft (society), but the expression bad Gemeinschaft (community) violates the meaning of the word. Lawyers may speak of domestic (*häusliche*) Gesellschaft (society) thinking only of the legalistic concept of a social association, but the domestic Gemeinschaft (community) or home life with its immeasurable influence upon the human soul has been felt by everyone who ever shared it. Likewise, each member of a bridal couple knows that he or she goes into marriage as a complete Gemeinschaft (community) of life (*communio totius vitae*). A Gesellschaft (society) of life would be a contradiction in and of itself. One keeps or enjoys another's Gesellschaft (society or company) but not his Gemeinschaft (community) in this sense. One becomes a part of a religious Gemeinschaft (community); religious Gesellschaften (associations, or societies) like any other groups formed for given purposes, exist only in so far as they, viewed from without, take their places among the institutions of a political body or as they represent conceptual elements of a theory; they do not touch upon the religious Gemeinschaft as such. There exists a Gemeinschaft (community) of language, of folkways, or mores, or of beliefs; but, by way of contrast, Gesellschaft (society or company) exists in the realm of business, travel, or sciences. So of special importance are the commercial Gesellschaften (societies or companies), whereas, even though a certain familiarity and Gemeinschaft (community) may exist among business partners, one could indeed hardly speak of commercial Gemeinschaft (community). To make the word combination, "joint-stock Gemeinschaft," would be abominable. On the other hand, there exists a Gemeinschaft (community) of ownership in fields, forest, and pasture. The Gemeinschaft (community) of property between man and wife cannot be called Gesellschaft (society) of property. Thus many differences become apparent.

In the most general way, one could speak of a Gemeinschaft (community) comprising the whole of mankind, such as the church wishes to be regarded. But human Gesellschaft (society) is conceived as mere coexistence of people independent of each other. Recently, the concept of Gesellschaft as opposed to and distinct from the state has been developed. This term will also be used in this treatise, but can only derive its adequate explanation from the underlying contrast to the Gemeinschaft of the people.

Gemeinschaft (community) is old; Gesellschaft (society) is new as a name as well as a phenomenon. This has been recognized by an author who otherwise taught political science in all its aspects without penetrating to its fundamentals. "The entire concept of Gesellschaft (society) in a social and political sense," says Bluntschli (*Staatswörterbuch* IV), "finds its natural foundation in the folkways, mores, and ideas of the third estate. It is not really the concept of a people (*Volks-Begriff*) but the concept of the third estate . . . Its Gesellschaft has become the origin and expression of common opinions and tendencies . . . Wherever urban culture blossoms and bears fruits, Gesellschaft appears as its indispensable organ. The rural people know little of it." On the other hand, all praise of rural life has pointed out that the Gemeinschaft (community) among people is stronger there and more alive; it is the lasting and genuine form of living together. In contrast to Gemeinschaft, Gesellschaft (society) is transitory and superficial. Accordingly, Gemeinschaft (community) should be understood as a living organism, Gesell-schaft (society) as a mechanical aggregate and artifact.

12 MIND AS THE INDIVIDUAL IMPORTATION OF THE SOCIAL PROCESS *

BY GEORGE HERBERT MEAD (1863–1931)
UNIVERSITY OF CHICAGO

THE self is not so much a substance as a process in which the conversation of gestures has been internalized within an organic form. This process does not exist for itself, but is simply a phase of the whole social organization of which the individual is a part. The organization of the social act has been imported into the organism and becomes then the mind of the individual. It still includes the attitudes of others, but now highly organized, so that they become what we call social attitudes rather than rôles of separate individuals. This process of relating one's own organism to the others in the interactions that are going on, in so far as it is imported into the conduct of the individual with the conversation of the "I" and the "me," constitutes the self.[1] The value of this importation of the conversation of gestures into the conduct of the individual lies in the superior co-ordination gained for society as a whole, and in the increased efficiency of the individual as a member of the group. It is the difference between the process which can take place in a group of rats or ants or bees, and that which can take place in a human community. The social process with its various implications is actually taken up into the experience of the individual so that that which is going on

---

* Reprinted by permission of the editor and of the publisher from *Mind, Self & Society: From the Standpoint of a Social Behaviorist*, ed. by Charles W. Morris (Chicago: University of Chicago Press, 1934), pp. 178–180, 186–192.

[1] According to this view, conscious communication develops out of unconscious communication within the social process; conversation in terms of significant gestures out of conversation in terms of non-significant gestures; and the development in such fashion of conscious communication is coincident with the development of minds and selves within the social process.

takes place more effectively, because in a certain sense it has been re-hearsed in the individual. He not only plays his part better under those conditions but he also reacts back on the organization of which he is a part.

The very nature of this conversation of gestures requires that the attitude of the other is changed through the attitude of the indi-vidual to the other's stimulus. In the conversation of gestures of the lower forms the play back and forth is noticeable, since the indi-vidual not only adjusts himself to the attitude of others, but also changes the attitudes of the others. The reaction of the individual in this conversation of gestures is one that in some degree is continually modifying the social process itself. It is this modification of the process which is of greatest interest in the experience of the indi-vidual. He takes the attitude of the other toward his own stimulus, and in taking that he finds it modified in that his response becomes a different one, and leads in turn to further change.

Fundamental attitudes are presumably those that are only changed gradually, and no one individual can reorganize the whole society; but one is continually affecting society by his own attitude because he does bring up the attitude of the group toward himself, responds to it, and through that response changes the attitude of the group. This is, of course, what we are constantly doing in our imagination, in our thought; we are utilizing our own attitude to bring about a different situation in the community of which we are a part; we are exerting ourselves, bringing forward our own opinion, criticizing the attitudes of others, and approving or disapproving. But we can do that only in so far as we can call out in ourselves the response of the community; we only have ideas in so far as we are able to take the attitude of the community and then respond to it. . . .

I have been presenting the self and the mind in terms of a social process, as the importation of the conversation of gestures into the conduct of the individual organism, so that the individual organism takes these organized attitudes of the others called out by its own attitude, in the form of its gestures, and in reacting to that response calls out other organized attitudes in the others in the community to which the individual belongs. This process can be characterized in a certain sense in terms of the "I" and the "me," the "me" being that group of organized attitudes to which the individual responds as an "I."

What I want particularly to emphasize is the temporal and logical pre-existence of the social process to the self-conscious individual that arises in it. . . . The conversation of gestures is a part of the social process which is going on. It is not something that the individual alone makes possible. What the development of language, especially the significant symbol, has rendered possible is just the taking over of this external social situation into the conduct of the individual himself. There follows from this the enormous development which belongs to human society, the possibility of the prevision of what is going to take place in the response of other individuals, and a preliminary adjustment to this by the individual. These, in turn, produce a different social situation which is again reflected in what I have termed the "me," so that the individual himself takes a different attitude.

Consider a politician or a statesman putting through some project in which he has the attitude of the community in himself. He knows how the community reacts to this proposal. He reacts to this expression of the community in his own experience—he feels with it. He has a set of organized attitudes which are those of the community. His own contribution, the "I" in this case, is a project of reorganization, a project which he brings forward to the community as it is reflected in himself. He himself changes, of course, in so far as he brings this project forward and makes it a political issue. There has now arisen a new social situation as a result of the project which he is presenting. The whole procedure takes place in his own experience as well as in the general experience of the community. He is successful to the degree that the final "me" reflects the attitude of all in the community. What I am pointing out is that what occurs takes place not simply in his own mind, but rather that his mind is the expression in his own conduct of this social situation, this great co-operative community process which is going on.

I want to avoid the implication that the individual is taking something that is objective and making it subjective. There is an actual process of living together on the part of all members of the community which takes place by means of gestures. The gestures are certain stages in the co-operative activities which mediate the whole process. Now, all that has taken place in the appearance of the mind is that this process has been in some degree taken over into the conduct of the particular individual. There is a certain symbol, such as the policeman uses when he directs traffic. That is something that is out there. It does not become subjective when the engineer, who is engaged by the city to examine its traffic regulations, takes the same attitude the policeman takes with reference to traffic, and takes the attitude also of the drivers and machines. We do imply that he has the driver's organization; he knows that stopping means slowing down, putting on the brakes. There is a definite set of parts of his organism so trained that under certain circumstances he brings the machine to a stop. The raising of the policeman's hand is the gesture which calls out the various acts by means of which the machine is checked. Those various acts are in the expert's own organization; he can take the attitude of both the policeman and the driver. Only in this sense has the social process been made "subjective." If the expert just did it as a child does, it would be play; but if it is done for the actual regulation of traffic, then there is the operation of what we term mind. Mind is nothing but the importation of this external process into the conduct of the individual so as to meet the problems that arise.

This peculiar organization arises out of a social process that is logically its antecedent. A community within which the organism acts in such a co-operative fashion that the action of one is the stimulus to the other to respond, and so on, is the antecedent of the peculiar type of organization we term a mind, or a self. Take the simple family relation, where there is the male and the female and the child which has to be cared for. Here is a process which can only go on through interactions within this group. It cannot be said that the individuals come first and the community later, for the individuals arise in the very process itself, just as much as the human body or any multi-cellular form is one in which differentiated cells arise. There has to be a life-process going on in order to have the differentiated cells; in the same way there has to be a social process going on in order that there may be individuals. It is just as true in society as it is in the physiological situation that there could not be the individual if there was not the process of which he is a part. Given such a social process, there is the possibility of human intelligence when this social process, in terms of the conversation of gestures, is taken over into the conduct of the individual—and then there arises, of course, a different type of individual in terms of the responses now possible. There might conceivably be an individual who simply plays as the child does, without getting into a social game; but the human individual is possible because there is a social process in which it can function responsibly. The attitudes are parts of the social reaction; the cries would not maintain themselves as vocal gestures unless they did call out certain responses in the others; the attitude itself could only exist as such in this interplay of gestures.

The mind is simply the interplay of such gestures in the form of significant symbols. We must remember that the gesture is there only in its relationship to the response, to the attitude. One would not have words unless there were such responses. Language would never have arisen as a set of bare arbitrary terms which were attached to certain stimuli. Words have arisen out of a social interrelationship. One of Gulliver's tales was of a community in which a machine was created into which the letters of the alphabet could be mechanically fed in an endless number of combinations, and then the members of the community gathered around to see how the letters arranged after each rotation, on the theory that they might come in the form of an Iliad or one of Shakespeare's plays, or some other great work. The assumption back of this would be that symbols are entirely independent of what we term their meaning. The assumption is baseless: there cannot be symbols unless there are responses. There would not be a call for assistance if there was not a tendency to respond to the cry of distress. It is such significant symbols, in the sense of a subset of social stimuli initiating a co-operative response, that do in a certain sense constitute our mind, provided that not only the symbol but also the responses are in our own nature. What the human being has succeeded in doing is in organizing the response to a certain symbol which is a part of the social act, so that he takes the attitude of the other person who co-operates with him. It is that which gives him a mind.

The sentinel of a herd is that member of the herd which is more sensitive to odor or sound than the others. At the approach of danger, he starts to run earlier than the others, who then follow along, in virtue of a herding tendency to run together. There is a social stimulus, a gesture, if you like, to which the other forms respond. The first form gets the odor earlier and starts to run, and its starting to run is a stimulus to the others to run also. It is all external; there is no mental process involved. The sentinel does not regard itself as the individual who is to give a signal; it just runs at a certain moment and so starts the others to run. But with a mind, the animal that gives the signal also takes the attitude of the others who respond to it. He knows what his signal means. A man who calls "fire" would be able to call out in himself the reaction he calls out in the other.

In so far as the man can take the attitude of the other—his attitude of response to fire, his sense of terror—that response to his own cry is something that makes of his conduct a mental affair, as over against the conduct of the others. . . . But the only thing that has happened here is that what takes place externally in the herd has been imported into the conduct of the man. There is the same signal and the same tendency to respond, but the man not only can give the signal but also can arouse in himself the attitude of the terrified escape, and through calling that out he can come back upon his own tendency to call out and can check it He can react upon himself in taking the organized attitude of the whole group in trying to escape from danger. There is nothing more subjective about it than that the response to his own stimulus can be found in his own conduct, and that he can utilize the conversation of gestures that takes place to determine his own conduct. If he can so act, he can set up a rational control, and thus make possible a far more highly organized society than otherwise. The process is one which does not utilize a man endowed with a consciousness where there was no consciousness before, but rather an individual who takes over the whole social process into his own conduct. That ability, of course, is dependent first of all on the symbol being one to which he can respond; and so far as we know, the vocal gesture has been the condition for the development of that type of symbol. Whether it can develop without the vocal gesture I cannot tell.

I want to be sure that we see that the content put into the mind is only a development and product of social interaction. It is a development which is of enormous importance, and which leads to complexities and complications of society which go almost beyond our power to trace, but originally it is nothing but the taking over of the attitude of the other. To the extent that the animal can take the attitude of the other and utilize that attitude for the control of his own conduct, we have what is termed mind; and that is the only apparatus involved in the appearance of the mind.

I know of no way in which intelligence or mind could arise or could have arisen, other than through the internalization by the individual of social processes of experience and behavior, that is, through this internalization of the conversation of significant gestures, as made possible by the individual's taking the attitudes of other individuals toward himself and toward what is being thought about. And if mind or thought has arisen in this way, then there neither can be nor could have been any mind or thought without language; and the early stages of the development of language must have been prior to the development of mind or thought.

13 THE SOCIAL STRUCTURE OF THE FAMILY *

BY TALCOTT PARSONS (1902–   )
HARVARD UNIVERSITY

THE scientific study of the social relationships of everyday life presents peculiar difficulties. We are continually living in and through them and hence do not find it easy to view them from the outside. The problem may be compared to grammar and the other aspects of language which interest the technical linguist. Every ordinary person speaks his native language reasonably correctly and without effort, without necessarily being even aware that those technical aspects exist. In the social field these considerations are preeminently applicable to the family, for no aspect of social life is more deeply imbedded in layers of sentiment and of motivation of which we are normally scarcely even aware. Hence the difficulty is often more a matter of the perspective in which the facts are seen than of their unfamiliarity or difficulty of ascertainment as such.

In attaining this perspective social science has been greatly aided by the comparative study of the structure and functioning of different societies. Seen in these terms the contemporary American family and kinship system is not simply the natural way to live but constitutes a highly exceptional mode of the patterning of relationships in this area.

It can perhaps be regarded as established that, with proper precautions, analysis of kinship terminology can serve as a highly useful approach to the study of the functioning social structure. In the case

* Reprinted by permission of the author, of the editor, and of the publisher from Parsons' chapter of the same title in Ruth Nanda Anshen, ed., *The Family: Its Function and Destiny* (New York: Harper & Brothers, 1949), chap. x, pp. 173–201; pp. 173–184 reprinted.

of the English language two precautions in particular, over and above those commonly observed, need to be explicitly mentioned; for such analysis alone cannot serve to bring out what is distinctively American because the terminology has been essentially stable since before the settlement of America, and today there is no significant terminological difference as between England and the United States. Moreover, the differences in this respect between English and the other modern European languages are minor. Hence all that an analysis of terminology can do is to indicate a very broad type within which the more distinctively American system falls.

As shown in the accompanying diagram [page 92] [1] the American family is perhaps best characterized as an open, multilineal, conjugal system.

The conjugal family unit of parents and children is one of basic significance in any kinship system. What is distinctive about our system is the absence of any important terminologically recognized units which cut across conjugal families, including some members and excluding others. The only instances of such units are *pairs* of conjugal families each with *one* common member. Terminologically, in common speech, it is significant that we have only the words "family," which generally [2] refers to the conjugal unit, and "relatives," which refers not to *any* solitary unit at all but only to anyone who is a kinsman.

[1] The diagramming conventions adopted in this chapter are somewhat different from those commonly used by anthropologists. They are imposed by the peculiar structural features of our system, especially

(a) Its openness, i.e., absence of preferential mating. Hence the two spouses of any given conjugal family are not structurally related by family of orientation and it is not possible to portray *the* system in terms of a limited number of lines of descent. Each marriage links "ego's" kinship system to a complete system.

(b) The consequent indefinite dispersion of the lines of descent.

The best that can be done in two dimensions is to take ego as a point of reference and show his significant kin. It is strictly impossible to diagram the system as a whole—that would require a space of n-dimensions. Similarly, vertical and horizontal or lateral axes have only a very limited meaning. Lines of descent and generations are significant. But there is a geometrically progressive increase in the number of lines of descent with each generation away from ego, and the distinctions cannot be made in terms of a linear continuum. I am indebted to Miss Ai-li Sung of Radcliffe College for assistance in drafting the diagram.

[2] The most important exception is its usage in upper class circles to denote what Warner calls a "lineage," i.e., a group possessing continuity over several generations, usually following the "name line," e.g., the "Adams family." See W. L. Warner and P. S. Lunt, *Social Life of a Modern Community* (New Haven: Yale University Press, 1941). The significance of this exception will be commented upon below. [See especially pp. 93–96, *infra.* — Ed.]

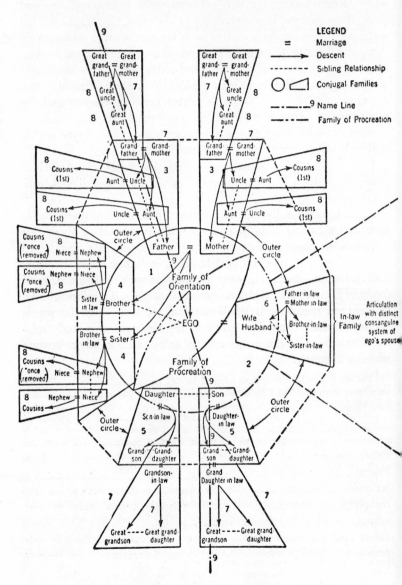

[Diagram of the American Family (see page 91).]

Types of Families:

1. Ego's family of orientation (1 only)
2. Ego's family of procreation (1 only)
3. First-degree ascendant families (2)
4. First-degree collateral families (number indefinite, 2 types)
5. First-degree descendant families (number indefinite, 2 types)
6. In-law family (1 only)
7. Second-degree ascendant and descendant families (4 ascendant, descendant indefinite, 4 types)
8. Second-degree collateral families (all children ego's cousins)

Structural Groupings of Families:

I. 1 + 2—Inner circle
II. 3, 4, 5 + 6—Outer circle
III. 1, 2, 3, 5, 7—Families in line of descent
IV. 4, 8—Collateral families
V. 2, 6—Articulation of consanguine systems

No difference according to sex of ego, except in the term for spouse and the fact that, if ego is female, name line does not extend below ego in line of descent.

Ours then is a conjugal [3] system in that it is made up exclusively of interlocking conjugal families. The principle of the structural relation of these families is founded on the fact that, as a consequence of the incest taboo, "ego" in the structurally normal [4] case is always a member not of one but of two conjugal families, those which Warner usefully distinguishes as the "family of orientation," into which he is born as a child, and the "family of procreation," which is founded by his marriage. Moreover, he is the *only* common member of the two families.

From ego's point of view, then, the core of the kinship system is constituted by families 1 and 2 in the diagram—in the one case his father, mother, brothers, and sisters; in the other his spouse (wife or husband according to ego's sex), sons, and daughters. Monogamy is reflected in the fact that parent and other parent's spouse are terminologically identical, modified only by the prefix "step" to take account of second or later marriages, and in the fact that the terms father and mother, husband and wife, can each apply to only *one* person at a time. It is also notable that no distinction on the basis of

[3] See Ralph Linton, *The Study of Man* (New York: D. Appleton-Century Company, 1936), chap. viii, for the very useful distinction between conjugal and consanguine kinship types.

[4] Excluding, of course, those who do not marry. But failure to marry has no positive structural consequences in relation to kinship—only negative.

birth order is made—all brothers are terminologically alike. But most notable of all is the fact that *none* of these seven kinship personalities is terminologically identified with *any* relative outside the particular conjugal family in which he is placed. A brother is specifically distinguished from any male cousin, the father from any uncle, the mother from any aunt, and so on. These two conjugal families may conveniently be treated as constituting the inner circle of the kinship structure. Relative priorities within them will be discussed below.

Now *each* member of ego's inner kinship circle is the connecting link with one other terminologically recognized conjugal family. Moreover, he links the family of orientation or procreation, as the case may be, with only one farther conjugal family, and each individual with a separate one. The kinship personalities of this outer circle, however, are not always terminologically separate, a fact which will be shown to be of paramount importance.

The first pair of outer-circle families, which may be called the first ascendant, are the families of orientation of ego's parents; besides the articulating personality, each consists of the four kinship personalities of grandfather, grandmother, uncle, and aunt. The most significant fact is the lack of terminological distinction between the paternal and the maternal families of orientation—grandparents, uncles, and aunts are alike regardless of which side they are on. The only important exception to this lies not in the kinship terminology as such but in the patrilineal inheritance of the family name, giving rise to a unilateral "name line." Since the same principle of lack of distinction by sex of intervening relatives applies to still higher ascendant generations—the four great- and eight great-great-grandfathers—it is perhaps more accurate to speak of a multilineal than of a bilateral system. Any one of an indefinite number of lines of descent may be treated as significant. Above all, the extension from the principle of bilaterality, as applied to the first ascendant (and descendant) families, to that of multilineality in succeeding generations is completely incompatible with any tendency to bifurcate the kin group on the basis of lines of descent.

The same fundamental principles govern the terminology of the first collateral families—the families of procreation of ego's siblings—and the first descendant families, the families of procreation of his children. It is noteworthy that siblings' spouses are terminologically assimilated to sibling status with the suffix "in-law"—generally not used in address or the more intimate occasions of reference—and that nephews and nieces are the same whether they are brothers' or sisters' children and regardless of the sex of ego. Similarly, spouses of children are assimilated to the status of children by the same terminological device, and sons' and daughters' children are all indiscriminately grandchildren. Finally, both siblings-in-law and children-in-law are terminologically segregated from any kinship status relative to ego except that in the particular conjugal family which is under consideration.

The last outer-circle family, the in-law family, has a very particular significance. It is the only one of those linked to ego's inner circle to which he is bound not by descent and consanguinity but only by affinity, and this fact is of paramount importance, signalizing as it does the openness of our system. In other words, preferential mating on a kinship basis is completely without structural significance, and every marriage in founding a new conjugal family brings together (in the type case) two completely unrelated kinship groups which are articulated on a kinship basis only in this one particular marriage. Seen from a somewhat more generalized point of view, if we take the total inner and outer circle group of ego's kin as a system, it is articulated to another entirely distinct system of the same structure by every peripheral relative (one who is not a connecting link between the inner and outer circles), except in the direct lines of descent. The consequence is a maximum of dispersion of the lines of descent and the prevention of the structuring of kinship groups on any other principle than the "onion" principle, which implies proportionately increasing distantness with each circle of linked conjugal families.[5]

Another way of throwing the significance of this basic open-multilineal structure into relief is to recall the fact that ego's family of orientation and his in-law family are, from the point of view of his children, both first ascendant families whose members are equally grandparents, aunts, and uncles.

[5] In any finite population, lines of descent are bound to cross somewhere, and in our society the marriage of close relatives is not infrequent. But there is no consistent pattern in this intermarriage, hence it is without structural consequences.

Most of the essentials of an open conjugal system can be maintained, while a high level of generation continuity in at least one line is also maintained, by a systematic discrimination between lines of descent—especially through primogeniture. The extent to which this has and has not occurred is the most important range of variation within the basic pattern and will have to be discussed in some detail below.

In principle it is possible to distinguish, beyond the outer circle, further layers of the so-called onion indefinitely. It is significant, however, that our kinship terminology ceases at this point to apply at all specific terms, fundamentally recognizing only two elements. The first is the line of descent designated by the ascendant and descendant family terms with the addition of the reduplicating prefix "great"—as in greatgrandfather and greatgrandson. The second is the indiscriminate category "cousins" into which all collaterals are thrown, with only the descriptive [6] devices of "first," "third," "once removed," and so forth to distinguish them by.

This onion structure of interlocking conjugal families differs above all from most other kinship systems in the fact that the conjugal family is so isolated by the unusual symmetry of its relationships to all the other conjugal units with each of which it is linked by one common member. It is not particularly closely integrated with any one or two of these in a larger solidary grouping which would bias this symmetry of relationship to others. Above all there is no strong emphasis on a line of descent which would ensure conformity of status of the kinship unit from generation to generation.[7]

How far can this distinctive terminology be said to reflect the actual institutional structure of kinship? In a broad way it certainly does this. We clearly have none of the extended kin groupings so prevalent among non-literate peoples, such as patrilineal or matrilineal clans; we have no exogamy except that based on degree of relationship; we have no preferential mating—all these are a matter of the simplest common knowledge. But to get a clearer conception of the more specific structure it is essential to turn to a different order of evidence.

In the first place, the importance of the isolated conjugal family is brought out by the fact that it is the normal household unit. This

[6] It should perhaps be stated explicitly that, though sometimes called a descriptive system by some of the older anthropologists, our terminology is by no means literally descriptive of exact biological relationships. Above all it fails to distinguish relatives whose relation to ego is traced through different lines of descent. But it also fails to distinguish by birth order, or to distinguish siblings' spouses from spouses' siblings—both are brothers- or sisters-in-law. Finally, as just noted, it stops making distinctions very soon and treats all collaterals as cousins.

[7] A well-known example of the latter type is the traditional Chinese gentry family with its three- or four-generation household, consisting of an older couple, their married sons, wives, and children, and perhaps even grandchildren in the male line. A different type is that common among European peasants; here the holding and corresponding status in the community is passed down intact to one son, and the others must leave the agricultural community.

means it is the unit of residence and the unit whose members as a matter of course pool a common basis of economic support—especially, as with us, money income. Moreover, in the typical case neither the household arrangements nor the source of income bears any specific relation to the family of orientation of either spouse, or, if there is any, it is about as likely to be to the one as to the other. But the typical conjugal family lives in a home segregated from those of both pairs of parents (if living) and is economically independent of both. In a large proportion of cases this geographical separation is considerable. Furthermore, the primary basis of economic support and of many other elements of social status lies typically in the husband's occupational status—his job, which typically he holds independently of any particularistic relation to kinsmen.

The isolation of the conjugal unit in this country is in strong contrast to that common in the historic structure of European society, where a much larger and more important element have inherited home, source of economic support, and specific occupational status (especially a farm or family enterprise) from their fathers. This of course has had to involve discrimination between siblings, since the whole complex of property and status has to be inherited intact.[8]

Hence considerable significance attaches to our patterns of inheritance of property. Here the important thing is the absence of any specific favoring of any particular line of descent. Formally, subject to protection of the interests of widows, complete testamentary freedom exists. The American law of intestacy, however, in specific contrast to the older English Common Law tradition, gives equal shares to all children, regardless of sex or the order of birth. But, even more important, the actual practice of wills overwhelmingly conforms to this pattern. Where deviations exist they are not bound up with the kinship structure as such but are determined by particular relationships or situations of need. There is also noticeable in our society a relative weakness of pressure on a person to leave all or even most property to kin.[9]

It is probably safe to assume that an essentially open system, with a primary stress on the conjugal family and a corresponding absence

[8] Though perhaps the commonest pattern, primogeniture has by no means been universal. Cf. Arensberg and Kimball, *Family and Community in Ireland* (Cambridge: Harvard University Press, 1940), and G. C. Homans, *English Villagers of the 13th Century* (Cambridge: Harvard University Press, 1941).

[9] Indeed a wealthy man who completely neglected philanthropies in his will would be criticized.

of groupings of collaterals cutting across conjugal families, has existed in Western society since the period when the kinship terminology of the European languages took shape. The above evidence, however, is sufficient to show that within this broad type the American system, by contrast with its European forebears, has developed far in the direction of a symmetrically multilineal type. The relative absence of any structural bias in favor of solidarity with the ascendant and descendant families in any one line of descent has enormously increased the structural isolation of the individual conjugal family. This isolation, a manifestation of the almost symmetrical onion-type structure, is the most distinctive feature of the American kinship system and underlies most of its peculiar functional and dynamic problems.

Before entering into a few of these, it should be made clear that the incidence of the fully developed type in the American social structure is uneven and that important tendencies to deviation from it are found in certain structural areas. In the first place, in spite of the extent to which American agriculture has become commercialized, the economic and social conditions of rural life place more of a premium on continuity of occupation and status from generation to generation than do urban conditions; hence, especially perhaps among the more solidly established rural population, something approaching Le Play's *famille souche* is not unusual.

Second, there are important upper-class elements in this country for which an élite status is closely bound up with the status of ancestry, hence the continuity of kinship solidarity in a—mainly patrilineal—line of descent, in lineages.[10] Therefore in these "family élite" elements the symmetry of the multilineal kinship structure is sharply skewed in the direction of a patrilineal system with a tendency to primogeniture—one in many respects resembling that historically prevalent among European aristocracies, though considerably looser. There is a tendency for this in turn to be bound up with family property, especially an ancestral home, and with continuity of status in a particular local community.

Finally, there is evidence that in lower-class situations, in different ways both rural and urban, there is another type of deviance from the main kinship pattern. This type is connected with a strong tendency to an instability of marriage and to a mother-centered type of

[10] Cf. Warner and Lunt, *op. cit.*, and Allison Davis and B. B. and M. R. Gardner, *Deep South* (Chicago: Chicago University Press, 1941).

family structure—found both in Negro and white population elements.[11] It would not disturb the multilineal symmetry of the system
but would favor a very different type of conjugal family, even if it
tended to be as nearly isolated as the main type from other kinship
groups. This situation, however, has not been at all adequately
studied from a functional point of view.

Thus what is here treated as the focal American type of kinship
structure is most conspicuously developed in the urban middle-class
areas of the society. This fact is strong evidence of the interdependence of kinship structure with other structural aspects of the same
society, notably the occupational system.

In approaching the functional analysis of the central American
kinship type, the focal point of departure must lie in the crucial fact
that ego is a member not of one but of two conjugal families. This
fact naturally is of central significance in all kinship systems, but in
our own it acquires a special importance because of the structural
prominence of the conjugal family and its peculiar isolation. In most
kinship systems many persons retain throughout the life cycle a fundamentally stable—though changing—status in one or more extended
kinship units.[12] In our system this is not the case for anyone.

The most immediate consequence lies in the structural significance
of the marriage relationship, especially in relation to the lines of descent and to the sibling tie. That is, in ours as compared with other
kinship systems, ego by his marriage is drastically segregated from
his family of orientation—both from his parents and their forebears
and from his siblings. His first kinship loyalty is unequivocally to his
spouse and then to their children if and when any are born. Moreover, his family of procreation, by virtue of a common household, income, and community status, becomes a solidary unit in the sense in

[11] Cf. Davis and Gardner, op. cit., chap. vi; E. Franklin Frazier, The Negro
Family in the United States (Chicago: Chicago University Press, 1939), and Robert
S. Lynd, Middletown in Transition (New York: Harcourt, Brace & Company, 1937).
Dr. Florence Kluckholm has called my attention to a fourth deviant type which she
calls the "suburban matriarchy." In certain suburban areas, especially with an upper-
middle class population, the husband and father is out of the home a large proportion of the time. He tends to leave by far the greater part of the responsibility for
children to his wife and also to participate in the affairs of the local community
either not at all or only at the insistence of his wife. This would apply to informal
social relationships where both entertaining and acceptance of invitations are primarily arranged by the wife or on her initiative.

[12] This, in a unilateral clan system, is conspicuously true, for example, of the members of the sex group on which the continuity of the clan rests. On the other hand,
the situation of the other, the out-marrying sex, is quite different.

which the segregation of the interests of individuals is relatively meaningless, whereas the segregation of these interests of ego from those of the family of orientation tends relatively to minimize solidarity with the latter.

For ego as an adult the strong emphasis on the marriage relationship at the expense of his relationship to parents and siblings is directly correlative with the symmetrical multilineality of the system. From the standpoint of the marriage pair, in other words, neither family of orientation, particularly neither parental couple, has a structurally sanctioned priority of status. Thus in a sense there is a balance-of-power situation in which the independence of the family of procreation is favored by the necessity of maintaining impartiality as between the two families of orientation.[13]

From this it seems legitimate to conclude that in a peculiar sense which is not equally applicable to other systems the marriage bond, in our society, is the main structural keystone of the kinship system. This results from the structural isolation of the conjugal family and the fact that the married couple is not supported by comparably strong kinship ties to other adults. Closely related to this situation is that of the choice of a marriage partner. It is not only an open system in that there is no preferential mating on a kinship basis, but, since the new marriage is not typically incorporated into an already existing kinship unit, the primary structural reasons for an important influence on marriage choice being exerted by the kin of the prospective partners are missing or at least minimized.

It is true that something approaching a system of arranged marriages does persist in some situations, especially where couples brought up in the same local community marry and expect to settle down there—or where there are other particularistic elements present, as in cases of "marrying the boss's daughter." Our open system, however, tends very strongly to a pattern of purely personal choice of marriage partner without important parental influence. With increasing social mobility—residential, occupational, and other—it has

[13] See Simmel's well-known essay on the significance of number in social relationships (*Soziologie,* chap. ii). This is an illuminating case of the "triadic" group. It is not, however, institutionally that of *tertius gaudens,* since that implies one "playing off the other two against each other," though informally it may sometimes approach that. Institutionally, however, what is most important is the requirement of impartiality between the two families of orientation. Essentially the same considerations apply as between an older couple and two or more of their married children's families of procreation—impartiality irrespective of sex or the order of birth is expected.

clearly become the dominant pattern. Though not positively required by the kinship structure, freedom of choice is not impeded by it, and the structure in various ways is probably connected with the motivation of this freedom, an important aspect of the "romantic love" complex.

A closely related functional problem touches the character of the marriage relationship itself. Social systems in which a considerable number of individuals are in a complex and delicate state of mutual interdependence tend greatly to limit the scope for "personal" emotional feelings, or at least its direct expression in action. Any considerable range of affective spontaneity would tend to impinge on the statuses and interests of too many others, with disequilibrating consequences for the system as a whole. This need to limit affective spontaneity is fundamentally the reason why arranged marriages tend to be found in kinship systems where the newly married couple is incorporated into a larger kin group, but it also strongly colors the character of the marriage relationship itself and tends to place the primary institutional sanctions upon matters of objective status and obligations to other kin, rather than on subjective sentiment.[14] Thus the structural isolation of the conjugal family tends to free the affective inclination of the couple from a whole series of hampering restrictions.

Nevertheless, these restrictive forces, which in other kinship systems inhibit affective expression, have positive functional significance in maintaining the solidarity of the effective kinship unit. Very definite expectations in the definition of the different roles, combined with a complex system of interrelated sanctions, both positive and negative, go far to guarantee stability and the maintenance of standards of performance. In the American kinship system this kind of institutionalized support of the role of marriage partner through its interlocking with other kinship roles is, if not entirely lacking, at least much weaker. A functionally equivalent substitute in motivation to conformity with the expectations of the role is clearly needed.

[14] This tendency for multiple-membered social systems to repress spontaneous manifestations of sentiment should not be taken too absolutely. In such phenomena as cliques, there is room for the following of personal inclinations within the framework of institutionalized statuses. It is probable, however, that it is more restrictive in groups where, as in kinship, the institutionalized relationships are particularistic and functionally diffuse than in universalistic and functionally specific systems such as modern occupational organizations. In the latter case, personal affective relationships can, within considerable limits, be institutionally ignored as belonging to the sphere of private affairs.

Hence it may be suggested that the institutional sanction placed on the proper subjective sentiments of spouses, in short the expectation that they have an obligation to be "in love," has that significance. This in turn is related to the personal choice of a marriage partner, since affective devotion—particularly in our culture—is linked to a presumption of the absence of any element of coercion.

14 THE SEPARATE CULTURE OF THE SCHOOL *

BY WILLARD WALLER (1899–1945)

BARNARD COLLEGE, COLUMBIA UNIVERSITY

TEACHERS have always known that it was not necessary for the students of strange customs to cross the seas to find material. Folklore and myth, tradition, taboo, magic rites, ceremonials of all sorts, collective representations, *participation mystique,* all abound in the front yard of every school, and occasionally they creep upstairs and are incorporated into the more formal portions of school life.

There are, in the school, complex rituals of personal relationships, a set of folkways, mores, and irrational sanctions, a moral code based upon them. There are games, which are sublimated wars, teams, and an elaborate set of ceremonies concerning them. There are traditions, and traditionalists waging their world-old battle against innovators. There are laws, and there is the problem of enforcing them. There is *Sittlichkeit.* There are specialized societies with a rigid structure and a limited membership. There are no reproductive groups, but there are customs regulating the relations of the sexes. All these things make up a world that is different from the world of adults. It is this separate culture of the young, having its locus in the school, which we propose to study. To work out all the details of this culture would be a task long and difficult, and, for our purpose, not altogether necessary. We shall be content to mark out the main lines of the cultural background of school life.

* Reprinted by permission of Mrs. T. H. Brady and of the publisher from *The Sociology of Teaching* (New York: John Wiley & Sons, Inc., 1932), pp. 103–114.

In part the discussion of the school in cultural terms has been anticipated in a preceding section. We have advanced the notion that the school is a center of cultural diffusion; we have shown that the school serves as a point from which the cultural standards of the larger group are mediated to the local community. The organization of higher and lower schools for the purpose of cultural diffusion may be thought of as analogous to the organization of wholesale and retail merchandising for the distribution of material goods. The goods, here certain cultural traits, are sent out from centers in job lots, to be distributed by retailers by their own methods at their own price. There is a certain amount of central control of education, as there is central control of the merchandising of certain material objects. We have noted also that the school is engaged in the transmission of a vast body of culture which is passed on from the old to the young. The school must pass on skills and it must implant attitudes; most of these are not new in the community. At any time and in any community the major portion of the work of the school is that of imposing these preexistent community standards upon children.

Certain cultural conflicts are at the center of the life of the school. These conflicts are of two sorts. The first and most obvious is that which arises from the peculiar function of the school in the process of cultural diffusion. A conflict arises between teachers and students because teachers represent the culture of the wider group and students are impregnated with the culture of the local community. Where the differences concern matters of religion or of fundamental morality, the struggle which then ensues may become quite sharp and may seriously affect the relation of the school to the community. A second and more universal conflict between students and teachers arises from the fact that teachers are adult and students are not, so that teachers are the bearers of the culture of the society of adults, and try to impose that culture upon students, whereas students represent the indigenous culture of the group of children.

The special culture of the young grows up in the play world of childhood. It is worth while to note that it arises in the interstices of the adult social world. Thrasher's *The Gang* is a study of the conflict between the established social order and the interstitial group which has sprung up and grown strong in the sections of society where the adult order does not hold. But this is by no means a complete explanation of the behavior norms of childhood groups. Another fact of importance is that the child does not experience the world in the same manner as does the adult. The child perceives the world differently from the adult in part because he sees it in smaller and simpler configurations. The adult sees social situations as falling into certain highly complex configurations; the child, with a simpler mental organization, does not see these, but breaks up his sensory data into different wholes. The sensory patterns of childhood, then, arise in part from imperfectly experienced adult situations. What the child appropriates from the cultural patterns around him must always be something which is within his power to comprehend. This is usually one of the simpler and more elementary forms of adult behavior, as the criminal behavior followed out by the gang, or it is a split-off part of a more complex whole common in the culture of adults.

The culture pattern followed out by children may be a survival, for when culture changes it often happens that what was formerly a serious activity for adults is continued in the play of children. Indian fighting, sword play, Hallowe'en festivities, fairy tales, and the use of the bow and arrow have lost their worth in the adult world, but they have retained a certain value in the mental world of childhood. Sometimes economic activities survive and are continued in play because they have great intrinsic interest and have disappeared from the adult world only because they were unable to hold their own in competition with more efficient and prosaic means of getting a living. This has been true of hunting and fishing. There is in the developmental process a gradual evolution in the complexity of social situations and of the adjustment which the person makes to them; the fact that these social situations sometimes reproduce the actual situations of an earlier state of society has led some common-sense observers to believe in the theory of recapitulation.

Between mental processes and the cultural milieu in which they take place there is at all times a nice adjustment. As one's mind approaches the adult form of organization, he is increasingly assimilated to the culture of adults. . . . Mental life develops by a series of "Aha moments." As a result of these moments of insight, material objects may pass through a long series of metamorphoses. The little round glass backed with mercury is for the very young child something to pound with; a little later it is a mystery, and later yet a thing with which to play a prank upon the teacher; at one time it is a thing that it is slightly disgraceful to be caught looking into; for the adult it is just a pocket mirror. It is this difference in mentality which determines the different uses of cultural products among groups of different age levels.

Age is not the only factor that separates people who nominally drink of the same cultural stream from actual community of culture. Mental ability, education, subtle differences of interests and of personality may likewise sort people into cultural pigeonholes. So completely is the individual immersed in the culture of his own age and social level that he often has difficulty in realizing that any other kind of culture exists. He is separated by invisible walls from those about him who follow different gods. Persons living in different segments of our culture, as determined by age and life situation, may find difficulty in communicating with each other or in understanding each other at all. The old cannot understand the young, the prudent cannot understand the heedless, the married can have little sympathy for the unmarried, parents can never commune with non-parents; each person in the world is surrounded by many with whom he must communicate by smoke signals and by only a few with whom he can converse. But the greatest chasm is that which separates young persons and old.[1]

[1] The fact that the world of the child is organized into configurations of a different kind from the configurations composing the base of the adult's universe seems to constitute, by the way, the best justification we have for lying to children. The greatest argument for the teaching of falsehood seems to be that different orders of truth exist for different mental levels. Children should therefore be taught the kind of truth they are able to understand. There is truth in this argument in that children are likely to break up into simpler configurations the complicated configuration which results for the adult mind in the weighing of virtue against vice, and they are likely to get a final result which is, for the adult, distorted and beside the point. No one who has seen the demoralization produced in some not overly intelligent youth by contact with cynical but well-balanced and earnest adults can fail to see that there is some argument for the simple virtues, even if they are based upon falsehoods. But one wonders whether demoralization is not even more likely to result from building up in the child's mind a structure of beliefs which he is likely to take sometime for complete lies because they are partly false. That such demoralization often occurs will be apparent to all who have ever been in a position to witness the changes wrought in the moral fiber of students when they enter the greater world or make the transition from secondary schools to universities. Nor should we fail to remark in this connection that the policy of lying to children presupposes that one should be intelligent enough and dexterous enough to deceive them completely. This is often not the case at all, for shrewd children, judging their elders by their behavior rather than by their words, are frequently able to cut through the adults' rationalizations to the amoral core of their behavior. Since children, even the shrewdest of them, do not make allowance for rationalizations as rationalizations, as phenomena beyond the conscious control of the individual, they judge their elders more harshly, sometimes, than they deserve. They think their elders both knaves and

The journey from the world of the boy to the world of the man is rarely smooth and continuous. But it has fewer sharp corners to turn if the members of the adult world are able to project themselves back into the psychic world of childhood. The adult who can live in the childish world with sufficient intensity to understand children from within can help them intelligently to develop those complex and unstable syntheses upon which the adult adjustment depends. Teachers have tried to make the transition easier by presenting to children a finely graded and continuously evolving culture, organized into ever more complex configurations. (They have succeeded very well in grading and sorting academic subject matter.) So have arisen those teacher-initiated and teacher-managed "activities," ceremonials, traditions, etc. So were produced, in fact, most of the things which we shall treat in discussing the culture of the school. The purpose of all these things is to soften the conflict of cultures between old and young.

Though an enlightened pedagogy may ameliorate the conflict of adults and children, it can never remove it altogether. In the most humane school some tension appears between teacher and students, resulting, apparently, from the rôle which the situation imposes upon the teacher in relation to his students. There are two items of the teacher's duty which make it especially likely that he will have to bring some pressure to bear upon students: he must see to it that there is no retrogression from the complexity of the social world worked out for students of a certain age level,[2] and he must strive gradually to increase that complexity as the child grows in age and approximates adult understanding and experience. Activities may reduce conflict, but not destroy it.

Children have something which can be regarded as a culture of their own. Its most important loci are the unsupervised play group and the school. The unsupervised group presents this culture in a

fools when those elders are in fact too high-minded to admit their selfishness to themselves. Perhaps, when all the alternatives are considered, we shall do better to stick to the simple virtues ourselves, and to speak truth, while taking such precautions as we may against unwarranted generalizations from facts which run contrary to the accepted views of ethics. The virtue that we shall so engender will be a tough-minded virtue. It may be less comprehensive than some would desire, but it will not be brittle.

[2] A strong tendency toward such retrogression in the direction of simpler and easier structures seems to exist, especially in the intermediate stages. This retrogression appears as "silliness." Much conflict between teachers and students arises from the desire of the teacher to eliminate "silliness."

much purer form than does the school, for the childish culture of the school is partly produced by adults, is sifted and selected by adults, and is always subject to a certain amount of control by teachers. The culture of the school is a curious mélange of the work of young artisans making culture for themselves and old artisans making culture for the young; it is also mingled with such bits of the greater culture as children have been able to appropriate. In turning to more concrete materials, we may note certain aspects of tradition in the school. It will illustrate well this mingling of cultures if we divide the tradition which clusters about the school into three classes: tradition which comes entirely, or almost entirely, from the outside; tradition which is in part from outside the school and in part indigenous; and tradition which is almost entirely indigenous. It is roughly true that tradition of the first class exists in the community at large, that of the second class among teachers, and that of the third class among students.

Tradition of the first class, that which for the particular school comes altogether from the outside, is a manifestation of a culture complex diffused throughout the whole of West European culture. The historic school has of course had a part in the formation of this complex, but any particular school is largely the creation of it. Tradition of this sort governs the very existence of schools, for, without such a culture complex, schools would not exist at all. This traditional culture complex governs also the general nature of the life in the schools. It determines that the old shall teach the young, and not that the young shall ever teach the old, which would be at least equally justifiable in a world that changes so rapidly that an education twenty years old is out of date. Tradition governs what is taught and it holds a firm control upon the manner in which it is taught. Tradition determines who shall teach; we have already discussed some of the traditional requirements for teaching. It is this same sort of tradition also which largely determines how students and teachers shall think of each other.

The best example of a mingled tradition in part absorbed from the general culture of the group and in part produced in the particular institution is the tradition of teachers. In so far as this tradition of teachers is derived from outside a particular school, it is drawn by teachers from the general culture, and from association with members of the teaching profession everywhere. In so far as it is a purely local product, it is produced by the teachers in the institution and is passed on from one teacher to another. We may mention some cardinal points of the teacher tradition as it is usually encountered, making due allowance for local variations. There is a teacher morality, and this morality regulates minutely the teacher's relations with his students and with other teachers; it affects his relations with other teachers especially where the standing of those teachers with students might be affected. There is a character ideal of the teacher; nearly every group which lives long in one stereotyped relation with other groups produces its character ideal, and this ideal for teachers is clearly observable. When teachers say of a colleague, "He's a school teacher," they mean that he conforms to this local character ideal. (It usually implies that the individual puts academic above other considerations, is conscientious in his duties, and exacting in the demands he makes upon himself and others.) There is a taboo on seeking popularity among students, and this taboo operates with dreadful force if it is thought that popularity seeking is complicated by disloyalty to the teacher group. There is a traditional attitude toward students; this attitude requires that a certain distance be kept between teachers and students. The desire to be fair is very likely not the strongest motive that teachers have for keeping students at a distance, but it is certainly one of the consequences of the policy, and it has in its own right the compelling value of an article of faith. None may violate the code of equality with impunity. Teachers have likewise a certain traditional attitude toward each other. The most obvious manifestation of this traditional attitude is the ceremoniousness of teachers toward each other and toward the administration of the school. It seems clear that this is the ceremoniousness of a fighting group which does not care to endanger its prestige with underlings by allowing any informality to arise within itself. Another interesting observation that has often been made about particular groups of teachers is that they discriminate markedly between veterans and new men. This distinction is in the folkways. Occasionally there is a more or less definite ceremony of initiation, more rarely, actual hazing.

The indigenous tradition of the school is found in its purest form among students. This tradition, when it has been originated on the spot, is passed on, largely by word of mouth, from one student to another. Some of the indigenous tradition has been originated by the faculty, and then imposed upon the students; once it has been accepted by students, however, it may be passed on by student groups.

Some of the traditional observances which students follow are not home-grown; there is a great literature of school life, and students occasionally appear who are obviously playing the parts of story-book heroes. Besides, there exists in the culture of any community a set of traditional attitudes toward school and school life, varying from one social class to another, and from family to family; these attitudes influence profoundly the attitudes which students have toward school life. Nevertheless the tradition of students is very largely indigenous within the particular school. Although this sort of tradition varies much in detail from one school to another, we may mention certain characteristics of the fundamental patterns.

Like teacher morality, student morality is the morality of a fight-ing group, but differences appear in that the student group is subor-dinate, and its morality is relevant to that situation. Social distance between student and teacher seems as definitely a part of the student code as of the teacher code. The student must not like the teacher too much, for that is naïveté. There is the well-known school-boy code, the rule that students must never give information to teachers which may lead to the punishment of another student. Certain folkways grow up in every group of school children, as the folkway of riding to grade school on a bicycle or of not riding to high school on a bicycle, and these folkways have a great influence over the behavior of all members of the group. These groups of children are arranged in stair-steps. Membership in the older group implies repudiation of the folkways of the younger group. No one more foolish than the high-school boy on a bicycle, or the college boy wearing a high-school letter! Interlocking groups look forward only, each group aping its elders and despising its juniors. In modern schools, there is a whole complex of traditions pertaining to activities; it seems that all activities are meritorious, that they are in some way connected with the dignity and honor of the school, that some activities are more meritorious than others.

Sometimes a whole social system is carried in the tradition of stu-dents, and such social systems are very resistant to change. The fag-ging system, or a system of any sort of hazing, may persist for dec-ades against the best efforts of highly efficient teachers and admin-istrators to change them. A collegiate institution comes to mind which has conducted such a struggle for upwards of a hundred years. We are led to believe that hazing, at least, having its roots in the desire of those already in the group to dominate new members (and having its parallel on the faculty), would be destined to have some place in the culture which the young work out for themselves even if it had no sanction in tradition. In other words, the manner in which the young experience the universe recreates a hazing problem in every generation of students. . . .

Less dignified than tradition, and less old, but of a fascinating diversity, are those bits of folklore which circulate among students. A few years ago there walked upon this very spot a marvellous being, a student who defied the school authorities, laughed when the principal flogged him, finally ran away from home and has never been seen again. There was formerly a teacher in this school who was so near-sighted that the boys played leap-frog in the rear of the classroom. Such and such a teacher has a glass eye. The principal has an artificial foot. A certain male teacher once killed a man in a boxing bout. Much of this folklore centers about teachers. By its spread to adults, which occurs only occasionally, it gives rise to some of the fantastic gossip concerning teachers which circulates in the small town.

The cultural anthropologists have taught us to analyze the actions of human beings living in a certain culture into culture patterns. Those partially formalized structures of behavior known as "activities" will serve as excellent examples of culture patterns existing in the school. Among the "activities" to be found in most public schools may be mentioned athletics, work on the school paper, oratory and debating, glee club work, Hi-Y work, dramatics, participation in social clubs, departmental clubs, literary societies, fraternities, etc. Each of these activities may be thought of as representing a more or less ritualized form of behavior carried out by the individual as a member of a group and, often, a representative of the larger group. There is a set form for these activities. There is merit in these activities, and that merit seems to rest ultimately upon the notion that group welfare and group prestige are involved in them; the honor of the high school is damaged if the team loses. ("Our team is our fame-protector, On boys, for we expect a touchdown from you—" is unpoetic, but explicit on this point.) But there is intrinsic, irrational merit in them, too, as in the trading of the Trobriand Islanders. There is distinction in these activities for individuals. That distinction rests in part upon the prominence which participation in them gives the individual in the eyes of the school at large, and in part upon the recognition which the adult group accords them. The variety of activities is almost endless, for each of the activities mentioned above has many subdivisions; these subdivisions are sometimes arranged in something of a hierarchy as in athletics, where the greatest distinction attaches to football, a little less to basketball, less yet to baseball and track. These activities are commonly justified on the grounds that they actually prepare for life, since they present actual life situations; their justification for the faculty is in their value as a means of control over restless students. It is noteworthy that a competitive spirit prevails in nearly all activities. Not all activities are really competitive, but the struggle for places may make them so, and the desirability of having some place in some school activity makes the competition for places keen. One "makes" the school orchestra or glee club quite as truly as one makes the football team.

These culture patterns of activities are partly artificial and faculty-determined, and partly spontaneous. In so far as they have been evolved by the faculty, they have been intended as means of control, as outlets for adolescent energies or substitutes for tabooed activities. They represent also the faculty's attempt to make school life interesting and to extend the influence of the school. Any activity, however, which is to affect the life of students at all deeply, any activity, then, which aspires to a greater influence than is exerted by the Latin Club or the Cercle Français, must have a spontaneous basis, and must appeal to students by presenting to them behavior patterns of considerable intrinsic interest. Each activity usually has some sort of faculty connection, and the status of the faculty adviser is thought to rise or fall with the prosperity or unprosperity of the activity which he promotes. Activities, then, increase in importance and gain recognition from the faculty through the efforts of interested faculty members, as well as through their own intrinsic appeal to students. (A change is taking place in our teacher idiom. The young teacher now refers to himself not as the teacher of a certain subject, but as the coach of a certain activity.)

Of all activities athletics is the chief and the most satisfactory. It is the most flourishing and the most revered culture pattern. It has been elaborated in more detail than any other culture pattern. Competitive athletics has many forms. At the head of the list stands football, still regarded as the most diagnostic test of the athletic prowess of any school. Then come basketball, baseball, track, lightweight football, lightweight basketball, girls' basketball, girls' track, etc. Each of these activities has importance because the particular school and its rivals are immersed in a culture stream of which competitive athletics is an important part. Each school has its traditional rivals, and a greater psychic weighting is attached to the games with traditional rivals than to those with other schools. Schools are arranged in a hierarchy, and may therefore win moral victories while actually suffering defeats. Pennsylvania wins, but Swarthmore triumphs.

Games, the most interesting phase of competitive athletics, are complex and elaborate cultural patterns. Other culture patterns reside in them. Some form of game is to be found in most cultures. The history of games is one of the most fascinating chapters of anthropology of the historical sort. Enthusiasts of the modern games played with balls claim for them a most ancient origin. (Basketball is an exception.) The game acquires a clearly defined pattern, and this is passed on with little variation. (Even minor changes in the rules usually meet with determined opposition.) Skill is relevant to the culture pattern of the game; if the form of the game is changed, skill vanishes. It is interesting, too, that a "form" which is partly cultural comes to reside in every feature of competitive athletics. The most flexible and skillful performance, with irrelevant motions most completely eliminated, represents "form" in a particular performance. Lack of form usually limits the perfectibility of a performance sufficiently to keep the athlete out of competition. Thus there is "form" for batting a baseball, for a drop-kick, for putting the shot. It is possible that an athlete, by long practice, might develop this form through trial and error and the gradual removal of imperfections in his performance. But it is more likely that the athlete gets this form through cultural diffusion. Form itself may represent the accumulated improvements in technique of many generations of athletes. Form, produced by the internal mechanisms making for the perfection of responses, has thus a cultural character as well.

Competition between schools in athletics comes to a focus in games. The game is in fact disguised war. There is a continual tendency for the game to revert to actual war. "Now go out and fight," says the coach. "Fight," says the school orator. "Fight," scream the spectators. Everyone treats the game as a fight and thinks of it as a fight except perhaps the referee. It is small wonder that the political order worked out for this conflict situation, the political order consisting of the rules and the referee to back them, is maintained with such difficulty and only by penalties which impose the direst disabilities upon the offenders. There is, it is true, a whole code of sportsmanship which arises from this conflict situation, a code which internalizes the rules and makes for the principle of fair play. This code of sportsmanship is a central part of the athletic tradition, and as such an important aspect of the cultural life of the school.

15 KINSEY AND THE MORES *

JOSEPH KIRK FOLSOM (1893–   )
VASSAR COLLEGE

KINSEY does not moralize *about sex behavior*. He does not defend the existing sex mores, nor does he propose any changes in them. But his description of how people actually live, and of their different attitudes toward sexual activities, makes clear that actually there are several codes of sex mores in society. Not only are there the differing codes of social classes and of nationalities, but also there are different qualities or categories of values. The concept of "right" versus "wrong" is only one of these, and it is not quite the same as the religious concept of "innocence" versus "sin." Among Germans and Russians strongly influenced by Lutheran or orthodox Christianity, there is the idea that all people are sinners; if one does not sin, one cannot repent; and repentance is a happier state than mere innocence.[1]

There is also the concept of "natural" versus "unnatural." To the lower level males, illicit sexual activities may be a "sin," and to many a "wrong" in the sense used by the upper level. But the lower level is also governed by the value of "natural" versus "perverted," which with them is much narrower in definition than with the upper class. Pre-marital intercourse may be a sin, but petting, deep kissing, and

---

* Reprinted by permission of the author, of the editor, and of the publisher from pp. 79–84 of Folsom's "Sociological Implications of the Report" in Albert Deutsch, ed., *Sex Habits of American Men: A Symposium on the Kinsey Report* (New York: Prentice-Hall, Inc., 1948), pp. 71–87. The "report" is Alfred C. Kinsey, Wardell B. Pomeroy, and Clyde E. Martin, *Sexual Behavior in the Human Male* (Philadelphia: W. B. Saunders Company, 1948).

[1] F. D. Borkenau, "On Lutheranism," *Horizon* (English), September, 1944.

masturbation are also "perverted," and it is worse to be perverted than merely sinful. The less educated especially condemn the college students not for having intercourse but for their long hours of erotic stimulation without intercourse.

Furthermore, codes of value differ according to the situation in which they are expressed. Anyone knows that on a public platform, through the radio, and in the movies, one can express only the traditional code of sex behavior; some license is allowed to doctors and psychiatrists, but not to clergymen or teachers. Yet in private conversation one may often excuse or even justify for individual cases something he has condemned in general terms on the platform. On the legitimate stage one can present solutions of socio-sexual problems which would be summarily cut from the movies. When Noel Coward's *Design for Living* was translated into a film, just two inserted words were enough to change the original meaning to the one acceptable to the then Will Hays directed Motion Picture Producers and Distributors of America and the various boards of censorship. The heroine, finding her solution to the triangle dilemma in a decision not to reject either of her rival lovers, loudly whispers "No sex." Perhaps never have two words so completely whitewashed a concept for the great American public. Spiritual love and affectionate companionship of a woman with two men—"all right." The public is not supposed to think about whether any of these persons had sex needs or where and how they found—*à la Kinsey*—their "outlets." Perhaps the lesser of imagined evils was that the lovers enjoyed their beloved platonically while they discreetly resorted to prostitutes; she, of course, being a woman, had no sex urge. Of course these differences between media represent in part social class differences.

For a city of 100,000 the Kinsey figures for contacts with prostitutes show an average of 3,190 per week, yet we are told prostitutes supply only about 10 per cent of pre-marital intercourse and 15 per cent of extra-marital intercourse. They find the greatest resort to prostitutes is among unmarried males of the grade school level of 36 to 40 years of age; yet even these get an equal amount of outlet from intercourse with non-prostitute companions.

Marital intercourse, the Kinsey report shows, provides only 85 per cent of the sexual outlet of the married population as a whole, and not more than 62 per cent of the upper level males' outlet by the age of 55. Considering the entire male population, only 52 per cent of its total outlet is derived from marital intercourse and nocturnal emissions, the only outlets which are both legal and morally approved. Probably about one-fourth the total outlet is definitely illegal.

Kinsey destroys false ideas about homosexuality. Most persons who practice homosexuality are described as heterosexuals who use it as a second best practice. *Fifty per cent of all males* who remain single to the age of 35 are found to have had *some* overt homosexual experience to the point of orgasm, but only 4 per cent of males are exclusively homosexual all their lives.

In the eyes of some critics, the Kinsey report, while rigorously confining itself to facts and avoiding moral judgments, is immoral in effect. They say it implies that whatever is, is moral. *It does no such thing.* What are its probable effects on our mores?

1. It does, in indirect discourse, contain a lecture to those who through official duty or through inclination, attempt to control sex behavior. It points out the futility of legal control where this contradicts the actual working, living, though unwritten, code of morality of a group. A moral code is more than a simple list of right and wrong acts for the ultimate subject; it also contains opinions as to what acts are right or wrong for the authority or bystander who is trying to get the subject to "do right." Thus even *if* the majority of the people of Connecticut should approve the old state law which makes it illegal to practice birth control, they would not believe it right to have police invade homes to see whether people were obeying the law. The Kinsey report is no more immoral than were the arguments against the Prohibition Amendment. To give up the effort to prevent individual acts of extra-marital intercourse, even those which are paid for, does not mean that public policy may not vigorously attack *organized* prostitution.

The long-run trend in a democracy is to give more freedom to the individual acting in an individual capacity, while putting stiffer controls upon the businesses, institutions, minor authorities, contracts, conspiracies, gangs and rackets which have power over individuals. If different groups within the country have different mores, they can support them by education and group opinion; no group should be allowed to impose its mores upon others by writing them into the law of the land.

2. The Kinsey report does "debunk" some of the medical and psychological arguments which have been used to reinforce certain

moral standards, and compels us to face the issue: will we still maintain these standards as values in themselves or on religious authority? Thus for example, what of the old taboos against heavy petting and masturbation?

3. The Kinsey report may make easier the development of a new, positive, democratic, morality of relations between the sexes. Its contribution to this end is mainly a negative one, but none the less important. Because of its preoccupation with the sexual orgasm as a unit of human behavior, with its numerical frequency patterns, etc., seen apart from its varied social contexts, this first Kinsey report has left many, particularly the anthropologists, unsatisfied. This is the kind of preoccupation which for years and years has distorted efforts toward more constructive and humane social relations between men and women. But Kinsey has given it its Aristotelian catharsis. After 800 pages of facts about genital behavior, we breathe a sigh and exclaim "So what!" It now becomes plainer than ever before that the methods of effecting orgasmic release of the sexual drive are one thing, the emotional and social relationships of human beings are quite another thing.

Western civilization has long placed high value upon the concepts of pre-marital "chastity" and post-marital "monogamy." What do they mean today?

On the college level, "chastity" seems to mean "technical virginity." There is only a slight anatomical difference between this and non-virginity, and as Kinsey points out, some males even consider themselves virgin when they effect genital union but avoid orgasm. In older times some such boundary line of morality was supported by the practical risks of venereal disease and pregnancy. Now that these risks are greatly reduced, especially on the higher educational level, as much evidence from Kinsey shows, can any such distinction of inches remain morally important?

"Monogamy," as a legal concept, is quite simple. You may not go through marriage procedure with a second partner while still married to another. If you do, you are punishable for bigamy, but then you find you are not really bigamous after all, because the marriage you are punished for is null and void. You merely attempted bigamy. But of course you might get away with this bogus marriage and deception for some time, so the law aims to deter you.

But, apart from the legal definition, does monogamy mean a paramount social and emotional relationship, or does it mean exclusiveness of coitus? If the genital definition be used, does monogamy exclude masturbation or nocturnal emissions accompanied by dreams of another partner, sexual contacts with animals, homosexuality? Does it exclude petting to the point of orgasm with a secondary partner, without actual union of the genitals? If, as is Kinsey's estimate, one-half of all married males have *at some time* during marriage had extra-marital intercourse, is half of the male sex in fact polygamous? Or is the still larger number polygamous who sometimes lust for such experience? Or does it take repeated or regular intercourse with outsiders to constitute a violation of monogamy? Or does the definition necessitate sexual relations with one particular partner who may thus attain a status rivaling that of the spouse?

May we perhaps agree with Porterfield and Salley[2] that the older universals of the sex mores are being replaced by numerous alternatives with the result that it becomes increasingly difficult and perhaps meaningless to define sex delinquency, except where cruelty or exploitation is involved?

But let us not fall into the simplified idea that changes in the mores are merely approaches to a better satisfaction of eternal and unchanging human needs. Human needs themselves change and expand. Men and women come to desire all kinds of things intensely merely because it becomes possible to have them. The attitude of "Why not?" may contain as much potential "punch" and drive as the concept of psychic "starvation." In sex there is no real biological starvation; people can live out their individual lives with much or with practically nothing. But in sex as in other fields individuals will demand the fullest measure of the possible. In the long run the limits will be set by nature and science, not by mores based upon the human ignorance and helplessness of the past.

[2] Austin L. Porterfield and H. E. Salley, "Current Folkways of Sexual Behavior," *American Journal of Sociology*, November, 1946.

16   DELINQUENT BEHAVIOR OF PEOPLE *

MABEL A. ELLIOTT (1898–   )
PENNSYLVANIA COLLEGE FOR WOMEN

NUMEROUS philosophers of criminology, if I may speak of them thus, have long held that every society has the criminals it deserves; that a given society or culture in itself provides the matrix or stimuli which induced the resultant delinquent behavior which the same society condemns. Practically everyone at first will believe that delinquency and crime are deviant behavior from the cultural norms, that is, deviant from the behavior defined as acceptable by the group. It is not so easy, however, for the law-abiding, the socially secure, and the high-principled citizens either to recognize or to admit that the peculiar aspects of their own culture, and the so-called norms of society itself plant the seeds for most of its own criminal activities. This topic I shall develop shortly. A second cultural characteristic of the delinquent behavior is that the crime rate itself is also related to the type of social organization in a given society and the degree of social consensus which characterizes the particular society. A third postulate with reference to the cultural aspects of crime is that there is a differential patterning of crime and delinquency in the various cultural groups. As a fourth premise, I shall maintain that it is true that just as social organization affects the crime rate, the converse is also true that social disorganization and the confusion in social values are also evidenced in an increasing crime rate. The fifth and most striking premise which may be maintained with reference to crime is that crime is a relatively constant characteristic of all classes of society, but that the dominant and powerful in-groups are seldom punished for their anti-social behavior.

Obviously there are many other facets to the problem of the delinquency of peoples which cannot be covered in the space allotted to this article. Please consider my remarks to be lifted out of the context of the larger whole of criminal theory. Now, however, let us

* Reprinted by permission of the author and of the editor from *Phylon, the Atlanta University Review of Race and Culture* (1949), 242–251.

consider these five postulates briefly: First, that a given society by its peculiar norms of behavior in itself is a stimulus to anti-social conduct. Naturally enough, the norms of conduct give us whatever basic stability our society may purport to possess. They give us our concepts of decency, our prevailing notions of monogamy and honesty, and whatever degree of law abiding behavior we achieve. We need to recognize, however, that the norms of behavior as expressed negatively in our restraining laws represent in an especial sense the ethical notions of the law-makers who, generally speaking, represent only a part of society, namely, the articulate upper-middle class. After all, who are the legislators? They are the successful members of the community who can afford to take time out from farm, business or profession to participate in a legislative program. Incidentally, only a well-to-do man can afford to be a legislator. Actually there is nothing particularly democratic about the moral and social values they seek to impose, although most legislators would undoubtedly be astounded if anybody, even I, made such a suggestion. My point is simply this: That as leaders and molders of public opinion the upper-middle class sometimes forgets that it represents itself and often fails to realize that the values which seem so pertinent and so important to maintaining the status quo are often neither so obvious nor so important to the illiterate, the unsuccessful and the impecunious. *Laws, therefore, often fail in their purpose, which is to induce conformity, because they represent the way legislators believe people ought to act or else be willing to take the consequences.* Legislators often fail similarly to realize that people obey laws which they accept as reasonable standards of conduct. Certain laws which are representative of particular class interests often seem to interfere with the accepted patterns of the lowest economic and social groups or other groups unconvinced of the law's validity as the case may be. The fate of the prohibition law is a case in point.

Please do not misunderstand me. I am not arguing that we should let down our fences in the realm of criminal law. Most offenses prohibited by law we should all be willing to admit as belonging to the category of socially dangerous behavior. What we need to recognize, however, is that such conduct will be recognized as socially dangerous by all classes only insofar as it is an accepted norm for all classes, and this can be accomplished only by making it possible for all persons to have greater participation in the creation of social norms. Surely the persons who live in squalor and poverty and are denied the benefit of adequate education have little opportunity to develop high-minded notions with reference to honesty, sex morality or the sanctity of human life. . . .

My second thesis, that the crime rate is related to the type of social organization and to the degree of social consensus, is in a sense a corollary of my last-mentioned premise. There are further implications in my second premise, however, and these may be illustrated briefly by the low crime rates which we find in relatively simple peasant societies and in primitive societies. Here conformity in social behavior is induced by the intimacy of social life, by the very impossibility of escaping detection, and by the enormous pressure of family and primary group controls. And even in our own society there is a striking difference in urban and rural crime rates. In 1948, for example, we find that the rural crimes included 153,757 known offenses in contrast to some 1,028,826 recorded offenses in urban areas. Thirty-six and one-half million lives were represented in the reports of rural crime rates, with approximately one-third of the population committing but slightly more than one-sixth of the reported offenses. The Federal Bureau of Investigation estimates, however, that the total number of offenses for the country as a whole was some half a million greater than the actual number of offenses reported since a number of very serious offenses including embezzlement, fraud and arson (chiefly urban crimes) were not included in these figures. If these were included the rural rate would be even lower, proportionately.

Larger cities report a much higher crime rate than smaller cities, although cities with a population of approximately 100,000 reported more aggravated assaults in ratio to population than larger cities and a higher larceny and burglary rate than in cities over 250,000. There may be certain reasons for these differentials and it is possible that fewer crimes go unreported in cities under 100,000 than is true in our larger cities. On the other hand, municipalities with a population of less than 25,000 had a lower crime rate than the open country which seems to indicate that the optimum population for inducing social conformity falls within the population range of the small city, small town and village. Police are more easily accessible in smaller cities. With all due regard to our statistics, we must admit of course that they are very inaccurate. But even so, there is the unmistakable fact that the bulk of crime occurs in cities.

Yet the disparity between urban-rural life is certainly decreasing with what Professor Kolb calls the "rurbanization" of rural life. And studies made of the relationship between crime rates and proximity to a large city show crime rates to decrease in ratio to the distance from our larger urban centers. Dr. Mapheus Smith, for example, made a study of crime rates in counties surrounding the larger cities in Kansas and found the rate to decrease with each successive tier of counties.[1]

Professor Sutherland's analysis of the crime rates in different areas as related to the distance from a city showed burglaries and bank robberies to decrease with the distance from urban centers, although there were relatively few bank robberies within the cities studied (Chicago, East St. Louis and Wichita). Since gangsters usually hide out in larger cities they seemingly operate within range of their respective hideouts. Other studies have also shown a close association between crime and urbanization.[2]

If we analyze our urban civilization further we find that within the cities the differential aspects of economic status, neighborhood, and educational level are closely linked to the crime rate. The sordid aspects of our industrial civilization as evidenced in economic insecurity, in poverty and slums which exist in easy access to wealth cannot but arouse desires among the economically handicapped for the material advantages from which their pay envelopes seem forever to exclude them. We all know that our much vaunted standard of living with its emphasis upon the amazing gadgets our generation has produced has also produced a desire for those objects. The increase in the educational level of our masses has contributed to a demand for a high standard of living, for higher wages and thus to the eventual ability to possess those gadgets. The stimulus that great wealth affords for those who live in close proximity but who can never hope to possess such means legally is undoubtedly a factor in producing the George Kelleys, the Capones, the Pretty Boy Floyds and the John Dillingers. Gangsters are in a sense frustrated personalities who are hell-bent on becoming millionaires. The high standard of living so characteristic of our culture is certainly a factor in our crime rate, just as surely as materialism is a part of our social values.

Another notable aspect of our culture is our lawlessness and our

[1] V. Mapheus Smith, "The Counties and Delinquency in Kansas," *Rural Sociology,* II, 310–322.

[2] *Cf.* Edwin H. Sutherland, *Principles of Criminology* (4th ed.; Philadelphia: J. P. Lippincott Company, 1947), pp. 135–138, for an extensive list of studies on rural-urban crime.

lawlessness in the name of the law which has been so strikingly related to our frontier mores. The discriminatory criminal law of the South seems to have arisen out of the caste system imposed upon two groups, first, the indentured white men, often transported criminals from England, and second upon the slaves because of fears of their uprising. The early Virginia pioneers legalized a dual crime code for the slave and the white man which became enmeshed in the cultural pattern for the South.

The luckless white outlaws from Virginia often pushed into the wilderness of North Carolina where they might escape the law. Here crimes became so frequent that lynch law arose in protest, first against the threats to life, property and decency imposed by the escaped indentured criminals. When life in North Carolina became more orderly with an influx of sturdy, decent folk, the less tractable elements of the population again sought the frontier, this time to the west along with an adventurous group of the better stock. No one supposes that all these frontiersmen were completely lawless. But even so the restive spirit of the pioneer created a pattern of freedom which rejected the restraining influences of group life, and this pattern of freedom was made possible by the vast open spaces, where pioneer man could exist without tribute to lawmakers or tax collectors, and if he moved with the first encroachments of later settlers he could refuse to bow to any human's opinions. With the ever receding frontier any who exerted himself could wrest a living from the wilderness. Where men settled down to the insistent demands of effective agricultural production, life became relatively calm and peaceful and eventually took on a general orderliness that became the way of life in the great Middle West. Certainly it is true that to the plains and mountain states to the west, many honest folk migrated. But here also came the flotsam, the outlaws, the ex-convicts and desperadoes. Legal, religious and educational institutions were virtually unknown when men first built their cabins on the prairie and in the forests of the Middle West and in consequence the quick decisive lynch law developed. This lynch law of the West was an attempt to expedite decency, to keep down holdups and to control the men who staged highway robberies or stole the money bags of cattle men returning from driving their cattle over the long trails to market. History is replete with examples of "Boot Hill" cemeteries and of men shot quickly and without remorse. Similarly, in mining communities the vigilante committees arose to repress the stage coach robberies which entailed so many losses of fabulous sums of silver and gold. In the United States we must remember the population swept westward before organized institutions could be set up to implement effective social controls and in this fact we may find the reason for the rise of lynch law, which was a matter of outraged citizens taking law into their own hands.

With the exhaustion of the free lands of the West many alterations in our economic and social life have transpired which we cannot here consider. It is important for us to realize, however, that with the disappearance of our frontier the defenses of a freedom-loving people shifted from the security of the great open spaces to the demand for security through social legislation and with this demand came an enormous expansion in the categories of criminal conduct. When the last homestead stake was filed a new era began. Instead of moving out of ear range of the encroaching neighbor the pioneer's lineal descendant attempted instead to solve his problems by writing laws and often with none too satisfactory results. For legislators have often failed to take into consideration the need for re-educating our population into a re-evaluation of basic social patterns before attempting to alter behavior by statutory enactment.

In the meantime our lawless heritage persists. Professor Sutherland shocked American sociologists and perhaps frightened the American businessman when he made a pronouncement a few years ago that ninety per cent of all businessmen are guilty of breaking laws for which they might receive serious penalties, fines or prison sentences. The unorganized social processes of pioneer society have left their cultural residue in the excessive opposition of big business to restrictive legislation although [big business seems quite] willing to restrain the activities of persons who threaten [its] status quo, as is witnessed by such enactments as the Taft-Hartley Act. But part of our crime rate is certainly to be explained by our unwillingness to accept the social restraints of laws, while at the same time each legislature increases the varieties and types of behavior which may be classified as crimes in a given political jurisdiction.

Pioneer society thus illustrates my third premise that there is a differential patterning of delinquency in different culture groups. For there are many other ways in which culture patterns affect crime, both by providing stimuli and by setting patterns for committing crimes. Victims of crime, according to Dr. von Hentig, seem literally to set the stage for crimes by making it both easy and possible to steal, to burglarize, or to commit rape.[3] Our newspapers stimulate crime by recounting the methods and emphasizing the details. Thus every sordid murder tends to set off a series of dreadful crimes. Our stores display goods in a fashion which permits easy theft, at the same time that they entice the honest customer.

Crimes also vary with different cultures. In America, for example, we rob banks. In Russia organized thieves specialize in foreigners' luggage. Differentials in economic well-being undoubtedly make for a greater Russian interest in foreign luggage than applies with organized criminal "mobs" in America. There is even a cultural aspect to methods employed in stealing and burglarizing. In America clever burglars are supplied with special tools to facilitate breaking locks. Russian burglars instead use a saw and *cut out the lock*. Stealing luggage from trains in Russia is a special skill. Luggage is placed on high racks opposite the windows in Russian trains, but with the aid of crane-like hooks, which reach through the train compartments, luggage is easily pulled five or six feet through the windows.

Behavior is also differently defined by different cultures as we all know and a given act may be interpreted as crime, misdemeanor or legitimate conduct—even within different sections of the same nation as is witnessed by our varying criminal codes. We also know how hard it was to enforce prohibition among our foreign born groups to whom the consumption of wine was as much a part of their dietary habits as coffee is to the American public.

This leads us to our third premise, namely, that crime is an index to social disorganization and to confusion in our social values. There are many earmarks of social disorganization in a world torn by conflicting ideologies, political theories, and cultural lag. When old cultural norms are questioned on the one hand and threatened on the other, the forces of reaction may tighten at the very time that social change is imminent. Similarly, wars and rumors of wars destroy the foundations of existing moral values. Sometimes the urge to survive outweighs all other values and seemingly undermines all the slow accumulation of ethics for which man has struggled so hard and so long.

Thus when political ideologies are in conflict, kind, well-mannered persons of high ideals may come to accept the role of traitor to their

---

[3] *Cf.* Hans von Hentig, *The Criminal and His Victim* (New Haven: Yale University Press, 1948), especially chap. xii, pp. 383–450.

own national group as was so frequently true in wartimes in Europe and likewise has been true in our own country. Brother turns against brother, father against son in the belief that an alien value is actually the higher good. Similarly conflicting economic values may lead to violence and to mass uprisings and the destruction of property in labor disputes, as we well know.

Wars and wartime afford the example, par excellence, of the relationship between social disorganization and delinquent behavior. In wartime the standards and patterns of peacetime life are grossly altered. Families are separated, illicit sex relations and prostitution increase markedly and reckless marriages take place to end shortly in divorce. Crime temporarily decreases because the young men—who commit most of the crimes—have gone to war. When the war is over the disruptions of war make their surest impact upon old behavior norms, for war transvalues values, and frequently in what seems to be in the negative direction. To kill, to maim, to destroy become major aims in war in order to defeat the enemy. But in addition to defeating the enemy these devices destroy much of the moral fabric of human society and initiate patterns of conduct which persist long after the armistice is signed.

With the veterans' return to civilian life crime rates are always markedly increased. In 1945, for example, there was a pronounced widespread increase in crime in the United States in all categories. In 1946 there was an even higher rise with a 7.4 per cent increase in urban crimes over 1945 and an upswing of 14.7 per cent in rural crime. War as an acculturating agency apparently contributed toward inducing much the same rates of anti-social behavior in rural and urban areas, for in 1947 rural crimes witnessed a general increase of 7.1 per cent, with a marked increase in every category except criminal homicide and auto theft. Unquestionably the sophistication of the rural-born soldier increased with his new experiences. In the meantime urban crime decreased 5.1 per cent. During 1948 high crime rates persisted within only two categories of behavior—negligent manslaughter and auto theft—which declined to below prewar averages. The increase in postwar murder rates, in particular, seems to bear an important relation to war, perhaps because the emotional reaction to killing declines with military training in the techniques of killing.

The disturbed family relationships of wartime along with other disturbing factors also create many problems of wartime juvenile delinquency as is well known. What is perhaps more important is the difficulty in dealing with young persons who have been trained to lie and to steal from the enemy during the war, and this is especially true in the occupied countries. This practice in deluding enemies which youngsters learned so avidly during wartime persists when the enemy has been scouted and seems to work when applied to neighbors, government officials, teachers, etc. At least European friends and educators tell me that cheating, lying and stealing have become serious problems in school administration and that re-education of young persons into an acceptance of prewar morals has become a very serious problem.

Just as wars are disruptive so, too, are there disruptions imposed by revolutions, by social uprising and by local community disorganization. When the values of a given society are seriously threatened, norms of conduct may seem virtually to disappear. For the time being, social organization may be practically non-existent. Whether the resultant behavior can be called delinquency may depend upon the moral and social perspective of the one who defines the conduct. If there is no state there is no law and the conduct though generally opposed to norms of social well-being may be technically difficult to punish. Here we have the old question of whether a crime is a crime unless it involves breaking the law. In any event, it is obvious that conduct generally defined as criminal increases where there is no restraint of law.

The fifth premise which I have offered with reference to delinquent behavior is the most startling, *viz.,* that delinquent behavior is relatively common in all classes of society although delinquents in the upper-middle and upper classes are seldom brought into court. This is true both of juveniles and of adult offenders according to Professor Austin Porterfield's study of delinquent offenses committed by two hundred college men and 137 women enrolled in colleges in Northern Texas. Exactly one hundred per cent of both the men and women admitted committing one or more offenses identical with those of fourteen hundred children who were referred either to the police station and/or the juvenile court. In fact, the college men in their pre-college days committed an average of 17.6 offenses and in their college days the average number was 11.2. In their pre-college days the women averaged 4.7 offenses. For chivalrous reasons, perhaps, the college women were not asked to record their post-enrollment delinquencies.

These Texas students included class officers, honor students, ministerial students, athletes and musicians and they were in every way representative of the rank and file of college men and women, from a wide range of economic backgrounds. Yet their offenses were practically identical with those of young persons brought into court. The offenses of the college students ranged in fact from truancy to serious sex offenses, shoplifting and murder. Yet, the only significant instance in which there were court charges was for traffic violations. Even in the case of murder, there was no charge.[4]

All this indicates that there is no close relationship between income and delinquency. Instead an important relationship exists between the social status of the offender and the reporting of his offense.[5]

Delinquents who get reported above all else offend the sensibilities of the persons who complain about them. By and large we seem to be most offended by the misconduct of those whom we do not esteem. This lack of esteem may be partly a matter of social position, but it may have its roots also in jealous rivalry.

The individual's family is often of primary importance in determining whether he will or will not be reported, or if reported, whether any serious charges will be made against him. Where the father is dead or the parents divorced, the family situation seems to militate against the child's status in the community and he is much more likely to be reported than otherwise. Juveniles brought into court are actually frequently reported to the court by their parents who more or less reject the child because he got into trouble. The juvenile court child tends to be the friendless child, from a socially unimportant family. This disparity in family pride and loyalty which exists in case of the delinquent from a good family in contrast to the rejection which the court-committed child experiences is unquestionably an important differential in the determining of the degree of social recompense which the community may exact from the child.[6]

Struck with the significant implications of Porterfield's study, James S. Wallerstein and Clement J. Wyle decided to find out to what extent the so-called law-abiding adults were law breakers. These researchers drew up a questionnaire which they submitted to

[4] *Cf.* Austin L. Porterfield, *Youth in Trouble* (Ft. Worth: Los Potishman Foundation, 1946), pp. 38–45.

[5] *Ibid.*, p. 45.

[6] *Ibid.*

persons in a wide range of professions and occupations, although the group was somewhat weighted by persons in the higher income brackets. Replies were received from 1,698 individuals, chiefly residents of metropolitan New York and its suburbs, but they were also scattered over New York State and several other states. The replies were anonymous to insure frankness and the anonymity apparently produced the desired results for 99 per cent admitted they had committed numerous adult offenses. The mean number of offenses committed after the age of sixteen by the men was 18, ranging from 8.2 for clergymen to 20.2 for laborers. Women laborers on the other hand were the lowest offenders among their sex with an average 9.8 offenses while women in military and government work admitted 14.4 delinquent acts, with a mean of eleven for the whole group.[7] Of course we are relying here on their willingness to report their offenses. In any event the reported offenses ranged from malicious mischief to serious felonies, such as burglary, robbery, tax evasions, auto theft. In conclusion the Messrs. Wallerstein and Wyle maintain that there is a large element of chance (and we may interpolate, social position) which determines who gets caught.

Unfortunately, the man or woman who is incarcerated is far more likely to become a confirmed criminal than is true in cases of the person whose delinquency goes undetected. A college student may be put on probation by the Dean, the boy who lives in a slum may be committed to an industrial school.[8]

A major conclusion from all this is that respectable people are relatively lawless and yet somehow they may become outstanding, even distinguished citizens.[9] The psychiatrist would undoubtedly tell us that the respectable group punishes others because they themselves feel guilty. The important fact which needs concern us here is that our criminal procedure is shot through with hypocrisy. On the other hand, it is also obvious that the total worth of the individual should be assessed in determining his value as a person. Men, including those we punish as criminals, should be known as much for their good deeds as for their bad, in making any plans for treating them effectively. Thus far this important consideration has escaped us.

[7] James S. Wallerstein and Clement J. Wyle, "Our Law Abiding Law Breakers," reprint from *Probation*, 1947.
[8] *Ibid.*
[9] *Ibid.*

17 THE PSYCHOTIC PERSON SEEN CULTURALLY *

BY JOHN DOLLARD (1900–   )
YALE UNIVERSITY

FROM the sociological point of view a psychotic person may be seen as one who has rejected existing social organization and developed a compensatory private version of culture. Up to the point of psychosis our hypothetical person accepts group valuations and meanings and responds to persons and objects in a way which is intelligible to us, therefore within the range of the "normal." For example, his "boss" is to him his boss, with a rôle which would be intelligible to all of us. After the psychosis, his boss takes on strange capacities for him, though not for us. The boss becomes something else, a different object, to be reacted to in an altogether different way. He may be thought of by the patient as in love with the patient, or as pursuing him, or as silently hating him, or as planning evil things, or as being gifted with various magical attributes—such as control of natural forces at long distance, being present though invisible, etc. This different slant of the psychotic person on social objects for which there is a standardized group valuation I ask to be allowed to refer to as a "private version of culture." It is not a mere disintegration of culture; it is organized and consistent, often even highly integrated and systematic. Again, before the psychosis, our potential psychotic person is joined with us in agreement on the way to respond to the simplest life-situations, as that milk is a food (not a poison) and that a wink is a sign of accord (not a secret accusation). After the psychosis, our common frame of reference is to a greater or less degree discarded. We find ourselves differing with the patient on matters which are from our point of view beyond dispute. He seems to take words and situations which seem patent enough to us in their meaning and to see them and react to them in a quite different way. We would say "crazily."

* Reprinted by permission of the author and of the editor from *The American Journal of Sociology*, XXXIX (1933–34), 637–648; excerpts taken from pp. 637–643, 647–648.

To be sure, we all differ from one another somewhat in our way of taking situations, but in the psychotic person the differences are radical and striking and seem at first blush not to be of the same order as "normal" differences.

With this said we can state the sense in which we are using the word "culture." We mean the shared world of experience characteristic for the group to which the person belongs. It implies common definitions of acts and objects, common views on good and evil actions, common assumptions regarding the meanings of words and experiences. This "platform" is seen here as deserted by the mentally ill person. This desertion cannot be seen in terms of conscious purpose and intent. It is a despairing reaction of the total personality in the face of an unendurable situation, in which his inner situation (wishes and impulse life) as well as the outer situation and its rigors must be taken into account. The revolting person has recourse to a massive redefinition of persons and social values and substitutes private for social definitions of objects and situations.[2]

If this is true, study of individual psychotic persons ought to show the process by which the ill person has developed the particular idea-system which he manifests, once ill, and it ought to be theoretically possible to compare point for point his idea-system with that held by the rest of us. We have before spoken of the "inner" and the "outer" situations of our mentally ill person. Let us note that the inner situation has been long in formation; it is the precipitate of the interaction of the drive life of the person with a long series of situations. This attitude-pattern of the subject will contain the answer to our question as to why a particular revision of culture is made by the subject once he becomes psychotic. The "outer" situation of hardships and stresses seems easier to define, though this, too, is deceptive; our subject may, for example, feel a particular stress in a much more significant way than we think we should (such as a death in the family). To follow this example for a moment, we strive to put ourselves in the position of the subject and express our evaluation thus, "Poor chap, no wonder he is in mental trouble, his wife being ill for such a long time and then dying just when he needed her most." This would be the outer or average cultural evaluation of

---

[1] Sigmund Freud, *Civilization and Its Discontents* (London: The Hogarth Press, 1930), pp. 41, 139.

[2] A later reaction will be that of the group in isolating and rejecting the sick person. This is the first step in the diagnosis of mental illness.

such a situation. But, from the standpoint of the inner life of the subject (conscious and unconscious), the event may seem quite different. It may be seen by him as a punishment, as another in a long series of frustrations, as a realization of his hostile wishes, etc. The point is that the latter evaluation, also cultural, is built up in the life-sequence of the person and is highly relevant to the fact of his illness. This inner evaluation points backward into the life of the person and indicates situations long past, and persons perhaps dead, who are still being reacted to in the present overt situation. This "inner" life of the person, conscious and unconscious, is what he brings to the events which are judged by us to have some sort of average potentiality (effect on us) in reality. This inner life is "cultural" and "social" down to its contact with the drive or impulse life of the individual.

The study of this inner life brings us immediately in contact with the "outer world" of the person as it once existed. Each new situation in the past has added some element to this patterned "inner life" as we find it now. Through a life-history of the person we try to make out what these earlier "external" situations were and what instinctual impulses (with their social definitions) he brought into each such former situation. We can get this kind of information from the subject (or at least some psychotic subjects); we can also go to those persons who were parts of the subject's earlier milieu and get their impressions of the same situations that are alleged to be important for him. Since the earliest and most important aspects of these "forming situations" will be found to have existed in the intimate milieu of the family, we are led to the intensive study of this unit as a condition of the thoroughgoing study of the individual.

One sometimes hears of *also* "getting the life-history," as though it were a foreign kind of datum in some way external to the subject as he is. This "also" attitude toward the life-history is a lamentable misunderstanding. I suppose there are aspects of a person which can be defined in biological concepts which could be said not to be germane to the life-history. The better assumption is, however, that one is dealing with a socially patterned and constellated organism and that all data from any conceptual level must be seen in its interrelations with all other data. (Such a datum might be a disease of childhood whose permanent significance . . . lies rather in the fact that it called forth unusual love and care from the mother.)

The results of preliminary study indicate that it would probably be profitable to seek to get a series of life-histories in this field—a very detailed one of the mental patient himself, and histories as detailed as may be from relevant members of his formative milieu. It is obvious that these life-histories would be found to intersect and interlock at many points, and that each would throw light upon the other. Since the family of the psychotic person is often (not always) sympathetically related to the mental hospital, the observer in the hospital can be in a preferred position for study. The patient is, of course, always accessible for study by virtue of his continued and enforced residence in the institution. Sympathetic observers with insight can hope to study in such situations without harm either to patients or milieu, and often with some prospect of gain in helpful insight both for the patient and relatives. It should be noted, however, that the object is not the invasion of the field of the psychiatrist, or the treatment of mental patients by the sociologist, but a study in how culture is transmitted and how, from our point of view, the personalities in question arose.

It has already been proposed that the psychotic person (in his psychosis) is responding to social organization. He rejects or reinterprets the ordinary social texture of expectations of action and substitutes his private definitions of situations and preferred ways of behavior.[3] One guess as to the motivation would be that the cultural world immediately facing the patient has somehow become dangerous or distasteful to such a degree that he can no longer endure it. He flies, therefore, into other reaction forms—but forms no less related to ordinary social ways of behaving for the fact that they seem to us bizarre. An additional point is the fact that no one knows the carriers of future psychoses until they are legally committed; until that time they appear to us as not distinctively differentiated from the mass of culture-bearers. It seems unnecessary to assume that the psychotic has been an undistinguished member of society up to the point of his commitment, and that thereafter he is no longer to be considered and studied from the angle of his rôle as a group member.

One of the commonest criteria defining the mentally ill person is disorientation for time, place, and person. The patient may not know where he is, for example, or who the interrogator is, or what month and day it is. Such knowledge is, of course, a minimal and

[3] Not all patients in mental hospitals are "psychotic" patients. For example, neurotics, alcoholics, extreme behavior problems, and others are also present.

highly important demand for social adjustment, and not to fulfil it is an especially serious mark of disorganization. But this is not the end of the matter. It is sometimes assumed in addition that nothing the patient does or says makes much sense, that he has in some way been moved off the continuum of objects which must be seen as functioning in reference to a social milieu. This view is probably erroneous. Often there is only the appearance of such disorganization, of such total cleavage from the milieu. We assume irrelevant utterance on the part of the patient because the subjective context for his remarks is lacking. But, perhaps, if we knew that, there would appear sense in the seeming nonsense. It is my impression that mentally ill people worry and talk about things they ought to worry and talk about—matters in every respect of significance and importance if one only knows how to understand them. To overlook this possibility is on a par with the behavior of the benighted traveler who hears a foreign language and calls it a lot of "hash." What mental patients talk about makes sense to them. It is to be viewed as a kind of confession, an attempt to explain, which at first we cannot understand. Perhaps such patients are really to be viewed as inventors, inventors of a variant culture and symbolism, strange to the rest of us. The fact that a mental patient thinks he is God or Napoleon may seem quaint or merely crazy, and we have an amused feeling of superiority to him. But we are merely affirming that he is "different" and that we do not understand him. Nor is it enough to talk from a different conceptual level and content ourselves with the formula that such ideas are the product of a "diseased brain," though that can sometimes be shown, or in more sophisticated form that we are facing here the results of "neural dissociation." We must emphasize that such ideas function for the patient. They get something done for him. They are part of his life-adjustment to surrounding social processes. They are part, if you will, of his continued wrestle with "culture" (in part, internalized). As such they command the respectful attention of the sociologist.

Residence in a mental hospital rapidly convinces one that, whatever else it may be worth while to define him as, the psychotic person is a storehouse of social experience. He reeks cultural implications. Bizarre and unintelligible references may be taken as challenges to our curiosity—as shards torn from life-contexts—as meanings in a strange personal currency which are nevertheless derived from our common speech. But such riddles are not easily solved unless we are contented with rough and ready definitions. If, for example, we are content with the conception that a personality disorder is related to a "broken home," that fact is rather readily established; but if we wish to know in just what sense the home is broken for this particular person and how the precise manner of breaking has impinged on him, we must resign ourselves to a long period of arduous investigation. Investigators who come in with a hundred life-histories after a couple of years in the field are justifiably suspected of being easily contented in their methods or of operating under pressure of quantitative ideologies which are for the time being inapplicable. . . .

It is, perhaps, important also to suggest that mentally ill persons are sick in two senses. They are medically "sick" in the sense that they can no longer fend for themselves in the outside community and that their illness is very conveniently treated by the same means as is used for persons with demonstrably somatic difficulties. It may be provisionally worth our while also to view them as sociologically "sick," by which I mean to suggest that there is a problem in how the culture "took on" with them. This distinction has no implications for treatment at the present time but points only to the research possibilities.[4] But problems in the field of cultural transmission are, it would seem, matters of first concern to the sociologist in any life-form in which they appear. Naturally, also, the sociologist can only study the mental patient when he is already receiving all that medical and psychiatric organization can do for him. There is very little that we can do for the patient now, but there is much that he can do for us if we enter the field of his study with even our present preliminary point of view. Sociologists, modest in their aspirations and properly trained, are likely to have a good reception from existing hospital organizations and the "chance to work," which is all we can ask for at present. "Proper training" would include the appreciation both of the imperative nature of the world presented to the organism by the pre-existing group and the full realization that custom, as it functions in the person, is affectively charged to the limit. The postulate might be that the mentally ill person is still and wholly a person, if a somewhat unusual one. Sociologists should view him calmly as any other person and ask how he got this way, and not be contented with an-

[4] Note, as an exception, the original proposal of Harry Stack Sullivan for revision of the hospital milieu for schizophrenic patients. See his "Socio-Psychiatric Research," *American Journal of Psychiatry*, X (May, 1931), 977-91.

swers which run counter to their view of the nature of the rest of the social world.

Mechanical techniques are not immediately needed for such study though they may, in the latter development of the field, be quite helpful. The sensitization of the observer both culturally and from the viewpoint of psychic dynamics is, however, crucial. Scientific success in such studies can come only to an observer who shares richly and realistically in cultural experience and who can define rather exactly his own position with relation to his "taking on" of culture. Systematic discussions (like this paper) and formal pedagogy alone are likely to be quite unavailing in reaching the necessary level of insight. They can only point out the object of study in a preliminary way.

Probably the nice problem in this field will prove to be the relative evaluation of the existing milieu, with its points of significant support and stress, and the force of highly fixed inner definitions tending toward pathological interpretations of existing situations and consequent pathological response. We may state it also as a problem of the "cleaving power" of the person to the objects from which he gets group support and maintains normal function.

SECTION THREE
Human Ecology

18 HUMAN ECOLOGY *

BY LOUIS WIRTH (1897–   )
UNIVERSITY OF CHICAGO

I

HUMAN ecology as an academically recognized intellectual discipline is considerably younger than the *Journal,* whose fiftieth
anniversary this issue celebrates. It borrowed its conceptual framework and much of its method from plant and animal ecology, which
are themselves but recent arrivals in the scientific world. When Ernst
Haeckel coined the name for the new branch of biological science in
1869, he sought to call attention to the fact that the structure and
behavior of organisms are significantly affected by their living together with other organisms of the same and other species and by
their habitat.

Whatever else men are, they are also animals, and as such they
exhibit the effects of physical aggregation and of their habitat. Much
of what subsequently became human ecology had already been
studied in a less systematic and scientific manner by geographers,
historians, and philosophers under the general theme of "environ-
mentalism." New impetus was given to the study of human ecology
by the interest aroused in the relationship between population and
the means of subsistence through the writings of Malthus and by the
new understanding of the web of life, including the survival and
development of species derived from Darwin and the theorists of
evolution.

Developments in demography during the nineteenth century and
the more accurate description of human settlements as furnished by
the human geographers, together with the beginnings of social surveys of specific communities, particularly in England, set the stage
for the systematic formulation of problems and the perfection of
methods out of which have grown the ecological studies of the last
generation.

* Reprinted by permission of the author and of the editor from *The American
Journal of Sociology,* L (1944–1945), 483–488.

Sociologists, both urban and rural, were at work studying the human community by methods which subsequently have been called ecological long before human ecology was recognized as a distinctive field of scientific activity. A series of significant maps on the spatial distribution of vital and social phenomena in England had appeared in Henry Mayhew's *London Labour and the London Poor*. Booth's *Survey of the Life and Labour of the People in London* had furnished a notable example of the importance of areal study of the great metropolis of London. Von Thünen's *Der isolierte Staat* had given a theoretical framework for the understanding of successive concentric zones of land use of a region. The device of graphically presenting population composition by means of pyramids had already been used by pioneers in the United States Census. There had been studies of urban land use, of housing, and the incidence of poverty, disease, and crime, and there had also been systematic interpretations of these phenomena on high theoretical levels, of which Henry George's *Progress and Poverty* is perhaps the outstanding example. Studies of the physical aspects of the human community had even found their way into sociological textbooks, exemplified by Albion W. Small and George Vincent's *An Introduction to the Study of Society*. C. J. Galpin, in his surveys of rural communities, notably in his *The Social Anatomy of an Agricultural Community,* had indicated the methods for depicting objectively the interrelations between the trade center and the hinterland. In addition, there had been numerous monographs of a more or less scientific nature on specific communities, towns, and cities in various parts of the country showing their growth, their social characteristics, their physical structure, and the incidence of problems such as housing and social disorganization.

It was not, however, until 1915, when Robert E. Park published his provocative paper on "The City: Suggestions for the Investigation of Human Behavior in City Environment" in this *Journal,* that what subsequently became recognized as the ecological study of the human community was systematically formulated. Park's suggestions stimulated a series of investigations which, in the course of a few years, led not merely to a rich body of objective data but also to an appreciation of the significance of the study of the community as a physical fact for the understanding of it as a social phenomenon and as a state of mind, and eventually to the recognition of the role that human ecology might play in the study of social life generally.

Human ecology, as Park conceived it, was not a branch of sociology but rather a perspective, a method, and a body of knowledge essential for the scientific study of social life, and hence, like social psychology, a general discipline basic to all the social sciences. He recognized its kinship to, and derivation from, geography and biology. But he emphasized that, unlike the former, human ecology was less concerned with the relationship between man and his habitat than with the relationship between man and man as affected, among other factors, by his habitat. In distinguishing it from plant and animal ecology, he stressed the unique characteristics of man and the human community. He noted that, unlike plants and animals, human beings in large measure make their own environment; they have relatively great powers of locomotion and thus are less attached to the immediate habitat in which by nature they are placed; they are conditioned by their capacity for symbolic communication, by rational behavior, and by the possession of an elaborate technology and culture. Moreover, in human aggregations we find the life of the individuals regulated by conscious controls, by rules, norms, and laws, and by formal organizations and institutions. These factors introduce into the study of human ecology complications unknown in the plant and animal world.

The focus of attention of ecological studies has been on localized or territorially delimited social structures and social phenomena. This has given to the community a central position in the conceptual framework of human ecology. Unfortunately this common-sense term, like all other common-sense terms when used in scientific discourse, has had the disadvantage of ambiguity. The early literature of human ecology was much concerned with the distinction between the community and the society. The former stressed the symbiotic relations, spatial and temporal dimensions, physical structure, competition and the division of labor; whereas the latter stressed communication, consensus, common norms, values, conscious social control, and collective action. Unfortunately these two ideal-typical aspects of human social life have frequently been confused with concrete realities. Thus there has been a failure to see that all communities are also societies and all human societies bear at least some of the characteristics of communities. Competition, for instance, among human beings never takes the form of a blind struggle for life and survival. Rather, it manifests itself as a more or less regulated and controlled struggle for a living and for status. Whereas in the plant and the animal world the mechanisms of collective behavior, such as there are, are built into the structure of the organisms and can truly be described in terms of reflexes and instincts, the behavior of the human world can be understood only in the light of habit, custom, institutions, morals, ethics, and laws.

Aside from the considerable theoretical literature that has developed in the field of human ecology, the contributions of the discipline have become increasingly manifest as aspects of specific studies of communities and regions. As the ecological interest and techniques developed, almost all American community studies have given increasing evidence of the use of ecological methods and knowledge. This is as true of the studies of rural and urban communities as it is of those of wider regions. It is not merely because the ecological aspect of human social life yields a degree of objective knowledge, in the sense of noncontroversial description of physical facts and offers possibilities for a high degree of mensuration and precision, but also because the relevance of the physical base of human social life is increasingly appreciated for the understanding of sociocultural phenomena that human ecology has found an increasingly important place in community studies and, for that matter, in all studies which have an areal dimension.

The emergence of human ecology as a scientific discipline and its recent developments have already been adequately reviewed by others.[1] It is necessary in this review to sketch merely the newly developing interests, problems, procedures, and findings of the discipline. As might be expected, the most important developments and achievements of human ecology are not to be found in studies which pass under that label but are associated with empirical studies of rural and urban communities and of regions undertaken by sociologists, by other social scientists, and by specialists in other practical fields such as market analysis, administration, and planning.

II

Considerable progress has been made in the methods of delimiting the territorial bounds of social phenomena and relationships. This

[1] See R. D. McKenzie, "The Field and Problems of Demography, Human Geography, and Human Ecology," chap. iv in *The Fields and Methods of Sociology,* ed. L. L. Bernard (New York: Long & Smith, Inc., 1934), pp. 52–66; and James A. Quinn, "Topical Summary of Current Literature on Human Ecology," *American Journal of Sociology,* XLVI, No. 2 (September, 1940), 191–226. [See also James A. Quinn, *Human Ecology* (New York: Prentice-Hall, 1950.)]

has called into being the concept of the natural area as distinguished from the administrative area. It has been found that the settlement of human beings, the patterning of social institutions, the incidence of social problems, and the intricate network of social interrelationships does not, except by accident, conform to arbitrarily delimited areas and that hence administrative areas only rarely coincide with the ecological or natural areas. In the study of urban life, for instance, the types of land use and the types of residential areas to be found in the city do not conform to the neat lines of precincts, wards, and other political and administrative boundaries. Neither do crime, disease, family disorganization, and, for that matter, political alignments fit themselves into the static patterns of formally adopted areal units. They have patterns of their own, and they shift in accordance with the total conditions of life. Human ecologists have developed the techniques of base maps, spot maps, and rate maps for the more accurate exploration and delineation of the actual incidence and distribution of these phenomena. Burgess' ideal concept of the growth of the city [2] and the many studies of delinquency, family disorganization, racial and economic distribution, housing, incomes, and standards of living in rural, as well as urban, areas have shown that students of social life cannot accept without considerable modification the presentation and analyses of data offered them by official agencies which must use arbitrary administrative areal units. The development of census tracts in cities, for instance, by the United States Bureau of the Census represents a recognition of the need for reducing large arbitrary areal units to the smallest possible units for the purpose of scientific investigation.

Particularly in the study of urban areas and metropolitan regions has it become necessary to discover the actual extent of the influence exerted by the center upon the periphery. This applies as much to social institutions as it does to technology and to population aggregates. A metropolis, through its intricate network of interrelationships, extends its range of influence upon a territory usually far beyond the orbit of the immediately surrounding urbanized fringe. Because the census gives us a picture of human settlements in accordance with where people sleep rather than where they work, we are likely to gain a false impression of the economic and social entity con-

[2] Robert E. Park, Ernest W. Burgess, et al., The City (Chicago: University of Chicago Press, 1925), chap. ii, "The Growth of the City: An Introduction to a Research Project."

stituting the metropolis and tend to conceive of it primarily as a political unit.

The recognition of the factors which underlie the distribution of people and which account for the differentiation of types of human settlements has important implications for social control, especially government. For instance, whereas the criminal is free to move about, irrespective of political boundaries, the police are hedged in by rigid lines of areal jurisdiction; and whereas disease germs are no respecters of administrative barriers, health officials are often handicapped by them. The no-man's land on the margin of two or more jurisdictions, that so frequently becomes the favorite location for contraband activities, is the result of the discrepancy between natural and administrative areas. The lack of coincidence between natural areas (which are defined by the range of actual functions and which are constantly in flux) and administrative areas (which are defined by law and are relatively static) is of particular concern to community organization and planning. Unless the area of community organization and planning is approximately coextensive with the area over which the phenomena to be organized or planned extend, there is bound to be confusion and ineffectiveness.

To the research in human ecology belongs much of the credit for the more realistic conception of the community and the region. The Fifteenth Census of the United States (1930), in its special monograph on *Metropolitan Districts*,[3] took explicit account of the regional scope of at least our larger urban centers. McKenzie's study of the metropolitan community[4] traced "some of the basic changes that have taken place in American cities since the advent of motor transportation" and "the more important structural changes that are taking place in American settlement"[5] as a result of new technological developments. By taking account of newspaper circulation as one of the factors determining the scope of the metropolitan region and the area of influence of urban institutions, this study suggested a series of subsequent investigations into the ecological aspects of social-psychological phenomena which had hitherto been neglected or were not thought to be subject to objective analysis. The numerous studies which followed on radio-listening areas and on the area of influence of urban institutions, such as the stock exchange, the professional

---

[3] Washington: Government Printing Office, 1932.
[4] *The Metropolitan Community* (New York: McGraw-Hill Book Co., Inc., 1933).
[5] *Ibid.*, p. ix.

organization, and the health, welfare, educational, governmental, and cultural agencies and institutions, gave ample evidence of the theoretical as well as practical usefulness of this approach.

Nowhere has the new conception of the metropolis found greater recognition than in the field of planning. *The Regional Survey of New York and Its Environs*,[6] the National Resources Committee's *Regional Factors in National Planning and Development*,[7] and its *Our Cities: Their Role in the National Economy*,[8] together with supplementary reports, and such technical planning manuals as *Action for Cities: A Guide for Community Planning*,[9] show the extent to which the ecological point of view, concepts, methods, and findings have penetrated into the art and science of planning. And what is true of urban studies is equally true of rural and wider regional analyses and planning enterprises.[10]

Even when planning was primarily physical planning it offered great hospitality to the methods and findings of human ecology; but since planning has developed to include the economic and social designing or redesigning of the community, human ecology has found an even more important place in it. Planning aims at the optimum use of resources and the rational integration of community life. Such knowledge as the human ecologist has been able to obtain about the location of industry, the distribution, segregation, and succession of population, the areas of influence of social institutions, and the interrelationship between the physical, the technological, the economic, the political, and the cultural aspects of community life has proved itself indispensable.

It should be noted, however, that human ecology has not been merely the handmaiden either of the other social sciences, on the one hand, or of such practical arts as planning, on the other. It has, in recent years, developed a substantial body of scientific knowledge in its own right and has also drawn upon other branches of social science for its data and hypotheses. Thus, for instance, studies of communication, public opinion, markets, and voting have contributed

---

[6] New York, 1927-31.

[7] Washington: Government Printing Office, 1935.

[8] Washington: Government Printing Office, 1937.

[9] Published under the sponsorship of the American Municipal Association, the American Society of Planning Officials, and the International City Managers' Association (Chicago: Public Administration Service, 1943).

[10] Cf. the studies of Rupert B. Vance, the "Rural Life Studies" prepared by the U. S. Department of Agriculture, Bureau of Agricultural Economics.

immensely to the formulation of the problems of human ecology, the data with which the discipline works, and the explanations and interpretations toward which it strives.

It should also be noted that, although the most intensive studies of human ecology have been concerned with urban and rural communities, human ecology has also been applied to larger areas and to world-wide phenomena. Thus the patterns of urbanization, the trends of migration, the interrelations between national states, the functions of frontiers, and the problems of minorities, among others, have been studied at least in a preliminary way by the methods of human ecology; and there is every reason to believe that in the future the knowledge gained from local small-scale research will be applied to the world as a whole.

III

The accumulation of vast bodies of precise, descriptive material and its graphic presentation by means of maps and diagrams has unfortunately led some investigators to assume that the facts are either self-explanatory or that one set of ecological facts can be adequately interpreted in terms of other ecological data. In the ecological studies of delinquency, insanity, family disorganization, religious life, political behavior, and social institutions it has sometimes been naïvely assumed that, once the spatial distribution of people, institutions, functions, and problems has been traced and their concentration and dispersion noted, there remains nothing for the ecologist to do but to relate these phenomena to other ecological data to arrive at valid explanations. This view overlooks the fact that social life is a complex interdependent whole. Material conditions of existence are, of course, important factors in the determination of social structure and personal characteristics and behavior. Subsistence, competition, the division of labor, spatial and temporal arrangements and distributions are important aspects of the material conditions of existence and, in turn, of social life. But they are not the whole of social life. On the contrary, as has been adequately demonstrated through numerous investigations, types of attitudes, personalities, cultural forms, and social organizations and institutions may have as significant an effect in shaping ecological patterns and processes as the latter have in conditioning social and social-psychological phenomena. Indeed, in view of our present-day knowledge concerning social causation, we might well be predisposed to follow the general principle that physical factors, while by no means negligible in their influence upon social life and psychological phenomena, are, at best, conditioning factors offering the possibilities and setting the limits for social and psychological existence and development. In other words, they set the stage for man, the actor. We are not yet far enough advanced to say with confidence what importance shall be ascribed to any one factor operating in the complex sphere of the social and the psychological, much less to evaluate the relative importance of physical as distinguished from social and psychological factors.

This does not, of course, mean that ecological studies are irrelevant to sociology and to the social sciences. They furnish the indispensable framework of knowledge upon which social and psychic existence rests. They often aid us in defining and localizing our problems. They aid us in uncovering interrelationships of which otherwise we might not be fully aware, and they suggest the selection of criteria for controlled study. It is as yet questionable to what extent ecological facts may serve as indices of social and psychological facts. For instance, the use of income, occupation, area of residence, home-ownership, rental, and duration of settlement may well be justified in the analysis of social status; but if social status is not to be thought of as identical with economic status and if, as we might well suspect, economic status itself is the resultant of factors among which those cited are only a few, then the use of such an index as rental for economic status, not to speak of social status, is likely to be misleading. Used judiciously, however, such an index may prove itself useful for scientific analysis, especially when its correlation with other facts of the same order has been established.

The studies showing significant differences in such phenomena as delinquency and mental disorders as between different areas of the city are of the utmost importance for the advance of scientific knowledge in these fields. The establishment of gradients for rates of personal and social disorganization passing from the center of the city out toward its periphery is a scientific achievement which carries us far beyond the common-sense knowledge we have had hitherto. But it would be absurd to say that there is something in the inlying areas themselves or in the fact that they are close to the center of the city that produces these high rates of delinquency or other forms of social disorganization. It is rather to the relative concentration and segregation of certain population groups living under certain conditions and in a certain culture that we must look for an explanation of these facts. Human ecology thus provides us with one of the hitherto neglected aspects of the matrix within which social events take place and hence with a conceptual framework and a battery of techniques through which these social phenomena can be more fully and adequately understood.

It would be vain, however, to expect human ecology to give us more than a segmental view of the group life of man which sociology seeks to depict and to understand. Working in co-operation with students of social organization and social psychology, human ecologists can furnish a more comprehensive and a more realistic analysis of society than would otherwise be possible. They can introduce into the study of social phenomena objective referents which will anchor the generalizations concerning society, for which all sociologists strive, more firmly in time, in space, and material reality. Human ecology is not a substitute for, but a supplement to, the other frames of reference and methods of social investigation. By introducing some of the spirit and much of the substance and methods appropriate to the natural sciences into the study of social phenomena, human ecology has called attention to the wide areas where social life can properly be studied as if the observer were not an integral part of the observed. This beneficent influence would be negated, however, if the human ecologists were to proceed as if they, together with the demographers and the statisticians, were the only true scientists among the sociologists, or as if they, unaided by others using different approaches, alone could comprehend and explain the complicated and elusive realities in the realm of the social.

19 REFUGEES BECOME AMERICANS *

BY MAURICE REA DAVIE (1893–   )
YALE UNIVERSITY
AND SAMUEL KOENIG (1899–   )
BROOKLYN COLLEGE

THE story of Mr. S—— is typical of that of thousands of the refugees from Nazi tyranny who came to the United States in the years immediately before the war.

Mr. S—— was an exporter in Germany. He lived in comfortable circumstances, but he was not rich. He was one of the heroes of the first World War and enjoyed considerable prestige. When the Nazis first came to power, he felt quite safe. But though he was transacting his business strictly according to the letter of the law, he was arrested in 1934 on a trumped-up charge of illegal trading with the government of Czechoslovakia. The trial was a farce, and he was dismissed. A second arrest in 1937 on the same charge was only slightly more serious. A third trial a few months later, before a hostile judge and prosecuting attorney and a jury wearing swastika bands, led to a sentence of ten months' imprisonment.

In the few days allowed by the court and the Gestapo to put his business affairs in order, he managed to escape to Czechoslovakia. After months of wandering, he and his wife finally reached a French port from which they sailed for America.

His joy and relief at reaching this country were immediately overcast by a feeling of despair at being in a new and completely foreign country where he had to make a new start. The English that he had learned so correctly at school was of no help. The porter at the dock and the cab driver could not understand him.

He decided that the thing to do first was to learn English and the way to do it was to mingle with people. He began by peddling, first pencils and later candy that his wife made. Then he tried jobs. The various social agencies to whom he went suggested retraining, particularly because his arm had been injured in the first World War; and he looked into this, too. His heart was not in it. He had been a businessman, and he was determined to get back to business. He talked to a great many businessmen and was impressed by their kindness, by

* Reprinted by permission of the authors and of the editor from "The Refugees Are Now Americans," Public Affairs Pamphlet No. 111 (2nd ed.; New York, 1946), pp. 1–19.

the freedom with which they gave information, and by the amount of time they were willing to spend with him. After a year and a half, with the financial help of another German refugee, he bought a small defense plant in a New England town and employed sixteen workers in the manufacture of war goods for the government.

He lives modestly and does not have the luxurious apartment that he had abroad, but he feels that he is sharing in the abundance of America and he has a sense of well-being.

This is but one story out of thousands that could be told about the most recent of American immigrants.

Few immigrant movements to the United States have been as dramatic as that of the refugees. Although small in numbers, the refugees have aroused unusual interest because of the tragic circumstances under which they emigrated. Fleeing from the oppression of fascism, they made Americans aware of the sinister events occurring in Europe and forewarned them of the impending world catastrophe. Arriving during a period of extreme economic depression, they met with considerable opposition, particularly on the part of professional and business people who feared their competition. Moreover, since the majority of them came from Nazi Germany, there was some suspicion as to their intentions in this country. And since many were Jews, they increased anti-Jewish feeling among certain elements in the population. All this has led to widespread rumors and charges. What are the facts regarding these refugees? How many came? Who are they? How are they adjusting to American life? What effect are they having on American economy and culture?

BACKGROUND OF THE REFUGEE MOVEMENT

Earlier Refugee Movements. This is by no means the first time that people have come to these shores to escape persecution. Early in our history the Pilgrim Fathers sought refuge here. Later came the Huguenots, who were driven out of France because of their religious beliefs. Numerous other religious groups, such as the Protestant minorities from England, Holland and Germany, sought freedom here from persecution. Among other groups who fled from oppression were the Scotch-Irish in colonial times and the German liberals of 1848. In later periods came the Eastern European Jews, escaping from pogroms and other mistreatment. After World War I, a series of refugee movements began, during which America received several thousand Armenians, escaping from the cruelty of the

Turkish regime, and "White" Russians, fleeing because of Bolshevism. With the rise and spread of Fascism and Nazism, a refugee movement of gigantic proportions was started which sent a considerable number of victims to the United States.

The Present Refugee Movement. All refugee movements have much in common. The refugees leave against their will. They are forced out by tyranny and oppression or by upheavals and wars. In some ways, however, the present-day refugee movement is in a class by itself. From a world-wide view, it is unprecedented in scope. Also unique is the fact that descent or "race" has forced people to leave their homelands. The individual is thus left with no choice, for while it is possible to change one's faith or political views, one cannot change one's ancestry.

Similarly without parallel is the doctrine of nationalism that resulted in pushing aside all conflicting loyalties, whether political, social, or religious. This extreme nationalism has led to depriving the nonconformist of the rights of citizenship, leaving him unprotected by any government. Being a man without a country was a rare and isolated occurrence in the past but has now become common.

The recent refugee movement has also been marked by (1) the extremely cruel treatment of the victims of political, religious, and "racial" persecution; (2) by the difficulty which these victims encountered in escaping and in finding a secure refuge as Nazism spread to ever larger areas; (3) by the reluctance of the countries not immediately affected to admit them because of the deep economic depression then existing; and (4) by the breaking up of families on a scale previously unknown. Such has been the refugee movement which began with the rise of Hitler to power in 1933.

The Assault on the Jews. The first victims of the Nazi assault on civilization were the Jews in Germany, a small minority numbering 499,682 according to the German census of June 16, 1933. Although they constituted only 0.8 per cent of the total population, they were a convenient scapegoat because of their geographical and occupational concentration. About 70 per cent were living in cities of 100,000 or more population, and about four-fifths resided in Prussia. Despite this concentration in large urban centers, no German city had so large a Jewish population as such European cities as Lodz, London, Moscow, Budapest, and Warsaw, or such American cities as New York, Chicago, and Philadelphia. Since the German Jews were concentrated in commerce and the liberal professions, their influence could easily be exaggerated. As a matter of fact, they constituted only 3.3 per cent of the Germans engaged in commerce, only 2.3 per cent of all engaged in the professions. Only in law and medicine, traditional professions among the Jews, did they constitute comparatively large proportions, 16.3 per cent and 10.9 per cent respectively. But though the Jews formed less than 1 per cent of the German population, they played an important role in scientific, political, and cultural life, far out of proportion to their numbers.

Against this helpless minority of half a million souls the force of Nazi fury was directed. Those who had sufficient foresight and the financial means migrated early with a considerable part of their possessions. Those who hesitated were first deprived of the means of livelihood and of their civil rights and property. Then they were ostracized and segregated, tortured in concentration camps, driven out, or killed. By the close of the war, there were only some 20,000 Jews remaining in Germany. The Nazis went so far as to persecute not only those who were Jews by religion but also those who had even one Jewish grandparent.

Refugees who succeeded in escaping from Nazi terror in Germany to other European countries soon found themselves pursued by the Nazi hordes invading one country after another, and were forced to flee again. The extension of Nazi domination also stirred up new refugee movements from the invaded countries where minorities, both Jewish and Christian, were subjected to the same kind of treatment as in Germany. What had taken the Nazis years to accomplish in Germany was brought about in Austria and Czechoslovakia in the course of a few months. Poland became the central slaughterhouse of Nazi victims. Practically no country in continental Europe escaped Nazi domination or influence.

War and fascism have uprooted and displaced many millions of people in Europe. Among them were millions seeking to escape from persecution. Only a small proportion of them succeeded in escaping the Nazi terror. Most were killed, either directly in extermination camps or indirectly through disease and starvation. Of the approximately 6,000,000 Jews living in Europe outside of the Soviet Union in 1933, over 4,000,000 were killed by one means or another. How many anti-Nazi Christians were killed is unknown, but the number was small compared to the Jews who were the main victims.

Of those who escaped the Nazis, many found shelter in various

European and overseas countries. Some countries, such as France, offered a temporary haven, and others, especially Sweden and Switzerland, a more lasting place of refuge. Estimates of the number of refugees, Jewish and non-Jewish, admitted into countries other than the United States vary widely. The following may be taken as rough guesses of the number admitted, at one time or another, into the most important refugee-receiving areas: France (including North Africa), 800,000; Palestine, 150,000; Great Britain, 140,000; Latin America, 125,000; Italy, 116,000; East African Colonies, 90,000; Switzerland, 80,000; Sweden, 44,000; Shanghai, 30,000; Spain, 18,000; and Canada, 6,000.

How Many Refugees Came to the United States?

There are no official figures on the number of refugees admitted to the United States, since refugees are not separately classified under our laws. All aliens are admitted to the United States either as immigrants for permanent residence or as non-immigrants for temporary stay. Refugees are subject to the same eligibility requirements as all other applicants for admission. Since it is the motive for immigrating that distinguishes the refugee from other immigrants, and since the United States Immigration and Naturalization Service does not record motives, it is necessary to resort to an estimate of the number of refugees.

This estimate is based on the number of arrivals in the United States since 1933 who were born in what came to be Axis-occupied or Axis-dominated countries. To this list of countries Spain has been added, since its civil war led to a fascist regime that resulted in a refugee movement from that country. Russia has been included because many individuals who had been born in Russia but were living as emigrees in other countries came here as refugees. The list of countries of refugee emigration thus includes all of Europe except Great Britain, Eire, Portugal, Sweden, and Switzerland. If all the immigrants admitted to the United States from the refugee countries between 1933 and 1944 were refugees, the maximum number of refugee immigrants . . . would be 318,235. Since, however, most of these countries were not Axis-occupied or -dominated as early as 1933, this estimate should be reduced by eliminating the number of immigrants arriving from European countries other than Germany prior to 1938. This year has been selected as marking the period when German aggression against other countries began and it became clear that there was no escape from Axis domination. Thus calculated, the total number of refugee immigrants admitted to the United States would be 243,862. . . . [The] period 1938–1941 marks the peak of refugee immigration. After the entry of the United States into the war only a few refugees were able to reach this country.

In addition to the refugees admitted on permanent visas as immigrants, some refugees arrived here as so-called "non-immigrants," or visitors, on temporary visas. The total number of visitors admitted from these same countries during the entire period of 1933–1944 was 293,976. Arrivals from Germany since 1933 and from the other countries since 1938 totalled 196,432. Even if we assume that all of them were refugees, the number of such non-immigrant refugees remaining in the United States is not large, because most of these non-immigrants left the country. Only 34,037 more visitors entered the country than left during the 1933–1944 period. Some of the visitors who left re-entered later on permanent visas, in which case they were included in the figures of immigrant aliens admitted. Although exact figures are lacking, official reports indicate that only about 15,000 refugees remain here on visitors' visas. These are mainly persons who were granted an extension of their permits because they were unable to return to their homelands.

Aside from the refugees who entered this country under our immigration laws, approximately 1,000 refugees were admitted in 1944 outside of the regular immigration procedure and placed in an emergency shelter at Fort Ontario, near Oswego, New York, under the authority of the War Refugee Board. This group was made up of persons of various nationalities who had fled from their homelands to southern Italy. They were brought here for the duration of the emergency.

Our immigration laws were not changed during the period of refugee immigration. Neither were the quota requirements altered. Indeed, owing to the economic depression and the threat of war, the enforcement of our laws became more severe. A new visa procedure was introduced to prevent the entry of aliens whose admission might endanger public safety. Visa control was centralized in the State Department, and all applications for admission were carefully examined. These new regulations were time-consuming, with the result that often individuals were unable to leave in time to save their lives. Some administrative measures, on the other hand, were adopted to make the immigration of refugees less difficult. In the case of children unaccompanied by their parents, the affidavit of designated child-caring agencies was accepted in place of the usual guarantee of support by individuals. About 1,000 children were brought over under this plan. In granting visas, preference was given to those who were able to escape so as to make full use of the places available under the quota. Our immigration laws were administered justly. They were not modified for the benefit of the refugees despite the tremendous urgency of the situation.

The figures given above refute the rumor that a million or more refugees have been admitted to the United States. Indeed, the total number of immigrants from all countries during 1933 to 1944 amounted to only 528,549, and that from Europe—the source of refugee movements—was only 365,955. Moreover, it is worth noting that during the period 1933–1944 only 16.8 per cent of the total number of aliens from Europe admissible under our quota law have entered the United States. This was due to a strict interpretation of the immigration laws because of the economic depression, and, later, because of wartime restrictions. In fact, . . . the total number of immigrants admitted during this period was smaller than at any other period during the last century.

What Proportion of the Refugees Are Jews? While Jews constitute a minority of all recent immigrants, they make up a majority of the refugee group. Assuming that all Jews from Europe were refugees, we find that the Jews would constitute 51.5 per cent of the gross estimate of the number of refugees. . . . If, however, the refined estimate is taken, they would make up 67.6 per cent of the total, which may be considered the more accurate estimate. This percentage does not include an appreciable number of Christians who were declared Jews by Nazi decrees. Among the Christian refugees in general, there are more Protestants than Catholics, the ratio being approximately three to two. . . .

The Germans and Austrians rank first among the refugees, and the Poles, Czechoslovaks, Russians, French, Italians, and Hungarians should follow in this order.

CHARACTERISTICS OF THE REFUGEES

Who Are the Refugees? The refugees differ in a number of ways from the immigrants who came to the United States in the two or three decades immediately preceding 1933. To begin with, they include more women. A larger proportion of the refugees are forty-five years of age or over. A higher percentage are married. Although the refugee movement is fundamentally a family type, there is a large number of separated families. There is also a large number of young children, since their escape was made easier by the help extended by various social agencies.

Refugees and Earlier Immigrants Compared. One of the most striking differences between the present-day refugees and other earlier immigrants is to be found in the kind of jobs they held before coming to this country. According to official immigration statistics, an unusually large proportion of the refugees were engaged in professional and commercial fields and white-collar occupations. The proportion of skilled workers was less than normal, while the proportion of farmers, unskilled laborers, and servants was far below average. Of those who had engaged in business and industry before coming to this country, some 25,000 were merchants and dealers, about 5,500 agents, and 1,800 manufacturers. Physicians were the most numerous among those in the professions, numbering about 5,000. Other professional groups included approximately 3,500 college professors and school teachers, 2,500 technical engineers, 2,400 clergymen, 1,900 scientists and literary men, 1,800 lawyers, 1,200 musicians, 800 actors, and 700 artists.

In contrast to the earlier immigrants, a good many of the refugees who came here were relatively well off. This was particularly true of the refugees who arrived in the middle 1930's, when it was still possible to rescue a part of one's fortune. Educationally, too, the refugees were exceptional. By far the most of them had gone beyond the elementary school level, and nearly half had attended college or graduate school. They were primarily a city group with a cosmopolitan outlook, many of them having come from the largest cities of the Continent. A considerable number of them had traveled widely and knew languages other than their own.

How Are the Refugees Distributed? Although the majority of the refugees, like other immigrants, arrived at the port of New York, they are to be found in practically every state of the Union. Following the distribution pattern of our immigrant population, they are concentrated in the East, particularly New York, New Jersey, Pennsylvania, and Massachusetts; in the Middle West, especially Ohio, Illinois, Wisconsin, and Michigan; and in the Far West, especially California. They have settled mostly in the larger cities although a good many live in small towns and rural areas. New York City, the largest center of immigrant population and the main port of entry, has absorbed a larger number of refugees than any other city in the United States. The distribution of the refugees throughout the country has been determined largely by the location of their relatives and friends, job opportunities, and the resettlement program of the various refugee service agencies.

THE REFUGEES BECOME AMERICANS

Difficulties Faced by Refugees. The task of becoming adjusted to American life is difficult enough for the ordinary immigrant in normal times. He finds himself in a strange environment, with different customs, laws, language, and ways of life to which he must adjust. The difficulties faced by the refugee, however, are much greater, for he has been forcibly uprooted and often has gone through indescribably horrible experiences. He is filled with fears and anxieties about the fate of relatives and friends left behind. His adjustment is made more difficult by the spread of propaganda against him from fascist countries. Being forced, in many instances, to leave his possessions behind, he often arrives here without means and finds it necessary to accept jobs beneath his former status. Thus, many a former businessman, manufacturer, or professional person has had to take a job as a peddler, janitor, doorman, or dishwasher. Many couples who previously had servants of their own took jobs as butlers and maids. Housewives who never before had been employed accepted factory jobs and other kinds of work. Not infrequently the main support of the family fell upon them. Not all of the refugees accepted these hardships with good grace, but most of them accepted their difficulties with a courage that was truly admirable.

Assistance by Refugee Service Organizations. Assisting the refugees in their adjustment have been a number of agencies and organizations supported by private funds. Some of these were social service and immigrant aid societies already established. Others have been created for the refugees to meet the special problems presented by them. Some of these agencies give aid to refugees in general and render a variety of services, including temporary financial relief, loans for establishing business enterprises and professional practice, retraining for new occupations, resettlement in other communities, and aid in family and general social adjustment, in immigration problems, and in job finding. Prominent are the large national refugee service organizations with their local cooperating committees throughout the country. Also noteworthy are the self-help and other organizations created and maintained by the refugees themselves.

Other refugee service agencies assist in solving the problems of special groups. Important among this type are committees aiding in the adjustment of such groups as physicians, scholars, lawyers, musicians, clergymen, teachers, writers, and artists. Some agencies have carried on rescue and relief work overseas, either aiding all groups or concentrating on helping in the rescue of intellectuals, labor leaders, or political refugees whose lives were in special danger. Other agencies have been concerned solely with bringing children over and supervising their adjustment.

The refugees have also been helped in many ways by relatives and friends. Only in the case of the special group in the emergency shelter at Oswego have public funds been used, and even here some of the costs have been paid by private funds.

What Refugees Do.   A majority of the refugees ultimately found work in business and the professions, even though many of them were forced at first to accept menial jobs. Owing to the shortage of manpower during the war period, practically all of those seeking employment eventually found work. Often they did not find it in the occupations for which they were trained abroad. Yet practically all have become self-supporting. Among the few still needing financial assistance are those either too old or too young to work and the physically or emotionally handicapped. Most of the refugees are wholly dependent upon their earnings. Only a small proportion have other sources of income.

Most of the refugees, according to the findings of the Study, now feel that their living conditions are as good as or better than those they enjoyed in Europe. This is particularly true of the skilled and unskilled workers, the younger persons, and those who have lived here a number of years. On the other hand, among the professional and business people, the older age groups, and those who have been here a comparatively short time, the majority report their living conditions as being the same or worse. Moreover, the great majority feel that their social position is about the same as or lower than it was in Europe. Thus, it would seem that most of the refugees feel that they have lost more in social than in economic standing.

Where They Live.   The refugees, unlike other recent immigrants, do not concentrate in special neighborhoods in the towns in which they live. Except in a few very large cities like New York and

Chicago, they do not form colonies, but scatter throughout the city. They do, however, show a tendency to settle in parts of the city where others of their own nationality group live, taking into account economic and social class lines.

In contrast to other immigrants of recent periods, the refugees tend to associate much more frequently with native Americans. This is unusual in view of the fact that they have been here a short time.

Integration into Community Life. The striking extent to which refugees have fitted into American community life may be explained partly by their relatively small numbers and wide distribution, partly by their superior educational and cultural background, but particularly by their desire to become assimilated. Reports from communities throughout the country reveal that refugees take part in all kinds of community activities. They readily intermarry with native Americans, especially with persons of their own religion and national background. Of those who have married since their arrival, 30 per cent of the men and 17 per cent of the women have married native Americans, unusually high percentages for a foreign-born group. The only age group that experiences real difficulty in adjusting to American life is, as might be expected, the older people.

Refugee women on the whole appear to adapt themselves more readily to American life than the men. The women are quicker in acquiring the language and adapting themselves to new customs. They find it easier to get jobs. They accept inferior types of work with more composure than the men, to whom this means a greater sense of loss and frustration. They encounter less prejudice in the labor and business fields because they are less likely to be considered as permanent competitors.

Although the refugees have acquired a knowledge of English with great rapidity, they frequently state that language has been one of their greatest difficulties in adjusting to American life. This is because they are not content with a superficial knowledge of the language. They are very anxious to master it and use it like an educated native American.

Refugee Children Adjust Readily. Most successful in adjusting to American life have been the young adults and the children. Reports from various communities throughout the country agree that refugee children fit into American life without difficulty and soon become practically indistinguishable from native-born children. Principals and teachers who have been interviewed say the same of the refugee children in school. They report that these children have learned English in a remarkably short period of time, that language has been, at most, only a temporary handicap, that they associate freely with other children, and present no special problem. Many of the teachers stated that the work of refugee children as a group has been above average. They feel that this is due to the superior educational background of their parents and the value the latter place upon education. They also feel that the refugee children have exercised a beneficial influence by stimulating interest in languages, art, literature, and scholarship.

Although most of the refugee children have recovered quite rapidly from the harrowing experiences abroad, some have found it difficult to overcome those experiences and have suffered from emotional upsets in various degrees. In general, however, these emotional disturbances have tended to disappear after a while as a sense of security is gained and unpleasant memories recede into the dim past. Refugee children, having few or no ties to the European background but merely recollections of an often unhappy childhood in Europe, do not know or long for any other life, as their parents may. They cannot, therefore, think of their future apart from America.

What America means to these children may be seen in the following story, written by a sixteen-year-old boy after nine months in this country:

November 10, 1938, was the most terrible day in my life. In the morning of that day I went as usual to school. At 10 o'clock I went home, beaten by Nazi boys. It was on this day the Nazis set fire to the Jewish synagogues throughout Germany. But this was not enough. At 11 o'clock they took my father to a concentration camp without giving any explanations. Later, six Nazis came to our door, brutally expelled us from our home, and destroyed everything in it.

My brother and I worked hard to support our mother. There were many days when we had nothing to eat. Those who have never known what famine is can't realize what a terrible thing it can be. Days, weeks, months went by, and still my father had to bear the terrible life of a concentration camp. Just at that time when we felt we could not endure the struggle any more, my dad was released from the camp. We were glad to see him, but the change in him was pathetic. His eyes were sunken. His face was drawn and haggard. His hair was gray, and he had aged twenty years and lost about 30 pounds.

After a great deal of effort my parents were able to send my sister and me to France. . . . Finally the train came. A last embrace and good-bye. One part of my heart was full of joy because of having escaped from a land of slavery, but the other part of my heart was dark, full of grief for my parents and all my folks who were left behind. . . .

We spent two years in children's homes in France. Finally, together with forty-three other children we were brought to the United States. When we arrived at the port of New York, every one of us felt overjoyed and our eyes were wet with tears, thrilled at the sight of this land of liberty and justice for all. My dreams were finally realized—being in America. How wonderful it was to be able to sleep at night without fear of being bombed or killed, to have enough to eat, and to be free as only in America one can be free!

[This boy and his sister are still in a foster home and have not yet heard from their parents, who fled to France and were put into a concentration camp.]

The Refugees Become Loyal Americans. The refugees, on the whole, have sought to identify themselves completely with America. About 95 per cent of them state that they have no intention of returning to their former homelands. The proportion varies with the nationality and occupation. Practically no German wants to return, and only a few Austrians, Poles, and Russians. More Czechs, Italians, Belgians, Netherlanders, and Frenchmen indicate that they want to go back. Artists, scholars, and political leaders predominate among those who wish to return. Jews are almost unanimous in their intention not to return.

Nearly all have shown great eagerness to become naturalized. Many of them took out their first papers almost immediately after their arrival. Only a few have failed to apply. Fully half of the refugees have been granted citizenship, the rest being in various stages of getting it. This is a remarkable record, considering the brief period of time they have been here. To the refugees, most of whom have been deprived of their full rights as citizens in their homelands, and many of whom had been rendered stateless, the attainment of American citizenship is a matter of great importance. The event is often marked by celebrations, the exchange of gifts, and notices in the foreign-language press. The refugees become enthusiastic citizens and show great appreciation of the democratic principles underlying our government, contrasting, from personal experience, the freedom of democracy with the tyranny of fascism.

Loyalty to the United States was also shown by the refugees who had been here too short a time to become citizens and hence were still aliens when America entered the war. Along with other aliens born in countries with which the United States was at war, they became technically "enemy aliens," with limitations on their personal freedom. Actually, however, they were "friendly aliens" of enemy nationality. This fact was soon recognized by the Department of Justice which, upon proof of loyalty, permitted them to become naturalized. The refugee community proved itself to be overwhelmingly on the side of democracy and aided in the war effort in every way. The Selective Training and Service Act made aliens as fully liable to service as citizens. Eligible refugees, aliens and citizens alike, therefore entered the armed forces to the same extent as native Americans. Many of them rendered special services because of their intimate knowledge of the languages, culture, psychology, and geography of enemy countries. Those who remained at home contributed generously to the various war activities on the home front. Important contributions were made by scientists and highly trained technicians, either in government services or in private industries. All regarded their contribution to the war effort as an expression of the gratitude they feel toward America.

20 MIGRATION WITHIN THE UNITED STATES *

BY PASCAL KIDDER WHELPTON (1893-   )
SCRIPPS FOUNDATION FOR RESEARCH IN
POPULATION PROBLEMS, MIAMI UNIVERSITY

AMERICANS have long had the reputation of being "on the move" to a greater extent than most people. Since the early 1600s the frontiers have gradually been pushed back, and the settled areas expanded from small communities on the Atlantic coast to all the

* Reprinted by permission of the author and of the editor from "A History of Population Growth in the United States," *The Scientific Monthly*, LXVII (1948), 277–288; pp. 282–285 used.

habitable portions of our 3,000,000 square miles. During most of the time the main movement was westward, in accordance with Horace Greeley's famous advice, "Turn your face to the great West, and there build up a home and fortune."

Interstate Migration.   The first reliable information regarding the amount of internal migration comes from the census of 1850, and is based on a comparison between the number of persons born in a state and the number (excluding foreigners) living in that state. In 1850 each state from Georgia to Maine (and Kentucky and Tennessee as well) was found to have sent its native sons to other states in greater degree than it had attracted the native sons of other states. In contrast, Florida and each state west of those mentioned had attracted natives from other states in larger numbers than it had sent its own natives to other states. The net loss through out-migration had been especially large for South Carolina, the number of persons living in South Carolina being only slightly more than half as large as the number born there. Vermont, Connecticut, Virginia, and North Carolina also had suffered a net loss of 25 percent or more. California had had the largest gain, for it contained more than ten times as many people as had been born within its boundaries! Ratios of more than 2 to 1 occurred for Michigan, Wisconsin, Iowa, Arkansas, and Texas.

Although a large westward movement continued after 1850, its influence gradually was offset by an increasing movement northward and eastward. By 1940 this had gone so far that the Northeastern states as a group had attracted about as many people born in other regions as they had lost to other regions (Fig. 1). The North Central region had gained somewhat in its exchange with the South and Northeast, but had lost heavily to the West. The South had lost slightly to the Northeast and more heavily to the North Center and West. The West had gained greatly from the North Center, moderately from the South, and slightly from the Northeast. Vermont and Iowa are the only states showing in 1940 a net loss of 20 percent or more through interstate migration, but 15 other states (mostly in the Midwest and Southeast) had lost more than 10 percent. California had benefited the most from migration, for nearly 3,400,000 persons—almost half its population—had been born in other states. Florida, Arizona, Nevada, Oregon, and Washington also owed much of their pre-1940 growth to a net inward movement.

During World War II the migration of the civilian population followed the general pattern just described but took place on a larger scale. Nearly 15,000,000 civilians were classified as migrants during the three years 1942–44, compared with about 14,000,000 during the five years 1935–39 and smaller numbers during preceding periods. Again it was California that attracted outsiders in greatest numbers, with some of its neighbors not far behind. In consequence, California now ranks third in population, having passed Ohio and Illinois since 1940; before 1950 it probably will pass Pennsylvania and rank second. [California did rank second in 1950. — *Ed.*]

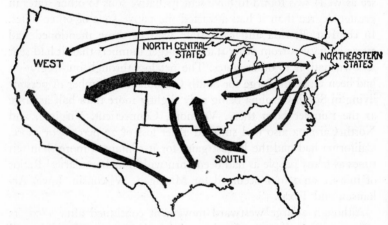

Fɪɢ. ɪ.—Interregional migration in the United States in terms of birthresidence index: 1940. 12,792,000 migrants. [From Henry S. Shryock, Jr., and Hope Tisdale Eldridge, "Internal Migration in Peace and War," *American Sociological Review,* XII (1947), 27–39, p. 28.—*Ed.*]

Migration by Color, Age, and Sex. The white and colored populations appear to have been equally mobile during recent decades, for in 1940 approximately one out of four persons in each group was living outside the state in which he was born. The situation changed temporarily during 1935–39, when the proportion of the population classified as migrating was half again as high among white persons (12.3 percent) as among colored persons (8.5 percent). From 1940 to 1947, however, about one person in five in each group has moved across county lines.

Migration rates were highest for young adults and lowest for elderly persons during 1935–39 and 1940–47, and probably during most other years also. Because an important proportion of the young adults who move have married previously and started their families, the migration rate for children under fourteen has been higher than that for persons middle-aged or older. Youngsters of high-school age (fourteen to seventeen) have been least likely to move among the population under fifty.

Although men are usually thought to be more foot-loose than women, the proportion that makes one or more moves has been about the same for each sex. This is confirmed by a comparison of state of birth and state of residence for 1940, and also by the census data on migration during 1935–39 and 1940–47. If the number of moves could be counted, however, it might be found substantially higher for males than for females.

The Rural-Urban Movement. For many decades a high proportion of the persons migrating within the nation were moving to new land, which they began to farm. During the nineteenth century the situation was completely changed by the industrial development, for it greatly stimulated the growth of cities. In 1790 nearly 95 percent of the population were classified as rural, and only 33,000 people lived in the largest city (New York). By 1850 the rural proportion had dropped below 85 percent, and New Yorkers numbered over 500,000. Since then the urban trend has been accelerated. By 1900 barely 60 percent of the population lived in rural areas, nearly 20 percent were in cities of 100,000 or more, and three cities were over the million mark. By 1940 only 43 percent were rural, 29 percent were in cities of 100,000 or more, and five cities were in the million class (Fig. 2).

The great urban growth came about in important degree through migration from other areas, but the net inward movement prior to 1935 can only be estimated roughly for cities with the most reliable birth statistics. Net migration to New York City probably accounted for 70–80 percent of its population increase from 1900 to 1910, and the excess of births over deaths for only 20–30 percent. (In this case, however, the majority of the migrants came from abroad rather than from other parts of the United States.) The proportions were almost reversed during 1910–30, when about 70 percent of the growth came from natural increase and only 30 percent from migration. The two were of approximately equal importance during 1920–30 and 1930–40.

Los Angeles is the outstanding example of a large city which has grown from migration. Its population was about 577,000 in 1920; 1,238,000 in 1930; and 1,504,000 in 1940. Of the 661,000 increase during 1920–30, approximately 90 percent came from net migration and

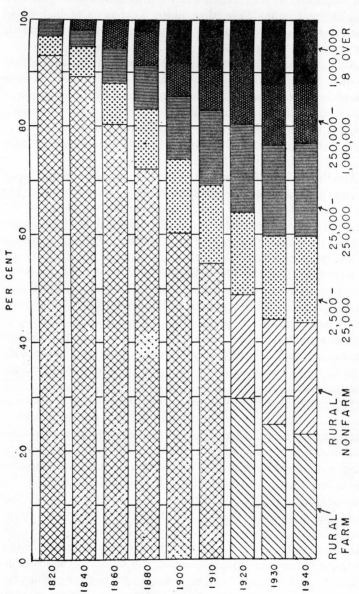

FIG. 2.—Proportion of the population in rural areas, and in cities of specified size, selected years, 1820–1940.

only 10 percent from an excess of births over deaths. The latter was somewhat more important during 1930–40; nevertheless, nearly 85 percent of the increase came from net migration.

The Urban Fringe. During the past 20–30 years automobile and paved roads have enabled people to live in the rural areas surrounding cities, but to continue to work in the cities. At the same time the development of tractors and other laborsaving machinery has reduced not only the proportion of the population on farms but the actual *number* of persons as well, the reduction exceeding 1,000,000 from 1920 to 1940, and 3,200,000 from 1940 to 1947. In consequence, the rural population has come to consist more and more of persons who are like city folk rather than farmers. The rural-nonfarm group was less than two thirds as numerous as the farm group in 1920, but outnumbers it by a wide margin (probably about 4,000,000) at present. The movement to rural areas around cities apparently has even checked the growth of cities, for the rate of increase from 1930 to 1940 for the rural-nonfarm population (nearly 15 percent) was almost double that of the urban population (less than 8 percent). A more striking illustration of this tendency is found in the 140 metropolitan districts, where the rate of gain from 1930 to 1940 was about 30 percent for the rural-nonfarm population, but less than 6 percent for the urban population.

Decentralization? Unless war can be prevented, or at least as long as atomic bombs can be used in war, it seems criminal from a military standpoint to permit further increases in the concentration of population in and around large cities. To stop the trend in this direction, however, probably will require government action of some type. Private enterprise apparently finds it more profitable in a large proportion of cases to expand facilities for production in or near large cities than elsewhere. To sacrifice lower costs during an unknown number of years in return for making the nation somewhat stronger from a military standpoint and the factory safer in case of war is a choice few business executives can make for various reasons. So far there has been much talk of the need for real decentralization of population and industry, but little or no progress toward bringing it about. Unless some agency capable of keeping world peace is developed, it is to be hoped that some feasible method of stimulating decentralization will be devised.

21 THE REGIONAL BALANCE OF MAN AND CULTURE *

BY HOWARD WASHINGTON ODUM (1884–   )
UNIVERSITY OF NORTH CAROLINA

THE role of regionalism in social problems may perhaps best be epitomized in the concept of the regional balance of man and Nature and of culture and technology. This has usually been featured
more specifically in what is called balanced economy. The heart of
the problem of regional balance is one of opportunity for people in
the places where they live and its attainment is essentially a matter
of the functional definition of social planning as well as regionalism.
"Planning for what" becomes essentially a symbol of inquiring into
the new order of world society and more specifically for each particular society. Still more specifically it is the chief problem of American society as represented by the United States of America.

The Basic Principle of Regional Balance.   But first, it is important
to recognize the broader, more general assumption that the key problem of all our postwar reconstruction and planning centers around
the quality and balance of people and culture, of economy and technology the world over. More appropriate for our purpose, the problem is one of regional equality and balance in the total integration of
world order. For it seems clear that a great deal, perhaps most, of
the tragic situations of maladjustment, disorganization, and pathology in the world is due to imbalance whether in terms of the lack of
natural ecological balance between plant and animal resources or
between man and Nature, or whether in terms of the "haves" and
"have nots" in advanced civilization. Inherent in the waste and
weakness of any region, in the conflict and lack of unity of the people, and in hazards of regional imbalance and pathology are lurking dangers and dilemmas capable of swelling to floodtide mass emotion, confusion, and revolution in the immediate postwar world and
after.

By the same token, the main strategy of planning will be found

* Reprinted by permission of the author and of the publisher from *Understanding
Society: The Principles of Dynamic Sociology* (New York: The Macmillan Company), 1947, pp. 620–624.

within the framework of regional balance and equality which must include not only economic opportunity but cultural development and the thing now so much stressed, namely, justice in world organization. Yet justice, admittedly basic to adequate and enduring arrangements, is not primarily something on the level of abstract morality or moralistic principles, but of the essential regional equality and balance of opportunity in the places where people live set in the framework of world standards and interrelationships.

As relating to the functional aspects of this thing we call the regional balance of man and culture, it seems demonstrably clear that many of the conferences for racial, religious, and world unity became in effect forces for disunity, centering on abstract demands on the one hand and concrete pleas for special priorities on the other, rather than realistic strategy for regional and racial balance and harmony within the framework of the people, their resources, situation, technology *and* high moral principles.

Balanced Culture and Economy. Now we turn to our main assumptions on the basis of the functional definitions of regionalism and planning and our illustrations from world regions and from the quest for the regional balance of America. In the first place, the assumptions of balance comprehend a great deal more than the technically defined balanced economy with its factors of balanced agriculture and industry and the other factors so well defined by the economists. These are assumed as basic to what Henry T. Buckle a long time ago called order and balance in a country and what administrative authorities have been seeking in balanced economies and parity programs. The heart of regional balance is found in the search for equal opportunity for all the people through the conservation, development and use of their resources in the places where they live, adequately adjusted to the interregional culture and economy of the other regions of the world or of the nation. The goal is, therefore, clearly one of balanced culture as well as economy, in which equality of opportunity in education, in public health and welfare, in the range of occupational outlook, and in the elimination of handicapping differentials between and among different groups of people and levels of culture.

The Integration of Diverse Cultures and Values. With reference to the functional definitions of regionalism, it is necessary to re-emphasize the fact that the primary objectives of regionalism are found in the end product of integration of regions more than in the mere study and development of regions themselves. The regions are studied and planned to the end that they may be more adequate in all aspects of resources and culture; yet regionalism itself is primarily interested in the total integration and balance of these regions. In the world order it is not so much a problem of conflict between universalism and regionalism as it is one of world order and organization brought out through the representation, initiative, and balance of world regions. In the case of American society it is not so much a question of centralization of authority in conflict with State rights as it is developing an adequate federalized central authority capable thereby of achieving realistic decentralization. In other words, it is necessary to have some sort of world order or organization before the world's regions can be integrated and before they may be cooperatively developed at their best. In American society there must be strong national character and organization before the Nation can be made stronger through the strength and integration of its diverse regions so that regionalism may supplant the older separatism and isolationism of sectional development.

Again, the People the Heart of Society. So, too, the global situation with reference to races, minority peoples and nationalities has made increasingly clear and vivid the organic significance of this regional quality and balance of the people everywhere. The assumptions of regional balance here are both culturally theoretical and administratively practical since it seems likely that one of the key tasks of the postwar planning world will be to rediscover and recognize the folk personality of millions of people who give new emphasis to *vox populi, vox dei,* or to the realistic verdict that only the people count. All this means that regional balance assumes a healthy diversity; that the way of each region is the way of its culture and that each culture is inseparably identified with its regional character.

This is not only nothing new but has always been recognized as a definitive part of understanding peoples and their institutions. It has always been recognized by the common people in their loyalties and devotion to their own customs and institutions and in their criticism of others. It has always been recognized by anthropologists and sociologists in their study of cultures. Regional attitudes and mores are so definite and powerful that they constitute rights and wrongs; they determine the nature of behavior and institutions. Intolerance, therefore, of the mores of a people reflects narrowness and provincialism of outlook. In the contemporary America there has recently developed an increasing tendency among urban intellectuals to belittle and to characterize as intolerable many of the mores of rural society, and for intellectuals everywhere to dictate the ways and means of living for minority peoples wherever they are. Manifestly, however, this is one source of conflict and imbalance in the world, for how can the United States dictate cultural order for Poland or the conflicting folk of the Balkan states or the South American republics? Or, how can the oversimplified plans for the reintegration of the cultures of India or the conflicting claims of Palestine be made to work? All this reflects a strange backwardness in an age of communication and intellectual liberalism. The depth and width of the growing chasm and threatened imbalance and the reasons for it would be unbelievable if the situation were not actually true.

This regional quality of culture, behavior, and institutions is, of course, universally applicable to all regions of world society. The recognition of this regional quality of world society, of its imbalance, and of the need for regional arrangements for world organization and peace, while relatively new, is rapidly becoming the basic consideration in nearly all plans for stabilizing world organization. Symbolic of the swelling tide of regionalism is the conviction of Sumner Welles that "an effective international organization can be constituted only through the creation of regional systems of nations . . . under an over-all international body, representative . . . of all regions." But in whatever instance, the point of emphasis is that it is through co-operative arrangement and the integration of diversified cultures that strength and stability are to be found.

Regionalism as a Tool for Decentralization and Redistribution of Wealth. Such a functional regionalism thus becomes a tool for attaining balance and equilibrium between people and resources, men and machines, the state and the folk. It is a tool of the democratic process in that it provides for the redistribution of the good things of life and of the opportunity to work within the framework of every people's geography and of their inherent cultural equipment. It is a tool for democratic world reconstruction in the postwar world, because it is through co-operative regionalism rather than economic nationalism that the society of tomorrow can be organized for human welfare instead of for military achievements. It is a tool for social planning, because it takes into consideration the rights, privileges, resources of people and areas, and stresses self-government and self-development as opposed to coercive centralized power. It is a tool for social planning, also because it offers specific technical work-able ways of developing and conserving resources for human-use ends. Since regionalism, as the opposite pole of sectionalism, isola-tion, and separatism, is as true of international as well of national affairs, it wants no self-sufficiency in economy. It wants no isola-tionism and separatism, and it wants no tragic imbalance between the folk and the state or between power and the people.

Regionalism and Planning. There are other assumptions of re-gionalism which it is not necessary to discuss in relation to our main premises. Assumed are the specifications of administrative regional-ism, regional planning, regional mercantilism and the science of the region which delineates regions, defines its terms, and sets up its adequate methods. There is the final point of emphasis which is that regional balance is essentially synonymous with the ends of social planning. There are many satisfactory definitions of planning in terms of its attitudes, two of which are appropriate here. One is a commonly used one which makes the objectives of planning the at-tainment of balance and equilibrium between competing factors and the substitution of effectiveness and abundance for inefficiency and scarcity. The other is one utilized by Patrick Geddes, which assumed planning to be the bridging of the distance between science and knowledge and practical problems. In both of these, as in all efforts toward world regional balance, there are implied skills, science, ex-pertness through which the facts and specifications are provided and through which then the distance is bridged.

SECTION FOUR

Race

22 RACIAL THEORY *

BY EDWARD BYRON REUTER (1882–1946)

FISK UNIVERSITY

WHILE racial differences have perhaps nowhere escaped observation and comment and have often been made the basis for differential treatment, scientific study appears to have had its beginning with the publication of Linnaeus' classification of species in 1758. His division of mankind into the *Sapiens,* the *Ferus,* and the *Monstrosus*—the wise, the wild, and the vicious—gave no new concept of race or race relations. It was grounded in common-sense observations, and the questions it raised were relevant to race, not to race relations. But it set a pattern of interest and defined a method of study; for well over one hundred years discussion was concerned exclusively or primarily with racial differences and problems of biological descent, and research was limited to the use of biological or pseudo-biological methods. In some measure the continued interest in racial classification must be understood in terms of its practical usefulness; particularly as subsidiary techniques developed, it gave an apparently objective basis for the reasoning in support of the differential treatment of racial groups. In 1854, a century after Linnaeus, Count Arthur Gobineau published a study, *The Inequality of Human Races,* which seemed to justify the dominant races of Europe in extending their control over other peoples.

In America racial discussion took a peculiarly concrete form that precluded any theoretically significant contribution. It was chiefly concerned with the Negro as a unique phenomenon, not with race or even with races; hence it could not rise to a truly scientific level. During the first one-half and particularly during the second one-quarter of the nineteenth century, race, as typified by the Negro, was a matter of political controversy rather than an object of analysis and research. The northern writers, generally uninformed and doctrinal, had little interest in research findings and objective realities, except as these could be used in the political controversy; the southern social students were equally not interested in cautious analytical

* Reprinted by permission from *The American Journal of Sociology,* L (1944–45), 452–461; excerpt used from pp. 453–459.

procedures: they were occupied in elaborating rationalizations of the institution of slavery. Following the emancipation of the slaves, an extensive racial literature concerned itself with the so-called Negro problem, but, except for a few scattered literary items, it made remarkably little contribution to an understanding of racial relations.

In a later period, racial comment shifted from the Negroes to the immigrants and the foreign-born elements of the population. But here the interest was in political or practical problems; the discussion was chiefly concerned with the concrete historical phenomena, hence made little contribution to an understanding of basic racial realities. The popular prejudices toward orientals, as toward European and other immigrants supposed to differ racially from the established population, were fostered and inflamed in the promotion of political and economic interests. Discussion emphasized racial and cultural differences, deplored the inevitable decline in the biological quality of the stock and the slender possibility of preserving national and cultural unity in a racially heterogeneous population. There were some scientific studies and some changes in theoretical conceptions, particularly in the period of the first World War, but they had little influence on public attitudes or national policy. The legislation defining a changed immigration policy was based on the tacit assumption that fundamental racial differences separated the old from the new immigrants and on the belief that the racial traits of the later immigrants made their assimilation difficult and undesirable.

In the decades around the end of the century—the formative years of sociology—social thought was almost completely dominated by the biological concepts and points of view. The idea of organic evolution was the common property of all literate people and was reaching the stage of general public acceptance; the Darwinian concepts of universal competition, lethal selection, and species adaptation seemed to provide an explanation of social organization and assure a continuous social evolution. Social Darwinism—the body of social theories called forth by the Darwinian principle—got its first coherent statement in Walter Bagehot's *Physics and Politics,* which was published in 1872 and read by all social students in England and America for a full generation. It undertook, by the application of the principles of natural selection and inheritance, to give a natural history of political society. Ludwig Gumplowicz' *Der Rassenkampf* appeared in 1883 and his *Grundriss der Soziologie* in 1885. Gustav Ratzenhofer's *Wesen und Zweck der Politik* was published in 1893 and *Die sozio-*

logische Erkenntniss in 1898. Benjamin Kidd's *Social Evolution,* which appeared in 1894, was a widely read and influential publication.

Certain prominent social Darwinians, notably G. Vacher de Lapouge, in *Les Selections social* (1896), were proponents of the doctrine that Nordic or Aryan races are inherently superior and that progress and civilization are dependent upon the racial composition of the population. This doctrine was further popularized by Houston Chamberlain's *Foundations of the Nineteenth Century* (1899), which exploited the Germans as a superior type of chosen people, and it achieved complete vulgarization in popular American books by Madison Grant, *The Passing of a Great Race* (1916), Lothrop Stoddard, *The Rising Tide of Color against White World-Supremacy* (1920), and other writers to the present day.

Another exploitation of the currently popular mode of thought appeared in the antidemocratic philosophy of eugenics, a pseudobiological exploitation of individual, class, and racial differences. In psychology the biological point of view received expression in the doctrine of human instincts, which, carried over into sociology, helped to delay the appearance of profitable methods for the study of human behavior and social phenomena. At a later date it reappeared in psychology in the form of mental testing; here the assumptions were that the obvious differences in performance and social behavior arise from differences in innate capacities and that the isolation and measurement of the native traits will provide the explanation of individual, cultural, and racial differences. This position was widely recognized as untenable in the second decade of the century but was not given up for another decade.

The dominance of the biological point of view was not conducive to serious and objective racial study; it directed attention along lines that prevented the emergence of significant questions and productive procedures. Classification emphasized differences; this led to the definition and measurement of physical and mental traits. But these racial traits had no meaning, or at least the meaning was not clear without interpretation. Interpretation involved the dubious procedure of explaining social reality in biological terms.

In the decades at the end of the nineteenth and the beginning of the twentieth centuries there was a growing realization that the social significance of race could not be discovered and understood by the enumeration and definition of physical characters and mental differences or through an examination of biological processes. The attempts to classify races had finally brought a realization of the fact that there are no pure races and that no valid classification of the empirical groups was possible. In a biological sense, pure races are hypothetical entities. There is no known group of men whose culture can be differentiated on the basis of any specific complex of racial traits. In civilized life, probably in all stages of culture, the significant differences among peoples are those of language, belief, custom, technology, and other items in the mode of life. These cultural acquisitions are quite independent of race; they are learned, used, transmitted, and discarded without changes in the germ plasm.

The cultural differences among peoples are wide and conspicuous, and they are not easily eradicated. Moreover, they excite prejudices and lead to antagonisms; the conflicting attitudes in the contact of culturally diverse peoples are quite as intense as those that arise in the contact of racially different groups. Such considerations suggested the study of the social heritage as a profitable approach in the analysis of racial realities. The emphasis on culture in the study of race definitely changed the locus of the problem; it moved racial study out of a biological and into a cultural frame of reference.

Social and cultural study developed slowly. It did not abruptly displace the biological methods and points of view, rather it grew up beside the older modes of analysis and report. In the theory of Durkheim, Tarde, and others the emphasis was placed on cultural rather than on biological facts in accounting for differences among peoples. The extensive, and in many ways admirable, ethnological writings of the later decades of the nineteenth century, drawing heavily on the accumulated store of travelers' tales and other descriptive accounts, extended the historical and factual information of the customs and institutions of strange and distant peoples. As ethnology came to be called "social anthropology" at the end of the century, it gave special attention to the invention, accumulation, diffusion, and transmission of behavior patterns. Culture came to be treated, at least by one dominant school, as a distinct and self-determining realm, the culture traits operating as a new set of race determiners.

The more genuinely sociological point of view and contribution came considerably later. If the publication of Ward's *Dynamic Sociology* in 1883 is taken as marking the beginning of a continuing scholarly interest in sociology in the United States, ethnological and cultural studies began a good generation earlier; they were numerous and important during the final quarter of the century. Moreover, sociology was slow to become a profitable research instrument: it was handicapped by its biological viewpoint and, until about 1920, by its humanitarian legacy of philanthropic ideas and sentiments and their expression in social-reform interests and movements.

As sociological study approached the status of scientific procedure, its emphasis shifted from the description of social structures to the study of social processes. The interest in differences was replaced by an interest in uniformities; the interest in traits, whether inherited or acquired, whether biological or cultural, gave way to an interest in relationships. Social traits were seen to form and change in the experience of living together; the problem of social research was seen to lie, not in the biological characters or cultural traits which get whatever meaning they have in social relations and their changes, but in the social and human attitudes, values, and experiences.

The development of racial theory followed closely the emergence of scientific sociology; it was promoted by and contributed to the growth of general theory. In some very large part the development of each was the work of the same men. The early conception of race in terms of concrete phenomena—the Negroes, the orientals, or other physically divergent types—gave way, in the second and later decades of the century, to generalized and impersonal conceptions. The efforts to examine racial realities objectively forced students to face and redefine the field, with the result that the problem became one of interaction and the relevant data became relations rather than traits. The traditional common-sense ideas were in a measure replaced by abstract and generalized conceptions of race and race relations which, for the first time, provided a framework and a basis for empirical research of a productive order.

In the period under discussion there has been a persistence of earlier interests and modes of thought, there have been various sporadic movements in response to new doctrines and methods in more or less related fields, and there have been some negative reactions to the direction of thought and efforts to counteract the movement toward objective analysis. But the trend of racial theory has been reasonably consistent: it has been away from physical concepts and biological processes, through cultural analysis, and into a sociological and social-psychological study of social interrelations. The progression may, perhaps, be further clarified by an enumeration and brief description of some significant aspects of the change in interests and conceptions that mark the advances in racial theory. The items to be mentioned cannot in all cases be stated in a disconnected serial order or as independent developments. They are, in reality, different phases of the same body of thought as it moved from a biological to a sociological frame of reference; they are often divergent offshoots of the same insights.

The interest in racial prejudice, which had its beginning around the turn of the century and has continued intermittently to the present time, requires only brief comment. It was a step away from the earlier preoccupation with physical traits, but, so far as the interest remained in the body of phenomena, it was not productive of results. Other efforts to explain the prejudices as instinctive reactions to strange and divergent types contributed little or nothing to social understanding. But some studies of prejudicial attitudes undertook an examination of the conditions and factors associated with their rise and persistence. Here the findings supplemented those of other research and blended with it in the emergence of modern racial theory. Race prejudice came to be seen and treated as a subjective aspect of competition and conflict, as a subjective barrier interrupting, or accompanying the interruption of, the processes of racial and cultural fusion.

Racial consciousness, race movements, racial ideologies, and other social-psychological and collective phenomena have received some study. Particularly in the later and recent periods, there has been considerable attention given to personality development in racial groups and to the general problem of racial relations in the American social order. But for the most part the points of view have been dictated by practical, rather than scientific, considerations, and the publications have been informative rather than enlightening.

The natural history of group contacts is not well defined. The knowledge is still more incomplete where the contacts are between peoples sharply contrasted in physical characters, historical experiences, cultural heritages, or social values. The variability in the external conditions of such contacts—the relative population numbers, the types of economy, the stages of technological advance, the nationalistic sentiments, the purposes and interests of the invading groups, and other factors—determines the types of dominance, the nature, speed, and duration of the stages of acculturation, the ease of assimilation, and other items in the concrete historical sequence. However, the social research and racial study of the last two or three decades have defined the general forms of contact with reasonable clarity.

Two or more groups, whether closely similar or widely divergent in physical or cultural characteristics, may occupy the same general area as relatively independent units. They may exist side by side with a minimum of biological fusion, cultural exchange, or social contact. Conflicts may arise in the event of trespass, but otherwise a high degree of isolation may be maintained over very considerable periods of time. The attitudes remain mutually hostile and intolerant; each group holds the other in contempt as something short of real men. The contacts are physical, geographic, and territorial, essentially the contacts that obtain among animals of different species occupying the same general area. The spatial distribution of each such group is determined in some part by the presence of the other groups, but only in the ecological sense of being an adjustment to their presence as to other external facts of the habitat.

Peoples unlike in physical type or culture may live and intermingle in a common area in a way that is symbiotic or mutually helpful, but with few or no personal contacts and social relations. The economies are separate, the adjustments are essentially biotic, the relations are exploitative or mutualistic but quite impersonal; each regards the other as of a different species. Such interactions as exist are characteristically non-social; there is no mutual understanding or personal sympathy; there is no interpenetration of personalities, hence no genuine human understanding.

Contrasted racial groups may establish and maintain economic and competitive relations which are in no real sense social or racial. Such tends to be the case where the Europeans, interested in trade and exploitation rather than in the occupation and settlement of an area, establish and maintain contacts with native peoples. If the traders desire goods that lie outside the orbit of the indigenous economy, the ecological order of the native peoples—the balance of population and cultural resources—may for a time remain undisturbed. The repercussions of contact are indirect. The introduction of strange artifacts may change the native order by creating new wants external to the traditional culture. The withdrawal of natives from the indigenous economy to supply commodities to exchange for the traders' goods presently disrupts the ecological balance. Particularly in the case of the alienation of land, the closed native economy gives way to a money economy, and values come to be defined by competition in the market rather than by tradition. In the process the native economy is demoralized, and the natives are in a measure acculturated. But the contacts are economic and exploitative rather than social; no race relations exist and no race problems arise.

In other situations, in order to profit quickly and in full measure from the resources of the area, it may be in the interests of the militaristically dominant group to exploit the vital power of a weak but numerous people. In these circumstances slavery or some other form of forced labor is used to develop a plantation economy or exploit other resources, or coercion through systematic impoverishment may bring the native people into the new economy. In such colonial areas there are numerous and often difficult problems of administration, but in general there are no race problems. The contacts of the natives with their exploiters may be friendly or they may be hostile; in either case they are external and impersonal. The natives are completely dominated, and a habit of collective obedience is established; in time they become accommodated to a semiservile status and a body of understandings and expectations develops which defines and supports the system and promotes harmonious working relations.

In areas of racial contact the native peoples become in varying degrees acculturated and, in larger or smaller numbers, assimilated. They gain a command of the language of the conquerors and conform in other respects to the culture standards of the ruling group. As they acquire the European heritage, they seek to penetrate the European world; they aspire to new and equal status in the culture area; they consider themselves as integral parts of the life of the area and feel entitled to the same treatment and opportunities as others of like attainment. As their developing social and political aspirations are denied, they become racially self-conscious, develop a sense of unity and solidarity, become a conflict group engaged in a struggle for status. It is at this stage in the contact of peoples that race problems, as distinct from economic and administrative problems, make their appearance and that race contacts take on the character of race relations.

The isolation and definition of race relations and race problems, as distinct from prior and nonsocial forms of contact, was a major step in racial theory. As the distinction came to be appreciated, racial studies entered a new phase. The relations of contrasted groups, seen as adjustments of ideas and aspirations, became meaningful; the contact of peoples could be separated from specific concrete phenomena, could be conceived as a natural process amenable to scientific analysis. It became generally clear that race relations, like all social and human relations, begin with language communication involving the interpenetration of personalities and result, inevitably, in a degree of unity, in a new society.

The recognition of diverse types of racial contacts and their appearance in some sort of a temporal sequence was a first step in the statement of a natural history. It differentiated biotic, economic, administrative, and other contacts from one another and indicated the type of unity or integration to which each gave rise. In doing so it differentiated each from a racial order, that is, an order among peoples of diverse physical or biological traits which is based on human and social relations.

The isolation of race relations from the various forms of nonsocial contact set new problems of a similar order. In the concrete reality, race relations are a confused complex, in varying degrees, of opposition and agreement, friction and harmony, conflict and co-operation. To work out the cycle of relations—the sequence of steps from the emergence of conflict to its disappearance in new and unified attitudes—was an obvious task if the study of race was to maintain or achieve scientific reputability. The problem was one of major dimensions and the studies so far made or in progress, while suggestive and useful, are, for the most part, in the nature of preliminary and tentative explorations.

The definition of an ecological interest and point of view, chiefly a development of the third decade of the century, was a distinctive contribution to social and racial theory. Human ecology was less the emergence of a new hypothesis than it was a reformulation of existing modes of analysis and their extension and use in a new area of study. The prompt prosecution of a series of studies developed the conceptual framework and defined a methodological procedure which, by isolating independent but coincident processes, contributed to the definition of the racial cycle and otherwise brought a measure of clarity into a confused area of social study.

Ecology came into social analysis from the biological sciences and, in lesser degree, from classical economics. In biology it was concerned to describe the spatial distribution of living forms and to define the factors and the impersonal processes determining the placement. In the biological struggle for existence, success is determined by superior competitive ability; the survivors are those who have the traits that fit them to succeed in the existing conditions. The inevitable end result of competition, in the presence of diverse characters and variable external conditions, is a distributional pattern: each form occupies, to the exclusion of competing forms, the area to which it is best adapted—the area in which, because of its specialized needs and distinctive traits, it can survive and propagate its kind. Ecology is then a description of distributional patterns and of the simple impersonal processes that create and maintain them.

In the human world, ecology includes all this and something more. The spatial distribution of human populations is rather obviously determined by impersonal factors; men live where they can secure the means of subsistence. Competition and survival, operating in and below the level of a social order, are the mechanisms that determine their placement. In civilized life the gross and direct aspects are in a measure concealed by cultural factors and human activities, and some new factors determining survival make their appearance. But man never escapes the universal principle. Its application is wider in the human than in the simpler orders of life. It determines the distribution and survival of forms of culture, its operation dictates the class structure, and the occupational placement of individuals and groups is a result of competitive struggle. The factors determining success in competition are numerous and they differ with the social situation; their operation is often indirect and sometimes subtle, but the process is continuous and universal. The isolation of impersonal factors and processes made it possible to discuss them in objective rather than in personal terms, hence made possible a search for rational and effective controls.

The development of the ecological studies provided a useful tool in racial analysis. Some of the superior studies were pieces of racial research. Their general influence was to increase the emphasis on natural factors and processes, reduce the emphasis on human prejudices and other personalized explanations of status, and make a larger area of racial phenomena understandable in mechanistic and impersonal terms.

Human hybridization with the associated body of social and cultural phenomena, long an area of confused and conflicting doctrines, has received some sociological study and clarification in the recent decades. The problem has been redefined, the physical and the cultural phenomena have been differentiated, and some of the social aspects have been analyzed and made generally intelligible. The studies made important contributions to racial and social theory: they provided valuable new insights, and they opened several new and productive lines of sociological research. From these studies, in a brief period, there emerged the generic sociological concept of marginality with its great contribution to the study and understanding of culture development and personality organization.

23 CONTEMPORARY HUMAN TYPES *

BY DOUGLAS G. HARING (1894–   )
SYRACUSE UNIVERSITY

SCHOOLBOOKS often repeat the ancient legend that there are five human races: white, yellow, red, brown, and black. Actually few 'whites' are very white, 'yellows' and 'reds' are neither yellow nor red, and 'blacks' range from creamy tan to deep chocolate brown. Of course, this naïve classification ignores all features other than skin color, which depends on two factors: the amounts of brown and yellow pigment, and the 'thickness' of the skin. Thin skins look pink where the red color of the blood shows through. Moderately pigmented thin skins appear bronzed; thicker skin with similar pigmentation has a yellowish cast. In all 'races' the pigments are identical chemically, but the amounts vary. Certain diseases that disturb bodily chemistry and allow pigment to accumulate may turn white skins brown. And a few individuals in every race—including the Negroes —manifest a hereditary absence of pigment known as albinism; these persons have white skin, pinkish eyes, and colorless hair.

Brown spots of varying area appear on the skin of many human beings. These pigmented areas are not 'defects'; roughly they are analogous to patches of light and dark fur in other mammals, and appear to be without significance. While individuals thus marked occur in all but the darkest-skinned human stocks, they are more numerous in China and Japan.

* Reprinted by permission of the author (the copyright owner) from *Racial Differences and Human Resemblances*, rev. ed. (booklet; Syracuse, N. Y.; Syracuse University Bookstore, 1947), pp. 7–14.

Human hair varies in color, texture, shape, and distribution on the body. Round hair is straight; the more highly elliptical the cross-section of the hair, the more it curls. Straight, wavy, curly, and 'frizzly' hair occur in all colors from straw-blonde through red and brown to black. Nearly all colors and forms of hair may accompany any of a variety of skin colors. A unique hair pattern characterizes the South African Bushmen and Hottentots; the scalp hair grows in tufts which form tight spiral curls instead of being distributed evenly on the scalp. Kinky black 'wool' does not always go with very dark skins; the Melanesians grow huge mops of 'frizzly' black or brownish hair, while the still darker Australian aborigines often have wavy brown hair like that common in Europe. Black hair is a peculiarly human feature that is rare in the animal world.

The kind and amount of hair of the beard and on the body vary greatly. Some males grow abundant beards, others almost none; beards may differ in color from the scalp hair. The 'white races' are the hairiest and many white persons have thick growths of hair on chest, legs, and arms. In Negroes and Eastern Asiatics this kind of hairy covering is almost unknown. Sometimes a nearly imperceptible down covers the skin; this may even be dark-colored against light skin, or, as among the Pygmies, light colored against a dark brown skin. Many African Negroes have skin that is velvety in texture and practically hairless.

The iris of the human eye is predominantly brown. Minorities in the populations of Europe, North Africa, and Central Asia exhibit eyes that range from pale blue through grey and greenish tints to light brown. The two eyes of the same person—even parts of a single iris—may differ in color. Light colored irises occur more frequently though not uniformly in individuals whose skin and hair also lack pigment.

Variations in the bony skeleton appear conspicuously in the differences between tall, thin, long-faced, long-limbed individuals, and short, wide-faced, plump, short-limbed persons—as well as the whole gamut of intermediate types. So universal and so common are these differences that most talk about race has ignored them. Nevertheless, these inherited bodily characteristics are just as important as skin color.

Stature varies from an average of four feet six inches among Pygmies to six feet two inches among some tribes of the Upper Nile. Shoulder breadth, pelvic measurements, relative massiveness of bones, and proportions of limbs and trunk vary widely in every part of the world. In all 'races,' however, homologous bones are arranged in the same distinctively human pattern. The number of bones is uniform, save for an extra bone in the skull in a very few local groups, and rarely, an extra bone in wrist or ankle. Teeth vary in minute details, but the basic pattern of human dentition is uniform.

Skulls range from long-narrow to short-broad, combined variously with different heights and differing degrees of slope of the forehead. Bony eyebrow ridges are frequent in Europeans and Australian blacks, but are absent in a large majority of Chinese. Proportions of the skull seem to vary with diet and methods of infant care; thus infants who are tied tightly to a wooden cradleboard may develop skulls flat in the back and rising to a high point—a fact which has led to erroneous racial classifications. Sometimes the teeth of the two jaws meet vertically, again they protrude somewhat. Chins slope at many different angles from the vertical. Noses vary from high and narrow with pronounced bridge and small nostrils to broad and flat with almost no bridge; some are convex in profile, others concave. A wag has remarked that in most Chinese a fly can walk on the level from one eye to the other, but must be a mountain climber to accomplish a like journey on many European faces.

Variations in the folds and tensions of the skin, in underlying musculature, and in local deposits of fat greatly alter the appearance of the face and body. For example, many Chinese and Japanese develop slight cheek-pads which impart a well-fed appearance even when the body is emaciated. Prehistoric carvings indicate the prevalence of another variation now infrequent, known as steatopygy; this variation involves heavy deposits of fat on the female buttocks which effect a startling change in bodily contour. There is no evidence of any accompanying specific effects on physiological functioning. In modern times extreme steatopygy occurs mostly among the natives of South Africa.

Eyelids manifest numerous minor variations. At the inner epicanthus (the junction of upper and lower eyelids nearest the nose) the two eyelids usually meet evenly; in some individuals, however, a fold of the upper lid covers the inner end of the lower one. About 2% of Europeans show this feature, while in China it characterizes from 20% to 50% of the population, depending on the locality. Hence it has been called the 'Mongoloid fold' and people often refer to the

Chinese as 'slant eyed' or 'almond eyed' even though a majority of Chinese lack this feature. In many Chinese the almond effect is enhanced by absence of the bridge of the nose. A Mongoloid fold may escape notice in a European because it may be combined with a high nasal bridge, beetling eyebrows, and blue eyes. These latter features prompted the Chinese to call Europeans 'dog eyed'—a characteristic naïvely verified when a European fondly boasts that his pet dog's eyes are 'almost human.' In turn, many Europeans exhibit another kind of fold of the eyelid that is rare in Chinese; this is the so-called Nordic fold, which is an extra fold of the upper lid that conceals the outer epicanthus (the junction of the two eyelids furthest from the nose).

Another highly variable feature is the external contour of the reproductive organs. These organs vary so widely that psychiatrists often discover individuals who have become neurotic because they feel themselves to be 'queer' in this respect. Actually many forms of these organs are 'normal' in the sense that they function adequately. Secondary sexual characteristics, such as male and female differences in beard, stature, breasts, breadth of pelvis, etc., also very widely in individuals. Some males approach the female bodily form with broad hips, narrow waist, and soft fleshy upper arms and legs. Some females approach the male contour in analogous manner. In general, Europeans and Polynesians exhibit wider differences between the sexes, while Eastern Asiatics approach a minimum of difference in bodily form between males and females. But in all human groups some individuals develop accentuated secondary sexual features and others attain minimum development.

Bodily chemistry also varies within ranges not yet clearly determined. Adequate studies of this aspect of racial differences are few. An example is the differing effects of the anti-malarial drug plasmochin upon persons differing in pigmentation. Injurious effects of this drug are almost nil when administered to very white-skinned persons; but as brunetteness increases, the drug produces increasing anemia and in very dark-skinned persons its effects are serious. Another aspect of bodily chemistry, the 'blood groups,' has been studied in many different populations. Group A is common among Europeans, Ainu aborigines of Japan, Australian blacks, and certain isolated tribes in India. Group B is observed most frequently among the peoples of Central and Eastern Asia, in South India and Indonesia, and some African tribes. Group O characterizes so-called Semites, the Lapps, most African and Oceanic Negroes, a few East Asiatic tribes, and American Indians. Group O, however, is extremely common everywhere, and the other types turn up occasionally in nearly all populations. Curiously, Group O is rare in apes and monkeys; only a few species of monkeys and about one chimpanzee in ten show this blood type. Apparently all these kinds of blood 'work' equally well. The clearest exception is one hereditary type called 'Rh negative' which may cause serious difficulties in pregnancy and childbirth if present in only one parent.

Resistance to disease differs widely. Diseases regarded as unimportant may flare into devastating epidemics when introduced suddenly to a population previously isolated. The survivors, however, develop resistance comparable to that of other peoples. Alleged 'racial immunities' to disease may be explained in terms of previous history of epidemics without resort to mystical 'racial' characteristics. Thus the relative immunity of Jews to tuberculosis is understood against the long history of confinement in European ghettos, which may have eliminated the family strains which were not resistant to that disease. This view is strengthened by the fact that rural populations suddenly placed in urban environments show high incidence of tuberculosis, and by the fact that Jews are of many different 'racial' types.[1]

To what extent do visceral and other internal organs vary? In general, internal organs vary much as do external features. In no human 'race,' however, are these variations so great that a surgeon about to operate on a specific organ would be in doubt as to the proper place for incision. The same organ turns up in the appropriate place and performs the same physiological function, whatever the 'race.' Perhaps such external variations as those in stature, bodily contour, skin, and hair are related to the relative activity of many endocrine or ductless glands; thus far, however, attempts to define 'race' in terms of glandular functioning are unsatisfactory.

Participation in human societies depends on ability to learn to such a degree that mental defectives are shut out of active social life because they cannot learn readily. This fact focuses interest upon the brain and nervous system; what is the significance of variations in size and structure of human brains? Unlike bones, brains are jellylike, difficult to observe and measure. Nor are brains obtained easily for purposes of research; people are squeamish about removal of the brains of deceased relatives to say nothing about relinquishing their

[1] Maurice R. Davie, *World Immigration* (New York, 1936), p. 158.

own cerebra for scientific experimentation. Much more needs to be learned about the import of minor anatomical variations in brain and nervous system. The relation of brain anatomy to many of the mental diseases popularly called 'insanity,' for example, is yet to be clarified. Some of the best prewar research came from the East Indies, where Dutch investigators studied brains from individuals of many 'races.' Like other students, they failed to discover specific racial differences.

In bulk mature human brains vary from 910 cc. to 2100 cc. Brain size, however, is proportional to body bulk; small persons have small brains. Brain size also is related to nutrition; individuals well-nourished from infancy develop brains larger than those of their ill-fed brothers or sisters. No one has shown that large brains function more efficiently than small brains, or vice versa. The efficiency of the nervous system depends on the delicacy of an extremely complex chemical and electrical balance within the system rather than upon the size of its parts. In basic pattern all human brains are the same, and apart from deformity or injury no specific detail of variation is known to affect ability to learn or to predetermine specific talents. The vast importance of minute chemical differences outwardly invisible is suggested by the well-known effects of alcohol upon behavior. As for size of brain, there is point to the analogy of a brain and a watch; the size of a brain is no more indicative of its performance than the size of a watch indicates its accuracy. Nor are structural details of brains related to external bodily features in any more significant way than differences in the mechanisms of watches are related to the decorations on the watch-cases. External anatomical details may be as irrelevant as the facetious but unchivalrous comment that ladies who are deficient in waves of the cerebral cortex compensate by adding waves to their coiffure. The function of cortical convolutions is not clear; an unproven guess is that by increasing the surface of the cerebrum they extend the range of associative memory and learning. All higher Primate species possess convoluted cortices—man most of all—and these species learn and remember more than do other animals. Within any species, however, individual differences in size and details of brain anatomy show little or no relation to differences in behavior and capacity for learning.

Conspicuous is the fact that, excepting pathological cases, all these human bodily variations 'work' for practical purposes. For example, tropical sunlight injures light-skinned persons and does not injure the dark-skinned. The white-skinned individual, however, can either stay indoors during the peak of the day or may wear a pith helmet. A tall man picks cherries from a tree more easily than a short man; but the short person can get a ladder and pick just as many cherries. Long slender fingers may be an asset to a pianist—or to a pickpocket —but stubby fingers have made good in both professions. All shapes of noses manage to breathe; all shapes of jaws chew and talk; mathematics, golf, or Sanskrit are learned equally well by the thin or the fat, the blonde or the brunette, the kinky-haired or the straight-haired. Even badly-mutilated bodies function effectively when the owner has courage and resourcefulness, as many a war casualty has demonstrated. Abraham Lincoln struck at the heart of the problem; asked what should be the length of a man's legs, he replied soberly, "I think they ought to be at least long enough to reach from his body to the ground."

Observations throughout the world show that all these variable features are combined in divers patterns. All normal human beings are fertile with mates of any physical type, and the offspring combine parental features in unpredictable ways. Negro-White matings have produced offspring who are tall, lanky, with red kinky hair, narrow noses, blue eyes, freckles, and dark brown skin; as well as other offspring with light skin, dark eyes, stocky build, straight black hair, broad nostrils, and protruding jaws. The children of Chinese-White matings combine the parental features in ways that seem just as strange. Tall Mongolians with round heads, heavy build, almost hairless bodies and straight black scalp hair have mated with small, slender, wiry, wavy-haired, long-headed Malays to produce offspring with hair and head form like the Mongol parent and the small wiry build of the Malay—as well as big-boned children with Malayan features and hair. Matings of Japanese with African blacks have resulted in bewildering combinations of the distinctive features of the two parents. Such mixed matings have occurred in all times and places. Consequently the majority of mankind exhibit features in combinations that can only be called scrambled. No known human hybrid is infertile like the mule.

Wars and migrations have provided the warp of history. Always they are accompanied by matings of contrasted physical types. Ever since the Hittites defeated the Jews in the seventh century B.C. the exaggerated 'Hittite nose' has appeared in many Jews, though it does not seem to have been originally a Jewish feature. Similarly, certain physical characteristics of Scottish Highlanders occur in a district of

India where a Scotch regiment was stationed for some years. In the belief that India needed the 'superior qualities' of the Scotch, the commanding officer encouraged his men in affairs with native girls. That sort of modification of 'typical features' of local populations is familiar in military history. So freely and frequently have both Negroes and Asiatics mingled with Europeans for centuries past that the family trees of most of the readers of these words probably include both Negroid and Mongoloid twigs in a not-too-remote past. Most of the variations appearing in mankind occur sporadically in any local population. In any one region, the accidents of history and of local isolation have produced specific combinations of features that differ from combinations observed elsewhere, so that to some extent all of the inhabitants in a long-settled population look somewhat alike. These more or less definite local patterns of bodily characteristics underlie the belief in clear-cut racial differences.

Attempts to classify mankind in a specific number of well-defined 'races' invariably fail. The great mixed populations defy attempts to fit all their members into any definite 'race.' No one can draw boundaries within which all 'whites,' all 'negroids,' or all 'mongoloids' fall. Classifications based on color are vitiated by the predominance of intermediate colors. If hair be used as a standard, the color groups are broken up. For example, skin color puts the aboriginal Australians with the Congo Negroes; but hair form puts them with the European 'whites.' Which is correct? Both—and neither.

Prior to the invention of the steamship, railway, motor-car, and airplane, small local populations often experienced long isolation from the outer world. Of necessity, these groups inbred. Contrary to popular superstition, inbreeding does not necessarily result in inferior offspring. In domesticated animals, for example, inbreeding fixes a type and may improve it. This happened among isolated human groups. Thus there developed tribes of common descent whose members all, or nearly all, manifested similar bodily characteristics. These were true races. The number of such races has been great, and different races have flourished at different historical periods.

In rich, accessible regions, however, no race remains pure. Travel, immigration, and invasion effect intermixture. The larger the population and the more different physical types it includes, the more hazily defined are the racial types. In modern times isolated pure races are very few. In general, the pure races, being isolated, have small opportunity to learn from others and hence contribute little to the achievements of civilization. The great civilized societies can draw ideas from the past and from diverse contemporary sources; hence inventions occur more frequently in such societies because inventors have a larger fund of knowledge with which to work. Such societies, in consequence of their very size and lack of isolation, are made up of heterogeneous populations. Historically, civilization and race mixture have gone together; achievements in civilization are the work of mixed peoples—not because mixed peoples are superior but because racial purity depends on isolation.

Despite scientific inaccuracy, convenience has led to a rough division of mankind into three major stocks and several minor groups. The *Caucasoids* include the light-skinned, highly variable Europeans and their descendants in the New World, South Africa, and Australia, and also the dark-skinned Hindus. The term *Mongoloid* denotes the Chinese, Mongols, Japanese, and aboriginal Americans, plus several variable minor stocks. *Negroids* include the many dark-skinned races of Africa and Oceania.

The inclusion of so many and varied physical types in these three general categories obviously involves fallacious classification. For example, many and diverse 'racial types' inhabit Europe, North Africa, Western Asia, and Northern India. Their resemblances are so vague and general that it is misleading to lump them together as "Caucasoids.' Among these peoples the blue-eyed, fair-skinned, light-haired individuals, though numerous in the Baltic area, constitute a decided minority. The brown-skinned Hindus are included because of historic affiliations and physical resemblances other than skin color. Similarly, 'Negroid' is an omnibus term for dark-skinned peoples as diverse as the Pygmies, the tall Melanesians with their Roman noses and mops of frizzly hair, and the long-limbed woolly-haired tribes of the African Congo. Under 'Mongoloid' are classified the tall northern Chinese and their Mongol neighbors, the short southern Chinese and the Japanese, the Burmese and various Malayan tribes—most of whom are broad-headed, with bridgeless noses, scant beards, and sallow of complexion—and also the varied physical types of the American Indians.

Bodily types that cannot be fitted into this somewhat Procrustean classification are observed among the following: the light-skinned, hairy Ainu of north Japan; the black Australians, who resemble white Europeans save for black skin and broad nostrils; the Polynesians of the Pacific islands; the South African Hottentots and Bushmen with their tufted hair and their steatopygous females; the Veddah aborigines of Ceylon; and others.

Any racial group, however defined, includes all sorts of personalities. Both geniuses and idiots occur in all races. Always there are the clever and the stupid, the honest and the deceitful, the arrogant and the meek, the pious and the godless, the alert and the lethargic. No so-called race monopolizes any of these qualities. The practical question about any individual is not, what is his physical type, but *what sort of person* is he? Opportunity and taste for learning, not bodily features, play the leading role in the development of personalities.

SECTION FIVE
Intergroup Relations

24 AN INDIAN'S SOLILOQUY *

BY BURT W. AGINSKY (1905–   )
THE CITY COLLEGE (OF NEW YORK)

WHILE doing field research in northern California with an Indian group which had suffered a great deal under the disruptive influences of Spanish and Americans, I became familiar with an old Indian man well over one hundred years of age. He had lived through a period which encompassed the days before any whites had come into his territory, the Spanish raids, the white massacres, the herding of his people upon reservations, and the variegated civilized tortures accompanying these deprivations. One day after a long period of discussion concerning the changing family situation he talked eloquently for a period of about two hours. As soon as it was possible I returned to my headquarters and recorded what he had said in as close an approximation as I could.

An old Pomo Indian once said to me: "What is a man? A man is nothing. Without his family he is of less importance than that bug crossing the trail, of less importance than the sputum or exuviae. At least they can be used to help poison [1] a man. A man must be with his family to amount to anything with us. If he had nobody else to help him, the first trouble he got into he would be killed by his enemies because there would be no relatives to help him fight the poison of the other group. No woman would marry him because her family would not let her marry a man with no family. He would be poorer than a newborn child; he would be poorer than a worm, and the family would not consider him worth anything. He would not bring renown or glory with him. He would not bring support of other relatives either. The family is important. If a man has a large family and a profession [2] and upbringing by a family that is known to produce good children, then he is somebody and every family is willing to have him marry a woman of their group. It is the family

---

* Reprinted by permission of the author and of the editor from *The American Journal of Sociology*, XLVI (1940–41), 43–44.

[1] Sorcery—black magic.

[2] Specialized occupation requiring years of training and preparation. Some of the specializations are deer-hunter, gambler, doctor, and money manufacturers.

that is important. In the white ways of doing things the family is not so important. The police and soldiers take care of protecting you, the courts give you justice, the post office carries messages for you, the school teaches you. Everything is taken care of, even your children, if you die; but with us the family must do all of that.

"Without the family we are nothing, and in the old days before the white people came the family was given the first consideration by anyone who was about to do anything at all. That is why we got along. We had no courts, judges, schools, and the other things you have, but we got along better than you. We had poison, but if we minded our own business and restrained ourselves we lived well. We were taught to leave people alone. We were taught to consider that other people had to live. We were taught that we would suffer from the devil, spirits, ghosts, or other people if we did not support one another. The family was everything, and no man ever forgot that. Each person was nothing, but as a group joined by blood the individual knew that he would get the support of all his relatives if anything happened. He also knew that if he was a bad person the head man of his family would pay another tribe to kill him so that there would be no trouble afterward and so that he would not get the family into trouble all of the time.

"That is why we were good people and why we were friends with the white people when they came. But the white people were different from us. They wanted to take the world for themselves. My grandfather told me that the white people were homeless and had no families. They came by themselves and settled on our property. They had no manners. They did not know how to get along with other people. They were strangers who were rough and common and did not know how to behave. But I have seen that these people of yours are even worse. They have taken everything away from the Indians, and they take everything away from one another. They do not help one another when they are in trouble, and they do not care what happens to other people. We were not like that. We would not let a person die of starvation when we had plenty of food. We would not bury our dead with no show. We would kill another person by poisoning him if he was an enemy, but we would not treat a stranger the way they treat their own brothers and sisters. Your people are hard to understand. My brother lived with your people for twenty years, and he said that he was used to you; but he cannot understand yet why you people act as you do. You are all the same in one way.

We are all the same in another. What is wrong with you? The white people have the land. They own the courts, they own everything, but they will not give the Indians enough money to live on. It is hard to understand.

"With us the family was everything. Now it is nothing. We are getting like the white people, and it is bad for the old people. We had no old peoples' homes like you. The old people were important. They were wise. Your old people must be fools."

25 ETHNOCENTRIC IDEOLOGY *

BY DANIEL J. LEVINSON (1920–)
HARVARD UNIVERSITY

THE term "prejudice" is not entirely adequate, since it has numerous meanings and connotations which might obscure or distort the ideas guiding this research. The term "ethnocentrism" is preferable because its traditional meaning comes much closer to that used here. First introduced and used descriptively by Sumner [1] in 1906, the term had the general meaning of provincialism or cultural narrowness; it meant a tendency in the individual to be "ethnically centered," to be rigid in his acceptance of the culturally "alike" and in his rejection of the "unlike."

The traditional conception of ethnocentrism, from which the present one is derived, differs in several important respects from the usual notion of prejudice. Prejudice is commonly regarded as a feeling of dislike against a specific group; ethnocentrism, on the other hand, refers to a relatively consistent frame of mind concerning "aliens" generally. Usually, in discussions of prejudice against groups there is specific reference to "race prejudice" or "prejudice against racial and

---

* Reprinted by permission of the author and of the publisher from his chapter on "The Study of Ethnocentric Ideology," in T. W. Adorno, E. Frenkel-Brunswik, D. J. Levinson, R. N. Sanford, and others, *The Authoritarian Personality* (New York: Harper & Brothers, 1950), chap. iv, pp. 102–150; pp. 102–104, 146–150 reprinted.

[1] W. G. Sumner, *Folkways* (Boston: Ginn & Company, 1906).

religious minorities." This terminology is used even by people who know that "race" is a socially harmful idea as ordinarily understood, and who know that many groups (zootsuiters, "Okies," and so forth) are discriminated against on neither racial nor religious grounds. Ethnocentrism refers to group relations generally; it has to do not only with numerous groups toward which the individual has hostile opinions and attitudes but, equally important, with groups toward which he is positively disposed.

A theory of ethnocentrism offers a starting point for the understanding of the psychological aspect of group relations—why individuals are inclined toward competition, or conflict, or harmonious interaction and so on. It is concerned with such questions as: What kinds of general attitudes do individuals have about their own and other groups? What underlying ideas or themes run through an individual's thinking about groups and group relations? How do these ideas develop? How are they related to trends in the individual's thinking about other social processes? What personality trends, if any, are they related to, and in what way? How are they related to membership in class, church, political party, and so forth?

The term "ethnocentrism" shifts the emphasis from "race" to "ethnic group." The everyday use of the term "race" has been criticized from many sides and on many grounds. It was originally suggested as one type of broad classification of human beings on the basis of skin color. Other anthropometric measures such as head shape and blood type were also suggested. Each of these organic bases of classification divides human beings (also known as the human "race") into groups which are mixed with respect to the other organic characteristics. Thus, the Negroes, a "race" according to the skin color criterion, are mixed with respect to head shape and blood type. But, apart from the arbitrariness of the organic basis of classification, the greatest dangers of the race concept lie in its hereditarian psychological implications and in its misapplication to cultures. Psychologically, the race theory implies, whether or not this is always made explicit, that people of a given race (e.g., skin color) are also very similar psychologically because they have a common hereditary family tree. This notion has been controverted in the past few decades by work in psychology on the problem of "heredity vs. environment" and by work in cultural anthropology on the tremendous psychological variations within any given culture. Furthermore, the term "race" is often applied to groups which are not races at all in the technical sense. Sometimes this term is applied to nations, e.g., "the German race" or even "the American race." Sometimes it is misused in connection with American ethnic minorities, such as Italians or Greeks. There is no adequate term, other than "ethnic," by which to describe cultures (that is, systems of social ways, institutions, traditions, language, and so forth) which are not nations, that is, which do not form politico-geographical entities. This confusion, which is more than merely terminological and which permeates much thinking on social problems, has plagued the Jews particularly; they are a good example of an ethnic group which is neither a formal nation nor a race. From the point of view of sociology, cultural anthropology, and social psychology, the important concepts are not race and heredity but social organization (national, regional, subcultural, communal) and the interaction of social forms and individual personalities. To the extent that relative uniformities in psychological characteristics are found within any cultural grouping, these uniformities must be explained primarily in terms of social organization rather than "racial heredity." The use and development of the concept of "ethnic group," as part of a broad educational program dealing with individual development and social change, can do much to clarify everyday thinking about social processes and problems. . . . Ethnocentrism is conceived as an ideological system pertaining to groups and group relations. A distinction is made between *ingroups* (those groups with which the individual identifies himself) and *outgroups* (with which he does not have a sense of belonging and which are regarded as antithetical to the ingroups). Outgroups are the objects of negative opinions and hostile attitudes; ingroups are the objects of positive opinions and uncritically supportive attitudes; and it is considered that outgroups should be socially subordinate to ingroups.

The basic questions for research . . . concern the inclusiveness of ideas regarding a given group, the *generality* of outgroup rejection, the *content* of ideas about ingroups and outgroups, and the amount of *stereotypy* in thinking about groups generally.[2] . . .

The term "group" is used in the widest sense to mean any set of people who constitute a psychological entity for any individual. If we regard the individual's conception of the social world as a sort of map containing various differentiated regions, then each region can be considered a group. This sociopsychological definition includes

[2] [Omitted here are sections (pp. 104–146) dealing with "Construction of Ethnocentrism (E) Scale," results of use of scale, and analysis of results.—Ed.]

sociological groups such as nations, classes, ethnic groups, political parties, and so on. But it also includes numbers-of-people who have one or more common characteristics but who are not formal groups in the sense of showing organization and regulation of ways. Thus, it is legitimate in a sociopsychological sense to consider as groups such sets of people as criminals, intellectuals, artists, politicians, eccentrics, and so on. Psychologically, they are groups in so far as they are social categories or regions in an individual's social outlook—objects of opinions, attitudes, affect, and striving.

"Ingroup" and "outgroup" are sociopsychological rather than purely sociological concepts, since they refer to identification and, so to speak, contraidentification, rather than to formal membership in the group. A person may be identified with groups to which he does not formally belong. This is exemplified by the type of socially upward mobile person who is identified with groups of higher status and power (class, profession, political faction) than those to which he now belongs; also by the person with motivated downward mobility [3] who identifies with lower status and power groups such as Negroes, Jews, "the proletariat," "the weak and suffering."

An individual may, of course, be concerned with many groups which are neither ingroups nor outgroups for him. One may feel sympathetic towards Negroes or the Catholic Church without actually identifying with them. Conversely, one may be opposed to many groups in the sense of feeling a difference in interest or values, or merely of feeling that their aims and existence are irrelevant to him; but these are not outgroups if there is not the sense of contraidentification, of basic conflict, of mutual exclusiveness, of violation of primary values.

A primary characteristic of ethnocentric ideology is the *generality* of outgroup rejection. It is as if the ethnocentric individual feels threatened by most of the groups to which he does not have a sense of belonging; if he cannot identify, he must oppose; if a group is not "acceptable," it is "alien." The ingroup-outgroup distinction thus be-

---

[3] The word "motivated" is used to distinguish this type of downward mobility—which is psychologically desired and sought—from a loss of status which is externally imposed by depression or economic failure (and in which the individual usually remains identified with the higher status group). Similarly, a person may want to rise in economic status primarily because of the desire for comfort, leisure, and so on; this is psychologically different from that upward mobility in which the desire for status and power, and identification with powerful groups, are primary motivating forces.

comes the basis for most of his social thinking, and people are categorized primarily according to the groups to which they belong. The outgroups are usually entirely subordinate (Negroes, Mexicans), or groups with relatively low status and power who are struggling to better their position in society. The major outgroups in America today appear to be Jews, Negroes, the lower socioeconomic class, labor unions, and political radicals, especially Communists. Other groups whose outgroup status varies somewhat are Catholics, artists, intellectuals; Oklahomans and Japanese (in the West); pacifists, Filipinos, Mexicans, homosexuals. Most other nations, especially the industrially backward, the socialistic, and those most different from the "Anglo-Saxon," tend to be considered outgroups. While there are probably considerable sectional, class, and individual differences regarding which groups are regarded as outgroups, it would appear that an individual who regards a few of these groups as outgroups will tend to reject most of them. An ethnocentric individual may have a particular dislike for one group, but he is likely nonetheless to have ethnocentric opinions and attitudes regarding many other groups.

Another general characteristic of ethnocentric ideology is the *shifting* of the outgroup among various levels of social organization. Once the social context for discussion has been set, ethnocentrists are likely to find an outgroup-ingroup distinction. Thus, in a context of international relations ethnocentrism takes the form of pseudopatriotism; "we" are the best people and the best country in the world, and we should either keep out of world affairs altogether (isolationism) or we should participate—but without losing our full sovereignty, power, and economic advantage (imperialism). And in either case we should have the biggest army and navy in the world, and atom bomb monopoly.

However, the superior American "we" breaks down when the context shifts to intranational affairs. In a religious context the ingroup-outgroup distinction may shift in various ways: religious-nonreligious, Christian-Jewish, Protestant-Catholic, among Protestant sects. Similar outgroup-ingroup distinctions can be found in various other phases of American life. It seems, then, that the individual who has a pseudopatriotic conception of America in relation to other nations actually regards most of America as an outgroup: various religions, non-whites, "the masses," too-educated people and too-uneducated people, criminals, radicals, and so on, tend largely to fall in the outgroup category. This is not to say that nonethnocentrists regard all these groups as ingroups; rather, the nonethnocentrist can take a supportive attitude without necessarily identifying, and he can be critical without a sense of alien-ness and of categorical difference.

The social world as most ethnocentrists see it is arranged like a series of concentric circles around a bull's-eye. Each circle represents an ingroup-outgroup distinction; each line serves as a barrier to exclude all outside groups from the center, and each group is in turn excluded by a slightly narrower one. A sample "map" illustrating the ever-narrowing ingroup would be the following: Whites, Americans, native-born Americans, Christians, Protestants, Californians, my family, and finally—I.

The ethnocentric "need for an outgroup" prevents that identification with humanity as a whole which is found in anti-ethnocentrism. (This lack in identification is related to the ethnocentrists' inability to approach individuals *as* individuals, and to their tendency to see and "prejudge" each individual only as a sample specimen of the reified group. Their experience of interpersonal relations involves, so to speak, the same stereotypy as their opinions regarding groups generally.) The inability to identify with humanity takes the political form of nationalism and cynicism about world government and permanent peace. It takes other forms, all based on ideas concerning the intrinsic evil (aggressiveness, laziness, power-seeking, etc.) of human nature; the idea that this evil is unchangeable is rationalized by pseudoscientific hereditarian theories of human nature. The evil, since it is unchangeable, must be attacked, stamped out, or segregated wherever it is found, lest it contaminate the good. The democratic alternative—humanitarianism—is not a vague and abstract "love for everybody" but the ability to like and dislike, to value and oppose, *individuals* on the basis of concrete *specific experience;* it necessarily involves the elimination of the stereotypical ingroup-outgroup distinction and all that goes with it.

What is the *content* of ethnocentric ideology regarding outgroups? There are, of course, individual differences here, and the same individual has different conceptions of, and attitudes toward, different outgroups. Nevertheless, certain common trends seem to exist, and these are generally the same as those found in anti-Semitic ideology. Most essentially, outgroups are seen as *threatening* and *power-seeking.* Accusations against them tend to be moralistic and, often, mutually contradictory. One of the main characteristics of most out-groups is that they are objectively *weaker* than the groups whom they supposedly threaten. Sometimes this weakness is perceived by the ethnocentrist, but this does not seem to lessen his sense of being threatened./The conflict as he sees it is between an ingroup trying to maintain or recapture its justly superior position, and an outgroup, resentful of past hurts, trying to do to others what they have done to it. But the conflict is seen as permanent and unresolvable; the only alternatives are dominance and submission; justice requires dominance by the superior ingroup, and the subordinate group will always remain resentful and rebellious. Because he considers hierarchy and power conflict "natural" he has difficulty in grasping a conception of group relations in which power considerations are largely eliminated and in which no group can control the lives of other groups.

The moralistic accusations against outgroups are similar to those that were seen in the case of anti-Semitism; again we find stereotypy, an absence of theories—save simple hereditarian ones—to explain why groups are as they are, and a readiness to place all the blame for group conflict upon outgroups.

The general outlook just described must, it would seem, have to do primarily with psychological trends within the ethnocentrist rather than with the actual characteristics of the outgroups. For one thing, many people who have had bad experiences with members of minority groups—and most of us have had unhappy experiences with members of most groups including ingroups—or who have heard derogatory remarks about these groups, do not have ethnocentric imagery and attitudes. It is not the experience as such that counts, but the way in which it is assimilated psychologically. Also, the prejudiced individual is prepared to reject groups with which he has never had contact; his approach to a new and strange person or culture is not one of curiosity, interest, and receptivity but rather one of doubt and rejection. The feeling of difference is transformed into a sense of threat and an attitude of hostility. The new group easily becomes an outgroup. The stereotypy, the illogicality, the large number of outgroups, the consistency of outgroup imagery—all these point to things in the psychological functioning of ethnocentrists which differentiate them from anti-ethnocentrists.

Ethnocentric ideology regarding ingroups shows similar trends, though often in an opposite direction, to that regarding outgroups.

The ingroups are conceived of as superior in morality, ability, and general development; they ought also to be superior in power and status, and when their status is lowered or threatened the ethnocentrist tends to feel persecuted and victimized. Attempts by subordinate groups to improve their status are regarded as threats; he cannot imagine that they are struggling for equality and mutual interaction because he does not think in these terms. The ingroup is idealized and blindly submitted to. Obedience and loyalty are the first requirements of the ingroup member. What is called power-seeking and clannishness in the outgroup is transformed into moral righteousness, self-defense, and loyalty in the ingroup. In all other respects the ingroup is regarded as the opposite of the outgroup: clean, unaggressive, hard-working and ambitious, honest, disciplined, well-mannered. The same values, then, are applied to both ingroups and outgroups, and in the same stereotyped way.

The interaction of ingroups and outgroups, and indeed all social interaction, is conceived in hierarchical and authoritarian terms. Groups as well as individuals must "find their level," and the greatest danger is that certain groups will attempt to rise above their natural position. The same conceptions are applied to ingroup structure and functioning. As in the army, there should be a series of levels, and individuals on a given level should submit to those above and dominate those below. The conception of the ideal family situation for the child is similar: uncritical obedience to the father and elders, pressures directed unilaterally from above to below, inhibition of spontaneity and emphasis on conformity to externally imposed values.

We can now consider the ethnocentric solution to problems of group conflict. The ingroup must be kept pure and strong. The only methods of doing this are to *liquidate* the outgroups altogether, to keep them entirely *subordinate,* or to *segregate* them in such a way as to minimize contact with the ingroups. The first method represents politicalized ethnocentrism—fascism and the dissolution of democratic values. This method so obviously violates traditional American values of nonviolence, fairness, and equal opportunity that it has found relatively little support in this country. The second and third methods are supported, however, by large numbers of ordinary citizens.

Attitudes that the main outgroups should be subordinated and segregated are characteristic of American ethnocentrism because, it would seem, they combine so well ethnocentric imagery and sense of threat on the one hand, and certain democratic values which still prevail even in ethnocentrists, on the other. The democratic values often prevent more drastic action, but they may also serve to permit discrimination and oppression behind a pseudodemocratic front.

From these considerations the following general statement emerges. *Ethnocentrism is based on a pervasive and rigid ingroup-outgroup distinction; it involves stereotyped negative imagery and hostile attitudes regarding outgroups, stereotyped positive imagery and submissive attitudes regarding ingroups, and a hierarchical, authoritarian view of group interaction in which ingroups are rightly dominant, outgroups subordinate.*

26 THE CHANGING STATUS OF THE NEGRO *

BY E. FRANKLIN FRAZIER (1894–   )
HOWARD UNIVERSITY

UP TO the first decade of the present century the vast majority of the Negroes were peasant folk dwelling on the plantations of the South. A third of the southern Negroes were illiterate while less than a half of the Negro children of school age were attending school. The lack of educational facilities together with the barriers that Emancipation and Reconstruction had erected between the races had tended to arrest the acculturation of the Negro.[1] This was all changed as the result of World War I which drew nearly a million Negroes out of the social and mental isolation of the world of the Negro folk. As Negroes have continued to be drawn into cities,

---

* Reprinted by permission of the author and of the publisher from *The Negro in the United States* (New York: The Macmillan Company, 1949), pp. 688–696.

[1] See Melville J. Herskovits, *Acculturation, A Study of Culture Contact* (New York, 1938), pp. 2–32, for a critical analysis of the processes involved in acculturation. See also Bronislaw Malinowski, *The Dynamics of Culture Change*, edited by Phyllis M. Kaberry, (New Haven, 1945), pp. vii ff., where the author emphasizes the fact that when two races with different cultures come into contact each takes over some elements of the culture of the other.

especially northern cities, the tempo and the character of their acculturation have changed. The tempo was quickened because they were
brought into contact with many phases of American culture with
which they had no contact in the rural isolation. Suddenly exposed
to a multiplicity of patterns of behavior and new modes of thought,
the Negro has often adopted bizarre forms of behavior in order to
secure recognition. Moreover, many of the newly acquired patterns
of behavior and ways of thinking have not affected the deeper layers
of his personality which were molded by the family and the folk culture. But on the whole the urbanized Negro has sought to conform
to the new environment. Thus, slowly the Negro, like the European
immigrant, has acquired the manners and customs of America and
as these new ways have become a part of his family heritage he has
been transformed into a new person. The extent to which this transformation has occurred has been in proportion to his schooling and
his participation in other phases of American culture.

Although the folk Negro has become transformed through education and wider participation in American life, the fact of his color
has continued to retard the degree of his integration into American
life. Despite the policy which defines as a Negro any person with
Negro ancestry, the mixed-blood in the United States as elsewhere
has enjoyed many advantages. Moreover, the mixed-blood has served
as a channel by which the culture of the whites has been communicated to the Negro group.[2] Under the conditions of city living, the
mobility of the Negroes of mixed ancestry has been increased. Because of the anonymity of the city they have been able to "pass"
for white or for southern Europeans and South Americans.[3] There
have been a number of estimates of the number of Negroes who
have passed into the white race; but it is impossible to know definitely the number who change their race.[4] It is well known that

[2] See Louis Wirth and Herbert Goldhamer, "The Hybrid and the Problem of
Miscegenation," in Otto Klineberg (Ed.), *Characteristics of the American Negro*
(New York, 1944), pp. 249–369, for the most comprehensive and critical analysis
of available information on Negro-white mixtures in the United States. See also
Edward B. Reuter, *The Mulatto in the United States* (Boston, 1918) and by the
same author, *Race Mixture* (New York, 1931).

[3] See Wirth and Goldhamer, *op. cit.,* pp. 312 ff.

[4] See John H. Burma, "The Measurement of Negro 'Passing,'" *The American
Journal of Sociology,* LII (July, 1946), pp. 18–22; and E. W. Eckard, "How Many
Negroes 'Pass,'" *The American Journal of Sociology,* LII (May, 1947), 498–500,
for the most reliable estimates on the number of Negroes who "pass" for white
each year.

many Negroes "pass" for white in order to secure employment in occupations which are closed to Negroes. Some Negroes experience considerable inner conflict in "passing" for white, while others feel completely at home in the white world. Those who feel an inner conflict despite their physical and cultural identification with whites remain as unassimilated as the dark Negroes. On the other hand, there are mixed-bloods who have identified themselves inwardly with whites and have become assimilated in the white race. The children of such people have no history or memories to connect them with Negroes.

Because of his high visibility, the Negro of dark complexion and pronounced negroid features experiences a different problem of integration. However, one should not overlook the fact that how the Negro appears is determined to a large extent by the manner in which the Negro is defined by our culture. As we have seen in the last chapter the categoric picture of the Negro as given in our culture has changed. The Negro who is presented, for example, in the advertisement of a popular brand of whiskey today is a kindly, dignified human being, entirely different from the grotesque apelike caricature of a human being that was used thirty or forty years ago to advertise shoe polish. Moreover, it should be noted that as Negroes dress as other Americans and acquire their manners and ways in their public conduct, their visibility tends to decrease. Finally, as Negroes are found increasingly in occupations and in rôles which they did not formerly occupy, the association of a dark complexion and negroid features with an inferior social status tends to disappear.

CHANGES IN THE NEGRO COMMUNITY

There have been important changes in the character of the Negro community and its relation to the white community which are facilitating the integration of the Negro into American life. First, it should be noted that a smaller proportion of the Negro population is concentrated in the South and the Negro population has become more evenly distributed in that region. Moreover, as we have shown during the course of this study, the Negro has become more integrated into the economic life of the nation. Forty years ago the Negro had lost his important position as a skilled worker in the South and he had no place in northern industry. As the result of World War I the Negro gained a foothold in industry and as the result of the development of the industrial unions and World War II, he has become

an important element among the industrial workers of the country
Moreover, as the result of his political power in the northern states
and Fair Employment Practices legislation the barriers to the em
ployment of Negroes are being removed. Thus the economic basis
for a separate communal life which was provided to some extent by
the concentration of Negroes in agriculture has been destroyed.

The increasing occupational differentiation of the Negro population is affecting the structure of the Negro community. Forty years
ago the Negroes were concentrated in agriculture and domestic
service. In the cities there had appeared, often in the neighborhood
of the Negro colleges, a small upper class comprised of a few professional men and the more stable and respectable elements of various
occupational statuses. As the result of the mass migrations to northern cities, the occupational differentiation of the Negro population
was accelerated. The process has continued until at present in the
North Negroes are found in most of the occupations. Even in the
South where the process has been much slower because of the lack
of political power and employment opportunities, education has provided the Negro with the knowledge and skills to serve the Negro
communities. As the result of these changes, in the North the various classes in the Negro communities are developing common interests with members of the same classes in the white community. For
example, Negro industrial workers are being integrated into the
unions and Negro and white social workers and teachers are being
drawn together outside their professional interests. The employment of Negro teachers in northern universities has been especially
significant for the changing status of the Negro. Although racial
barriers have prevented similar developments in the South there is
a growing recognition of the individual Negro's occupational and
professional status which is providing a basis of common interests
between the races. Despite these changes, Negro life continues to
flow within the separate institutions of the more or less segregated
Negro community. In the South the separate public schools and recreational facilities erect barriers between children who might otherwise forget racial differences. There are also the separate churches,
theaters, and even separate businesses which serve the wants of the
Negro. Even in the North where the public educational and recreational facilities favor the integration of the Negro into the American community, the separate churches and social clubs and other
associations embodying the cultural interests of the community main-

tain the separation of the races. While these separate institutions have played an important rôle in the acculturation of the Negro since they have provided the channels through which the Negro has taken over American patterns, they are nevertheless barriers to the integration of the Negro into American life. The persistence of segregation in the case of certain types of institutions while other types of institutions absorb the Negro seems to be related to certain fundamental facts of human relationships.

INTEGRATION: FROM SECONDARY TO PRIMARY GROUP CONTACTS

An attempt has been made to define the typical stages in the developing relationships of immigrants or minority groups and the dominant white group in the United States. Bogardus has developed the theory of a "race-relation cycle" based upon the recurrent behavior on the part of native white Americans toward the Oriental and the Mexican.[5] In the first phase there was an attitude of curiosity toward the stranger; and in the second stage, the stranger was welcomed because of the demand for his labor. In the third stage, however, the immigrant became the object of industrial and social antagonism because he was a competitor and sought improvement in his status. There followed a fourth phase when through legislation the immigrant was excluded or restricted in his enjoyment of economic, political, and social rights. In the fifth phase, there appeared "fair-play" movements which helped immigrants to retain confidence in American ideals and helped Americans to maintain their reputation before the world. Then followed a phase of acquiescence in which antagonism died down, and a final phase in which the children of immigrants had to face the problem of assimilation.

It is possible to relate the development of Negro-white relations to the stages described in the "race-relations cycle." For example, many features of present Negro-white relations indicate that they have entered the fifth, sixth and final stages depending upon the section of the country. However, instead of attempting to fit Negro-white relations in the various parts of the country into this scheme, we shall undertake to discover in what areas of human relations integration is progressing most rapidly and in what areas there is greater resistance to integration. This procedure appears to be more profitable

[5] Emory S. Bogardus, "A Race-Relations Cycle," *The American Journal of Sociology*, XXXV, 612–17.

since it involves at the same time the rôle of the institutions in the Negro community in the process of integration.

The process of integrating the Negro into American life may be represented by a gradient as indicated in the title of this section. The Negro is being integrated first into those areas of American life involving secondary contacts as opposed to primary contacts,[6] or secular as opposed to sacred relations. Yet the fact of status is involved in the relations of the races. It appears that as a rule status is more important where contacts are primary or tend to be intimate than where contacts are impersonal. The Negro was first integrated into the economic organization when he performed a specialized form of labor as a slave. Antagonism developed toward him as a competitor and this antagonism has continued on a wide scale until the last decade or so. But gradually the Negro worker is being integrated into industry. In fact, it is in the economic relations of American life that the Negro is gaining his greatest acceptance today. In the South where the CIO is carrying on an educational campaign against discrimination in connection with its union drive and has an established policy of nonsegregated unions, there is a growing acceptance of the Negro's right to work according to his skill and on the basis of equal pay. There is still a barrier to the employment of Negroes in "white collar" occupations along with whites because of the status involved in such occupations. On the other hand, in the North the Negro is gradually winning the right to work in "white collar" occupations. Increasingly, the public is becoming accustomed to being served by Negro clerks and white workers are exhibiting less opposition to Negro workers in such occupations.

However, in the South the barriers to the admission of Negroes to theaters and other public recreational institutions show few signs of weakening. Even in the District of Columbia, Negroes are excluded from theaters and movie houses despite nationwide protest. The fight against the segregated public schools in the capital of the world's greatest democracy is only beginning to enlist the support of national leaders. There is no likelihood that the separate public schools in the South will be abolished soon, though there is a growing opinion among white students in the state institutions of some southern states

---

[6] See Charles H. Cooley, *Social Organization* (New York, 1909), chap. iii, on the nature of primary group relations, and Ellsworth Faris, "The Primary Group: Essence and Accident," *American Journal of Sociology*, XXXVIII (July, 1932), 41–50, for a critique of the concept of primary groups.

that Negro students should be admitted. In the North where there has been no legal segregation in the matter of public education, there have been segregated schools and the employment of Negro teachers has been restricted or Negro teachers have been placed in Negro areas. Throughout the North opposition to this type of segregation and discrimination has been growing in recent years. Indicative of the changes which are occurring is the recent action of the states of New Jersey and New York in abolishing all forms of segregation in public education. Moreover, in the North the exclusion of Negroes from public places of amusement and recreation is not as great today as formerly.

While these changes are taking place in regard to public institutions where contacts are secondary or more or less impersonal and secular, there is little evidence that even in the North the Negro is gaining acceptance in those institutions and associations where contacts are more intimate and personal. For example, it appears that Negroes will be "integrated" into theaters and public places of recreation and amusement in northern cities sooner than in the churches. During the past decade or so Negro actors have increasingly been integrated on the American stage while the traditional opposition to Negroes in the audience has been diminishing.[7] Despite the professions of the Christian churches concerning brotherhood and even their interracial programs, churches consist largely of family groups and embody the cultural traditions of certain classes. The same might be said concerning the Negro church organizations which derive their support from family groups and embody the cultural traditions of the Negro minority. Moreover, the Negro churches like other separate institutions in the Negro world represent certain vested interests which Negroes particularly functionaries of these institutions are unwilling to surrender.[8]

When one considers the various associations in which human relations are free and informal and more especially the most intimate of social groups, the family, where human relations tend to be sacred, one can get a measure of the moral isolation of the Negro in American life. Probably, the Negro has felt more keenly his moral isolation in the midst of American life than the various forms of oppression and discrimination because these are only a reflection of his moral

[7] See Edith J. R. Isaacs, *The Negro in the American Theatre* (New York, 1947).
[8] E. Franklin Frazier, "Human, All Too Human. The Negro's Vested Interest in Segregation," *Survey Graphic,* January, 1947.

isolation. To be counted in or to belong, as Sterling Brown has pointed out, is what the Negro wants in America at the present time.[9] Of course, other racial and ethnic minorities experience to some degree the same moral isolation. But other racial minorities such as the Chinese and Indians are not numerous and have an ancestral cultural heritage and the ethnic minorities are all defined as white and are being assimilated. The Negro is a large racial minority without an ancestral cultural heritage to fall back on. While he is essentially an American, he is still regarded as an alien without even the romantic sentiment with which the Chinese or Indian is invested. The more the Negro escapes from the world of the folk and conforms to the dominant American patterns of behavior and thought, the more keenly he feels his moral isolation. The more he participates in American life, the more he feels that certain areas of intimate association with whites are closed to him.

Yet there are signs that among certain groups, especially in the larger cosmopolitan communities, the barriers to intimate association are being broken down. For example, among the more liberal and radical labor groups, Negroes participate freely in their social activities and are at home within their family circle. Then, too, among certain intellectual and artistic groups, the participation of Negroes on a basis of complete intimacy and acceptance has increasingly become a commonplace occurrence. As the Negro achieves competence in the various professional fields, there is a growing disposition to accept him as a social equal, generally within a restricted circle, since prejudices against such contacts are strong among the more conventional members of the professional groups. The final and strongest barrier to complete acceptance is, of course, the disapproval of intermarriage. There is little reliable information on this phase of race relations. Probably not more than three per cent of Negro marriages in the large northern cities are across race lines. The vast majority of whites and Negroes who intermarry are found in semiskilled and unskilled occupations. More Negro men than Negro women marry across race lines; and about a third of the white bridegrooms are foreign born. The members of the professional classes of both races who intermarry are generally the more sophisticated and emancipated members of the middle class. There is as much opposition among the conventional members of the Negro upper and middle classes to

[9] See Sterling A. Brown, "Count Us In" in Rayford W. Logan (Ed.), *What the Negro Wants* (Chapel Hill, 1944), pp. 308–44.

intermarriage as among the same elements in the white group. Despite these barriers to intermarriage it should be noted that intermarriage is not regarded with the same provincial attitude either among whites or among Negroes as in the past.

27 GROUP LIFE WITHIN THE AMERICAN PATTERN *

BY OSCAR HANDLIN (1915–   )
HARVARD UNIVERSITY

"THESE people associate as easily as they breathe," wrote Fredrika Bremer of the Americans in 1853. After two years of travel in the United States, what seemed most striking and characteristic to the Swedish novelist was the variety and spontaneity of group activity on this side of the Atlantic. There, she sensed, lay a key to the unique qualities of New World democracy.

Up to our own times, this feature of American life has continued to impress the Europeans who have made comparisons with their own uniform and stratified societies. Indeed, there seems, in retrospect, to have been a striking connection between the development of democracy in the United States and the growth in the number and scope of autonomous associations.

Such associations were not here at the start. American history began with the Puritan conception of Commonwealth of the 17th century, the ideal of which was the completely uniform society of the town meeting—one state, one community, one church. But the conditions of colonization exerted a steadily disruptive effect, broke up closely-knit, homogeneous communities. The constant influx of outsiders and the unsettling frontier left this country with a society in which no form of association was completely coterminous with every other. Every man was a stranger to some extent and "belonging" was a relative term. The result was the persistent sprouting of all sorts of

* Reprinted by permission of the author and of the editor from *Commentary*, VIII (1949), 411–417.

religious, cultural, and social groups among which the prospective member had the capacity freely to choose.

Out of enormous diversity grew an exhilarating sense of spontaneity, a taste for experimentation and improvisation, and the urge toward liberty.

Freedom of association then shielded the citizen against the naked exercise of power by his government. In the United States, the individual was not compelled alone to confront the state. Between the isolated man and his government stood a wide array of intermediaries. A person was not simply a citizen of the United States, and nothing more. He was also a Mason, an Odd Fellow, or a Tall Cedar of Lebanon; a Catholic, a Methodist, or a Jew; a Yankee or Irishman, a Democrat or Republican. And having these affiliations did not detract from his Americanism. In these groups, he could play a significant role that was free of pressure from the state. Competition among organizations created a situation in which diversity was normal rather than eccentric. It left great areas of social activity—the most important areas—free for the expression of the widest differences.

Today this variety of association, so productive of benefits in the past, seems threatened by a sustained assault from many complex and subtle sources. The unsettling mobility of new people in new places has, in some measure, subsided, while fresh forces press for uniformity. The very nature of metropolitan life tends to weaken the family and all the institutions derivative from it. Our role in world affairs has paradoxically generated an intense longing for cultural homogeneity, a longing that imparts an altogether new, exclusive connotation to nationalism. Fear, in a period of hazardous changes, gives rise to the reluctance to tolerate dissent. The media of mass communication assume forms which leave no room for the self-expression of small groups; compare the necessary audience of radio and movie with the twenty-thousand circulation of the very largest dailies a hundred years ago. All these developments place a premium on conformity, encourage the conception of an assimilating society that digests and obliterates the separate accents of distinctive groups in every aspect of social life.

What is most troubling in such sappings of the old structure of American institutional life is the effect upon the status of the individual in our society. For these trends coincide with mounting pressure by the state upon its citizens. Today the activities of the polity enter into every area of social existence. No man, in birth, marriage, or death, in education or the search for a livelihood, escapes its oversight and control. Whether this ubiquitous concern of government with the affairs of those governed be beneficent or not, it certainly alters the role of the individual in society.

For the state, particularly the democratic state, regards its members not as members of groups but as isolated, anonymous entities. Precisely to the extent that it abstains from granting privileges, from making distinctions, from recognizing inequalities in law or differences in status, it also assumes that its citizens are equal and alike. The whole tendency of government action is thus to create uniformity; and that tendency is immensely fortified by the fact that the state has now at its disposal the instruments of mass communication with their own intrinsic inclination to homogeneity. It is very likely, therefore, that the impulse toward conformity which seemed, for a time, a war phenomenon may instead be the outcome of deeper, more permanent trends.

In the totalitarian society, the issue is clear-cut: everything the state does is hostile to the individual, who must resist to preserve his elementary human dignity. But our society still cherishes the nonconformist, still recognizes the right to be different, indeed insists that there is a high social value to diversity. Furthermore, in a democracy the state that threatens to crush the individual is also the instrument of his preservation, and in many areas is alone capable of furnishing services that enhance his human dignity.

The problem of man in a democracy is therefore one of setting limits, of resisting encroachments upon the free personality without weakening the capacity of the state to act constructively on behalf of its citizens. Undoubtedly the extent to which associations independent of the state continue to have vitality in American life will play a part in setting the limits and determining the scope of state action.

These fundamental developments will, among other things, determine the fate of the ethnic group, a group which discovers its identity and maintains its coherence on the basis of the inheritance of a common culture. Such groups have played an important part in our past, and an evaluation of that part may illuminate their future.

Understanding of the ethnic group has been distorted by the fact that it has most often been studied in its pathological features, in its relations to prejudice and discrimination. Some scholars indeed regard these groups as altogether the products of prejudice and having no existence except as a response to fear. Arnold and Caroline Rose thus argue in *America Divided:* "Certain groups . . . are hated by most other people, and we . . . label them 'minorities.'"

The use of the term "minority" in this context is itself misleading. The word was inappropriately borrowed from the discussions of European nationalism in the period of the First World War. But one could speak of a Ukrainian minority in Poland because one could point to a definable majority of Poles. In the United States, there is no ethnic majority. How can one properly speak of minorities?

Once we erase the implications of the term "minority," it becomes clear that, while some ethnic groups are discriminated against, there is no necessary connection between prejudice and the existence of the ethnic group. Groups which are now subjected to prejudice were not always in that position. Some existed and led full lives as groups for long periods before the onset of prejudice. There were, for instance, no significant manifestations of anti-Semitism in the United States before 1870, perhaps not really before 1910. Yet even by the earlier date, the whole range of communal institutions, the ways of communal action, the sense of identity as an ethnic group, were already strong.

The case of the Italians in America was similar. Virulent feelings of hostility toward these people developed and occasionally broke out in violent mob action in the quarter-century after 1880. But until that time the group flourished and enjoyed a rather high social status. Such illustrations demonstrate that the awareness of group identity is not simply a response to prejudice but rather arises from other reasons independent of it.

The same conclusion emerges from the history of other ethnic groups that have outlived the prejudice once directed against them. The Quakers, at one time bitterly persecuted in America, by the 18th century had been fully accepted and were highly regarded. Yet they continued to act as an ethnic group. They avoided marriage outside their own group; distinctive religious and cultural forms, even distinctive manners of dress, separated them from their neighbors; and they showed a striking degree of economic stratification. Furthermore, the Quakers did not hesitate to take a stand as a group on controversial social and political issues. In many parts of the country, these features of Quaker life still persist. But they do not seem to evoke, do not seem at all related to, prejudice, even in periods of war when Quaker pacifism leaves this group particularly vulnerable as a target. Clearly it is not prejudice that holds the Quakers together but some positive common tie.

Some groups have long retained their identity without having had any experience of prejudice. Thus as New England's Yankees spread through America in the 19th century, they behaved very much like immigrants from abroad: wherever they went, they formed their own churches, their own political associations, and such spontaneous organizations as the New England Societies that played significant social roles until quite recently.

As a matter of fact it would appear that some small ethnic groups, far from being subjected to prejudice, actually occupied favored positions in their communities—for instance, the "Brahmins" in Boston and the Dutch in early 19th-century New York. The relationship of the ethnic group to prejudice could take any one of a number of forms or not exist at all. There was no necessary connection.

The activities of ethnic groups, as of other associations, have however occasionally become the objects of hostile movements of some intensity. The history of the United States is dotted with eras of inter-group tensions, eras marked by the growth of intolerance, by sporadic disorders, and by discriminatory political action. But it is significant that these movements did not, until our own times, question the right of the group to exist or to act; they objected rather to some trespass, real or fancied, that seemed to go beyond the legitimate bounds of group action.

The most prevalent objection has been to any kind of secrecy. The suspicion that beneath an innocent surface was a sinister purpose cloaked by secrecy has always aroused violent distrust among Americans. This was true with regard not only to groups of immigrants, but also to associations of the native born. It accounts, in part, for the early hostility to labor unions. It also accounts for the bitter campaign a hundred and fifty years ago against the eminently respectable Society of the Cincinnati. And, after 1828, it produced a decade of merciless political warfare against the Masonic societies. Underlying all these movements was the conviction that legitimate associational activities could be carried on in the public gaze, that secrecy was *prima facie* evidence of illegitimate intent.

A second common objection has been to foreign ties that carried the imputation of disloyalty. Americans for generations judged that there was an inherent contradiction between the principles of their society and those of the societies of Europe, and they were always vigilant lest the Old World somehow attack the New. Groups of any kind, the first loyalty of which lay across the Atlantic, by that fact alone became the objects of distrust. This was the source of the attacks upon the Jacobin societies of the 1790's. More generally, it has been at the root of the recurrent tides of anti-Catholic sentiment in the past century. The center of the Ku Klux Klan movement in the 1920's was in the same districts of the Middle West that had been instrumental in rejecting the League of Nations and that became the core of isolationism in the 1930's. Fear of possible treachery also accounts for the paradoxical simultaneous attacks on the Wall Street Bankers and the Socialist Reds, alike tainted by European connections.

Allied to objections to the secret and the "foreign," was the objection to any form of extra-legal coercion. While the effort to prohibit by law associations that depended upon binding oaths was not successful, they were persistently distrusted. Some of the fear of the Roman Catholic Church also derived from lurid suspicions as to the function of confession and the nature of the discipline that bound its clergy. These fears rested on the assumption that associations ought to hold together simply by the will of their members without the support of any form of sanction.

Finally, against ethnic as against other groups, was directed the suspicion of exclusiveness or special privilege. There was a dislike of any imputation that some individuals, by being situated in a favored group, escaped some of the burdens or enjoyed more of the privileges of Americans.

These various grounds of objection form a consistent pattern that limits ethnic group action. Resentment aims at the aspects of conspiracy, of unacknowledged objectives which may not be compatible with those of the whole society. Fear rises at the thought of an *imperium in imperio,* a government within a government, using hidden means of its own for coercion. Hostility is directed at the Pope, at the Elders of Zion, at the International Reds who would subvert the principles of free society in the United States.

The delimitation of these objections reveals, however, that there is an area of free association within which groups may act as such. If the individual retains his freedom of access and resignation, if the aims and actions of the group are open and above-board, it has a recognized place in American life, a recognized function to serve.

The existence of the ethnic group is then not a pathological response to prejudice, but the reaction of men of diverse cultural origins to a free society that encouraged their diversity. The characteristic attributes of the ethnic group and its function in society must be considered from that point of view.

Membership in the ethnic group comes through the family by which the group's culture is transmitted. There is, therefore, in all these groups a strong sense of family feeling, concern with ancestry and traditional inheritance. In the fact that each generation brings up its children under similar conditions is the source of the community of culture and ideology that distinguishes these groups. The influence of upbringing also accounts for a certain amount of occupational stratification. Sons have an advantage in following the callings of their fathers, and, with regard to occupational preferences, tend to absorb the values of their surroundings. To the extent that these values are common to the whole group, there is an inclination to concentrate in certain occupations.

Familial ties and common cultural, economic, social, and intellectual attitudes, lead the group into a wide array of associational activities which express its awareness of its own identity. The variety of sects that is characteristic of American religion springs from such ethnic roots rather than from theological differences. A sense of inner responsibility for the group has produced innumerable charitable institutions. Like traditions give rise to cultural associations, and the desire for comradeship leads to purely social and fraternal societies.

Common ideology and common interests sometimes encourage concerted political action as well. Most usually the group is moved to exert itself in matters of particular moment to its own members. But the ethnic group has by no means confined itself to such matters; often its most significant activity has been in areas of very general concern. Thus New Englanders in the last half of the 19th century were responsible for the agitation of the prohibition issue in the Middle West, and a German political convention in the heart of Texas did not hesitate, shortly before the Civil War, to proclaim slavery an evil and to demand its immediate abolition.

Ethnic institutions, once organized, acquire a vitality of their own and tend to attach members in some degree of closeness to the ethnic group. Since such associations are also a selective element in determining the contacts and limiting the acquaintances of the members of the group, they produce a tendency toward endogamy, not because of any abstract attitudes toward intermarriage, but because marriages are likely to be most numerous where the highest rate of contact exists.

In the past, these ethnic groupings have served a significant function. They have eased the situation of great masses of men and have helped them adjust to the violent changes of our society in the last hundred years. *Vereine* of immigrants and hereditary societies of New Englanders alike provided a milieu in which individuals, in some of their actions, were relieved of the necessity of getting on with strangers. Such groups set up little islands of security in which the like-minded could find relief from the ceaseless tension of the surrounding world. The existence of these islands of security reduced the frequency of trouble-breeding contacts with strangers and made it possible to have diversity without disrupting the social fabric, to have unity without imposing an artificial uniformity. It was this that Fredrika Bremer had in mind when she noted: "Free association is evidently an organizing and conservative principle of life, called forth to give law and centralization to the floating atoms, to the disintegrated elements. The United States thus provides at the same time for the highest development of the individual and of the community at large."

The absence of a full institutional life among ethnic groups not free to develop their own associations seriously impeded their adjustment. The Negroes were distinctive in this respect. The relics of their slave status, combined with the romantic assumption of the abolitionists that there were no real differences between the Negroes and other Americans, long deprived this group of the opportunity to build a life of its own. The failure to distinguish between uniformity and equality left it with a truncated social experience. The Negroes confronted an unreal alternative between complete segregation, on the one hand, and participation, usually at an inferior status, in "white" activities. It is significant that the autonomous churches which developed spontaneously from within the group provided until recently the most genuine media of social action for the great mass of American Negroes.

The problem of the role of ethnic groups was small in our consciousness until the 1930's because the stream of immigration until then automatically kept redefining their nature. The end of immigration has complicated the situation. Americans have not in these two decades grown less varied, but the source of their diversity is no longer the addition of large numbers of overseas newcomers. Differences are now more likely to spring from internal sources, from the recollection of dissimilar religious and cultural experiences, for instance. That is why so many Americans now face the problem of explaining to themselves the quality of their ethnic allegiances.

Certain general factors are already apparent. Not all ethnic groups cover the same ground. Some are far more inclusive in the range of their associational activities than others. Whether a group will support its own press, its own schools, churches, and hospitals, depends on the breadth of the meaningful differences it wishes to maintain. There is no reason why that breadth should be the same for all groups.

Furthermore, we are likely to see considerable fluidity in the structure of these groups in the future. With the disappearance of the most visible sources of identification—accent, name, manners—the strength of compulsory allegiances will wane. Few men will by reason of any overt marks find themselves forced into a group against their wills. In the future, identification with the ethnic group, even in the case of the Negroes, is far more likely to be voluntary, to represent the conscious recognition of the strength of some cultural ties.

Finally, it is likely that in the future individuals may often recognize affiliations with more than one ethnic group. In the 19th century, for example, there were immigrants who participated in both Jewish and German societies, who felt a closeness to both traditions. But often the claim to such multiple allegiances was merely the prerogative of politicians who searched their genealogies for vote-getting grandmothers. Now, however, a rising rate of intermarriage will undoubtedly make that kind of affiliation more common.

These changes may alter some aspects of the behavior of the ethnic group. But they are not likely to diminish its vitality or to curtail its associational activities. In man's present situation this is one of the surviving signs of his individuality, of his significance as a person. Here he may find the affirmation that he is not simply the anonymous citizen, a serial number on a dog tag or social security card, but the son of parents, with roots in the past, with a meaning larger than his own life. The islands of security the group can provide may in that sense be more necessary now than ever.

The variety and vitality of associational activity after 1900 distressed the advocates of a narrow one hundred per cent Americanism. Yet, granted the diversity of the American people, it was sense-less to expect that they should all be served in the same way. Those who objected to "ghettos" in American life, who demanded thorough assimilation, ultimately, therefore, became advocates of immigration restriction and went along the racist road of the Klan . . .

We have seen the terminus of that road in the *Gleichschaltung* of the totalitarian state. Having rejected that, we must accept the consequences of its alternative. As long as the individual retains the right to be different, he will follow the inclinations of his upbringing and find attractive the society of those like himself. Variety of association will continue to reflect variety of people.

Does this analysis apply to the Jews? Substantial groups of American Jews deny its relevance to their own experience. From two disparate sources come earnest objections that the Jews are not an ethnic group. Those who think of themselves as members of a religious community with interests confined to creedal matters will complain that the Jews are not so much as an ethnic group. Those who think of themselves as members of a national entity of some sort will complain that the Jews are not so little as an ethnic group. Both objections reveal an unwillingness to look at the substance of Jewish existence in the United States.

The insistence that the Jews constitute simply a religious sect is unrealistic in view of the fact that the organized aspects of all religious life in America revolve about an ethnic rather than a dogmatic axis. The most significant differentiation among Christians in the United States is that between Protestant and Catholics. Yet Unitarians and Episcopalians are both counted Protestants and find themselves closely linked in the social life of their communities, not because they are theologically closer to each other than they are to the Roman Catholics, but because they number the same kind of people among their communicants, because they share a wide common culture, and because their children frequently intermarry.

The same judgment may be made of the Jews. It would be futile to seek among them any creedal common denominator. Many Jews are identified as such with no reference to their religious beliefs and many Jewish activities have no religious focus at all.

The nationalistic conception rests on the argument of uniqueness: the experience of the Jews in the United States, it is urged, has not been like that of other groups. Significantly, that very claim is characteristic of all ethnic groups; each is proud of its uniqueness. No two groups, of course, are the same; in that sense each is unique. But the social experience of the Jews in America has run the same essential course as that of other ethnic groups; the development of religion, of fraternal, charitable, and cultural life, even of national-istic movements, demonstrates that.

The claim to uniqueness is invalid. It is also dangerous. For it is, in reverse, the charge of the American anti-Semite. Only those Jews who regard their life in America as temporary and conditional can seriously continue to put it forth. It would seem that the only basis on which the Jews may continue to lead their lives as a group and still partake of the life of American society as a whole is, as it was in the past, as one among the many ethnic groups of which our society is compounded.

In these terms, there is ample room for group activity wherever common interests dictate. Jews will in the future, as they and others have in the past, follow the inclination of their culture, tradition, and training in religion, in social action, and in politics. So long as their activities, in any sphere, do not bear the aspects of compulsion or conspiracy, other Americans will see in them only the continuation of a traditional means of American expression.

28 TECHNIQUES OF RACE RELATIONS *

BY DONALD YOUNG (1898–   )
RUSSELL SAGE FOUNDATION

MOST Negro and white Americans who object to the prevailing patterns of race relations express concern about existing and impending evils, but seem only casually interested in the practical details of procedures by which changes might be brought about. It is natural that there should be disagreement about immediate objec-tives and ultimate goals and that differences of opinion about the comparative merits of the possible strategic approaches to desired

* Reprinted by permission of the author and of the editor from *Proceedings of the American Philosophical Society*, XCI (1947), 150–161; pp. 150–151, 154–161 reproduced.

changes should persist. On these questions personal judgment will continue to determine individual opinions, for they necessarily depend on what people want and the price they are willing to pay. Granted that unanimity on these questions does not exist, it still seems that individuals of any view would want to know about practical means of influencing racial attitudes and behavior.

The accomplishments of any group desirous of altering interracial behavior will be far below the level of potentiality unless the details of race relations techniques are understood and tactically well used. When a group, perhaps a mayor's committee on race relations, a labor union, a race improvement association or a government agency concerned with the Negro, has decided on its goal and appropriate strategy, the effectiveness of its program is still dependent on materials, tools, and craftsmanship. Assuming, for example, that the officials of a labor union want to reduce Negro-white hostility within their local, what should they do? How much can they rely on particular kinds of argument, union regulation, cooperative measures by the management, experimental demonstration, interracial education, and various possible penalties and rewards? What measures have been tried elsewhere and with what success? If one puts oneself in the place of an official charged with planning and operating a program for a definite interracial purpose, the specificity of the problems and the need for technical knowledge and skill become evident. Thousands of public and private officials today have just such responsibility, and they are operating mainly by hunch and homemade rule of thumb with only random, unorganized information about the experiences of others in similar situations.

Dependence on untested preconceptions of the ways in which attitudes and behavior may be changed and failure to check on the effectiveness of their operations are characteristic of those who are working to reduce interracial hostility and conflict. Because the trend of Negro-white relations in the United States consistently has been toward improvement of the Negro's status, it has been possible to claim uncritically that this improvement is evidence of the efficiency of any and all pertinent programs. The reduction in the number of Negro deaths by lynching is probably only slightly related to purposeful activities by racial reformers, and certainly it is impossible to measure the influence of any one reform organization on the number of lynchings, yet its reduction has been cited as evidence of the effectiveness of interracial work. Similarly, wider employment opportunities for Negroes offer convenient if specious reassurance that the time and money spent to remove racial barriers in industry have not been poorly used. These two illustrations should not convey the impression that organizations for the improvement of race relations have been ineffectual, for their accomplishments more than justify their existence. Because they have been moving with the social current, however, it is difficult to tell what parts of their programs have really aided the progress made. Some parts may even have been retarding in their influence.

The practitioners' dependence on their own preconceptions is partly the fault of the social scientists. It is logically their function to find out why people behave as they do in specific racial situations, to formulate principles underlying such behavior so that they may be applied in developing means for its control, and to measure the effectiveness of the procedures used in attempts to modify interracial behavior patterns. This, however, is not what most social scientists interested in race relations have been doing; for the most part they have been busy describing racial situations, generalizing broadly on occasion, nearly always deploring inequities and commonly identifying themselves with reformatory programs to which their scholarly work usually has contributed little more than raw data illustrative of intergroup injustice. The standard studies of lynching, for example, suggest greater concern with the moral issue involved than with scientific understanding of this form of coercive mob behavior. But criticism of social scientists for not being scientific in this area should recognize that all the fields of knowledge which are now at a more advanced level have developed from somewhat similar but now outmoded beginnings. The early humanitarian emphasis on the insane and feebleminded in the study of mental qualities is comparable. Research in any area of human behavior seems necessarily to receive its impetus from a pressing concern with a social problem which leads first to broad studies of its extent and general nature and thence to objective testing of specific hypotheses as details are clarified and methods improved.[1] . . .

During the war there was a heartening if quantitatively slight in-

[1] The interests and approaches of social scientists and other writers on race relations in recent years may be judged by consideration of the titles of books and articles listed in the selected bibliography prepared by Julia Waxman, *Race relations* (Chicago: Julius Rosenwald Fund, 1945).

crease in the production of technical guides for executives, admin-
istrators, teachers, and others faced with problems of race. One of
the first and best was a pamphlet prepared by an economist, John A.
Davis, to explain to employers specific procedures for introducing
minority workers into new jobs.[2] An anthropologist and a specialist
in police administration collaborated in the preparation of a manual
on police techniques for preventing riots and improving relations
between different racial, religious, and nationality groups.[3] The War
Department prepared a manual on leadership of Negro soldiers designed to give officers the best available information on practical
procedures. Sociologists, psychologists, anthropologists and others
experienced in race relations as well as professional military men
contributed to this publication.[4] The Navy Department also issued
a technical guide on Negro-white relations for the use of all Naval
officers.[5] The Bureau for Intercultural Education has sponsored a
number of publications giving detailed advice on ways of reducing
interracial intolerance; included in an extensive series of teachers'
aids are a volume on the educational development of cultural democracy,[6] and one on the controlling factors in race prejudice.[7] A
yearbook published by the Department of Supervisors and Directors
of Instruction of the National Education Association contains an
excellent chapter of specific suggestions for the implementation of
programs in intercultural education.[8] Labor groups are showing increasing awareness of the need for practical guides for the use of
their members in programs for intergroup cooperation.[9] Other guides
are addressed to community leaders and members of local organizations. The American Council on Race Relations has issued a book-

[2] John A. Davis, *How management can integrate Negroes in war industries* (New
York State War Council, Committee on Discrimination in Employment, 1942). A
well selected, brief bibliography is included.
[3] J. E. Weckler and Theo E. Hall, *The police and minority groups* (Chicago: The
International City Manager's Association, 1944).
[4] *Leadership and the Negro soldier* (Army Service Forces Manual M5, 1944).
[5] *Guide to command of Negro Naval personnel* (Navy Department, Bureau of
Naval Personnel, 1944).
[6] William E. Vickery and Stewart G. Cole, *Intercultural education in American
schools* (New York: Harper & Brothers, 1943).
[7] Hortense Powdermaker, *Probing our prejudices* (New York: Harper & Brothers,
1944).
[8] Marion Edman, "The Role of the Instructional Leader," chap. XXIV in *Americans all: Studies in intercultural education,* 301–306 (Washington, 1942).
[9] For example, see Theresa Wolfson et al., *Overcoming prejudice* (New York:
American Labor Education Service, 1946).

let [10] designed to help communities examine and solve their own intergroup problems. In the belief that scattered individual efforts could be made more effective by technical assistance, the Writers' War Board early in 1945 distributed a kit containing five speeches, a quiz, a parody, and a pamphlet for use in promoting racial and religious tolerance through meetings, articles, radio speeches, or even letters to local newspapers. The campaign against anti-Semitism has been responsible for much of the rising interest in techniques of racial adjustment, and reference should be made to a resulting publication which explains the principles of "racial scapegoating" and suggests ways for counteracting it.[11] There are numerous other publications emphasizing definite things to do to prevent interracial conflict and to minimize its consequences when it does break out, but enough have been cited to exemplify a new and hopeful trend toward practicality in thinking on race relations.

One book which makes only passing reference to the Negro should be read by all concerned with Negro-white relations even though they deny the slightest interest in the minority on which it is based, American residents of Japanese origin. In *The Governing of Men,* Dr. Alexander H. Leighton, psychiatrist and anthropologist, tells the story of the relocation center at Poston, Arizona, and draws from his intensive study of this community principles of behavior and administrative recommendations which deserve the most thoughtful consideration by every person with any responsibility in Negro-white relations.[12] The results of the Poston study may not be wholly transferable to any other minority situation; in all likelihood they are not perfect even for Poston. The ultimate is hardly to be achieved in a path-breaking study. The point is that a painstaking attempt was made to find out what was going on in a minority community under great stress, what principles of human behavior were involved, and how desired objectives could best be achieved. The emphasis on techniques for the accomplishment of definite objectives is without parallel among the countless studies of the Negro in the United States.

It would be premature in our present state of knowledge to attempt a positive and inclusive statement of principles and methods for the guidance of workers in Negro-white relations. However, decisions

[10] Robert C. Weaver, *Community relations manual* (Chicago: American Council on Race Relations, Community Services Division, 1945).

[11] *A B C's of Scapegoating,* with a foreword by Gordon W. Allport (Chicago: Central YMCA College [n.d.; 1943 or 1944]).

[12] Alexander H. Leighton, *The Governing of Men* (Princeton Univ. Press, 1945).

on tactical details are having to be made daily not only by professional workers but also by public spirited citizens who feel obligated to make whatever contribution they may to national unity and by individuals in government and private business who realize that their normal activities involve interracial responsibilities. The laymen among them, at least, may be aided by an exposition of the most common sources of operative confusion.

One weakness of many interracial activities is failure to accept the principle that problems of race relations are essentially the same as any other problems of group relations. In spite of differences in detail, the principles and procedures which tend to reduce group hostilities and increase cooperation in the area of race are essentially the same as those which work in any other area of group conflict. Of course, the background and present status of the Negro American are in many respects unique, but the same is true of any other distinctive group in the population, such as the white sharecropper, the Mexican of the southwest, or the distressed coal miner of southern Illinois. The assumption that problems of Negro-white adjustment are somehow generically unique is practically certain to be fatal to cooperation since it implies belief in some kind of racial dogma which sets Negro and white apart from each other. National unity can hardly be achieved on such a premise.

Race improvement programs already recognized as outmoded illustrate the difficulties created by falling into the error of assuming that work with Negroes requires tactics of a special order. Until recently, it was almost universally believed that Negro health programs must take into account inborn susceptibilities of the Negro to a number of diseases, especially tuberculosis. It is now recognized that certain diseases are relatively prevalent among Negroes because of the way they live and that these diseases yield to the same health measures that are effective among the white population, with only such changes as are necessary to adapt them to any particular socio-economic group. Similarly, not so many years ago leading educators were convinced that Negro education either because of differential mental qualities or environmental limitations had to be of a special character, mainly that typified by the original Hampton-Tuskegee vocational idea; now it is accepted as a matter of course that Negro schooling should follow the general educational pattern, varying with the ability and opportunity of the individual, not his race. A third historical example is the attitude of resignation toward Negro morality and crime which was once so completely dominant that even many of the most kindly disposed white people assumed that little could be done beyond protective and paternalistic control of the most shocking derelictions. It is only relatively recently that we have discovered that the conditions which produce disease, illiteracy, and crime fundamentally are the same for Negroes as for others.

Among racial democrats any belief that inborn racial differences in mental ability and temperament have been demonstrated has been dissipated, but in its place there is an uneasy suspicion that Negroes as a race may have minor and practically undiscernible qualities which cannot be entirely ignored although they must never be mentioned in public. More open is the conviction that Negro behavior differs so much in degree from that of the assumed typical American that it might as well be considered a difference in kind. As many Negroes suspect, this may be partly an unconscious rationalization of suppressed belief in unproven biological differences, and partly a manifestation of guilt for the discriminations which have actually produced such differences as do exist. Whatever the origin, it shows up in a tendency to be apologetic for the Negro, defensive of his inadequacies and protective as of a child. For example, programs designed to enhance white appreciation of him most frequently emphasize not the accomplishments of a man earning his own way but racial specialties like the spirituals or ordinary achievements in the arts, sciences, and working world which would be worthy of exceptional mention only if the product of precocity.

No matter how well intended, such evidences of lack of confidence that Negro-white relations can follow ordinary human patterns are ruinous to any program for national unity. If cooperative interracial adjustment is the purpose of a radio script, an interracial meeting, an employment policy, a welfare program, or any other plan, it should be scrutinized microscopically to make certain that it takes Negroes for granted as normal human beings differing only in physical appearance and in some aspects of their cultural conditioning.

Acceptance of the concept of the unity of mankind has a corollary which seems equally obvious as a tactical principle but it is more often disregarded than heeded: Emphasis in education or in any kind of informative propaganda on Negro accomplishments popularly regarded as racially characteristic is an influence in the direction of differentiation and retards the process of integration. Such emphasis in its effect on popular attitudes if not in its logic contradicts the idea of unity and reinforces stereotypes which give support to doctrines of racism. No one doubts that the usual derogatory stereotypes of the Negro are a barrier to the improvement of his status. It is much less easy to understand that favorable stereotypes of the Negro as a born singer of spirituals and work songs, a natural creator of hot jazz and blues, a dancer endowed with a superior sense of rhythm or a superb athlete by racial inheritance also mark him as unique and help to maintain the cleavage between black and white. Such credits imply a biological theory of race differences just as surely as do unfavorable stereotypes, but this implication is too often overlooked. The cosmopolitan sophisticate can appreciate the folk contributions of Negroes, which are so constantly presented to the public to win friends and influence opinion, without drawing divisive inferences; but most white Americans accept such arts as gifts of a more primitive race and not as products of civilization. Many Negroes sense this differentiating inference and are disturbed by being put on display with their specialties. When the Negro has become secure in a better status his special cultural gifts to American life will no longer be a danger to him, but meanwhile they should be handled with care. There need not be complete avoidance of accomplishments characterized as Negro, but the current emphasis on them should be reduced and supplemented by greater stress on achievements of individual Negroes to which no racial tag can be attached.

Interracial tactics should be designed so that white people and Negroes may become increasingly used to each other under the normal circumstances of community life to the end that an individual's race will not be the focus of attention in any contact. Emphasis on the Negro as a Negro or on white people as white people works against this purpose. Notice of a Negro waiter, janitor, gardener, or other traditional service employee is only secondarily attracted to race, and so it should be with Negro stenographers, clerks, lawyers, businessmen, or public officials. Race relations can be eased as people get used to seeing Negroes in these capacities and in stores, hotels, parks, trains, and other public places, provided of course that the numbers are not overwhelming and that individuals conform to the customs of the locality in appearance and behavior.

It is possible and frequently relatively easy to introduce Negroes into new places and roles in such a way that the public will become accustomed to the change without serious incident. Negroes are widely employed in the postal service without public notice. Negro policemen and firemen are becoming increasingly common although it is not so long since such employment was generally thought daring. At the beginning of the war Negro Army officers attracted curious and uneasy stares on the street; a Texas enlisted man is said to have been court-martialed for trying to take the uniform off the first Negro officer he saw because he did not know that Negroes could be commissioned. There are sufficient numbers of schools in which Negroes instruct white pupils, hotels and restaurants which serve both Negroes and whites, businesses in which Negroes work with white fellow employees, stores which are patronized by members of both races, and so on, to demonstrate the practicality of increasing the areas of accustomed contacts. Both skill and luck, however, usually are needed in the introductory stage.

The Negroes who break the ice should be similar in personal traits and qualities to their new white associates, that is, they should be distinguishable only by color. The entry should be matter-of-fact without fanfare or apology. Preparatory announcement, debate, and stage setting should be kept at the minimum justified by advance estimates of possible difficulty. Once the first step has been taken, those in authority should be watchful for incidents which might grow in importance and respectfully firm with potential trouble makers. And the proportionate numbers of the minority can be a crucial factor. Of course, interracial situations have adjusted themselves smoothly when none of these precautions were observed, and trouble has arisen in spite of careful planning. The odds, however, are made more favorable by conscious effort to ease new interracial contacts until they become routine, always remembering that every situation has its own peculiarities and that one sure way of blocking Negro advance is to make it a crucial issue in the minds of the controlling white community.

Harping on conflict and mistreatment is another way of emphasizing racial cleavages. The right of Negroes to protest discrimination and the obligation of responsible citizens to fight injustice must be maintained, but fine judgment in tactics is required when defense measures threaten to cost more than they gain.[13] The constant pub-

[13] In the early years of the war the constant one-sided criticism of the War Department by the Negro press reinforced the conviction that stringent racial separation among troops was essential. Racial issues were made extra difficult to resolve by this punishment of officials. Later when the Negro press increased its rewards of praise for specific racial improvements the response in better relations and positive actions

licizing of general evidences of prejudice and of specific instances of racial inhumanity stimulates corrective action by some individuals but it also unconsciously reinforces the feeling in others that Negroes and whites are inevitably in separate camps.

Negro leaders might well give thought to the prevailing tactics in the battle against anti-Semitism which avoid newspaper trials in even flagrant cases of discrimination in favor of direct off the record protest to persons in a position to do something about it. Some of the so-called tolerance organizations with Jewish support have a tendency to fight more loudly against discriminatory treatment of non-Jewish minorities than of Jews. The argument that it is not entirely to the Negro's advantage to have a disproportionate share of the struggle against racial bigotry waged over his shoulder may not be without merit.

Protests must be made; the public cannot be encouraged to feel that all is sweetness and light on the Negro-white front; and it is to the advantage of those who are negotiating for racial advances to have a softening-up barrage of protests and threats fired ahead of them. Furthermore, the Negro does not yet have the financial and other resources necessary for a campaign similar to that against anti-Semitism. Pounding away with protests is the least expensive method of fighting at his command. The problem is one of fixing the point of diminishing returns—of determining the circumstances under which protests raise barriers between the races, increase the spirit of hostility in both groups or lose force through becoming too commonplace to be emotionally effective.

It is good technique to keep members of both races accurately informed about interracial questions. There is no better way to answer false assertions, kill tension-breeding rumors, and build a solid foundation for democratic action. This principle is generally accepted, but it is commonly misused because of fear that if the truth is not entirely laudatory of the Negro it may lead to greater prejudice. Also, because Negroes are sensitive and quick to infer insults from even the most objective statements at variance with their customary propaganda, racial liberals are reluctant to risk giving offense. The twisting or omitting of facts, exaggeration and plain prevarication in defensive arguments about race and crime, industrial skill, educational and scientific achievement, military accomplishment, literary and artistic

---

was promptly noticeable, even though criticisms continued to be freely printed when the editors thought they were deserved.

products, etc. are commonplace. But the unvarnished truth alone contradicts racial dogma, checks rumors, and in precluding specious rebuttal is more effective than the most kindly white lie. Unless the established facts are adhered to rigidly, and both weaknesses and strengths honestly included in interracial educational campaigns, the main results are likely to be a lack of public confidence and a weak foundation for action programs.

A second reason for the misuse of informational techniques in interracial activities is the aforementioned American faith that facts alone must modify attitudes in a uniform, predictable direction. This faith has made too many practitioners forget that varying and even opposite conclusions can be drawn from any set of data; for example, evidence of the Negro's industrial capacity may lead to the conclusion that he should be industrially integrated or that barriers should be erected to protect white men in their jobs, depending on the background, prejudices and personal motivations of the analyst.

Probably it has been necessary to reply at length and in detail to the racial nonsense of the pseudoscientists who did Hitler's work, but there is no justification for the complacency with which the public has been deluged with the negative evidence of research on race differences in ability, as a cure for the diseases of race prejudice. Just as men have long been able to compromise creed and practice, they are finding it possible to compromise conflicts between the facts of science and their personal preferences. Oral or written demonstrations of the lack of any known biological foundation for racist theories have their utility in counteracting false popular notions, but are not decisive in racial attitudes and practices.[14] Instruction in the psychological and social facts of everyday interracial behavior is much more practical.

It is always good tactics for members of both races to work in association on interracial questions. Any minority not crushed in spirit resents outside domination even for the best of purposes; and fewer mistakes will be made if there is free consultation and cooperation

[14] For example, it is commonplace knowledge even among racists that no unmixed *race* of humans now exists in the biological meaning of the word, i.e., a group of people with common physical characteristics because of common ancestry. Yet they continue to be racists because no matter what biological nonsense they prate, they are really concerned with groups which have socio-psychological if not ancestral reality. Science can destroy racist theories with ease, but racism persists because it neither originated from nor ever has been dependent upon the results of scientific study.

between the races in any project of mutual concern. Neither group admits any particular objection to this practice, but inter-group participation frequently appears grudging and superficial, as if it were more a gesture than a sincere effort made with confidence that good would come of it. Probably the main reason there is not more and better cooperation is that it is so hard to find the right people of whom to ask assistance and advice.

White interracial workers have a spotty record in their choice of Negro consultants and associates. In the first place, there are as few Negroes as whites with recognized wisdom and skill in race relations who do not have personal axes to grind. Second, those Negroes who make a profession or a hobby out of guiding white men's interracial thoughts and dollars are well known, ever-present, and not easily avoided. Although their customarily cautious advice is usually safe, it is also generally orthodox to the point of stagnation. A third difficulty is that Negro aid which will not be troublesome is often what is wanted. Above all, white people probably make their greatest mistakes in choosing Negro associates because of a naive faith that all Negroes are expert in matters of race. The simple rule that works best when seeking aid in an unfamiliar group is to think through the qualities and skills needed and then search for the person who meets the requirements, just as one would in filling a vacancy in any business. Both white and colored individuals with something to contribute . . . can always be found if they are honestly sought.

Negroes seem more sophisticated in their selection of white associates. They know what they want from the white man, and it is usually not advice or interracial skill but the advantages afforded by money, prestige, and power. These are rare commodities among Negroes and largely have to be imported from across the racial line. While Negroes on the whole are not unwilling to accept white cooperation in efforts to improve their status, they are doubtful about the possibility of getting much help and seem to prefer to carry on alone. White staff members are not wanted in Negro improvement organizations although boards of directors may be racially mixed and funds secured mainly from white sources.[15] This tendency reflects many things: a natural clannishness, suspicion of white sincerity, desire to avoid embarrassing situations, an understandable attempt to protect the professional jobs which are open to Negroes, and an urge

[15] The March on Washington movement advertised that contributions from white people would not be accepted.

on the part of Negroes to control as much of their own destiny as possible. It would seem tactically wiser to encourage the identification of white liberals with all movements for the improvement of Negro-white relations, strictly on the basis of individual qualifications.

The white tendency to regard all Negroes as expert in race relations and as morally obligated to exhibit racial altruism is productive of indignation and discouraging disillusionment when contrary behavior is observed. In Negro-white cooperation for a common democratic purpose, disillusionment can be avoided only if members of both races assume that their fellows of another color are only human. There is no more reason to expect Negroes to be omniscient and socially minded than to condemn white individuals unheard as ignorant bigots. Similarly, there is no more justification for uncritical acceptance of advice on interracial tactics from a Negro source than there is for rejecting suggestions of white origin. Interracial discussions, however, are now dominated by a tacit rule that Negroes know best how to meet the difficulties against which they protest and may not be openly disputed by a white man without raising suspicion of reactionism—a rule reminiscent of the white southerner's claim that he alone knows how to handle the Negro. Interracial cooperation in the improvement of race relations will continue at a low level of efficiency until the participants come much closer to accepting each other on the basis of individual knowledge and experience.

Finally, the most elementary tactical principle of all is that organized, coordinated action is the most effective form of operation. The more agencies there are working for the adjustment of race relations the better the chance of success for all, provided that they know about each other's activities and cooperate in their common purposes. It is not necessary and probably not desirable that all similar agencies, such as those working through the schools or those fighting for civil rights, be welded into one national body. Constant clearing of information, consideration of the possibilities of mutual supplementation and support, and strict avoidance of interagency sniping constitute about all the coordination that is essential. In the educational field, for example, it is all to the good that three national agencies—the American Council on Education, the National Education Association, and the Bureau for Intercultural Education—all work in the interracial field, so long as they remain alert to the dangers of competition and take advantage of opportunities for cooperation as they arise. And these three agencies at the national level each have been able to work with innumerable less extensive agencies where good will prevailed, without any compulsive element in the relationship. The American preference for voluntary, loose association of agencies engaged in a common cause holds in race relations, as elsewhere, and is no handicap to coordination of programs if professional jealousies can be subordinated.

The need for interagency coordination cannot be fulfilled without business-like intra-agency organization. Every activity should be carefully examined periodically to see that the results are satisfactory and in proportion to the cost. It should not be assumed that any well intentioned plan is working as hoped. In any proposed undertaking the first question should always be whether similar work has been done previously and if so, with what techniques and what results. Usually all that can be determined is that scattered precedents exist and that there are many practically unsupported testimonials and some criticisms regarding each. Because of the uncertainty about the effectiveness of interracial techniques, discussed in the first part of this paper, there is exceptional need for controlled experimentation before embarking on full-scale operations and for definite provisions for gauging the results of all projects.

Racial democrats cannot afford to trust to good hearts and good luck. Their opponents, the nativists and racialists, know what they want and they know the strategies and tactics most useful in accomplishing their purposes. They know the value of organization and the futility of wasting time in criticism of others who are on their side even though they may be ultimate competitors for the spoils. Severe national crises in the United States always have been followed by a surge of racialism whose advocates had the advantage of relatively unorganized opposition. It is true that such groups ultimately lost their influence, as in the cases of the Know-Nothing Party of the 1850's, the American Protective Association of the last part of the nineteenth century, and the modern Ku Klux Klan; but credit for their belated defeat is to be ascribed to the general social trend rather than to any purposeful attack by liberal elements. For the first time in American history there is now a chance that following a national crisis the forces of racial liberalism will be reasonably well organized in support of a composite program under which a multitude of private and governmental agencies will be working by varied approaches and techniques for essentially identical purposes.

This favorable position of the liberals is attributable largely to the great role of conflicting racial ideologies in World War II, and to the fact that the dangers of rising anti-Semitism spurred the most sophisticated and advantageously situated minority in this country into the best financed and best organized campaign for minority civil rights the nation ever has known. General recognition by minority leaders in recent years that from a purely selfish point of view no one minority can afford to be unmindful of the rights of any other has also advanced the Negro cause. But Negroes themselves and their co-workers for the improvement of Negro status are giving evidence of an increasingly practical and cooperative spirit.

During World War II two conferences were held in the South which were indicative of a trend toward a rational united front among racial liberals which has significant potentialities. A group of southern Negro leaders met in Durham, North Carolina, in October, 1942, to prepare a statement which could serve as "a basis for interracial cooperation and development in the South." The conferees were from varied ideological camps, yet they reached agreement on a clear statement of the racial issues in the war, in political and civil rights, industry and labor, agriculture, education, military service, and social welfare and health. There was a minimum of emphasis on emotionalized shibboleths and a maximum of attention to specific goals. At the very least, a basis for practical . . . action was laid.

In April of the following year a group of southern white liberal leaders met in Atlanta, Georgia, to consider the Durham statement, which they found "so frank and courageous, so free from any suggestion of threat and ultimatum" and so indicative of good will that cooperation was gladly offered. The statement resulting from the Atlanta conference did not attempt to parallel the Durham statement but suggested that there were some differences of opinion, expressed agreement on certain issues and reached this conclusion: "It is futile to imagine or to assert that the problem will solve itself. The need is for a positive program arrived at in an atmosphere of understanding, cooperation, and a mutual respect." [16] The Southern Regional Council with headquarters in Atlanta is a war-born agency which functions in accordance with the philosophy of the Durham and Atlanta statements.

[16] For the full text of the Atlanta and Durham statements, see C. S. Johnson and Associates, *To Stem This Tide,* Appendices I and II (Boston and Chicago: The Pilgrim Press, 1942).

The American Council on Race Relations, organized in 1944 with its main office in Chicago, "aims at the progressive elimination of discriminatory practices which breed racial tension" by helping local communities in their own efforts to solve interracial problems in cooperation with existing local and national agencies. While this organization is primarily concerned with Negro-white relations, it recognizes the common elements in discrimination against all minorities and in spite of limited facilities already has been active in situations involving groups of Japanese and of Mexican origin. It assumes that Negro-white relations are not independent of a community's other racial attitudes and behavior, and that all interracial agencies have basically similar objectives and can profit by a maximum of cooperation. It is the first national agency created to serve as a clearing house for interracial experience and technical knowledge, supplying materials and skilled workers on request insofar as its facilities permit, and assisting other agencies to coordinate their work with a minimum of duplication or conflict.

The Southern Regional Council and the American Council on Race Relations are not nearly adequate for the tasks which face them, even in conjunction with the many agencies with more restricted programs whose work they supplement. These Councils are woefully short of money, personnel, and materials; their policies and techniques are far from perfect; and they have yet to receive a full measure of cooperation from the organizations and individuals who are seeking the same ends by different paths. With all their limitations, however, these two agencies are performing functions previously allowed to go by default and they indicate that racial liberals are beginning to want to be as well organized and as practical in their work as the situation demands. What will happen after the war depends to no small degree on the development and support of these two Councils.

Unfortunately there are signs which suggest that the rational, organized approach to race relations may be overwhelmed by disagreements, suspicions, prejudice, and conflicts among those who are alike in wanting progress toward racial democracy. Perhaps the most portentous of these signs is the evidence that many professional liberals are intolerant of all who do not see eye to eye with them. Never before has it been possible for Negro Americans and those concerned with their welfare to speak so frankly and protest discriminations so violently, with so little fear of public disapproval and so much psychological reward as has been the case in the past few years. In the exercise of this new-found freedom there is a carelessness of the freedom of others.

Respect for the integrity of others is the obligation of those who demand full status for themselves. It is dangerous enough to democracy to demand, as so many advocates of individual freedom now do, that advocates of racist dogma should be hunted down and prevented by force from presenting their views. To refuse to give full freedom and respect to fellow liberals who differ in their concept of liberalism is fatal to the common cause both because it sanctions a pattern of repression and because it divides natural allies who need each other's support. It is to be devoutly hoped that those who fight intolerance will themselves have tolerance enough to work together.

SECTION SIX
Social Class

29 SOCIAL CLASS IN AMERICA *

BY W. LLOYD WARNER (1898–   )
UNIVERSITY OF CHICAGO
MARCHIA MEEKER (1916–   )
ILLINOIS INSTITUTE OF TECHNOLOGY
AND KENNETH EELLS (1913–   )
SAN DIEGO STATE COLLEGE

CLASS AMONG THE NEW ENGLAND YANKEES

STUDIES of communities in New England clearly demonstrate the presence of a well-defined social-class system.[1] At the top is an aristocracy of birth and wealth. This is the so-called "old family" class. The people of Yankee City say the families who belong to it have been in the community for a long time—for at least three generations and preferably many generations more than three. "Old family" means not only old to the community but old to the class. Present members of the class were born into it; the families into which they were born can trace their lineage through many generations participating in a way of life characteristic of the upper class back to a generation marking the lowly beginnings out of which their family came. Although the men of this level are occupied gainfully, usually as large merchants, financiers, or in the higher professions, the wealth of the family, inherited from the husband's or the wife's side, and often from both, has been in the family for a long time. Ideally, it should stem from the sea trade when Yankee City's merchants and sea captains made large fortunes, built great Georgian houses on elm-lined Hill Street, and filled their houses and gardens with the proper symbols of their high position. They became the 400, the Brahmins, the Hill Streeters to whom others looked up; and they, well-mannered or not, looked down on the rest. They counted themselves, and were so counted, equals of similar levels in Salem,

---

* Reprinted by permission of the authors and of the publishers from *Social Class in America: A Manual of Procedure for the Measurement of Social Status* (Chicago: Science Research Associates, 1949), pp. 11–24.

[1] See chap. xv [in Warner, Meeker, and Eells, *Social Class in America*] for a description of the several volumes of "Yankee City Series." New and poorly organized towns sometimes have class systems which have no old-family (upper-upper) class.

Boston, Providence, and other New England cities. Their sons and daughters married into the old families from these towns and at times, when family fortune was low or love was great, they married wealthy sons and daughters from the newly rich who occupied the class level below them. This was a happy event for the fathers and mothers of such fortunate young people in the lower half of the upper class, an event well publicized and sometimes not too discreetly bragged about by the parents of the lower-upper-class children, an occasion to be explained by the mothers from the old families in terms of the spiritual demands of romantic love and by their friends as "a good deal and a fair exchange all the way around for everyone concerned."

The new families, the lower level of the upper class, came up through the new industries—shoes, textiles, silverware—and finance. Their fathers were some of the men who established New England's trading and financial dominance throughout America. When New York's Wall Street rose to power, many of them transferred their activities to this new center of dominance. Except that they aspire to old-family status, if not for themselves then for their children, these men and their families have a design for living similar to the old-family group. But they are consciously aware that their money is too new and too recently earned to have the sacrosanct quality of wealth inherited from a long line of ancestors. They know, as do those about them, that, while a certain amount of wealth is necessary, birth and old family are what really matter. Each of them can cite critical cases to prove that particular individuals have no money at all, yet belong to the top class because they have the right lineage and right name. While they recognize the worth and importance of birth, they feel that somehow their family's achievements should be better rewarded than by a mere second place in relation to those who need do little more than be born and stay alive.

The presence of an old-family class in a community forces the newly rich to wait their turn if they aspire to "higher things." Meanwhile, they must learn how to act, fill their lives with good deeds, spend their money on approved philanthropy, and reduce their arrogance to manageable proportions.

The families of the upper and lower strata of the upper classes are organized into social cliques and exclusive clubs. The men gather fortnightly in dining clubs where they discuss matters that concern them. The women belong to small clubs or to the Garden Club and give their interest to subjects which symbolize their high status and evoke those sentiments necessary in each individual if the class is to maintain itself. Both sexes join philanthropic organizations whose good deeds are an asset to the community and an expression of the dominance and importance of the top class to those socially beneath them. They are the members of the Episcopalian and Unitarian and, occasionally, the Congregational and Presbyterian churches.

Below them are the members of the solid, highly respectable upper-middle class, the people who get things done and provide the active front in civic affairs for the classes above them. They aspire to the classes above and hope their good deeds, civic activities, and high moral principles will somehow be recognized far beyond the usual pat on the back and that they will be invited by those above them into the intimacies of upper-class cliques and exclusive clubs. Such recognition might increase their status and would be likely to make them members of the lower-upper group. The fact that this rarely happens seldom stops members of this level, once activated, from continuing to try. The men tend to be owners of stores and belong to the large proprietor and professional levels. Their incomes average less than those of the lower-upper class, this latter group having a larger income than any other group, including the old-family level.

These three strata, the two upper classes and the upper-middle, constitute the levels above the Common Man. There is a considerable distance socially between them and the mass of the people immediately below them. They comprise three of the six classes present in the community. Although in number of levels they constitute half the community, in population they have no more than a sixth, and sometimes less, of the Common Man's population. The three levels combined include approximately 13 per cent of the total population.

The lower-middle class, the top of the Common Man level, is composed of clerks and other white-collar workers, small tradesmen, and a fraction of skilled workers. Their small houses fill "the side streets" down from Hill Street, where the upper classes and some of the upper-middle live, and are noticeably absent from the better suburbs where the upper-middle concentrate. "Side Streeter" is a term often used by those above them to imply an inferior way of life and an inconsequential status. They have accumulated little property but are frequently home owners. Some of the more successful members of ethnic groups, such as the Italians, Irish, French-Canadians, have reached this level. Only a few members of these cultural minorities have gone beyond it; none of them has reached the old-family level.

The old-family class (upper-upper) is smaller in size than the new-family class (lower-upper) below them. It has 1.4 per cent, while the lower-upper class has 1.6 per cent, of the total population. Ten per cent of the population belongs to the upper-middle class, and 28 per cent to the lower-middle level. The upper-lower is the most populous class, with 34 per cent, and the lower-lower has 25 per cent of all the people in the town.

The prospects of the upper-middle-class children for higher education are not as good as those of the classes above. One hundred per cent of the children of the two upper classes take courses in the local high school that prepare them for college, and 88 per cent of the upper-middle do; but only 44 per cent of the lower-middle take these courses, 28 per cent of the upper-lower, and 26 per cent of the lower-lower. These percentages provide a good index of the position of the lower-middle class, ranking it well below the three upper classes, but placing it well above the upper-lower and the lower-lower.[2]

The upper-lower class, least differentiated from the adjacent levels and hardest to distinguish in the hierarchy, but clearly present, is composed of the "poor but honest workers" who more often than not are only semi-skilled or unskilled. Their relative place in the hierarchy of class is well portrayed by comparing them with the classes superior to them and with the lower-lower class beneath them in the category of how they spend their money.

A glance at the ranking of the proportion of the incomes of each class spent on ten items (including such things as rent and shelter, food, clothing, and education, among others) shows, for example, that this class ranks second for the percentage of the money spent on food, the lower-lower class being first and the rank order of the other classes following lower-middle according to their place in the social hierarchy. The money spent on rent and shelter by upper-lower class is also second to the lower-lower's first, the other classes' rank order and position in the hierarchy being in exact correspondence. To give a bird's-eye view of the way this class spends its money, the rank of the upper-lower, for the percentage of its budget spent on a number of common and important items, has been placed in parentheses after every item in the list which follows: food (2), rent (2), clothing (4),

[2] See W. Lloyd Warner and Paul S. Lunt, *The Social Life of a Modern Community*, Vol. I, "Yankee City Series" (New Haven: Yale University Press, 1941), pp. 58–72.

automobiles (5), taxes (5), medical aid (5), education (4), and amusements (4–5). For the major items of expenditure the amount of money spent by this class out of its budget corresponds fairly closely with its place in the class hierarchy, second to the first of the lower-lower class for the major necessities of food and shelter, and ordinarily, but not always, fourth or fifth to the classes above for the items that give an opportunity for cutting down the amounts spent on them. Their feelings about doing the right thing, of being respectable and rearing their children to do better than they have, coupled with the limitations of their income, are well reflected in how they select and reject what can be purchased on the American market.[3]

The lower-lower class, referred to as "Riverbrookers" or the "low-down Yankees who live in the clam flats," have a "bad reputation" among those who are socially above them. This evaluation includes beliefs that they are lazy, shiftless, and won't work, all opposites of the good middle-class virtues belonging to the essence of the Protestant ethic. They are thought to be improvident and unwilling or unable to save their money for a rainy day and, therefore, often dependent on the philanthropy of the private or public agency and on poor relief. They are sometimes said to "live like animals" because it is believed that their sexual mores are not too exacting and that pre-marital intercourse, post-marital infidelity, and high rates of illegitimacy, sometimes too publicly mixed with incest, characterize their personal and family lives. It is certain that they deserve only part of this reputation. Research shows many of them guilty of no more than being poor and lacking in the desire to get ahead, this latter trait being common among those above them. For these reasons and others, this class is ranked in Yankee City below the level of the Common Man (lower-middle and upper-lower). For most of the indexes of status it ranks sixth and last.

CLASS IN THE DEMOCRATIC MIDDLE WEST AND FAR WEST

Cities large and small in the states west of the Alleghenies sometimes have class systems which do not possess an old-family (upper-upper) class. The period of settlement has not always been sufficient for an old-family level, based on the security of birth and inherited

---

[3] The evidence for the statements in this paragraph can be found in *The Social Life of a Modern Community*, pp. 287–300.

wealth, to entrench itself. Ordinarily, it takes several generations for an old-family class to gain and hold the prestige and power necessary to impress the rest of the community sufficiently with the marks of its "breeding" to be able to confer top status on those born into it. The family, its name, and its lineage must have had time to become identified in the public mind as being above ordinary mortals.

While such identification is necessary for the emergence of an old-family (upper-upper) class and for its establishment, it is also necessary for the community to be large enough for the principles of exclusion to operate. For example, those in the old-family group must be sufficiently numerous for all the varieties of social participation to be possible without the use of new-family members; the family names must be old enough to be easily identified; and above all there should always be present young people of marriageable age to become mates of others of their own class and a sufficient number of children to allow mothers to select playmates and companions of their own class for their children.

When a community in the more recently settled regions of the United States is sufficiently large, when it has grown slowly and at an average rate, the chances are higher that it has an old-family class. If it lacks any one of these factors, including size, social and economic complexity, and steady and normal growth, the old-family class is not likely to develop.

One of the best tests of the presence of an old-family level is to determine whether members of the new-family category admit, perhaps grudgingly and enviously and with hostile derogatory remarks, that the old-family level looks down on them and that it is considered a mark of advancement and prestige by those in the new-family group to move into it and be invited to the homes and social affairs of the old families. When a member of the new-family class says, "We've only been here two generations, but we still aren't old-family," and when he or she goes on to say that "they (old family) consider themselves better than people like us and the poor dopes around here let them get away with it," such evidence indicates that an old-family group is present and able to enforce recognition of its superior position upon its most aggressive and hostile competitors, the members of the lower-upper, or new-family, class.

When the old-family group is present and its position is not recognized as superordinate to the new families, the two tend to be coordinate and view each other as equals. The old-family people adroitly let it be known that their riches are not material possessions alone but are old-family lineage; the new families display their wealth, accent their power, and prepare their children for the development of a future lineage by giving them the proper training at home and later sending them to the "right" schools and marrying them into the "right" families.

Such communities usually have a five-class pyramid, including an upper class, two middle, and two lower classes.[4]

Jonesville, located in the Middle West, approximately a hundred years old, is an example of a typical five-class community. The farmers around Jonesville use it as their market, and it is the seat of government for Abraham County. Its population of over 6,000 people is supported by servicing the needs of the farmers and by one large and a few small factories.

At the top of the status structure is an upper class commonly referred to as "the 400." It is composed of old-family and new-family segments. Neither can successfully claim superiority to the other. Below this level is an upper-middle class which functions like the same level in Yankee City and is composed of the same kind of people, the only difference being the recognition that the distance to the top is shorter for them and the time necessary to get there much less. The Common Man level, composed of lower-middle and upper-lower-class people, and the lower-lower level are replicas of the same classes in Yankee City. The only difference is that the Jonesville ethnics in these classes are Norwegian Lutherans and Catholic Poles, the Catholic Irish and Germans having been absorbed for the most part in the larger population; whereas in Yankee City the ethnic population is far more heterogeneous, and the Catholic Irish are less assimilated largely because of more opposition to them, and because the church has more control over their private lives.

The present description of Jonesville's class order can be brief and no more than introductory because all the materials used to demonstrate how to measure social class are taken from Jonesville. The interested reader will obtain a clear picture in the chapters which follow of what the classes are, who is in them, the social and economic characteristics of each class, and how the people of the town think about their status order.

The communities of the mountain states and Pacific Coast are new,

[4] It is conceivable that in smaller communities there may be only three, or even two, classes present.

and many of them have changed their economic form from mining to other enterprises; consequently, their class orders are similar to those found in the Middle West. The older and larger far western communities which have had a continuing, solid growth of population which has not destroyed the original group are likely to have the old-family level at the top with the other classes present; the newer and smaller communities and those disturbed by the destruction of their original status structure by large population gains are less likely to have an old-family class reigning above all others. San Francisco is a clear example of the old-family type; Los Angeles, of the more amorphous, less well-organized class structure.

CLASS IN THE DEEP SOUTH

Studies in the Deep South demonstrate that, in the older regions where social changes until recently have been less rapid and less disturbing to the status order, most of the towns above a few thousand population have a six-class system in which an old-family elite is socially dominant.

For example, in a study of a Mississippi community, a market town for a cotton-growing region around it, Davis and the Gardners found a six-class system.[5] Perhaps the southern status order is best described by Chart I on page 253 which gives the names used by the people of the community for each class and succinctly tells how the members of each class regard themselves and the rest of the class order.

The people of the two upper classes make a clear distinction between an old aristocracy and an aristocracy which is not old. There is no doubt that the first is above the other; the upper-middle class views the two upper ones much as the upper classes do themselves but groups them in one level with two divisions, the older level above the other; the lower-middle class separates them but considers them co-ordinate; the bottom two classes, at a greater social distance than the others, group all the levels above the Common Man as "society" and one class. An examination of the terms used

[5] Allison Davis, Burleigh B. Gardner, and Mary R. Gardner, *Deep South* (Chicago: University of Chicago Press, 1941). Also read: John Dollard, *Caste and Class in a Southern Town* (New Haven: Yale University Press, 1937); Mozell Hill, "The All-Negro Society in Oklahoma" (Unpublished Ph.D. dissertation, University of Chicago, 1936); Harry J. Walker, "Changes in Race Accommodation in a Southern Community" (Unpublished Ph.D. dissertation, University of Chicago, 1945).

CHART I

THE SOCIAL PERSPECTIVES OF THE SOCIAL CLASSES *

UPPER-UPPER CLASS		LOWER-UPPER CLASS
"Old aristocracy"	UU	"Old aristocracy"
"Aristocracy," but not "old"	LU	"Aristocracy," but not "old"
"Nice, respectable people"	UM	"Nice, respectable people"
"Good people, but 'nobody'"	LM	"Good people, but 'nobody'"
	UL	
"Po' whites"	LL	"Po' whites"

UPPER-MIDDLE CLASS		LOWER-MIDDLE CLASS
"Society" "Old families"	UU	
"Society" but not "old families"	LU	"Old aristocracy" (older) "Broken-down aristocracy" (younger)
"People who should be upper class"	UM	"People who think they are somebody"
"People who don't have much money"	LM	"We poor folk"
	UL	"People poorer than us"
"No 'count lot"	LL	"No 'count lot"

UPPER-LOWER CLASS		LOWER-LOWER CLASS
	UU	
	LU	
"Society" or the "folks with money"	UM	"Society" or the "folks with money"
"People who are up because they have a little money"	LM	"Way-high-ups," but not "Society"
"Poor but honest folk"	UL	"Snobs trying to push up"
"Shiftless people"	LL	"People just as good as anybody"

* Allison Davis, Burleigh B. Gardner, and Mary R. Gardner, *Deep South* (Chicago: University of Chicago Press, 1941), p. 65.

by the several classes for the other classes shows that similar principles are operating.

The status system of most communities in the South is further complicated by a color-caste system which orders and systematically controls the relations of those categorized as Negroes and whites.[6]

[6] [See Bertram W. Doyle, *The Etiquette of Race Relations in the South: A Study in Social Control* (Chicago: University of Chicago Press, 1937).]

The Generalities of American Class

It is now time to ask what are the basic characteristics of social status common to the communities of all regions in the United States and . . . what the variations are among the several systems. Economic factors are significant . . . in determining the class position of any family or person, influencing the kind of behavior we find in any class, and contributing their share to the present form of our status system. But, while significant and necessary, the economic factors are not sufficient to predict where a particular family or individual will be or to explain completely the phenomena of social class. . . . Money must be translated into socially approved behavior and possessions, and they in turn must be translated into intimate participation with, and acceptance by, members of a superior class.

This is well illustrated by what is supposed to be a true story of what happened to a Mr. John Smith, a newly rich man in a far western community. He wanted to get into a particular social club of some distinction and significance in the city. By indirection he let it be known, and was told by his friends in the club they had submitted his name to the membership committee.

Mr. Abner Grey, one of the leading members of the club and active on its membership committee, was a warm supporter of an important philanthropy in this city. It was brought to his attention that Mr. Smith, rather than contributing the large donation that had been expected of him, had given only a nominal sum to the charity.

When Mr. Smith heard nothing more about his application, he again approached one of the board members. After much evasion, he was told that Mr. Grey was the most influential man on the board and he would be wise to see that gentleman. After trying several times to make an appointment with Mr. Grey, he finally burst into Grey's offices unannounced.

"Why the hell, Abner, am I being kept out of the X club?"

Mr. Grey politely evaded the question. He asked Mr. Smith to be seated. He inquired after Mr. Smith's health, about the health of his wife, and inquired about other matter of simple convention.

Finally, Mr. Smith said, "Ab, why the hell am I being kept out of your club?"

"But, John, you're not. Everyone in the X club thinks you're a fine fellow."

"Well, what's wrong?"

"Well, John, we don't think you've got the *kind* of money necessary for being a good member of the X club. We don't think you'd be happy in the X club."

"Like hell I haven't. I could buy and sell a half dozen of some of your board members."

"I know that, John, but that isn't what I said. I did not say the amount of money. I said the kind of money."

"What do you mean?"

"Well, John, my co-workers on the charity drive tell me you only gave a few dollars to our campaign, and we had you down for a few thousand."

For a moment Mr. Smith was silent. Then he grinned. So did Mr. Grey. Smith took out his fountain pen and checkbook. "How much?"

At the next meeting of the X club Mr. Smith was unanimously elected to its membership.

Mr. Smith translated his money into philanthropy acceptable to the dominant group, he received their sponsorship, and finally became a participant in the club. The "right" kind of house, the "right" neighborhood, the "right" furniture, the proper behavior—all are symbols that can ultimately be translated into social acceptance by those who have sufficient money to aspire to higher levels than they presently enjoy.

To belong to a particular level in the social-class system of America means that a family or individual has gained acceptance as an equal by those who belong in the class. The behavior in this class and the participation of those in it must be rated by the rest of the community as being at a particular place in the social scale.

Although our democratic heritage makes us disapprove, our class order helps control a number of important functions. It unequally divides the highly and lowly valued things of our society among the several classes according to their rank. Our marriage rules conform to the rules of class, for the majority of marriages are between people of the same class. No class system, however, is so rigid that it completely prohibits marriages above and below one's own class. Furthermore, an open class system such as ours permits a person during his lifetime to move up or down from the level into which he was born. Vertical social mobility for individuals or families is characteristic of all class systems. The principal forms of mobility in this country are through the use of money, education, occupation, talent, skill, philanthropy, sex, and marriage. Although economic mobility is still important, it seems likely now that more people move to higher positions by education than by any other route. We have indicated before this that the mere possession of money is insufficient for gaining and keeping a higher social position. This is equally true of all other forms of mobility. In every case there must be social acceptance.

Class varies from community to community. The new city is less likely than an old one to have a well-organized class order; this is also true for cities whose growth has been rapid as compared with those which have not been disturbed by huge increases in population from other regions or countries or by the rapid displacement of old industries by new ones. The mill town's status hierarchy is more likely to follow the occupational hierarchy of the mill than the levels of evaluated participation found in market towns or those with diversified industries. Suburbs of large metropolises tend to respond to selective factors which reduce the number of classes to one or a very few. They do not represent or express all the cultural factors which make up the social pattern of an ordinary city.

Yet systematic studies [7] from coast to coast, in cities large and small and of many economic types, indicate that, despite the variations and diversity, class levels do exist and that they conform to a particular pattern of organization.

30 CLASS CIRCULATION AND SOCIAL CHANGE *

BY GAETANO MOSCA (1858–1941)

WHAT we see is that as soon as there is a shift in the balance of political forces—when, that is, a need is felt that capacities different from the old should assert themselves in the management of the state, when the old capacities, therefore, lose some of their impor-

---

[7] [See chap. xv in Warner, Meeker, and Eells, *Social Class in America.—Ed.*]

* Reprinted by permission of the publisher from *The Ruling Class* (*Elementi di Scienza Politica*), transl. by Hannah D. Kahn, ed. and rev. by Arthur Livingston (New York: McGraw-Hill Book Company, 1939), pp. 65–69.

tance or changes in their distribution occur—then the manner in which the ruling class is constituted changes also. If a new source of wealth develops in a society, if the practical importance of knowledge grows, if an old religion declines or a new one is born, if a new current of ideas spreads, then, simultaneously, far-reaching dislocations occur in the ruling class. One might say, indeed, that the whole history of civilized mankind comes down to a conflict between the tendency of dominant elements to monopolize political power and transmit possession of it by inheritance, and the tendency toward a dislocation of old forces and an insurgence of new forces; and this conflict produces an unending ferment of endosmosis and exosmosis between the upper classes and certain portions of the lower. Ruling classes decline inevitably when they cease to find scope for the capacities through which they rose to power, when they can no longer render the social services which they once rendered, or when their talents and the services they render lose in importance in the social environment in which they live.[1] So the Roman aristocracy declined when it was no longer the exclusive source of higher officers for the army, of administrators for the commonwealth, of governors for the provinces. So the Venetian aristocracy declined when its nobles ceased to command the galleys and no longer passed the greater part of their lives in sailing the seas and in trading and fighting. . . .

The best-known and perhaps the most important example of a society tending toward crystallization is the period in Roman history that used to be called the Low Empire. There, after several centuries of almost complete social immobility, a division between two classes grew sharper and sharper, the one made up of great landowners and high officials, the other made up of slaves, farmers and urban plebeians. What is even more striking, public office and social position became hereditary by custom before they became hereditary by law, and the trend was rapidly generalized during the period mentioned.[2]

On the other hand it may happen in the history of a nation that commerce with foreign peoples, forced emigrations, discoveries, wars, create new poverty and new wealth, disseminate knowledge of things that were previously unknown or cause infiltrations of new moral, intellectual and religious currents. Or again—as a result of such in-

---

[1] [Cf. writings of archeologists] Lenormant, Maspero, and Brugsch.
[2] Marquardt, *Manuel des antiquités romaines;* Fustel de Coulanges, *Nouvelles recherches sur quelques problèmes d'histoire.*

filtrations or through a slow process of inner growth, or from both causes—it may happen that a new learning arises, or that certain elements of an old, long forgotten learning return to favor so that new ideas and new beliefs come to the fore and upset the intellectual habits on which the obedience of the masses has been founded. The ruling class may also be vanquished and destroyed in whole or in part by foreign invasions, or, when the circumstances just mentioned arise, it be driven from power by the advent of new social elements who are strong in fresh political forces. Then, naturally, there comes a period of renovation, or, if one prefer, of revolution, during which individual energies have free play and certain individuals, more passionate, more energetic, more intrepid or merely shrewder than others, force their way from the bottom of the social ladder to the topmost rungs.

Once such a movement has set in, it cannot be stopped immediately. The example of individuals who have started from nowhere and reached prominent positions fires new ambitions, new greeds, new energies, and this molecular rejuvenation of the ruling class continues vigorously until a long period of social stability slows it down again. We need hardly mention examples of nations in such periods of renovation. In our age that would be superfluous. Rapid restocking of ruling classes is a frequent and very striking phenomenon in countries that have been recently colonized. When social life begins in such environments, there is no ready-made ruling class, and while such a class is in process of formation, admittance to it is gained very easily. Monopolization of land and other agencies of production is, if not quite impossible, at any rate more difficult than elsewhere. That is why, at least during a certain period, the Greek colonies offered a wide outlet for all Greek energy and enterprise. That is why, in the United States, where the colonizing of new lands continued through the whole nineteenth century and new industries were continually springing up, examples of men who started with nothing and have attained fame and wealth are still frequent—all of which helps to foster in the people of that country the illusion that democracy is a fact.

Suppose now that a society gradually passes from its feverish state to calm. Since the human being's psychological tendencies are always the same, those who belong to the ruling class will begin to acquire a group spirit. They will become more and more exclusive and learn better and better the art of monopolizing to their advantage the

qualities and capacities that are essential to acquiring power and holding it. Then, at last, the force that is essentially conservative appears
—the force of habit. Many people become resigned to a lowly station,
while the members of certain privileged families or classes grow convinced that they have almost an absolute right to high station and
command.

A philanthropist would certainly be tempted to inquire whether
mankind is happier—or less unhappy—during periods of social stability and crystallization, when everyone is almost fated to remain in
the social station to which he was born, or during the directly opposite periods of renovation and revolution, which permit all to aspire to the most exalted positions and some to attain them. Such an
inquiry would be difficult. The answer would have to take account
of many qualifications and exceptions, and might perhaps always be
influenced by the personal preferences of the observer. We shall
therefore be careful not to venture on any answer of our own. Besides, even if we could reach an undebatable conclusion, it would
have a very slight practical utility; for the sad fact is that what the
philosophers and theologians call free will—in other words, spontaneous choice by individuals—has so far had, and will perhaps always
have, little influence, if any at all, in hastening either the ending or
the beginning of one of the historical periods mentioned.

31 GENERAL CAUSES OF VERTICAL MOBILITY *

BY PITIRIM ALEXANDROVITCH SOROKIN (1889–)
HARVARD UNIVERSITY

SINCE vertical mobility is an inherent and perennial trait of all organized and stratified groups, its causes are also inherent and
perennial though somewhat different for different groups. Among
these may be mentioned the following.

(1) In groups electing or appointing the members of their upper
strata for *a definite term, this feature of their organization is the*

* Reprinted by permission of the author and of the publisher from *Society, Culture,
and Personality* (New York: Harper & Brothers, 1947), pp. 435–437.

basic cause of their horizontal and vertical mobility. On the expiration of the term, the previous incumbents must be replaced. Hence the inevitability of new persons being elevated to high positions. If the candidates are recruited from all the strata of the group, the vertical current circulates from the bottom to the top of the pyramid and now and then elevates to the upper positions members of the lower strata. If the candidates are limited to the middle and upper strata, the current catches up only the members within these strata.

(2) A similar cause operates in the Roman Catholic Church, whose high dignitaries are *elected or appointed for life* but, being celibate, do not transmit their position to their issue. After the death of a Pope, bishop, or cardinal their positions must be filled by persons recruited from the lower strata of the Church. Here again *the cause of vertical mobility is inherent in the very organization of the group.*

(3) In many groups vertical mobility is caused by *an insufficient self-perpetuation of the upper strata.* Through a low birth rate or through high mortality a number of vacancies are created within the upper layers which can be filled only by persons recruited from the lower layers. In such groups the insufficient self-perpetuation of the upper classes creates an "upward draft" that picks up and promotes persons from the lower classes. For instance, in Sparta the number of Spartiates (the upper social order) before the Persian Wars was 8000. Through high mortality and possibly a low birth rate it had decreased by *ca.* 420 B.C. to 6000; by *ca.* 371 B.C. to 1500; and by 244 B.C. to 700, of which only 100 were full-fledged Homoioi. Among the Roman patricians (the upper social order) only about 15 families survived to the time of Caesar. Even among the equestrian and noble families that arose during the age of Augustus most were extinct by the time of Claudius. The number of full-fledged citizens of Athens decreased from 16,000 at the beginning of the Peloponnesian Wars to some 2500 by the time of Sulla.[1] In all such cases the vacancies had to be filled by persons from the lower strata.

Similarly, in medieval and modern Europe most of the aristocratic families became extinct within 300 years. Of 500 English aristocratic families of the fifteenth century hardly any exist at the present time.[2] In specific aristocracies such as military castes and royal dynasties, extinction has often been due to a notable degree, to the dangerous character of their position and hence to an unusually high propor-

---

[1] *Cf.* my *Mobility*, pp. 357 ff., for an exhaustive series of facts of this kind.
[2] *Ibid.*, pp. 347–360.

tion of deaths through violence. While for the entire population of the United States suicide and other forms of violence constituted only 7.2 per cent of the total causes of death, for the monarchs of Rome, Byzantium, Turkey, England, Austria, Prussia, Russia, and Germany they fluctuated between 20 and 66.3 per cent. For the presidents of Bolivia they represented 40 per cent; for presidents of the United States and France, 12.1 per cent; for prominent military men of various countries, 20 per cent; for statesmen, 10 per cent, and for Roman Catholic Popes, 9 per cent.[3]

In recent decades the upper classes of the West have also possessed a birth rate often insufficient to fill the vacancies created by death.[4]

The foregoing observations demonstrate that a "social vacuum" is incessantly created through the inability of the upper strata to perpetuate themselves sufficiently to fill the vacancies and that these must be filled through promotions from the lower strata. This factor does not operate in all social groups, because in some the upper strata (for instance, the Brahmin caste of India) reproduce themselves sufficiently to fill the vacancies.

(4) *The next general cause is the unfitness of many individuals to perform the proper functions of their social stratum, arising from the dissimilarity of parents and children, and from the profound change which many persons undergo in the course of their life.* If the members of a group, especially those of the upper strata, regularly fail to discharge satisfactorily their duties and functions, the group will progressively suffer and eventually disintegrate. If the government of a state shows increasing incapacity; if the commanders of an army display a lack of organizational, strategic, and other military ability; if the leaders of a religious organization exhibit greed, sensuality, and ignorance, the state, the army, and the church are bound to suffer. If, on the other hand, their lower strata contain "born rulers," "born military geniuses," or genuine spiritual leaders, such persons are likewise unsuited to their lower positions. Directly or indirectly they will undermine the group from below. In other words, *a fairly high degree of correspondence between the social positions of the members and their ability to perform the proper functions of their strata is a prerequisite for the continued existence of the group. When the discrepancy becomes too great, the group must*

[3] *Cf.* my *Mobility,* p. 356.
[4] *Ibid.,* pp. 347–356.

either correct it by reallocating its members according to their ability or else to suffer, even perish. Hence the unavoidableness of vertical mobility under the circumstances in question.[5]

Several forces generate such discrepancies in the life process of every group. One such force is the *dissimilarity between the parents and children in regard to the specific ability necessary for the successful discharge of the functions of their stratum.* A portion—perhaps the lesser portion—of the children are born with qualities dissimilar from those of their parents. For example, the children of Hippocrates, Socrates, Aristotle, and many other eminent thinkers lacked the genius of their parents; the children of many capable rulers, such as Peter the Great, Charles V, and Napoleon, failed to display any of the ability possessed by their parents; and the children of builders of business empires not infrequently are wastrels.[6] Conversely, the children of slaves may be born rulers.

To prevent an unduly large accumulation of unfit persons, the group is forced continuously to shift a part of its members to the strata corresponding to their abilities, to demote the incapable children of capable parents and to promote the capable children of incapable parents. The concrete methods of promotion and demotion are of various sorts: on the one hand, impoverishment, outcasting, dethronement, discharge, revolutionary overthrow, failure to reelect, etc.; on the other, normal promotion, elevation through revolutions or palace coups, election, etc.

Owing to physical or mental sickness, accidents, excess, and other causes, *persons sometimes undergo a profound change in the course of their lifetime* whereby they lose their ability properly to perform their functions. Hence the need of replacing such persons with different ones. In this way again a steady stream of vertical mobility is

[5] A. Toynbee (*cf.* his *Study of History,* Vol. III, *passim*) has demonstrated that in all civilizations during the period of their growth their "creative minority" adequately meets challenges to the group's existence and growth, but that in periods of decline this creative minority is replaced by an uncreative "dominant minority" that fails to meet the challenges successfully.

[6] Ibn Khaldun made the generalization, on the basis of his observations of the life cycle of prominent Arabian families, that the son of the founder of a great family is often a mere continuator of his father's work, and that the grandsons and great-grandsons are regularly wastrels. See Ibn Khaldun, *Prolégomènes historiques, Notices et Extraits des manuscrits de la Bibliothèque Imperial* (Paris, 1862), XIX, 287. Pareto's cycle of the *speculatori* and *rentieri* is merely a special case of the general rule of the dissimilarity between parents and children. For the facts and the literature, cf. my *Mobility,* pp. 360 ff., and *Dynamics,* IV, 505 ff.

generated: sick monarchs and other rulers are eliminated; the rich become poor; religious and ethical leaders lose their prestige, and so on.

(5) *Another cause of vertical mobility is an incessant change in the environment—especially in the sociocultural environment—of groups and their individual members.* Changes in the sociocultural environment ceaselessly create favorable conditions for some members and unfavorable conditions for others, leading respectively to their promotion and demotion. Rich deposits of oil or manganese among a population that is aware of their industrial and economic uses serve to enrich the owners of such land. The invention of the automobile has enriched many of its manufacturers and impoverished many manufacturers of horse-drawn vehicles. A whimsical change in public taste makes millionaires out of Sinatras and beggars out of many "old-fashioned" singers. The replacement of a monarchy by a republic elevates a host of adherents of the republic and drags down many a monarchical aristocracy. A declaration of war automatically demotes many a pacifist and elevates to the rank of hero many a belligerent. Victory or defeat in war is followed by a mass displacement of groups and their members. The vicissitudes of the stock market enrich many a gambler and ruin many an unlucky investor. In general, any change in the economic, political, scientific, technical, ethical, religious, judicial, aesthetic, philosophical, and other sociocultural conditions of a group, as well as any profound change in its physical and biological condition (such as epidemics, floods, droughts, and earthquakes), cause a horizontal and vertical displacement of its members.

This dynamism of sociocultural life alone is sufficient to produce an incessant stream of vertical mobility within any group or constellation of groups. Considering that other factors of mobility—such as election or appointment for a limited term, the dissimilarity of parents and children, and the profound changes experienced by persons in the course of their lifetime—are also more or less inherent in the component of members of the groups, *the main cause of vertical mobility is seen to be immanent, or inherent, in the sociocultural groups themselves.* Even in a constant natural milieu, with an adequate self-perpetuation of the upper strata, vertical mobility would inevitably occur in all organized groups. *Factors external to the group may reinforce or hinder it, but they are merely secondary.*

SECTION SEVEN
Collective Behavior

32 FOUR GREAT TYPES OF SOCIAL PROCESS *

BY ROBERT E. PARK (1864–1944)
AND ERNEST W. BURGESS (1886–   )
UNIVERSITY OF CHICAGO

OF THE four great types of interaction—competition, conflict, accommodation, and assimilation—competition is the elementary, universal and fundamental form. Social contact, as we have seen, initiates interaction. But competition, strictly speaking, is *interaction without social contact*. If this seems, in view of what has already been said, something of a paradox, it is because in human society competition is always complicated with other processes, that is to say, with conflict, assimilation, and accommodation. . . . Competition takes the form of conflict or rivalry only when it becomes conscious, when competitors identify one another as rivals or as enemies.

This suggests what is meant by the statement that competition is interaction *without social contact*. It is only when minds meet, only when the meaning that is in one mind is communicated to another mind so that these minds mutually influence one another, that social contact, properly speaking, may be said to exist. . . .

Competition and Competitive Co-operation. Social contact, which inevitably initiates conflict, accommodation, or assimilation, invariably creates also sympathies, prejudices, personal and moral relations which modify, complicate, and control competition. On the other hand, within the limits which the cultural process creates, and custom, law, and tradition impose, competition invariably tends to create an impersonal social order in which each individual, being free to pursue his own profit, and, in a sense, compelled to do so, makes every other individual a means to that end. In doing so, however, he inevitably contributes through the mutual exchange of services so established to the common welfare. It is just the nature of the trading transaction to isolate the motive of profit and make it the basis

---

* Reprinted by permission of the junior author and of the publisher from *Introduction to the Science of Sociology* (2nd ed.; Chicago: University of Chicago Press, 1924), pp. 506–510.

of business organization, and so far as this motive becomes dominant and exclusive, business relations inevitably assume the impersonal character so generally ascribed to them.

"Competition," says Walker, "is opposed to sentiment. Whenever any economic agent does or forbears anything under the influence of any sentiment other than the desire of giving the least and gaining the most he can in exchange, be that sentiment patriotism, or gratitude, or charity, or vanity, leading him to do otherwise than as self interest would prompt, in that case also, the rule of competition is departed from. Another rule is for the time substituted." [1]

This is the significance of the familiar sayings to the effect that one "must not mix business with sentiment," that "business is business," "corporations are heartless," etc. It is just because corporations are "heartless," that is to say impersonal, that they represent the most advanced, efficient, and responsible form of business organization. But it is for this same reason that they can and need to be regulated in behalf of those interests of the community that cannot be translated immediately into terms of profit and loss to the individual. . . .

In the plant community, competition is unrestricted.

Competition and Freedom. The economic organization of society, so far as it is an effect of free competition, is an ecological organization. There is a human as well as a plant and an animal ecology. . . .

Competition is universal in the world of living things. Under ordinary circumstances it goes on unobserved even by the individuals who are most concerned. It is only in periods of crisis, when men are making new and conscious efforts to control the conditions of their common life, that the forces with which they are competing get identified with persons, and competition is converted into conflict. It is in what has been described as the *political process* that society consciously deals with its crises.[2] War is the political process par excellence. It is in war that the great decisions are made. Political organizations exist for the purpose of dealing with conflict situations. Parties, parliaments and courts, public discussion and voting are to be considered simply as substitutes for war.

Accommodation, Assimilation, and Competition. Accommodation, on the other hand, is the process by which the individuals and groups make the necessary internal adjustments to social situations

[1] Francis A. Walker, *Political Economy* (New York, 1887), p. 92.
[2] See chap. i, pp. 51–54. [Park and Burgess, *op. cit.*—Ed.]

which have been created by competition and conflict. War and elections change situations. When changes thus effected are decisive and are accepted, conflict subsides and the tensions it created are resolved in the process of accommodation into profound modifications of the competing units, i.e., individuals and groups. A man once thoroughly defeated is, as has often been noted, "never the same again." Conquest, subjugation, and defeat are psychological as well as social processes. They establish a new order by changing, not merely the status, but the attitudes of the parties involved. Eventually the new order gets itself fixed in habit and custom and is then transmitted as part of the established social order to succeeding generations. Neither the physical nor the social world is made to satisfy at once all the wishes of the natural man. The rights of property, vested interests of every sort, the family organization, slavery, caste and class, the whole social organization, in fact, represent accommodations, that is to say, limitations of the natural wishes of the individual. These socially inherited accommodations have presumably grown up in the pains and struggles of previous generations, but they have been transmitted to and accepted by succeeding generations as part of the natural, inevitable social order. All of these are forms of control in which competition is limited by status.

Conflict is then to be identified with the political order and with conscious control. Accommodation . . . is associated with the social order that is fixed and established in custom and the mores.

Assimilation, as distinguished from accommodation, implies a more thoroughgoing transformation of the personality—a transformation which takes place gradually under the influence of social contacts of the most concrete and intimate sort.

Accommodation may be regarded, like religious conversion, as a kind of mutation. The wishes are the same but their organization is different. Assimilation takes place not so much as a result of changes in the organization as in the content, i.e., the memories, of the personality. The individual units, as a result of intimate association, interpenetrate, so to speak, and come in this way into possession of a common experience and a common tradition. The permanence and solidarity of the group rest finally upon this body of common experience and tradition. It is the rôle of history to preserve this body of common experience and tradition, to criticise and reinterpret it in the light of new experience and changing conditions, and in this way to preserve the continuity of the social and political life.

The relation of social structures to the processes of competition, conflict, accommodation, and assimilation may be represented schematically as follows:

SOCIAL PROCESS	SOCIAL ORDER
Competition	The economic equilibrium
Conflict	The political order
Accommodation	Social organization
Assimilation	Personality and the cultural heritage

33 THE AGITATOR UTILIZES SOCIAL MALAISE *

BY LEO LOWENTHAL (1900–   )
COLUMBIA UNIVERSITY
AND NORBERT GUTERMAN (1900–   )
INSTITUTE OF SOCIAL RESEARCH

THE analyst of agitation . . . faces the problem: are these merely fleeting, insubstantial, purely accidental and personal emotions blown up by the agitator into genuine complaints or are they themselves a constant rooted in the social structure? The answer seems unavoidable: these feelings cannot be dismissed as either accidental or imposed, they are basic to modern society. Distrust, dependence, exclusion, anxiety, and disillusionment blend together to form a fundamental condition of modern life: malaise.

When we define the discontent utilized by agitation as malaise, we are, so to speak, on our own for we cannot justify this definition by explicit references to agitational statements. It is an hypothesis, but it is a highly plausible one, because its only alternative would be to see the maze of agitational statements as a lunatic product beyond analysis. Moreover, it helps to account for certain recurrent charac-

* Reprinted by permission of the authors and of the publisher from *Prophets of Deceit: A Study of the Techniques of the American Agitator* (New York: Harper & Brothers, 1949), pp. 14–19.

teristics of agitation: its diffuseness, its pseudo-spontaneity, its flexibility in utilizing a variety of grievances, and its substitution of a personal enemy for an objective condition.

The agitator does not spin his grumblings out of thin air. The modern individual's sense of isolation, his so-called spiritual homelessness, his bewilderment in the face of the seemingly impersonal forces of which he feel himself a helpless victim, his weakening sense of values—all these motifs often recur in modern sociological writings. This malaise reflects the stresses imposed on the individual by the profound transformations taking place in our economic and social structure—the replacement of the class of small independent producers by gigantic industrial bureaucracies, the decay of the patriarchal family, the breakdown of primary personal ties between individuals in an increasingly mechanized world, the compartmentalization and atomization of group life, and the substitution of mass culture for traditional patterns.

These objective causes have been operating for a long time with steadily increasing intensity. They are ubiquitous and apparently permanent, yet they are difficult to grasp because they are only indirectly related to specific hardships or frustrations. Their accumulated psychological effect is something akin to a chronic disturbance, an habitual and not clearly defined malaise which seems to acquire a life of its own and which the victim cannot trace to any known source.

On the plane of immediate awareness, the malaise seems to originate in the individual's own depths and is experienced by him as an apparently isolated and purely psychic or spiritual crisis. It enhances his sense of antagonism to the rest of the world. Those groups in our society that are at present most susceptible to agitation seem to experience this malaise with particular acuteness—perhaps precisely because they do not confront social coercion in its more direct forms.

Although malaise actually reflects social reality, it also veils and distorts it. Malaise is neither an illusion of the audience nor a mere imposition by the agitator; it is a psychological symptom of an oppressive situation. The agitator does not try to diagnose the relationship of this symptom to the underlying social situation. Instead he tricks his audience into accepting the very situation that produced its malaise. Under the guise of a protest against the oppressive situation, the agitator binds his audience to it. Since this pseudo-protest never produces a genuine solution, it merely leads the audience to seek permanent relief from a permanent predicament by means of irrational outbursts. The agitator does not create the malaise, but he aggravates and fixates it because he bars the path to overcoming it.

Those afflicted by the malaise ascribe social evil not to an unjust or obsolete form of society or to a poor organization of an adequate society, but rather to activities of individuals or groups motivated by innate impulses. For the agitator these impulses are biological in nature, they function beyond and above history: Jews, for instance, are evil—a "fact" which the agitator simply takes for granted as an inherent condition that requires no explanation or development. Abstract intellectual theories do not seem to the masses as immediately "real" as their own emotional reactions. It is for this reason that the emotions expressed in agitation appear to function as an independent force, which exists prior to the articulation of any particular issue, is expressed by this articulation, and continues to exist after it.

Malaise can be compared to a skin disease. The patient who suffers from such a disease has an instinctive urge to scratch his skin. If he follows the orders of a competent doctor, he will refrain from scratching and seek a cure for the cause of his itch. But if he succumbs to his unreflective reaction, he will scratch all the more vigorously. This irrational exercise of self-violence will give him a certain kind of relief, but it will . . . increase his need to scratch and will in no way cure his disease. The agitator says: keep scratching.

The agitator exploits not primarily the feelings generated by specific hardships or frustrations, but more fundamentally those diffuse feelings of malaise which pervade all modern life. The malaise which is experienced as an internal psychic condition, can, however, be explained only by the social process in its totality. Such an explanation—following the classical method of articulating causes of discontent in universal and verifiable terms and then proposing definite methods to remove them—is beyond the resources of the agitator.

Here the agitator turns to account what might appear his greatest disadvantage—his inability to relate the discontent to an obvious causal base. While most other political movements promise a cure for a specific, and therefore limited, social ailment, the modern agitator, because he himself indirectly voices the malaise, can give the impression that he aims to cure some chronic, ultimate condition. And so, he insinuates, while others fumble with the symptoms, he attacks the very roots of the disease in that he voices the totality of modern feeling.

Because the malaise originates in the deepest layers of the individual psyche, it can appear to be an expression of frustrated spontaneity and essential spiritual needs. The agitator, implicitly working on this assumption, thus claims in effect that he represents the most general interests of society, while his opponents, who concern themselves with such limited, specific matters as housing or unemployment or wages, represent only selfish class interests. He can excoriate the others for their seemingly materialistic attitude, since he, on the contrary, has at heart only the nation and the race.

He can thus identify himself with any symbol suggesting spiritual spontaneity and, by extension, with any symbol suggesting that he strives to gratify suppressed instinctual impulses. He can appear as the enemy of those unjust constraints of civilization that operate on a deeper, more intimate level than those imposed by social institutions, and he can represent himself as a romantic defender of ancient traditions today trampled down by modern industrialism.

This alleged spirituality is vague enough to include or exclude anything at all, to be dissociated from history and to be associated with the most primitive biological instincts. In its name the agitator can appeal to the Promethean energies of sacrifice and promise to satisfy the essential needs for participation in communal life, for spiritual security, spontaneity, sincerity, and independence. He can easily switch from money and unemployment to spiritual matters.

. . . there is something deeper, more substantial which has been removed from the foundation of our national life than the mere loss of money and loss of jobs . . . Charity means seeking first the kingdom of God and His justice rather than seeking banks filled with gold.[1]

Malaise is a consequence of the depersonalization and permanent insecurity of modern life. Yet it has never been felt among people so strongly as in the past few decades. The inchoate protest, the sense of disenchantment, and the vague complaints and forebodings that are already perceptible in late nineteenth century art and literature have been diffused into general consciousness. There they function as a kind of vulgarized romanticism, a *Weltschmerz in perpetuum,* a sickly sense of disturbance that is subterranean but explosive. The intermittent and unexpected acts of violence on the part of the individual and the similar acts of violence to which whole nations

[1] Charles E. Coughlin, *Father Coughlin's Radio Discourses,* pp. 236–237.

can be brought are indices of this underground torment. Vaguely sensing that something has gone astray in modern life but also strongly convinced that he lacks the power to right whatever is wrong (even if it were possible to discover what is wrong), the individual lives in a sort of eternal adolescent uneasiness.

The agitator gravitates toward malaise like a fly to dung. He does not blink its existence as so many liberals do; he finds no comfort in the illusion that this is the best of all possible worlds. On the contrary, he grovels in it, he relishes it, he distorts and deepens and exaggerates the malaise to the point where it becomes almost a paranoiac relationship to the external world. For once the agitator's audience has been driven to this paranoiac point, it is ripe for his ministrations.

The prevalence of malaise in recent decades is reflected in growing doubt with relation to those universal beliefs that bound western society together.[2] Religion, the central chord of western society, is today often justified even by its most zealous defenders on grounds of expediency. Religion is proposed not as a transcendent revelation of the nature of man and the world, but as a means of weathering the storms of life, or of deepening one's spiritual experience, or of preserving social order, or of warding off anxiety. Its claim to acceptance is that it offers spiritual comfort. A similar development may be found in morality. There are today no commonly accepted—commonly accepted as a matter of course and beyond the need for discussion—moral values. Such a pragmatic maxim as "honesty is the best policy" is itself striking evidence of the disintegration of moral axioms. And much the same is also true for economic concepts: the businessman still believes in fair competition, but in his "dream life . . . the sure fix is replacing the open market."[3]

As a result, the old beliefs, even when preserved as ritualistic fetishes, have become so hollow that they cannot serve as spurs to conscience or internalized sources of authority. Now authority stands openly as a coercive force and against it is arrayed a phalanx of repressed impulses that storm the gates of the psyche seeking outlets of gratification.

When, for whatever reasons, direct expression of feelings is in-

[2] Cf. Max Horkheimer, Eclipse of Reason (New York: Oxford University Press, 1947).
[3] C. Wright Mills, "The Competitive Personality," Partisan Review, XIII, 4 (1946), 436.

hibited, they are projected through some apparently unrelated materials. We may accordingly assume that if the audience is not aware of the causes of the malaise, this is due not only to the inherent complexity of these causes, but chiefly to unconscious inhibitions, which probably originate in a reluctance to struggle against seemingly superior forces. So the agitator sanctions immediate resentments and seemingly paves the way for the relief of the malaise through discharge of the audience's aggressive impulses; but simultaneously he perpetuates the malaise by blocking the way toward real understanding of its cause.

All such utilizations of malaise are possible only on condition that the audience does not become aware of its roots in modern society. The malaise remains in the background of agitation, the raw material of which is supplied by the audience's stereotyped projections of the malaise. Instead of trying to go back to their sources, to treat them as symptoms of a bad condition, the agitator treats them as needs that he promises to satisfy. He is therefore not burdened with the task of correcting the audience's inadequate ideas; on the contrary, he can let himself be carried along by its "natural" current.

34 OBSERVATIONS ON THE SOCIOLOGY OF SOCIAL MOVEMENTS *

BY RUDOLF HEBERLE (1896–   )
LOUISIANA STATE UNIVERSITY

OUR concern is to find those characteristics essential in social movements of major importance which serve us as prototypes and to develop, rather than define, a type concept.

In constructing this concept, I shall emphasize that social movements are a particular kind of social group. This may not be the most common way of perceiving these phenomena, but to me it seems to be the sociologically relevant aspect. I consider social move-

* Reprinted by permission of the author and of the editor from *American Sociological Review*, XIV (1949), 346–357; pp. 349–356 used.

ments as a species of "social collectives" (Tönnies); these are un-organized, or as we shall see, only partly organized groups, yet large enough to persist even if old members drop out and new members enter.

All the Western languages use the metaphoric term "movement" for the phenomenon which we want to define: "Soziale Bewegung," "mouvement social," "sociala rörelse," etc. The connotation is that there is a commotion, a stirring among the people, an unrest, a desire to approach a visualized goal. A "movement" therefore is a collective ready for action by which some kind of change is to be achieved, some innovation to be made, or a previous condition to be restored.

If we posit as an essential characteristic of a social movement direct orientation toward a change in the social order, that is, in the patterns of human relations, in social institutions and social norms, we can exclude a large number of phenomena which have some similarity to social movements but are concerned with the propagation of a new style in art, a new health fad and similar innovations which have no immediate social relevance.

We further maintain that mere like sentiments and like actions which occur independently among a large number of people do not constitute a movement; nor does mere imitative mass-action. A sense of group identity and solidarity is required: only when the acting individuals have become aware of the fact that they have social sentiments and goals in common and when they think of themselves as being united with each other in action for a common goal do we acknowledge the existence of a social movement. The theoretical problem is very similar to that of determining the characteristics of a fully developed social class: the "consciousness of class" among people in like class position is what really constitutes a class as a social entity.

Of course, any social movement has gone through initial stages where these conditions were only partly fulfilled. Thus, it may for example be doubtful whether there is a Negro movement in this country. However, the various endeavors to improve the social status of Negroes show many analogies to the early phases of other kinds of social movements.[1]

---

[1] Since about seven out of ten male Negroes in the labor force are wage earners one is tempted to say that the Negro's struggle is practically part of the labor movement. A very large proportion of the Negro workers are, however, not em-

There arises the question: how comprehensive a "program" must a movement have in order to be considered as a genuine social movement? To this we merely answer: the more comprehensive, the more will it conform to the ideal type. The problem is similar to that of distinguishing a political party from a mere "pressure group": a party is bound to have a program or platform which gives consideration to all important political issues, while a "pressure group" may be formed for a specific, limited purpose. It is true that political groups have been formed which under the name of a party represented merely the interests of real estate owners or vegetarians, but no successful and lasting party has ever been formed without a comprehensive political program.[2] A social movement therefore is bound to develop not merely an "economic" or a "political" program but one which concerns all important socially relevant issues.

Another question that may be raised concerns the duration of a movement: are short-lived group actions, such as a "wildcat strike," a race riot or a *coup d'état* to be considered social movements? It seems that the characteristics of comprehensiveness in aim, of orientation towards a new social order, and of intensity of we-feeling would lead to a negative conclusion.

We may refer here to the recent experience of the Resistance movements in various countries, composed of men and women of different political tendencies who were united in the common fight against Nazi and Fascist rule; they were really only temporary alliances which tended to break up as soon as the objective of liberation had been achieved. Had the German Opposition to Hitler not been crushed after the unsuccessful *coup d'état* of July 20, 1944, it could not possibly have held together for any length of time after an overthrow of the Hitler regime. However this is not to say that short-lived movements are not phenomena worthy of study; on the contrary, because of their simplicity a great deal can be gained from

ployed in capitalistic enterprises (e.g., the domestic servants and many agricultural workers) and therefore not proletarians in the technical sense. The analogy with the early phases of the labor movement lies in the importance of local and individual action and in the presence of white sponsors in many organized groups working for the improvement of the Negro's lot. There are, however, in the situation of the American Negro also some striking analogies to the situation of national minorities in Eastern Europe before and immediately after the first world war.

[2] See Schattschneider, "Pressure Groups," *Annals of the American Academy of Political and Social Science,* September 1948. The author very adroitly states that parties mobilize majorities, while pressure groups organize minorities. Also: MacIver, "Pressure Groups" in *Encyclopedia of the Social Sciences.*

studying them for an understanding of social movements in the strict sense. Besides, strikes, riots, *coups d'état* and similar kinds of short-lived group action do occur within the framework of social movements. In fact they are usually among the first symptoms of social unrest, and they form part of the "tactical" devices.

The concept of social movement will gain further in clarity when we determine the distinctions and relations between social movements and political parties. No clear distinction between the two types of groups can be made if one accepts the older concept of a party which received its classical definition by Burke as "a body of men united, for promoting by their joint endeavours the national interest, upon some particular principle in which they are all agreed." [3] By this definition the two major parties in the United States would of course not be political parties at all. And political parties according to this definition would be identical with political movements. It would be more realistic to define political party as a group of people who "propose to act in concert in the competitive struggle for political power." [4]

The uniting or binding factor in a party may either be a set of political principles in which all members are agreed, or it may be a complex of common "interests" or simply the desire to secure offices and patronage for members of the group, or it may be an emotional-affectual attachment to a leader of real or imagined extraordinary qualifications.[5] Genuine social movements on the other hand are always integrated by a set of constitutive ideas, although the elements of patronage and leadership are by no means absent.

By definition a party must be related to a larger social entity, typically a corporate group. Parties can appear in all kinds of corporate groups, as Max Weber points out, but by definition a political party can exist only within a state. This is an essential characteristic which distinguishes a party from a social movement; the latter needs not be restricted to a particular state or national society.

However, the appearance of international federations of political parties like the Second and Third International which belong to the same social-political movement constitutes one of the most serious

[3] Edmund Burke, *Thoughts on the Cause of the Present Discontents* (Cambridge University Press edition, 1930), p. 96.

[4] Joseph Schumpeter, *Capitalism, Socialism and Democracy* (1942), p. 283.

[5] See Max Weber's excellent discussion in *The Theory of Social and Economic Organization* (Oxford University Press, 1947), pp. 407 ff.

political problems in a world society of national states. The phenomenon is related to that of the "ultramontane" orientation of Catholic parties.[6]

Burke, in the context mentioned above, makes a very important statement about political parties: "Without a proscription of others, they are bound to give to their own party the preference in all things; and by no means, for private considerations, to accept any offers of power in which the whole body is not included." The main intention of this remark was, of course, to give strength to the emerging institution of parliamentary government; but by implication Burke also takes the position that a party is to consider itself as part of a larger whole, that it has to recognize legitimate opposition and competition from other parties—a criterion which also enters into Schumpeter's concept. The new totalitarian "parties" do not correspond to this concept in so far as they are very definitely bent upon the "proscription of others." It may very well be that under the impact of such movements, parties in the traditional sense will go out of existence in a large part of the world and be replaced by new kinds of groups for which we have no better term than that of "political order," as they show strong resemblance to certain militant religious orders.

Parties in the broadest sense of the term are not always organized bodies, nor are all individuals who consider themselves as supporters of a political party necessarily members of a formally organized group. However, the two main functions of a political party in a modern state make some kind of organization necessary. The preparation of bills in the legislature, the nomination of candidates, the mobilization of voters require delegation of certain powers to individuals who can act as agents for the group and also require some ways of enforcing discipline among members.

This necessity increases with the size of the party, and that again is largely a consequence of the extension of the franchise. As long as only relatively few, and mostly wealthy and educated people, voted, a party could rely on the existing ties of kinship, neighborhood, and friendship. This became impossible with the expansion of the electorate. The general trend therefore has been from informal and often

[6] The ultramontanism of the Zentrum (Center Party) in Germany was one of the major points in Nazi propaganda. The National Socialists themselves, however, committed the same sin against nationalism by creating affiliated national-socialist parties in various European countries. The substitution of the "Ethnic community" idea for the nation idea facilitated these "fifth column" activities.

short-lived groupings towards more and more elaborate formal organization, culminating in such highly bureaucratized party organizations as the German Social Democratic Party and in highly complex and integrated structures like the Fascist Parties.

A movement on the other hand is by definition an unorganized
group, a "social collective," as Tönnies calls those groups which are
large enough to persist and retain their identity in spite of turnover
in membership and yet are lacking designated organs, being held
together by sentiments and common interests rather than by institutionalized social controls.[7] The National Socialists, for example,
made a distinction between the NSDAP, which was a registered, incorporated association, and the "movement" which included all followers of Adolf Hitler, irrespective of party membership.[8]

The empirical interrelations between the two types of groups are
manifold and often complex. The following four can be discerned as
basic types:

1. A party can be part of a broader social movement, like the Socialist labor parties which form one of the branches of the labor movement; or

2. It may be independent from a particular movement and embody
eventually in its membership in whole or in part several social movements; this has been the tendency in the major American parties; or

3. The same social movement may be represented in several different political parties: e.g., the proletarian movement in the Socialistic and Communistic parties, the Socialist Movement in various
political parties.

4. Finally, a social movement may reject on principle the affiliation
with any political party, as for example the anarcho-syndicalistic movement or the I.W.W.

As a rule, a major social movement tends to form its own political
party or at least to affiliate itself with an existing party.

There are also likely to be other formally organized groups com-

[7] This was the predominant conception of "movement" within the German Youth
Movement; the Wandervogel and other groups objected to elaborate formal organization which they considered to be the characteristic of the Youth Guidance groups
which they opposed.

[8] It is significant that in national socialist treatises on parties one can find such
remarks as: movements become parties unwillingly through participation in parliamentary work. This obviously betrays syndicalistic contempt for rational debate
and deliberation and a preference for direct action. See Hans Fritz Roeder, *Parteien
und Parteienstaat in Deutschland* (Munich, 1929).

prised within a social movement, because concerted action of large numbers of individuals is not possible without delegation of certain functions to certain individuals who can act as "organs" of the group. Sometimes these organized groups are attached to a political party as "affiliated" and "auxiliary" organizations, like the youth organizations in political movements; sometimes they are formally and perhaps even de facto independent of the party, like the trade unions and consumers' cooperatives in some European labor movements. Sometimes the two types of groups, although not formally interrelated, may be tightly interlocked through double memberships and through the occupation of controlling positions in one organization by leaders in the other.[9] . . .

In addition, there will be found numerous small informal groups, such as friendship circles, luncheon and dinner clubs, cliques, personal followings of outstanding leaders, etc., many of whom may be very important in the actual functioning of the movement.[10]

These "structural" aspects—and there are many more—deserve certainly more attention than they usually receive. I believe, for instance, that our Denazification policy in Germany could have been more effective had it been based upon more thorough knowledge and understanding of the structure of the Hitler movement. Or, to take another example, we should realize that the labor movement, especially in European countries but also in some sections of the U. S. A., has grown into a complex structure of separate but interrelated organized and unorganized groups which form the institutional framework for a large part of the modern worker's life, not only in the shop or office but also in his leisure time. These facts have to be taken into account when one attempts to understand what a movement means to its participants. In many cases the "movement" has taken the place of the gemeinschaft-like groups which were so abundant in pre-industrial society.

The analysis of structure and organization, which has been intentionally emphasized in this paper, has of course to be complemented by inquiries into the ideologies, the tactics, the socio-psychic

[9] This was the essential device of coordination (*Gleichschaltung*) of all kinds of associations with the NSDAP after the seizure of power, but it was also a device of penetration or infiltration before that time.

[10] As examples may serve: The "Christlich-Deutsche Tischgesellschaft" which played an important role in the Prussian resistance against Napoleon I, and, more recently, the "Mittwochsgesellschaft" to which belonged General Beck and other leaders of the German opposition to Hitler.

foundations and "texture"[11] of a movement. All these aspects are closely interrelated among each other and with structure. The nature of the final objectives, the role which the organized cadres of the movement are to play in the future social order, and the ways and means by which the goal is to be reached—all these traits will be reflected in the structure and organization of the movement.[12]

In the study of ideologies considerable refinement of methods has been attained during the past half-century, largely through the sociology of knowledge and the theory of the political "myth."[13] No longer do we judge the social effectiveness of ideas by standards of logical consistency or empirical truthfulness. We have learned through bitter experience that even absurd and scientifically refutable ideas can become immensely effective tools in arousing men into action and in building up sentiments of solidarity and loyalty.[14]

As sociologists we are primarily interested in studying the ways in which ideas are accepted by the masses and the extent to which they became "constitutive" values[15] in social movements.

[11] I am using the term "texture" in order to denote the quality of sociopsychic interrelations between members of a group which are partly a consequence of the prevailing attitudes of the individuals to the group. Here the concepts of community (*Gemeinschaft*) and association (society) can be very usefully applied.

[12] Observe for example the differences in the structure and organization of the Social Democratic and the Communist movements, or the difference between the traditional craft unions and the I.W.W.

[13] In view of the tendency among contemporary writers to use the term "myth" indiscriminately in reference to various kinds of beliefs concerning social and political matters, it seems advisable to draw attention to Sorel's original theory. In *Reflexions sur la violence* (ed. 1907, pp. 32–33) Sorel says: "The men who participate in the great social movements represent to themselves their future action in the form of visions of battle ("images de batailles") assuring themselves of the triumph of their cause. I proposed to give the name "myths" to these constructions, the knowledge of which offers so much of importance to the historian: The general strike of the syndicalists and the catastrophic revolution of Marx are myths." . . . The full meaning of the concept can of course only be understood by knowing Sorel's use of it in his critique of democratic Socialism and of bourgeois society.

[14] We are in our days of social-psychology and propaganda technique confronted with the experience of purposively manufactured ideologies of the Fascist and Nazi type, consisting of ideas which are often not believed in by those who propagate them, nor shared by all who call themselves members or followers of the movement in question.

In a case like this, the simple device of asking members of the movement what they see in it, what induced them to join it, may result merely in the reproduction of the official propaganda line of the movement. It seems to me that this may have happened in the case of Prof. Abel's study of the Hitler movement which has been one of the main sources for Hadley Cantril's socio-psychological analysis of Nazism.

[15] I owe this concept to Ernst Jurkat, *Das Soziologische Wertproblem* (Phil. Diss., Kiel. ca. 1930).

It is generally recognized, as mentioned before, that the chances of an idea to become part of the creed of a mass movement depend not so much upon its intrinsic value as upon its appeal to the interests, sentiments, and resentments of certain strata and groups. This again will largely depend on constellations of several factors which may vary greatly in the course of time and from place to place.

The particular significance of an appeal to a certain social class or classes is now generally recognized. It has its explanation in the fact that major social and political changes will always affect the distribution of the societal income and wealth and thereby induce changes in the relative power position of the classes to one another. Social movements, even if not primarily concerned with the welfare of a particular class, are therefore as a rule closely affiliated to certain social classes and opposed by others.

However, it has been maintained that in this country sectional conflicts have been more important in the formation of political alignments than have class antagonisms.[16] This, I believe, is a kind of optical illusion, caused by an inadequate conception of the nature of social classes. In the analysis of the interrelation between social classes, socio-political movements and parties, not much can be achieved by the use of the popular, but pre-sociological notions of upper, middle and lower classes. These mean one thing in one community and other things in others. What we need are concrete class concepts; even a broad concept like "the farmers" will not do for our purposes. Farmers in the U. S. A. fall into quite a large number of economic classes: e.g., ranchers, planters, sharecroppers, commercial family farmers, self-sufficient farmers, etc. Each of these have specific economic interests and constitute at the same time quite distinct social classes between which there is little intermarriage or other social intercourse. It so happens that frequently rather large areas are inhabited by one subclass of farmers, whose political tendencies may vary from those in adjoining areas where a different subclass predominates. This creates the illusion of sectionalism.[17] Similar considerations apply to the class differentiations between "big busi-

[16] A. N. Holcombe, *Political Parties of Today* (New York, 1926); also his later book: *The Middle Classes in American Politics*. Stuart Rice, *Quantitative Methods in Politics* (1928), esp. pp. 125–135, 154.

[17] Compare my *From Democracy to Nazism* (1945), especially the chapter on Ecology of Political Parties, where I have shown that "sectional" variations in political behavior are essentially conditioned by variations in the class structure of rural society.

ness" and "small business," commercial and manufacturing entrepreneurs and so forth. Even among wage earners we should distinguish between those employed in capitalistic enterprises (the "proletariat" in the technical sense) and those in other kinds of employment. The former are likely to be more "class conscious" and therefore inclined to be politically more radically opposed to the dominant classes than the latter.[18]

The "white collar workers" or salaried employees are of course not a group of homogeneous class position although the majority of them in the more highly industrialized areas tend more and more to take the side of labor.

The correlation between classes, parties and movements is sometimes obscured by two phenomena which occur particularly in times when the established structure of a society is crumbling. One is the emergence of "deserters" from the ruling classes as leaders in revolutionary movements.[19] The other is the development of activistic counter-revolutionary movements and parties whose initial support comes from the "déclassés": discharged soldiers without a vocation, bankrupt farmers, and other individuals whose career plans are thwarted or who have lost their former social position (e.g., the Fascists and early Nazis).

Other factors, e.g., religious objections to the ideas of a movement or party, the memory of past historical experiences, the degree of social integration through kinship and neighborhood relations in the community may "disturb" the expected correlation. "Quantitative" studies have to be carefully planned with regard to the configurations of these factors in each area, or their findings are bound to be misleading.

Since the social stratification in this country is much less complex than in Europe, since class lines and class consciousness are not so clearly developed, and finally since the major party-forming issues in the past have been conflicts within the bourgeoisie or middle class [20]

[18] See for instance Dewey Anderson and Percy E. Davidson, *Ballots and the Democratic Class Struggle* (1943), pp. 119 f. and 136. A recent unpublished study by Samuel A. Pratt under the direction of Professor Charles P. Loomis at Michigan State College has shown that wage earners in certain "light" and small-scale industries in Germany were in the election of 1932 less inclined to vote Communistic than wage earners in the "heavy" and large-scale industries.

[19] A. Meusel, "Die Abtrünnigen," in *Koelner Vierteljahrshefte für Soziologie*, III, 1923.

[20] In the United States most of the farmers belong to this class. In Europe one can—or could at least until ten years ago—distinguish "capitalistic" farmers, peasants

rather than between major classes, it is much more difficult to analyze the relations between classes, movements, and parties in the U. S. A. than it would be in most European countries, where each of the major social classes stands for a different ideal social system [21] and consequently is likely to align itself with that party whose political philosophy comes closest to this ideal.

The relation between social movements and social classes is then, like that between classes and parties and parties and movements, not one of coincidence or identity but of overlapping and more or less close association. Furthermore, these relations should not be considered as static but rather as constantly changing as the movement grows or declines.

Social movements, like political parties, have the incidental, but sociologically important function of contributing to the formation of the political élite. As an example we may refer again to the trade unions. While their immediate aims have been improvements in the conditions of life and labor for their members, they have been a training ground for a new élite which in our era has contributed a very considerable number of statesmen in all the European countries and in the United Nations organization. But these distinguished leaders are only a very small part of the larger élite which is constantly being created in the labor movement, from the "Local" up to the "International." A hundred years ago Lorenz Stein thought that the proletariat would not be capable of ruling because its leaders lacked experience which, he believed, came only with the responsibilities involved in property ownership; he could not, of course, foresee that the "Social Movement" would itself become a training ground for leadership.

One can even go further and show that the movement has changed the character of the class, by endowing the workers with pride in their own institutions, by training the masses for political action, by improving their understanding of economic and political issues—in short, by integrating them into the (national) community. Furthermore, as the labor movement gains in strength and grows into a complete network of organized groups and institutions it attracts individuals from other classes—especially from among the intellectuals, who devote their work to the service of the movement as lawyers,

---

and grand-seigneurs or Landedelleute, the latter two tending to adhere to pre-capitalistic values and often supporting anti-capitalistic movements.

[21] Werner Sombart, *Sozialismus und Sociale Bewegung* (1919), p. 1.

journalists, artists, educators, research workers, even as organizers and as managers of various enterprises. The labor movement of to-day consists no longer of proletarians who have "nothing to lose but their chains."

35 MASS INTERESTS IN PACIFISM "VERY EASILY FAIL" *

BY MAX WEBER (1864–1920)
UNIVERSITY OF HEIDELBERG

ECONOMICALLY, in a polity without state-socialism the "mass" of partners need be as little interested in pacifism as is any single stratum.

The Attic *demos*—and not they alone—lived economically off war. War brought them soldiers' pay and, in case of victory, tribute from the subjects. This tribute was actually distributed among the full citizens in the hardly veiled form of attendance-fees at popular assemblies, court hearings, and public festivities. Here, every full citizen could directly grasp the interest in imperialist policy and power. Nowadays, the yields flowing from abroad to the partners of a polity, including those of imperialist origin and those actually representing "tribute," do not result in a constellation of interests so comprehensible to the masses. For under the present economic order, the tribute to "creditor nations" assumes the form of interest payments on debts or of capital profits transferred from abroad to the propertied strata of the "creditor nation." Were one to think these tributes cancelled for countries like England, France, and Germany, it would mean a very palpable decline of purchasing power for home products. This would influence the labor market of the respective workers in an unfavorable manner.

In spite of this, labor in creditor nations is of strongly pacifist mind and on the whole shows no interest whatsoever in the continuation

* Reprinted by permission of the translators and of the publisher from H. H. Gerth and C. Wright Mills, translators and eds., *From Max Weber, Essays in Sociology* (New York: Oxford University Press, Inc., 1946; London: Kegan Paul, Trench, Trubner & Co., Ltd., 1947), pp. 170–172.

and compulsory collection of such tributes from foreign debtor communities that are in arrears. Nor does labor show an interest in forcibly participating in the exploitation of foreign colonial territories and in sharing public commissions. If this is the case, it is a natural outcome of the immediate class situation, on the one hand, and, on the other, of the internal social and political situation of communities in a capitalist era. Those entitled to tribute belong to the opponent class, who dominate the community. Every successful imperialist policy of coercing the outside normally—or at least at first—also strengthens the domestic "prestige" and therewith the power and influence of those classes, status groups, and parties, under whose leadership the success has been attained.

In addition to the sources determined by the social and political constellation, there are economic sources of pacifist sympathy among the masses, especially among the proletariat. Every investment of capital in the production of war engines and war material creates job and income opportunities; every administrative agency may become a factor directly contributing to prosperity in a particular case and, even more so, indirectly contributing to prosperity by increasing demand and fostering the intensity of business enterprise. This may become a source of enhanced confidence in the economic opportunities of the participating industries, which may lead to a speculative boom.

The administration, however, withdraws capital from alternate uses and makes it more difficult to satisfy demands in other fields. Above all, the means of war are raised by way of levies, which the ruling strata, by virtue of their social and political power, usually know how to transfer to the masses, quite apart from the limits set to the regimentation of property for "mercantilist" considerations.

Countries little burdened by military expenses (the United States) and especially the small countries (Switzerland, for example) often experience a stronger economic expansion than do other Powers. Moreover, occasionally small countries are more readily admitted to the economic exploitation of foreign countries because they do not arouse the fear that political intervention might follow economic intrusion.

Experience shows that the pacifist interests of petty bourgeois and proletarian strata very often and very easily fail. This is partly because of the easier accessibility of all unorganized "masses" to emotional influences and partly because of the indefinite notion (which they entertain) of some unexpected opportunity somehow arising through war. Specific interests, like the hope entertained in over-populated countries of acquiring territories for emigration, are, of course, also important in this connection. Another contributing cause is the fact that the "masses," in contrast to other interest-groups, subjectively risk a smaller stake in the game. In case of a lost war, the "monarch" has to fear for his throne, republican power-holders and groups having vested interests in a "republican constitution" have to fear the victorious "general." The majority of the propertied bourgeoisie have to fear economic loss from the brakes' being placed upon "business as usual." Under certain circumstances, should disorganization follow defeat, the ruling stratum of notables has to fear a violent shift in power in favor of the propertyless. The "masses" as such, at least in their subjective conception and in the extreme case, have nothing concrete to lose but their lives. The valuation and effect of this danger strongly fluctuates in their own minds. On the whole, it can easily be reduced to zero through emotional influence.

The fervor of this emotional influence does not, in the main, have an economic origin. It is based upon sentiments of prestige, which often extend deep down to the petty bourgeois masses of political structures rich in the historical attainment of power-positions. The attachment to all this political prestige may fuse with a specific belief in responsibility towards succeeding generations. The great power structures *per se* are then held to have a responsibility of their own for the way in which power and prestige are distributed between their own and foreign polities. It goes without saying that all those groups who hold the power to steer common conduct within a polity will most strongly instill themselves with this ideal fervor of power prestige. They remain the specific and most reliable bearers of the idea of the state as an imperialist power structure demanding unqualified devotion.

36 THE RANGE OF SOCIAL SURVEYS AND POLLS IN THE UNITED STATES

BY MILDRED BERNICE PARTEN (1902–   )
UNIVERSITY OF ROCHESTER

THE American public's economic and social conditions—its income, purchases, employment status, health, housing, migration, family composition, fertility, and countless other conditions and characteristics—have become focal points for recent surveys. Furthermore, what the people think, feel, do, and plan to do about these and projected situations is of increasing interest to survey sponsors. This interest is being expressed in a great variety of attitude and opinion studies. Public opinion on social, economic, military, international, and political issues; people's preferences for various commodities, radio and movie programs, news commentators, movie stars, political candidates; the public's habits with respect to shopping, reading magazines, listening to the radio, going to the movies, driving cars, and almost every other field of human activity are being subjected to systematic investigation by social surveyors.

Of great significance also are the numerous surveys aimed at developing new survey techniques, improving upon known methods, and finding new applications for techniques already in use. Many surveyors are aware of the criticisms leveled against their findings because of the shortcomings of their techniques. Since millions of dollars are being spent yearly for surveys, surveyors cannot afford to let these criticisms go unanswered. Thus they are constantly experimenting with the ways of extracting reliable, valid, and accurate information and views whose significance cannot be doubted. They are experimenting with ways of choosing true cross-sections of the population and developing tests of adequacy and efficiency.

The information secured in surveys may consist of extremely diverse data. It may vary from easily defined or observable objective facts about the informant to relatively complex feeling tones or atti-

* This selection and the succeeding one reprinted by permission of the author and of the publisher from *Surveys, Polls, and Samples* (New York: Harper & Brothers, 1950), pp. 1–3, 419–424. This selection is from pp. 1–3.

tudes which the individual holds with regard to certain persons, situations, or events. It may be reported in terms of simple categorical answers to questions of fact or opinion, or it may be expressed in units on scales devised to quantify human reactions or situations.

More than a million people are interviewed annually by pollers. The public has given freely of its time and has even seemed to enjoy expressing its views. It has expected nothing in return. Most of the findings of surveys are published long after the survey interviews, but many other results never are available to the general public.

One national organization, however, recognized the potential interest of the public in what people in general think, feel, and do; hence it has been releasing syndicated newspaper reports weekly, or several times a week, ever since the middle nineteen-thirties. These releases, as well as radio programs relating to surveys and polls, have done much to acquaint the public with this phase of American social science. In 1944 a poll conducted by one of the national polling agencies revealed that over half the informants had heard of public opinion polls.[1] Of these, about three-fourths seemed to feel that polls were a good thing for the country. A very small minority seemed to disapprove. But whether they approved or disapproved or were neutral, most of them were ignorant about the purposes and methods of polls. Were it not for the attempts of pollers to predict the winning candidates in presidential elections and the wide publicity given to their forecasts, the public opinion poll might have received unqualified acceptance even on the part of the originally skeptical groups. Two times the nation has developed great confidence in the ability of pollers to foretell how people were going to vote, only to find that the forecasts were wrong. This confidence in the second instance was built up from the record of several hundred or more successful forecasts of city, state, or other local election results, as well as of three national presidential elections. The election pollers had such excellent records that they had begun to believe in their own infallibility. They claimed for themselves the title of "scientific pollers" to distinguish themselves from their "unscientific" predecessors. To be sure, they employed techniques which were far in advance of those used by the earlier polls. Being social scientists, they continued to experiment with techniques and to improve them. Being businessmen also, they felt justified in capitalizing on the growing body of knowledge.

[1] E. F. Goldman, "Poll on the Polls," *Public Opinion Quarterly*, VIII (1944–1945), 461–467.

As scientists they knew that numerous factors [2] . . . could affect the outcome of an election, but as commercial enterprisers they were willing to make specific predictions to satisfy their public. It is unfortunate that the public was not informed as to where the science of polling ended and the personal judgment of pollers entered into the forecasts. After a careful analysis of several surveys of the reactions of the public to opinion polls—before and after the 1948 presidential election—Sheatsley [3] concluded that the public has adopted a surprisingly tolerant attitude toward the polls. People are still willing and even curious to be interviewed, and the majority also regard the polls as accurate. Selected groups such as some Congressmen and newspaper editors who were hostile to polls before 1948 were even more so after the election. Clients of polling agencies seemed to follow a middle course. A mail survey of 200 leaders in advertising, marketing and public relations revealed that about half of the respondents blamed the failure of the forecasts upon bad judgment in interpreting results rather than on faulty techniques. Almost a third felt there was a basic lack of validity in public opinion measurement techniques, but as a whole they felt that the setback was only temporary.[4] Within six months after the election forecast fiasco, market research agencies as well as public opinion polls were functioning at their 1948 levels.

While some surveyors are still proceeding on the assumption that their methods are peculiar to their own fields of investigation, such as marketing research, social research, psychological measurement, election polling, or radio audience surveys, many others are coming to utilize the experience and techniques of workers in other fields. This practice proves advantageous because all have a common primary goal, that of securing information from and about the general public or a selected portion of it.

[2] See Parten, *op. cit.*, chap. 12.—*Ed.*
[3] Paul B. Sheatsley, "The Public Relations of the Polls," *International Journal of Opinion and Attitude Research*, I (1947), 1–17.
[4] *Tide*, "Leadership Survey," January 7, 1949.

37 SOURCES OF ERROR IN ELECTION POLL PREDICTIONS *

BY MILDRED BERNICE PARTEN (1906–   )
UNIVERSITY OF ROCHESTER

SOME pollers hold the view that the prediction of election outcomes is outside the scope of scientific polling. With the present limited knowledge about voting behavior it is true that a large element of guesswork and personal judgment enters into the election predictions. This need not always be the case because with each passing year knowledge of the factors controlling turnout and voting behavior is being advanced. Even when almost everything is known about voting behavior, pollers may find that several forecasts are necessary to cover the various contingencies which may arise the day of the election or the evening before. The public should be informed about the various elements which could turn an election one way or another. They should know that some of these factors are beyond the ability of the poller to foresee. They should be told where polling ends and guessing begins. The pollers of the future may present their predictions with such limiting phrases as "Assuming that 75 per cent of the eligible voters vote," or "If there is no concerted effort to influence the vote near the polling booths," or "If the weather is fair in the following states," or "Providing the popular vote is at least 50 million," or "Assuming that the people who are undecided as of November 1st are going to vote just like those who have already decided on their preferences." Insofar as certain elements are unpredictable the pollers could show how their predictions of the election outcome could vary, depending on the course of these extraneous influences. If, to satisfy the general public or the bettors the poller selects a single figure for his prediction, he should caution the public that the figure is his best guess but that the results may differ from this figure, depending upon which factors loom largest on election day. Below are some of the reasons presidential election pollers may forecast incorrectly even though the polling techniques—such as

* Op. cit., pp. 419–424.

sampling methods, ascertainment of true opinions, interview procedures, interpretations, and all other polling operations—are unbiased and adequate.

1. The turnout on election day may not be predicted correctly. If a disproportionate number of one party's members stay at home on election day the prediction of votes may be in error. Much has been done in recent years to discover what factors cause people to stay away from the polls and what kinds of people do so. Evidently not enough was known in 1948 because all the pollers expressed surprise at the small turnout.

The turnout may be affected by such a factor as *overconfidence*— the feeling that the preferred candidate will be elected regardless of whether a given voter votes. In 1948 when all the major polls had assured the public that the election was "in the bag" and that Dewey was going to win, a significant number of normally Republican places had low turnouts.

Apathy may affect the turnout; the voter may not be interested in either candidate so he does not bother to vote. This is especially true if apathy toward the candidate is associated with overconfidence that the preferred party will win.

Fear that the preferred candidate may not be elected unless everyone turns out to vote for him may bring out many voters who otherwise might stay home. Voters may also be afraid that a candidate whom they dislike will get in unless they vote against him. So even if they feel neutral to the candidate they vote for, they may come forth with their protest vote.

Enthusiasm—a desire to show by a vote how much a candidate or his policies are appreciated or how much his opponent is disliked— may affect the number who go to the polls.

By 1948 techniques for determining the intensity of feelings toward candidates and issues had been well developed. According to *Fortune* editors (December, 1948), the Roper poll had revealed that enthusiasm for Dewey was not very great. The data had shown also that the public as a whole favored the New Deal and its program. But the editors had mistakenly assumed that the public wanted Dewey to administer the programs.

At one time pollers thought that a small national turnout on election day was favorable to the Republican party. The 1948 presidential vote was the smallest per capita for twenty-eight years, but still the Democrats won. So merely the *number* of people going to the polls cannot be used for forecasting the probable winner; it is the number of people with given sympathies that is important.

Closely allied to turnout is the *failure to vote* for a given position or issue. Even the number who go to the polls and who profess attachment to a given party cannot be relied upon to produce a vote for a given candidate. In 1948, about 683,000 people who voted did not cast a ballot for President. To be sure, this might have been an oversight on the part of some, but for others it indicated a disapproval of both candidates or enthusiasm for a local candidate or issue.

2. The vote on a given candidate may be affected by the entire ballot. Certain candidates or issues on the ballot may draw a large vote because they are popular with the voters while other candidates or issues about which the voters are more neutral may receive large votes merely because they are sponsored by the same political group as the more popular candidate or issue. In presidential elections, city, country, or state candidates of the same party as the President often "ride in on his coattails." If enthusiasm for the presidential candidate is not high but if strong local candidates are listed on the ballot, the reverse situation might result—the presidential candidates might be swept into office on the coattails of popular Congressmen or other state candidates or issues. One of the functions of forecasters is to determine which candidate or issue has the greatest appeal to voters.

3. If the interviews are conducted too long in advance of election day the forecast may be wrong. Polling results may be correct as of the date the poll was taken, but if shifts in opinion occur between the date of the poll and the actual election, the forecast may easily be wrong. Pollers are aware of these shifts and so they usually continue sampling right up to the day before election. The telegraphic polls described elsewhere are particularly useful for these last-minute polls. According to published reports on the 1948 election forecasts, all three of the well-known national pollers stopped polling too soon. One poller, Mr. Roper, took his last poll in September. Crossley's interviewing took place three weeks before the election, and the field work for the Gallup poll ended more than a week before the election. All these pollers had observed a trend toward Truman during the months preceding the election but, as Crossley pointed out, they did not believe the trend would be sufficiently accelerated to overcome the 5-point lead Dewey had in mid-October.

4. The adjustments made by pollers to allow for trends toward or away from a given candidate between the last interviews and the election may be incorrect. Although the Gallup poll reported a sample of some 60,000 interviews during the period preceding the 1948 November poll, these interviews were spread over two months. Since Truman seemed to be gaining in popularity with each successive sample, Gallup had to guess whether this swing would continue at the same rate right up to election day, whether it would slow down, or whether it would stop or greatly accelerate toward the end of the campaign.

Even if the poll had been taken the day before the election, the poller had to be prepared for shifts which might result from an election eve broadcast or from events which might swing the vote even on election day. A sudden drop in the price of a farm commodity, a Pearl Harbor, a stock market crash, or extensive efforts on the part of one political group or its supporters to get out the vote might upset the best predictions. Even if sudden upsetting factors do not occur, the vote forecaster must guess how to project his figures to carry him beyond his interviews into the day of the election. In a Congressional investigation conducted after the 1944 presidential election, one poller reported that his published forecast of the election was 2 percentage points higher for Dewey than the figure he had obtained through interviews. He justified this on the ground that the trend was toward Dewey and this was his best guess as to what would happen by election time.

5. Events or speeches on election eve or election day sometimes cannot be foreseen by pollers. In an Australian election reported by Morgan [1] voters were handed printed cards by party officials showing them how to mark the ballots on several rather complicated issues being submitted to a referendum. The discrepancy between how the people voted and what they had told pollers was, in one instance, about 8 percentage points. The results of the election corroborated the findings of the polls on several issues in which public opinion and the printed card agreed, but when the two were in disagreement the card won out at the polls. Efficient forecasters need to know about plans such as cards, or other techniques to influence votes during election day. To the extent that such methods come as a surprise to pollers, to that extent may their prognostications be upset.

[1] Roy Morgan, "Last-Minute Changes in Voting Intention," *Public Opinion Quarterly,* XII (1948), 470–480.

6. Pollers may make poor guesses as to what the "undecided" groups will do on election day. Several studies have been made about what happens to the people who have not made up their minds about voting when questioned by interviewers. Techniques have been used such as having interviewers carry a secret ballot box with them, questioning the undecided about what he did or how he voted in the last election, and studying the characteristics of the undecided so that a reasonable guess may be made as to how he is likely to vote, if at all, on election day. In the 1948 election the pollers said that they had divided the undecided cases in the same proportion as the decided votes were distributed among the candidates. After the election, the pollers were of the opinion that most of the undecided votes had swung to Truman. Use of the techniques available to the pollers at that time should have given greater insight into what the undecided were likely to do. If there was no way of determining, the pollers might have warned the public of the possibilities if the undecided all turned toward one candidate. When one poller stopped polling, 15 per cent of the persons interviewed were still undecided. As many as 7 per cent were undecided when the last polls were taken.

7. The election results might be too close to be detectable or predictable from samples. The polls claim that errors of sampling in their polls are almost certain not to exceed 4 percentage points. If the sample happens to be that extreme deviate of one case in a thousand that may occur by the laws of chance, the poll findings may be incorrect. If one major party candidate were to receive 48 per cent of the popular vote and the other 49 per cent, sampling polls could not be reliable within such close percentages. The problem is multiplied manyfold, however, when the forecasters attempt to predict electoral votes. In all the states in which the popular vote for the leading candidates is very close, samples might fall down. In the 1948 presidential election, Truman won over Dewey in Ohio by only about 6000 votes in a total of about 3 million. In Illinois and California Truman led by slightly more than 30,000 votes in a total of about 4 million in each State. Such close margins would require extremely large samples to detect accurately.

8. Any one or more of the techniques of polls may be faulty and thus tend to produce biased results even as of the date of the poll. Quota sampling in which interviewers tend to select biased samples of the voting population, or in which weights assigned various population groups are incorrect, may produce inaccurate results. The

greater the time between the federal census and the election . . . the more hazardous the choice of weights used by pollers who employ . . . sampling techniques requiring up-to-date census data.

Other distortions can result from the use of mail ballots with inadequate protection from self-selected samples, from faulty interviewing or recording of results, from failure to reveal honest or true opinions or to gauge intensity of feeling, and from failure of analysts to interpret the meaning of the figures obtained. Thus, in addition to unpredictable factors, preventable errors arising at every stage of polling procedure may permanently distort the findings and the fore casts based upon them.[2]

38 THE ANALYSIS OF PROPAGANDA A CLINICAL SUMMARY *

BY ALFRED MCCLUNG LEE (1906–   )[1]
BROOKLYN COLLEGE

IN ONE sense, propaganda can be thought of as a use of expression-forms in such a way as to convey ideas rapidly to many people. Through graphic symbols, music, pageantry, and combinations of words the propagandist makes impressions upon masses of people. These impressions are sometimes vivid. They are frequently charged with emotion. They may be wholly or partially "true," confusing, or "false."

[2] See selected references in Parten, *op. cit.*, p. 424, and excellent bibliography, pp. 537–602.—*Ed.*

* Reprinted by permission of the editor from *The American Journal of Sociology*, LI (1945–46), 126–135.

[1] My colleagues in the Institute for Propaganda Analysis during my tenure as executive director aided me in many ways to develop the conceptions of propaganda, analytical techniques, and opinion modification set forth in this article. I want to mention indebtedness especially to Kirtley F. Mather, Harvard University, Institute president; F. Ernest Johnson, Columbia University and Federal Council of Churches, vice-president; Clyde R. Miller, Columbia University, secretary of the board; Clyde Beals, *Fortune Magazine,* former Institute editor; and Barrington Moore, Jr., U. S. Department of Justice, former Institute research assistant. Helpful with comments and suggestions on the manuscript were these Institute board members: Ralph D. Casey, University of Minnesota; Maurice R. Davie, Yale University; Forrest E. Long, National Safety Council and New York University; Peter H. Odegard, Amherst College and the U. S. Treasury Department; and Robert K. Speer, New York University.

If such impressions were transmitted in a detailed and accurate manner rather than in the shorthand of the propagandist, few would bother to listen; most would be bored. In moments given to decision, vividness and emotion-arousing symbolism frequently override common-sense demands for accuracy and for an opportunity to question and discuss.

This communication shorthand, through the purposeful use of omnibus symbols, facilitates and may even be said to be one of the elements making it possible for us to develop—for better or for worse —modern mass-political and mass-business action. It is an efficient way of attracting votes [2] and retail sales. Regardless of the intrinsic virtues of a political candidate or a brand of canned goods, a social reform or a religious doctrine, people are powerfully influenced in their judgment of these items by the impressions made by omnibus symbols, that is, by glittering generalities and name-calling symbols. Such impressions would be more accurate if derived from careful exposition, but few people have the necessary patience to read such expositions.

The word "propaganda" as used in this article is a colorless and yet descriptive term for a type of mass persuasion. [3] Those who contrast something they call "education" with something "quite different" that they call "propaganda" usually reveal before long that they

[2] Paul F. Lazarsfeld ("The Election Is Over," *Public Opinion Quarterly*, VIII [1944], 317–30) concludes (p. 330) that "elections are decided by the events occurring in the entire period between two Presidential elections and not by the campaign. . . . Only a very small percentage of people can be considered so truly undecided that propaganda can still convert them, and those are likely to be of a special kind." But, in this, Lazarsfeld neglects the role of propaganda in interpreting significant events "occurring in the entire period," in relating those events to popular sentiments and desires. As Kimball Young notes, in his *Social Psychology* (2d ed.; New York: F. S. Crofts & Co., 1944), p. 505, propaganda is "part of the larger process of legend- and myth-making." It is not merely a phase of a campaign; it is ever present in society.

[3] The meaning used here is much like that which "propaganda" originally acquired as a label for one of the departments of Roman Catholic pontifical administration. Pope Gregory XV formally established the Sacra Congregatio de Propaganda Fide on June 22, 1622, with his Bull, *Inscrutabili Divinae*. The body had gradually evolved to this point under a Cardinalitial Commission de Propaganda Fide, appointed by Gregory XIII (1572–85). This powerful department is "charged with the spread of Catholicism and with the regulation of ecclesiastical affairs in non-Catholic countries. The intrinsic importance of its duties and the extraordinary extent of its authority and of the territory under its jurisdiction have caused the cardinal prefect of propaganda to be known as the 'red pope' " (see Mgr. Umberto Benigni, "Propaganda, Sacred Congregation of," *Catholic Encyclopedia* [New York: Encyclopedia Press, 1913], XII, 456–61; p. 456 quoted). As a result of financial distress

are attempting to give to their own ideas about politics, economics, social philosophy, or whatnot a virtuous and respected label, "education," which may be unwarranted, and to attach "propaganda" as a "bad" label to ideas to which they are opposed. As Edrita Fried [4] points out in her analysis of propaganda techniques utilized in World War II, the "distrust which the public exhibits toward anything they sense to be propaganda is constantly anticipated by the propagandists."

Science and propaganda have also been contrasted, but here again one frequently has reason to suspect the conscious or unconscious support of an otherwise questionable position: that the word "science" becomes a manipulable virtue word and the word "propaganda" is treated as an evil label. It is naturally possible to contrast the merits of scientific conclusions, based upon adequate observations, with those of casual opinions—when these differ—that are spun out of random observations, prejudices, personal interests, and imaginings. But the student of propaganda and of social processes realizes that both scientific conclusions and purely imagined ideas are woven together into propaganda. Propaganda ideas or symbols may be true or false, good or bad, in your interest or against the interests you assume to be those of yourself and of the groups to which you belong, the interests you take to be those of "society" or at least those "best for society." [5]

---

among missions, a Society de Propaganda Fide came into being May 3, 1822, at Lyons, France.

It is because of this background that the Merriam Dictionary defines propaganda as "any organized or concerted group effort or movement to spread a particular doctrine or system of doctrines or principles." The term fell into popular disrepute during World War I, according to H. D. Lasswell, "when inconvenient news and opinion was stigmatized as 'enemy propaganda'" (see his "The Study and Practice of Propaganda," in Lasswell, R. D. Casey, and B. L. Smith, *Propaganda and Promotional Activities* [Minneapolis: University of Minnesota Press, 1935], pp. 3–27; p. 3 quoted).

Because of this situation, the Merriam Dictionary also notes, in the edition quoted above, that "now, often" propaganda refers to "secret or clandestine dissemination of ideas, information, gossip, or the like for the purpose of helping or injuring a person, an institution, a cause, etc." But this propagandistic service of the word "propaganda," it is the belief of the present author, should not stand in the way of its original, more technical, and more objective use.

[4] "Techniques of Persuasion," in *Propaganda by Short Wave,* ed. by H. L. Childs and J. B. Whitton (Princeton: Princeton University Press, 1942), pp. 261–301; p. 266 quoted.

[5] See the author's "Interest Criteria in Propaganda Analysis," *American Sociological Review,* X (1945), 282–288.

Propaganda, to offer a more formal definition, is the use of words, symbols, ideas, events, and personalities with the intention of forwarding or attacking an interest, cause, project, institution, or person in the eyes and minds of a public.[6] From a slightly different standpoint, propaganda is the expression of a point of view overtly stated or covertly implied for the purpose of influencing the thought and action of others. As viewed by the object of the propagandist, propaganda can also be thought of as the barrage of words, symbols, ideas, and events with which members of publics are assailed in efforts to change attitudes, prejudices, opinions, loyalties, and modes of living.

In the work of the Institute for Propaganda Analysis, five ways of looking upon propaganda for analytical purposes evolved. While they have not been previously brought together in a systematic statement, these types of analysis are the (1) societal,[7] (2) social-psychological,[8] (3) communications,[9] (4) psychological[10] and (5) technical.[11] As the following discussion indicates, these ways of analyzing propaganda overlap somewhat, but they have the merit of pointing to the necessary elements in any adequate analysis of propaganda and of suggesting the broad significance of propaganda analysis as an application or orientation of social science.

[6] This and the other definition given represent efforts to bring together useful elements from many of the definitions that have been put forward. Leonard W. Doob, in his *Propaganda: Its Psychology and Technique* (New York: Henry Holt, 1935), recognized the element of purpose in his "Principle of the Intention of the Propagandist," which he stated thus: "In intentional propaganda, the propagandist is aware of his interested aim; in unintentional propaganda, he does not appreciate the social effect of his own actions." In view of the fact that propagandists can seldom predict or even suspect and appreciate the "social effect" of their actions, this distinction does not appear valid. It is therefore more useful to indicate that a propagandist is always intentional in a general way but that this does not imply a grasp of the probable or actual consequences of his actions. If a person unconsciously serves the purposes of a propagandist, it would be more accurate to label him a "propaganda instrument" or possibly a "fellow-traveler" or "front" rather than an "unintentional propagandist."

[7] See, e.g., *Propaganda Analysis,* esp. IV (1940–42), Nos. 4, 8, 11.

[8] *Ibid.,* esp. III (1939–40), 105–11, and IV (1940–42), Nos. 4, 11.

[9] *Ibid.,* esp. I (1937–38), 12–32, 53–64; and IV (1940–42), Nos. 1, 3, 4, 9, 12, 13.

[10] *Ibid.,* esp. II (1938–39), 13–28, 61–77; and III (1939–40), 19–28, 43–52.

[11] *Ibid.,* esp. I (1937–38), ix–xiii, 5–18. See also A. M. and E. B. Lee, *The Fine Art of Propaganda* (New York: Harcourt, Brace & Co., and Institute for Propaganda Analysis, 1939), esp. chaps. iii–ix.

I. SOCIETAL APPROACH

Propaganda grows out of and plays a part in social tensions and struggles, and its effectiveness is controlled in this societal sense by the trend of popular sentiments and by the limits to societal change set by environmental conditions. Given such differences as those in this country between management and workers, patients and physicians, men and women, Negroes and whites, business leaders and politicians, uneducated and educated, and the various religious organizations, we must apparently regard as inevitable the continuous jockeyings by individuals for position and advantage in terms of group interest. Much of the contents of our newspapers, magazines, books, motion pictures, and radio programs contain the facts and rationalizations, claims and counterclaims, of the propagandas utilized in such struggles.

Donald C. Blaisdell and Jane Greverus have listed noteworthy characteristics of a typical social struggle, the struggle for power between government and business, in their *Economic Power and Political Pressures*,[12] written for the Temporary National Economic Committee, as follows: (*a*) invisibility of most of the action; (*b*) continuity of the struggle and the staying power of the contestants; (*c*) varying intensity; and (*d*) constantly shifting battleground.

Since other broad societal struggles have somewhat similar characteristics, it will be well to describe these in more detail, as follows:

(a) **Invisibility.** As Blaisdell and Greverus point out, "The factors which influence legislators . . . are the legislator's own political convictions, his mail from his district or State, the lobbyists who approach him in his office or in the halls of the Capitol, or the witnesses who appear before him in committee. None of these activities is carried on with the publicity devoted to formal congressional action." And, as Edward L. Bernays, a propagandist, has pointed out in his *Propaganda* (1928), "Propaganda is the executive arm of the invisible government." From kindergarten charts and motion pictures to scholarly monographs, in legislative halls and newspaper editorial rooms, as instigators of barrages of telegrams or of an impressive delegation, propagandists exhibit fully the various techniques of using this "executive arm of the invisible government."

(b) **Continuity.** "From the first days of the Republic to the present," Blaisdell and Greverus observe, "the contest [between govern-

---

[12] Washington: U. S. Government Printing Office, 1941, pp. 6–8.

ment and business] has never ceased. . . . There have been periods
which seemed relatively peaceful, but for the most part the peace was
on the surface, and indicated temporary gains on the part of business
when it controlled the Government and was not forced to resort to
secondary weapons to accomplish its will." In this struggle the greater
staying power of business . . . has "paid off" time after time.

(c) **Intensity.** "The strength and bitterness of the conflict are usually determined primarily by the philosophy of the temporary leaders
of government. . . . Their interpretations of events, their political
debts, their view of the future—all these things and many more determine the intensity of their participation. The philosophy of business
is not subject to change to nearly the same extent. Business wants government to leave it alone, and also wants to be able to use governmental authority in its own internecine competitions. This is a pervasive, single-minded philosophy, adhered to by businessmen generally, and providing a real rallying point for their energies." The
strategic significance of varying intensity in a struggle should not be
underrated.

(d) **Shifting Battleground.** "The first battle of the conflict occurs
in the choice of legislators. The second takes place in the legislature
itself. If business loses that, it resorts to the administrative agencies
charged with the enforcement of the law; if it loses there, or sometimes while it is fighting there, it has recourse to the courts; and if
it loses again, the struggle reverts to the legislature, taking the form
of an attempt to amend or repeal the law. The forces of propaganda
are, of course, in constant use." To mobilize pressure upon governmental units, the battleground shifts from arena to arena in the struggle for public support, for co-operating organizations, for the machinery of propaganda.

The societal approach involves, briefly, these analytical procedures:

(a) The investigator should discover first, to the extent possible,
the nature of the underlying social tensions and struggles that have
given rise to the propaganda.

(b) He should then determine who is fighting or competing with
whom and for what purposes, as nearly as this can be done. Are the
discoverable purposes ones with which the investigator wishes to be
identified, ones that he wants to oppose, or ones to which he can permit himself to be indifferent? [13]

---

[13] The persistent assumption of many sociological writers that their interest
criteria are only those of "social welfare" or "societal health," that they need not
compensate for individual and especially group and class biases, is regarded as an
untenable one (see n. 5 above).

(c) Is the apparent issue in the struggle a distractive or a fundamental one? See the discussion below of "selecting the issue" in connection with the "technical approach" to propaganda analysis.

(d) In what other conflicts or tensions have these particular propagandists become involved? This information will appear as the investigation of (a), (b), and (c) proceeds. It will help to relate the tension under investigation to other tensions.

In the arena thus defined by society, with its tensions and struggles and its slowly changing structure, the propagandist searches for "strings" by which he can tug at common motivations of men and make them believe and behave in the ways he wishes. This swings our focus to the "social-psychological approach."

2. SOCIAL-PSYCHOLOGICAL APPROACH

Within societal limitations, propaganda's effectiveness depends upon either luck or the propagandist's "intuitive" or conscious knowledge of how his audiences will react to mass-communication stimuli.[14] To guide a propagandist, a knowledge of sentiments—the basic emotional patterns underlying thought and action, defined by cultural and other environmental factors—is even more useful than the reports of public opinions, which are the "surface" answers of people to questions put by strangers. Not only are sentiments deep, largely unverbalized, and withal powerful in the determination of opinion and behavior, but they are also in many cases ambivalent. They help to define the love *and* hate with which we regard persons close to us and many other ambivalences that are sometimes merely dismissed with the label "mixed emotions" or "vacillating opinions." Opinions of the sort gathered by public opinion interviewers are significant chiefly as indications of what people . . . answer offhand to comparative strangers. . . . A student who did not understand the social-psychological background of opinion reports before Pearl Harbor Sunday, 1941, would scarcely have been prepared for the dramatic manner in which the Japanese attack "changed everything."

[14] By "intuitive" is meant the manner in which folkways and folk beliefs become ingrained in the minds of people, especially during their formative years. Those patterns become integral parts of their mental processes and are not used objectively and thoughtfully in many cases but automatically and without questioning. When not equipped with such knowledge, a propagandist has great difficulty in convincing an audience. And to synthesize such mental equipment requires an amount of preparation, study, and care that emphasizes the complexity of a society's and even of a group's cultural equipment.

The social-psychological appeals that a propagandist can make are exemplified by the chief ones used by proponents of prohibition in this country. In the hands of Dry propagandists, prohibition comes (1) to offer a religiously sanctioned scapegoat in the form of Liquor; (2) to provide religiously sanctioned child-substitutes, those who need to be protected from Alcohol; (3) to cater to exaggerated needs for perfection; (4) to furnish a formula for simplification, a security-giving orientation in an all-too-complex world; (5) to give a pattern for regression, a retreat in fantasy to a life-period in which Drys fancy they were more content and especially more secure; (6) to permit a flight from reality into the prohibition movement's mysticism; and (7) to encourage the identification of adherents with the movement as a whole and with each other.[15]

To sum up, the social-psychological approach to propaganda analysis can be presented in the form of these analytical questions that may be used to develop an understanding of many specific propagandas:

(a) What are the sentiments, mores, and moral idealizations to which the propagandist is attempting to appeal and with which he is attempting to identify his proposals?

(b) Do such sentiments, mores, and moral idealizations now exist in the minds of enough people, or have they changed to an extent that may counteract the effectiveness of the propagandist's efforts?

(c) To what other common psychological patterns does he appeal? Can he use them effectively?

(d) In making such appeals, what is the propagandist attempting to accomplish? With whose interests is his effort in line?

Once one has determined the nature of the propaganda's societal setting, the struggles out of which it arises, and the nature of its social-psychological dynamics, the appeals that give it emotional drive, the next question is: What are the mediums through which the propagandist transmits his messages? This is covered by the "communications approach."

3. COMMUNICATORY APPROACH

As in advertising, so in the whole broader field of publicity in general, the mediums through which messages may be carried delimit

[15] For a more detailed exposition and analysis of these specific appeals see the present author's "Techniques of Social Reform: An Analysis of the New Prohibition Drive," *American Sociological Review*, IX (1944), 65-77, esp. 74-75. For another

the potential size of the audiences. In turning the potential audience into actual and receptive readers or listeners, naturally much depends upon the message itself and general social conditions. Mediums also have another characteristic: They are owned and operated by human beings who also have special interests. Few messages pass unchanged from the propagandist through agencies of mass communication to a mass public.

To make a message course speedily and powerfully through communication mediums, one must have one or more of these three aids: (a) suitable events associated with the message to make its reporting appear to be imperative or desirable, (b) plausible propaganda theories associated with such events that will be sure to remain attached to reports and interpretations, and (c) organizational support that will further emphasize the message's importance.

Through the communications approach to propaganda analysis, the attempt is made to ascertain the kind and character of the publicity mediums being used and especially to learn the actual degree of currency being achieved by the propaganda. In addition to indicating the skill of the propagandist, this knowledge also leads to information concerning identities of interest between the propagandist and those who control advertising appropriations for direct-propaganda purposes and those who control the mediums themselves and thus can make them receptive to free publicity, both direct and indirect.

The communications approach to propaganda analysis can be summarized, at least for the purposes of suggesting its scope, in the form of these analytical questions:

(a) What is the publicity potential of the available mediums?

(b) To what extent can the propagandists enlarge and to what extent are they extending the number and importance of the mediums?

(c) How is the use of the mediums being financed?

(d) What are the policies of the available mediums? How significant are these policies?

(e) How well are the propagandists using the mediums? In other words, does their actual audience absorb all the potential audiences?

The last question naturally verges on the problems discussed above in connection with the social-psychological approach. It raises the issue of how effective a grasp the propagandist has upon the sentiment, moretic, and moral idioms—upon the techniques that will ap-

example see "Propaganda for Blitzkrieg," *Propaganda Analysis,* III (1939–40), 105–11.

peal to the sentiments, mores, and moral idealizations—of the masses he wishes to reach.

The three overlapping approaches to propaganda analysis that have been sketched mark out the most significant social aspects of a given propaganda program. They point to avenues for analyzing the tensions and struggles out of which propagandas arise and in which they have a part; the common patterns of popular motivation to which the propagandist appeals; and the channels through which the propagandist places and keeps his message before the publics he wants to influence. Because the strengths and weaknesses of the propagandist himself play powerful roles in determining the success of his program, it is desirable next to turn to an approach to propaganda analysis by way of this technician himself—in other words, the "psychological approach."

4. Psychological Approach

A propagandist tries to capitalize upon what he regards as his strengths, and he has to work within his own limitations or at least find ways of adjusting to them. To understand adequately the problems inherent in studying the propagandist himself is far from a simple assignment; psychology and psychiatry must be called into play. For our present purposes it is impossible to do more than to suggest briefly the vast complex of considerations this represents and then to offer (a) a group of principles and (b) a group of analytical questions.

Who is the propagandist? Or who are the propagandists? Sometimes this alone is difficult to learn, but there is one shortcut to this information: Read what the sharpest opponents of a propaganda program have to say. They will attack, in part, in terms of personalities. And although many of the things they say will be inaccurate or at least torn out of context and unfair, their comments frequently point to "prime movers" in a propaganda program and aid in characterizing such operators.

In using a psychological approach, it is well to remember the limitations outlined above upon the effectiveness of the propagandist. He must work under societal, social-psychological, and communications conditions that are largely defined for him and which he can do relatively little to alter. As Abraham Lincoln once put it: "I claim not to have controlled events, but confess plainly that events have controlled me." And even Napoleon Bonaparte, whose epochal blunders cost so much in lives and substance, had a glimpse of his own role when he said: "I declare myself the most enslaved man in the world. My master has no pity, and by my master I mean the Nature of Things." This was an effort at self-justification, but it was probably an accurate one.

Granted such insights into the nature of leadership and of societal change, the propaganda leader still figures as a person who can do the possible or can sell many people on attempting to do the impossible, who can use his energy and ability to minimize the pains to society of a forthcoming change or who can be sufficiently a blunderer to dissipate the efforts of followers and even to bring to them and to society additional maladjustments.

The foregoing can now be summed up in the following statements of principle:

(a) Social struggles and their resulting propagandas attract personalities of types that find needed self-expression in their appeals, promises, and activities.

(b) The personality types thus attracted in turn have strengths and limitations that are felt throughout the movement.

(c) The functions of propagandists in a movement can be labeled, according to typical roles: agitator, professional promoter, "front," bureaucrat, "heeler," and "fellow-traveler." Professional promoters and bureaucrats, especially the latter, tend to infiltrate a movement more and more as it passes from a dynamic, driving, pioneering stage to a more retentive, institutionalized, job-holding stage in its life-history.

In addition to the application of these principles, the following questions are also helpful for analytical purposes:

(a) To identify the propaganda personalities involved, what do the sharpest opponents of the propaganda program have to say?

(b) Does the propagandist give any evidence of working within societal possibilities? Or does he promote a program regardless of possibilities and consequences? These questions must be answered in a broad and objective fashion.

(c) If the propagandist is effective, in the sense of creating a sizable impact with his efforts, what will be the consequences of his work?

After pursuing these ways of analyzing propaganda and the propagandist in their social setting, it is then appropriate to turn to the analysis of the techniques and tactics used by propagandists. This type of propaganda analysis is called here the "technical approach."

5. Technical Approach

Propagandists use certain "tricks of the trade," or "propaganda techniques," which can be described rather simply and, with practice, can be easily identified.[16] Some of the propaganda devices now so subtly and effectively used both for and against our interests are as old as language, as political agitation, and as social struggles. All are used in one form or another by all of us in our daily dealings with one another.

Propagandists seize upon the methods we ordinarily use to convince one another; but they analyze and refine them and experiment with them until such homely devices of folk origin develop into tremendously powerful weapons for swaying popular opinions and actions.

In order to avoid technical language and to make our findings more generally useful, popular terms for common propaganda devices are retained here. Considerable experience with them by scientific analysts, businessmen, teachers, and college and high-school students indicates that the list, as now revised, has at least three necessary qualifications that fit it for our purposes: The techniques described are workable. Anyone, with practice, can use them. Even though they do not represent an exhaustive or conclusive list, they give the intelligent beginner in propaganda analysis a good start, so far as the technical approach is concerned. His own experiences with these eleven techniques will then permit him to develop his analytical ability further.[17]

Some of the chief devices used both in popular argument and by professional propagandists are the eleven following, which fall roughly into four groupings:[18]

[16] This approach is sometimes labeled "content analysis," but such a term limits the approach unduly to rhetorical considerations.

[17] The character of these techniques should not be confused with that of the traditional "logical fallacies." Propaganda techniques may be used for delusive, as well as for constructive, purposes; they refer to common patterns of persuasion and promotion or destruction. In short, these propaganda techniques are meant to be descriptions of patterns of behavior without concern at this point for their moral or social values. On the other hand, the "fallacies" of the logicians are practices in intellectual disrepute.

[18] *The Fine Art of Propaganda* and other publications of the Institute for Propaganda Analysis discuss seven propaganda devices. These seven are: name-calling, glittering generality, transfer, testimonial, plain folks, card-stacking, and band wagon. Considerable subsequent experimentation with the teaching of propaganda analysis to college students and to non-college audiences indicates that the new list of eleven techniques, while not represented as an exhaustive one, is more satisfactory,

A. Techniques of basic procedure
  1. Selecting the issue
  2. Case-making
  3. Simplification
B. Use of omnibus words (basic propaganda shorthand)
  4. Name-calling
  5. Glittering generality
C. Techniques of identification
  6. Transfer
  7. Testimonial
  8. Plain folks
  9. Band wagon
D. Strategic techniques
  10. Hot potato
  11. Stalling

The three techniques of basic procedure (A) are functional steps through which propagandists habitually go, more or less consciously, in organizing or reorganizing a propaganda program, as is shown in more detail below. The role of omnibus words (B) as a kind of basic propaganda shorthand is mentioned at the outset of this article. These protean labels, both name-calling words and glittering generalities, with other supporting and parallel symbols, carry much of the direct burden of the propagandist's message. Through the four techniques of identification (C), a propaganda project is identified with a preferred or detested institution or personality (transfer or testimonial), with the masses of the plain folks or with what "everybody" accepts or rejects (plain folks or band wagon). And the two strategic techniques (D) help to characterize the many ways in which a propagandist attempts to counteract the effectiveness of his opposition's work.

For the sake of brevity, these eleven techniques will merely be defined here:

1. *Selecting the issue* refers to the effort of the propagandist to select and state the issue upon which he chooses to make his stand in a social competition or conflict. From a current tactical standpoint, the issue that is accepted by a public as the crucial one in a contest has considerable bearing upon where the struggle begins, its support, and the relative advantages of such a starting-point to the partisans. Little wonder, therefore, that propagandists consider selecting the issue—in reality selecting the battleground—as primary business in a campaign and a matter on which to keep constant watch throughout the struggle. After all, shifts in the battle—in issues, in fields, and in terms of conflict—must constantly be planned and prepared.

---

particularly when seen in perspective in relation to the other four approaches to propaganda analysis: the societal, social-psychological, communications, and psychological. Because of its connotations of unfairness, *card-stacking* has been replaced by *case-making*. Naturally, many other techniques and strategies suggest themselves, but it is useful to keep the list from becoming too long and unwieldy.

2. *Case-making* is frequently the second step in propagandizing. It is the ordering of facts or falsehoods, illustrations or distractions or distortions, logical or illogical statements, in such a sequence that the best or worst possible impression will be made. Case-making is what lawyers do in preparing their cases for judge and jury, what political strategists do in working out campaign manuals and speech instructions for their candidates. Case-making accepts the issue or issues selected and uses the available arts of logic, interpretation, factual selection, and rhetoric to make the propagandist's cause appear great, noble, and honorable, or at least acceptable and necessary, and to make the opposition's cause appear dastardly, uncivilized, money-grubbing, unprincipled, or at least unnecessary.

3. *Simplification* refers to the reduction of propaganda materials to formulas which approach in brevity and dogmatism as nearly as possible the form of a slogan. Inaccuracy is not necessarily inherent in simplification, but the propagandist can seldom deal in shades of gray, in "maybes" or "perhapses." In his language, everything tends to become black *or* white, good *or* bad, yes *or* no. Simplification short-circuits the sound common sense of medical evidence, of psychiatric findings, or of engineering principles, because such common sense involves approximations, and that may "confuse" a public.

4. *Name-calling* is the practice of shortcutting discussion by giving an idea a bad label, to make us reject and condemn an idea without examining the evidence.

5. *Glittering generality* is the practice of shortcutting discussion by associating an idea with a "virtue word" in order to make us accept the proposal without examining the evidence further.

6. and 7. *Transfer* and *testimonial* are two ways of gaining some identity between a propagandist's project and an honored institution, symbol, or personality or—if attack is the purpose—between the opposition's project and a hated institution, symbol, or personality. Transfer carries the authority, sanction, and prestige of a respected institution over to something else, in order to make the latter more readily acceptable, or it does the opposite. Testimonial consists in having some respected or hated person say that a given idea or program or product or person is good or bad. Both transfer and testimonial thus function to bring about shifts in the loyalties of groups; they are means for identifying new groups with the propagandist's project in terms of the groups' own enthusiasms and loyalties. Either can be used to build up guilt—or virtue-by-association. The two

other techniques of identification achieve their aims somewhat differently.

8. and 9. *Plain folks* and *band wagon* are ways of indicating an allegedly existing identity or community of interest between the propaganda spokesman and his audience. Plain folks is the method by which a speaker attempts to convince his audience that he and his ideas are good because they are "of the people." The band-wagon technique, on the other hand, is a means for making us follow the crowd and accept a propagandist's program as a whole because of its popularity and without taking the time to examine and weigh the evidence. The plain-folks technique calls for the identification of the propagandist himself with his audience; the band-wagon device involves the identifying of members of his audience with the group "now on the band wagon."

10. *Hot potato* is a popular term for buck-passing, and for the sort of thing implied in the question, "Have you stopped beating your wife?" Something similar has been called by D. E. Saunders[19] the "propaganda of provocation." The hot potato is the technique through which a propagandist springs an event, a trap, a situation upon his opponent that will be interpreted by most people to the discredit of the opponent. The event, trap, or situation need not be fictitious. From the standpoint of effectiveness, it is better if the propagandist makes skilful use of events beyond his control. The hot potato depends for its power chiefly upon timing and interpretation.

11. *Stalling* involves a play for time, the use of plausible delaying tactics that may permit the opposition to lose vigor, interest, or support before the real struggle occurs. It may take the form of the appointment of an investigating committee,[20] the insistence upon adhering to "the proper sequence" (red tape), as well as the more familiar and sometimes endless memo-passing.

What can the propaganda analyst do with these eleven techniques when he has learned to spot them? Knowledge of them gives the analyst an opportunity to detect shortcuts in argument. Once these shortcuts and others are detected and understood, it is then possible for the analyst to decide whether or not they are being used against his interests, against the interests of "society."

---

[19] See "Speaking of Rudolf Hess," *Propaganda Analysis*, IV (1940–42), No. 76.

[20] Committees can also be used for other purposes in propaganda, especially as propaganda "sounding boards." Congressional committees, with their carefully staged investigations, have been useful to a wide range of special interests in this fashion.

The technical approach to propaganda analysis in particular and the other four approaches in general can be summed up briefly in the following list of analytical questions:

What is the source of the propaganda? In other words, who is the propagandist, and for what organization or cause is he working?

What is the social setting of the propaganda?

What is the over-all point of view of the propaganda? What is its objective? Is its objective socially possible? With what other objectives than its primary one is it identified?

What propaganda techniques is the propagandist trying to use?

In what ways does he use the techniques of basic procedure—selecting the issue, case-making, and simplification?

For what purposes is he using name-calling, glittering generality, transfer, testimonial, plain folks, band wagon, hot potato, and/or stalling?

What group's interests do the propagandist's objectives assist?

39 SOCIAL ACTION AND EDUCATION *

BY DAN W. DODSON (1907–)
NEW YORK UNIVERSITY

TODAY we realize that there is no dichotomy between social action and education. The one is a necessary complement to the other. For a long time, Educational Sociology leadership has contended that education had not taken place until behavior was changed. The criteria of health education, for instance, must be the improvement of health in the community. The criteria of the effectiveness of programs in human relations are not to be measured in the bales of literature produced, the speeches made, or even the development of "conflict-free ritualized" relations between children in school, but rather in the improvement of intergroup relations in the social milieu in which people function, namely the community.

In order to accomplish this change of patterns of community life,

* Reprinted (slightly shortened) by permission from *The Journal of Educational Sociology*, XXII (1949–50), 346–351; full article on pp. 345–351.

it is not sufficient to change individuals' attitudes. There must be a concern with the change of the group and institutional structure through which prejudices and cleavages are channeled. There is considerable evidence to indicate that the production of social change today depends less upon attitudes of individuals than upon moving the position of social institutions. If documentation of this point is needed one has only to look at the way in which the peoples of the world are pleading for peace and note the difficulty of moving the position of the institutions of government in that direction. Yet the major emphasis on peace education is focused toward changing individuals' attitudes. The one thing we learned about integration as a result of the war, was that where management at the top took a firm, positive stand there was no difficulty in integrating Negroes and whites. In public housing in New York City some one hundred thousand families are living in peace and harmony on a completely integrated basis because management, which was public, took the position from the beginning that this is "public housing" and being *public,* it is open to whoever qualifies, irrespective of race, creed, or color. In the four and one-half years during which I was Executive Director of the Mayor's Committee on Unity, there were not more than two evictions growing out of disputes between people of different ethnic backgrounds and neither of these disputes had its origin in ethnic differences. The institutional position in the community, unlike the individual's position—except where the individual is cloutered within the vestments of an institutional office—represents vested interests and usually represents the *status quo.* There is no formula yet known to this author where vested interests give up their preferred position without resistance. We have not learned Joshua's technique of bringing down the walls of Jericho by blowing the horn.

The foregoing statements have not been made to depreciate the role of education as a cultural dynamic. It is obvious that when behaviors are changed, people are educated. The emphasis has been, however, designed to place social action as a necessary complement to education and in many respects, scarcely distinguishable from it.

TECHNIQUES OF SOCIAL ACTION

An assessment of the techniques of social action is difficult to make at the present time. A few suggestions, however, will suffice to indicate the directions in which it is important in human relations.

(1) **Action Through Involvement.** With the rapid development of the field of group dynamics, considerable technology is being designed to produce social change by involving those who represent the interests which must be changed in a *social process*. There are varying degrees of effectiveness of such a procedure. Consideration is needed to know which levels of intergroup conflict can be changed and which cannot through such a process. It is the author's opinion that types of conflict in the realm of values *per se* can be changed much more rapidly by this procedure than those which involve giving up vested interests. The social technician also faces the problem of whether he is using the processes or whether *he* is being used by forces which wish to use the process as a stall. One of the finer points of judgment in the field of social action is, undoubtedly, that of deciding when or to what extent to "trust the process." The *involvement-in-process* approach is rapidly slanting education toward community-school programs in which the dichotomy between the school (in the sense of scholastics) and community is being erased. At the Center for Human Relations Studies, we are undertaking a project in cooperation with the Board of Education of New York City in which we are working in the community and in the school without too clear lines of demarcation as to where one begins and the other ends. This approach is based on the assumption that it would be impossible to move the school without moving the community and *vice versa*.

(2) **The Pressure Group Technique.** There are times when it is clear that the social technician cannot trust the process. In these instances to bother with involvement would represent a waste of time. Thus there is no alternative but to resort to the "soap box" or whatever means are available to change institutional patterns. In some respects, of course, this represents a negative approach to communal well-being. It is unfortunate that to this point we have no panacea, particularly in the larger communities, for bad government except "vote and throw the rascals out." Agencies of government as well as other institutional structures know this public apathy well. As a consequence, they are particularly sensitive to pressure group technique. There is scarcely a larger community but that the average citizen would come nearer getting change effected by knowing the pressure groups in the community than by the merits of his program—this includes the school.

At this point the technician must weigh in the balance the outcome of the long and short range effect of his action. Indeed, in the immediate and short run there is a heightening of tension as groups clash over differences. The ultimate assessment must be in terms of whether the broken barriers make up for such increase in group consciousness. When the Mayor's Committee on Unity started the fight against discrimination in colleges and universities in New York State, we faced frankly the possibility that the agitation and discussion would create a greater consciousness of who were Jews, Negroes, etc., and who were not, than had been true before. But it was clear that we were fighting a losing battle and that the quotas were becoming more rigid instead of flexible, hence the decision to make a fight of it. This has been undoubtedly true in many of the legislative cases which the NAACP has won against the South—cases which have made great advances in intergroup relations.

(3) **Legislation and Legal Action.** Fortunately the people of the country had heard little of Sumner and the mores and differed from the social scientist as to what could be accomplished through legislation. It is now clear that legislation and legal action can be some of the most formidable tools in social change. It may be true that attitudes cannot be changed by law, but it is being increasingly demonstrated, as indicated above, that the change of institutional policies and regulation of institutional practice (things which *can* be changed by law) goes a long way in by-passing the bias of individuals. Thus, the attitude of the employer is not so important if his institution cannot discriminate in its employment practices. Furthermore, by breaking the barriers to integration, individuals are brought together on an unselfconscious basis so that they have an opportunity to know each other in roles different from group stereotypes. Perhaps the most important facet of legislation is the fact that there is "public definition of policy" as a guide, not only to one institution, but to all the institutions in the community. As I indicated in the article on "Religious Prejudice in American Colleges," [1] no college felt that it could afford to remove the barriers to minority groups alone, but with public definition of policy on admission practices, all the institutions in the state were able to bring their policies in line at the same time and the fears of none were kindled. Another significant illustration of this pattern is demonstrated in New Jersey. Over a long period of years with all of the education, preaching, pleading, hoping, praying and trusting, the segregation of Negroes and whites in the public

[1] *American Mercury*, July 1946.

schools was becoming increasingly evident. It was when the position of the social institutions of public education were changed through the development of the new state constitution and legislation, that segregation started on its way out. This is not to say that education did not have its effect nor to depreciate its value, but it is to say that in the last analysis the job is not completed nor significantly improved in most cases until the institutional patterns are changed.

It should be clear from these suggested aspects of social action that fruitful approaches to human relations are being developed by forging of new conceptions of the function of education and not the least significant of the new conceptions is the closing of the gap between education *per se* and social action.

SECTION EIGHT

Institutions

40 A SOCIETAL PERSPECTIVE ON INSTITUTIONS *

BY WILLIAM GRAHAM SUMNER (1840–1910)
AND ALBERT GALLOWAY KELLER (1874–   )
YALE UNIVERSITY

HERE are the processes of variation, selection, and transmission. The first originates in the individual, who throws out tentatives in response to need felt personally; the third takes place through the eye and ear, and passes the mores over from generation to generation and also between contemporaries. The process of selection demands a little more attention, even in a summary. It is mainly automatic and unplanful, especially on the primitive stage; but so, for that matter, are variation and transmission. If purposeful reasoning, followed by action in the light of it, comes in anywhere, it is in variation, when that factor takes the form of experimentation. Selection, automatic or not, calls for conflict and competition, which are furnished primarily by the struggle for existence and then by the struggle for a better quality of existence. Competition never ends; and it is well that it does not if the attainment of better adjustment, which must be through the agency of selection, is desirable. The crudest form of selection is by way of violence, or war; it is also the final resort at any period, the last argument, the *ultima ratio*. Codes and institutions go down to destruction along with the men who practise them. Selection takes place also through peaceful competition, industrial, political, and other. Chiefly in these lighter forms does it reveal a certain relation between sets of mores that should be borne in mind throughout any study of societal evolution. This relation is as follows.

The mores that have to do with self-maintenance, being closest to natural conditions, are checked up more speedily and obviously on the life-conditions than are the rest of the mores. Poor methods in hunting are revealed to be such much more readily than are inexpedient religious practices. Causes of discomfort and failure are here more easily identifiable, impressing even the untrained mind. Hence

* Reprinted by permission from *The Science of Society* (New Haven: Yale University Press, 1927), I, pp. 36–37, 40–41.

the maintenance-mores tend to follow changing life-conditions pretty closely; that is, they are least insulated against selection, least subject to benumbing tradition, more sensitive. They are adjustable as the rest of the mores are not. The rest of the mores, however, take their tone from the maintenance-mores, as from a sort of basic theme; the former experience a strain toward consistency with the latter. The superstructure—those mores which are farther removed from the ground of natural conditions—must conform to the foundation-lines of the maintenance-mores. This is a relation which will be illustrated frequently, as we go on. It follows that selection operates indirectly upon the forms of property, marriage, religion, and government, as compared with its action upon forms of industry. If the industrial type changes from, say, a pastoral economy to an agricultural, gradually there appears a characteristic alteration in those customs which are more remote from pragmatic test. There is a pastoral type of general societal organization, as well as of industry. An appreciation of this relation amounts to the possession of a key to not a few doors that one wants to open as he explores the structure of society.

If society is to be studied in the evolutionary series of its institutions, the length of the perspective involved means that the individual is pretty much lost to sight. The subject-matter of a science of society can be nothing else than a society. It is a pity that everything cannot be studied at once, but the human mind is not constituted so as to do that. A society lives and evolves in accordance with laws of its own; the individual can be left to the sciences which make a business of investigating his body and mind. We believe societal phenomena to be due to the operation of impersonal, automatically acting forces which transcend altogether the range of individual powers and control and produce effects characteristic of themselves alone. Such a conception provides, to our view, the sole reason for existence of a science of society and assures to it a distinctive range of its own. The individual cannot be left utterly out of account any more than can the molecular composition of an ivory ball used in a physics experiment; but if the object of study is the ball, or the society, it is just and proper to deal with it as an entity, not as a sum of its constituent elements.

The individual has a function of surpassing importance as a source of variation in the mores; he is the indispensable leader-off in the evolutionary process, for without variation no process can take place. He may even set afloat a mutation. For present purposes, however, it is immaterial how or through what agency a variant derives its origin. When it comes into the range of our investigation, concurrence has taken place some time since; it is already a mass-phenomenon, to be dealt with as such. We are convinced that this way of looking at things frees our treatment from a current tendency, which we regard as confusing and unproductive, to refer societal results to conscious, reasoned, and purposeful action on the part of the individual. There is a view of society—as of woods from among the trees—which may be got by pre-occupation with the individual, his psychology, and his "choices"; then there is another—as of the woods from a detached position—which promises superior clarity and perspective in that it envisages society as a whole. The latter we regard as a more commanding vantage-point for the observation and assessment, not only of historic societal phenomena, but also of those formations and dissolutions that are taking place as our own day passes.

If we extend our perspective, look over and beyond the individual, and think in terms of societies, we can see, for example in the late world-conflict,[1] the alignment and confrontation of societies in pursuit of their group-interests under their codes—vast forms going about their prodigious affairs, unconcerned, above the fighting, dying, unregarded mortals. The movements of the contending societies are seen to be impersonal and automatic, after the manner of bodies acted upon by gravitation or capillary attraction, and the individual is lost to identification as he blends into the composite mass. The world-conflict, thus seen—and, as we believe, correctly seen—appears as a powerful selective agency in the evolution, not alone of the several societies, but of human society itself. Here was a vast laboratory of selection—the greatest laboratory the student of society has ever seen or heard of—for what was going on before his face was no less than the most gigantic exhibition of selection between codes of mores that the world has ever witnessed. Such a crisis-time affords glimpses of the cosmic process—glimpses that one can never catch, of truth that will remain veiled to him, so long as he does not ascend in thought to a plane where individuals and their doings cease to distract him. And what is true of a crisis-time is true, in its measure, of any other time also.

In adhering to this point of view, we present a way of looking at

---

[1] A. G. Keller, *War to Peace,* ix, chs. ii–iv. [Reference is to World War I.—Ed.]

the succession of societal phenomena, including those that are contemporary, which must be judged by what is rendered visible. No
amount of preliminary defense of the method adopted counts for
anything. The contention is that the life of society is so long and
wide that a far-reaching perspective of mass-phenomena is required
in order to make out the course and sense of its evolution.

41   ASSOCIATIONS AND INTERESTS *

BY ROBERT MORRISON MACIVER (1882–   )
COLUMBIA UNIVERSITY
CHARLES H. PAGE (1909–   )
SMITH COLLEGE

THE CLASSIFICATION OF ASSOCIATIONS

ASSOCIATIONS in a **Complex Society.** In a complex society, associations tend to be specialized so that each stands for a particular type of interest or interest complex. In primitive society, where
there is less division of labor and where change is slower, there are
few associations and they are more inclusive. They are communal or
semicommunal in the range of their interest. A newly developed interest does not so often create, as with us, a new association, but is
incorporated in the general body of interests pursued by the existing
organization. Thus in primitive life, associations lack the specific,
limited functional character which our own possess. They take such
forms as age-groups, kin-groups, sex-groups, groups for the performance of communal rites and ceremonies, secret societies, rather than
the economic or professional or political or cultural varieties familiar
to ourselves. This contrast will be shown more fully in Book Three,
the final one of this volume, devoted to the subject of social change.
Meantime, it may suffice to note that the functional differentiation of
modern organized groups makes it possible for us to classify them
according to the characteristic interests they severally pursue.

* Reprinted by permission of the authors and of the publisher from *Society:
An Introductory Analysis* (New York: Rinehart and Company, 1949), pp. 443–452.
This is a shortened version of a chapter with the same title.

Some Specific Problems of Classification. In classifying associations in terms of the nature of their interests, however, we are confronted with certain difficulties. There are four particularly important precautions we should have in mind in depicting the interest characteristic of any organized group.

(1) *The professed interest not always the determinant interest:* The group's ostensible interest is not always determinant; the professed or formulated aims of an association do not necessarily reveal the full or even the true character of the goal that it chiefly seeks. But at least a part of this difficulty disappears when we take as the basis of classification the immediate field of interest rather than the remote objectives or purposes, when in particular we avoid the confusion of interests and motivations. It would indeed be a hazardous task to classify associations in terms of professed objectives or ulterior aims. For one thing, a disparity not infrequently arises because the association, passing through historical changes, clings traditionally to older formulations—as religious bodies are particularly apt to do— or because the leaders idealize its aims, in the desire to broaden its appeal, to strengthen its public position, to secure funds, and so forth. Such idealization is seen not only in the platforms of political parties but also in the pronouncements of many other organizations. Often an organization will stress the more altruistic of the objects which lie within the field of its interest. A department store will proclaim that it exists to serve the community. A professional organization will emphasize the necessity of rigid qualifications for membership on the ground that the service of the public must be safeguarded while it is more or less silent on the competitive economic advantage thereby gained.

(2) *Professed interest modified by variant conditions:* We should also observe that we are far from expressing the distinctive character of any individual association when we have placed it in its interest category. The character of an individual association is often very subtle, and it is only in the light of a considerable study of its activities that its actual purpose and proper distinctiveness can be found. Moreover, in every case the interest it pursues is colored or modified by the personalities of the constituents and the social make-up of the community in which it functions. Often certain features of organizations are not brought into the focus of consciousness by the members or even by the leaders. For example, an organization which has gradually abandoned a traditional basis of solidar-

ity may gropingly move in a new direction and gain a new kind of solidarity, related to but different from that which its leaders believe and certainly state that it possesses. This situation is illustrated in the history of certain semireligious organizations such as the Y.M.C.A. and the Y.W.C.A. Shall we classify them as religious or recreational or generally educational or in a broad sense as "social" clubs? What element is focal or dominant in the interest complex? For reasons just suggested it is difficult to answer. The Y.M.C.A. or the Y.W.C.A. is a characteristic association, a certain "kind" of association with its own social "flavor." But it is a different kind in a rural area and in, say, a metropolitan area. In each region it has responded to certain social exigencies, seeking in the face of competing social agencies still to represent something, something in some way different from the rest, for when an organization loses its specific identity it loses its most important reason for existence in our highly organized society.

An associated problem of classification, arising out of the changing relation of associations to interests, is revealed in the struggle to survive of those interests which have fulfilled their original *raison d'être*. Organizations of people, like the individuals themselves, are tenacious of life. They refuse to die when their day is past. New interests are thus sought within them which will justify their existence in a continuing purpose. This organizational "will to live" centers in the officials, in the occupants of the "bureaucratic structure."[1] A political association is organized to achieve some piece of legislation; it is attained but the association lingers on. Thus a league for the enfranchisement of women turns into a party organization when the women gain the vote; or a reform movement to eliminate the "machine" becomes itself a machine after achieving its initial goal. An ancient guild is rendered obsolete by industrial change, yet it survives as an "honorable company," to perpetuate traditional ceremonies at annual dinners—once an economic organization, it has passed over into another category. This list can be easily extended—patriotic societies, veterans' groups, hooded organizations, and many others have sought and found new interests when the old have disappeared.

(3) *The main interest sometimes hard to determine:* A more important obstacle to a satisfactory classification is presented by those

---

[1] For the development of this point see [MacIver and Page, *op. cit.*, chap. x.— *Ed.*]

organizations which stand for a variety of different interests in such a way that it is hard to designate any one as dominant. Shall we classify a denominational college as a religious organization? Sometimes religion is the primary interest, sometimes merely the historical matrix. Shall we assign an organization for workers' education as economic or as cultural? It may exist to train union leaders or to inculcate the principles of Marx or to provide a general education—and it may combine all these interests in one. Shall we call a businessmen's club an association for social intercourse or an economic association? One aspect may be dominant at one time, the other at another. These are examples of the difficulty which frequently occurs when we seek to place associations in the categories described below. This difficulty leads up to our final caution.

(4) *Some important interests do not create specific associations:* We are making interests the basis of our classification, but the correspondence of interest and association is not, even in our specialized society, a simple one. There are some strong interests, such as the interest of power and of distinction, which do not normally create specific associations but ramify through associations of every kind. The dynastic state might be termed a "power organization," but the quest of power in some form invades every political system, underlies the interest of wealth which is the direct object of economic association, and in fact is found wherever organization of any kind exists. We might call certain kinds of clubs "prestige organizations," but as the interest of prestige is fostered no less in many other kinds of association, and particularly as men do not pursue prestige except through the medium of other interests, such an attribution would only confuse our classification. Again, the interest of companionship or of social intercourse is so pervasive that it is in some degree satisfied by every association and thus it is often dubious whether or not it is the main determinant. In our classification below, we take the club as the type-form association corresponding to this interest, but social intercourse is not the focus of all bodies called clubs and, on the other hand, there are various groups ostensibly established for other objects, from library associations to spelling bees, from charity leagues to sewing meetings, which are sustained mainly by this interest. The main interest of a group cannot be inferred from the name we apply to it. A gang, for example, may be little more than a boys' brotherhood, or it may be essentially an economic organization, exploiting a neighborhood by illegal means for economic ends.

Associations Classified by Interests. We may now turn to the classification as set forth in Chart [I]. We suggest that the reader consult this chart as he considers the following explanation.

(1) *Explanation of our general classification:* We first divide associations into *unspecialized* and *specialized*. Here we refer to the fact that they may stand for the total interests of a group or class or, on the other hand, they may represent either a particular interest or a particular method of pursuing interests. We include the state among specialized associations because, in spite of the vast range of its interests, it works through the special agencies of law and government.[2] As we have already pointed out, unspecialized associations are less characteristic of modern society—and less effective within it—than specialized associations.

The latter are classified in terms of the distinction between *primary* and *secondary* interests. By the former we mean those interests which have for men a final value, which are *ends* in themselves. By the latter we mean those interests which by their intrinsic nature are *means* to other interests. We do *not* mean that primary interests are more pervasive or necessarily even more significant in social life than secondary interests, or that the one or the other type functions in isolation from the other. The fuller significance of this division will appear [as] . . . we develop the distinction between *civilization,* as the sphere of secondary interests, and *culture,* as the sphere of primary interests.[3] Here a preliminary statement about these categories is in order.

Our distinction is one of ends and means. One difficulty in applying the distinction lies in the fact that *any* object we seek can become the "end" of our search, so that we look for no utility beyond it. We may seek wealth merely to possess it and not for its ulterior services; we may construct instruments or mechanisms (perhaps even social mechanisms) because we enjoy doing so and not because they will aid us to achieve other objects. But this is a problem of individual motivations, not of social organization. As aspects of the latter, the economic system would not exist but for the interests which underlie it, and technological mechanisms would be idle and soon forgotten toys but for their service as man's instruments. We divide these sec-

---

[2] For the state as an association see [*ibid.,* chap. xviii; see also chap xxi].

[3] For the further development of this distinction see R. M. MacIver, *Social Causation* (Boston, 1942), chap. x; and for its application to the problems of government in complex society, the same author's *The Web of Government* (New York, 1947), pp. 421–430.

CHART [I] General Classification of Interests and Associations

Interests	*Associations*
A. Unspecialized	Class and caste organizations
	Tribal and quasi-political organizations of simpler societies
	Age-groups and sex-groups
	The patriarchal family
	(Perhaps also such organizations as vigilante groups, civic welfare associations, etc.)
B. Specialized	
I. *Secondary* (civilizational or utilitarian)	
(a) Economic interests	Type form: *The business*
	Industrial, financial, and agricultural organizations, including unions
	Occupational and professional associations [a]
	Protective and insurance societies
	Charity and philanthropic societies [b]
	Gangs, "rackets," etc.
(b) Political interests	Type form: *The state*
	Municipal and other territorial divisions of the state
	Parties, lobbies, propagandist groups
(c) Technological interests	Associations for technical research, and for the solution of practical problems of many kinds [c]
II. *Intermediate*	
Educational interests	Type form: *The school*
	Colleges, universities, study groups, reformatories, etc.
III. *Primary* (cultural)	
(a) Social intercourse	Type form: *The club*
	Various organizations ostensibly for the pursuit of other interests
(b) Health and recreation	Associations for sports, games, dancing, gymnastic and other exercises, for diversions and amusements [d]
(c) Sex and reproduction	Type form: *The family*
(d) Religion	Type form: *The church*
	Religious propagandist associations
	Monasteries, etc. [e]
(e) Aesthetic interests, art, music, literature, etc.	Corresponding associations
(f) Science and philosophy	Learned societies

[a] These combine economic and technological interest; where the latter are dominant the associations fall in I (c).

[b] The economic interest is usually, though by no means always, the focus of these

ondary or *utilitarian* interests into three classes, the *economic,* the *political,* and the *technological.* We have placed another large group of interests, the *educational,* in an intermediate position between secondary and primary, since they involve both means and ends, since they are both utilitarian and cultural. All genuine education, elementary or higher, technical or "liberal," is at the same time an instrumental equipment for living and itself a cultural mode of life. We set the cultural or primary interests over against the secondary interests. We pursue the cultural goals apart from external pressure or necessity. Again, cultural interests may serve us merely as means, but, sociologically, their utilitarian service is incidental to the fact that we, or some of us, pursue them for their own sakes, because, that is, they bring us some *direct* satisfaction.

(2) *Other modes of classification in terms of interests:* While the specific nature of the interest is the main clue to the character of the corresponding association, as set out in Chart [I], there are other ways of classifying interests that throw further light on the relation between them and associations. Thus the direct social interest in *persons* is the distinguishing feature of *primary groups,* whereas the interest in the *impersonal* means and ends of living characterizes the *large-scale association.*[4] . . . Again, we can distinguish interests according to their degree of duration in the life history of their members. In terms of this criterion, associations within the same field may be transient, rapidly successive, or permanent. They may be permanent, as established *forms* of social organization like the family, though the individual instances are mortal, or they may be long-lived, potentially immortal, as individual structures, like the corporation. In Chart [II] we neglect the types of interest in order to classify associations according to their *durability.*

The classification in our first chart ([I]) is meant to serve as an introduction to the organized aspects of the social structure. . . .

---

associations. The fact that it is the economic welfare of others than the members which is sought does not affect the classification.

c The technological interest is generally subordinate to the economic, i.e., it is a means to a means. Hence it is usually pursued through subagencies of the economic order. Sometimes it is organized, under political auspices, through such divisions as a department of agriculture, bureau of standards, atomic commissions, etc.

d The interest of health and of recreation may of course be entirely dissociated. The interest of recreation is, on the other hand, often associated with the aesthetic interests, so that various associations could be classified under III (b) or under III (e).

e The monastery is a quasi-community, but if religion is the main determinant of its activities as well as the basis of organization, we can retain it under III (d).

[4] [See MacIver and Page, *op. cit.,* chap. x.—*Ed.*]

CHART [II] Associations Classified According to the Durability
of the Interest

Interests	*Associations*
(a) Interests realizable once for all—definite temporary objectives	Associations for the achievement of a specific reform, reconstruction, etc., political or other (e.g., antislavery); for a celebration, erection of a memorial, etc., for an emergency such as a flood, economic crisis, war
(b) Interests peculiar to a definite number of original or potential members—the "broken plate" situation [a]	Groups composed of the members of a school or college class or year, of army veterans, of the survivors of a shipwreck, etc.
(c) Interests limited to age-periods of a relatively short range	School and college teams, debating societies, etc.; boy scout, junior leagues, etc.—associations continuous as individual structures but with rapidly successive memberships
(d) Interests limited by the tenure or life span of some original or present member [c]	Partnerships of various kinds; groups of friends; the family—permanent as a social system embodied in successive individual associations [b]
(e) Interests unlimited by a time span	The corporation; most large-scale organizations, state, church, occupational associations, scientific associations, etc.—associations individually continuous through the recruitment and incorporation of new members

[a] The reference here is to an illustration given by G. Simmel in *Soziologie* (Munich, 1923), p. 60. A group of industrialists were seated at a banquet when a plate was dropped and shattered into fragments. It was observed that the number of pieces corresponded to the number of those present. Each received one fragment, and the group agreed that at the death of any member his fragment was to be returned, the plate being thus gradually pieced together until the last surviving member fitted in the last fragment and shattered again the whole plate.

[b] The larger patriarchal family or the "joint family" does not fall within this class, but the modern individual family does. We speak of the family in another sense, as when we say that a person is a member of an "old" family, but in this sense the family is not an association.

[c] Observe particularly the difference between the groups under (b) and under (d). The interest which creates an association under (b) is unique, peculiar to the members, and dies with the association. It has therefore little significance for the social structure. The interest under (d) is universal in its appeal and particularizes itself in a multitude of individual associations. The interest under (b) is in fact the social bond itself, whereas the interest under (d) is the perennial source of the social bond.

Intra-Associational Conflict of Interests

Social Cohesion and Conflict. The interest for which an association stands is the primary ground of its unity, the basis of its particular cohesion or solidarity. This unity is reinforced by other bonds,
by the shared tradition and prestige of the association or the associates, by the sustenance of the general need of social relationships
that it may provide, by the particular habituations and attitudes that
it supports, by the other common interests the members share in
whole or in part. But at the same time forces are generated or revealed within the association that cause tensions and strains in its
solidarity.

Conflicts develop in the field of the particular interest the association promotes and conflicts arise from oppositions between that
interest and other interests of the members. Like the greater communal manifestations of social cohesion—class, ethnic and racial
group, and crowd, as well as the community itself—the unity of the
association is imperfect and unstable, representing, while it endures,
the victory of integrative over disintegrative processes. A study of
the conflicts and harmonies of interest that appear within the life of
associations could be for the student an excellent preparation for the
investigation of that greater unstable equilibrium which is the social
order itself.

Types of Interest-Conflict within Associations. Here we select for
brief discussion three main types of interest-conflict. These three
types occur persistently in the history of organized groups, especially
in the variety of associations that grow up in modern complex
society.

(1) *Conflicts within the interest-complex:* The first arises from a
lack of harmony between the objectives that fall within the interest-
complex. A clear illustration is frequently presented within professional or occupational associations. The economic interest, the maintenance or enhancement of the emoluments of the service they render, is often difficult to reconcile with the professional interest proper,
the quality and extent of the professional service.

The medical profession offers a peculiarly interesting situation.
If it could achieve its professional ideal, it would thereby reduce to a
minimum the need for its therapeutic service while enlarging greatly
its preventive service. The former is mainly private practice, the latter
is largely socialized, provided through clinics, hospitals, state depart-

ments, public and semi-public institutions of various kinds. Here a dilemma is apt to arise not only because private practice is more in accord with the traditions of the profession but also because it tends, under prevailing conditions, to be more remunerative. If economic interest alone determined the policy of a professional organization, whether medical or other, we would have simply a conflict between the associational interest and the public interest. But the members of a medical association, like those of other professional groups, are concerned with the efficacy of the service the group represents. Hence there arises a conflict of interests within the association itself in the attempt to work out a policy that will reconcile or adjust the economic interest and the professional ideal. The problem has a peculiar character in this case, since under competitive conditions the livelihood of the physician depends on the length of treatment, on the seriousness of cases, and generally on the amount of disease prevalent in the community.[5]

Similar problems of the adjustment of interests arise within bar associations, educational organizations, business firms, labor unions, and other bodies. The conflict is seen very clearly in political groups. It is only in the extreme exploitative political organizations, such as that centering round a "boss," that the economic interest drives out almost altogether the professional interest, that of the standard of service. When this happens any "professional" organization becomes an association of another and frequently of a socially detrimental type.[6]

(2) *Conflicts between relevant and irrelevant interests:* The second type of conflict arises where the specific interest of the association demands a course of action which is opposed to some other interests not relevant to the association as such but nevertheless entertained by some members of the group. A highly qualified Negro, let us say, seeks admission to a university. He possesses the requisite qualifications, for racial difference is no bar to scholarship. But other consid-

---

[5] See, for example, J. Rorty, *American Medicine Mobilizers* (New York, 1937); C. Binger, *The Doctor's Job* (New York, 1945); and for brief reviews of the question, R. H. Shrylock, "Freedom and Interference in Medicine," *The Annals of the American Academy of Political and Social Science,* November, 1938; W. T. Foster, *Doctors, Dollars, and Disease,* Public Affairs Pamphlet No. 10 (rev.; New York, 1944).

[6] The conflict of interests in the professions is stressed in a large literature. Many illustrations may be found, for example, in A. M. Carr-Saunders and P. A. Wilson, *The Professions* (New York, 1933); E. L. Brown, *Lawyers and the Promotion of Justice* (New York, 1938); and L. Wilson, *The Academic Man* (New York, 1942).

erations that have nothing to do with the express purpose of the association enter in and create within the association a conflict concerning policy. In one form or another such conflicts are constantly occurring. Outside interests prevent the association from pursuing with single-mindedness its stated objectives. Group prejudices modify the devotion of the association to its avowed purpose. Individual jealousies and predilections thwart the interest which is the *raison d'être* of the organization. Thus confusion and disharmony appear within its councils.

We may include in the same general category the conflict which arises owing to the fact that the interests of the officials or leaders are not identical with those of the other members, or cease to be identical once they have enjoyed the fruits of office. The officials may be anxious to enhance their authority, though this course may lead to policies detrimental to the general associational interest. Or they may have an economic interest at variance with the interest, economic or other, of the group. The degree of maladjustment varies not only with the personalities involved, but also with the nature of the interest. A particularly significant illustration is furnished by groups founded on principles of equality, whether economic, political, or religious. Organization is essential to each and hence a bureaucratic structure emerges. It has even been maintained that officials, as soon as they acquire power, are driven by the logic of their position to antidemocratic attitudes, and thus no democratic or socialist organization can ever translate its principles into effective practice.[7] The argument is too sweeping, but the numerous instances adduced by the proponents of this "iron law of oligarchy" sufficiently illustrate the serious conflicts and confusions created by the dilemma of leadership.

(3) *Conflicts between alternative policies in the pursuit of interests:* A third source of conflict is found in the constant necessity of the new adaptation of means to ends. By the end we here understand the provisional basis of agreement regarding the interest of the association, which has to be translated into action by means of a policy. A group meets to decide a course of action in a given situation. The group interest has already been defined and redefined by past decisions, has been canalized in the series of adjustments which the group has undergone. But a new occasion often demands more than a routine following of the channel. Being different, it demands a fresh

[7] R. Michels, *Political Parties* (Eng. tr.; New York, 1915).

decision, a new expression of policy. The members meet on the assumption that all are agreed regarding the end—the problem is the appropriate means. A business must decide how to deal with a new competitive threat. A club must raise funds to meet a deficit. A church must decide how to act in the face of a declining membership. A settlement house must adapt itself to a changing neighborhood or to the "competition" of state agencies. A political party, say a revolutionary party, must adjust its strategy to changing historical circumstances.

In these situations, the agreement on ends is implicit, taken for granted. But the agreement on means must be explicit. This necessity inevitably evokes differences of temperament and viewpoint within the group. Shall the club raise the necessary funds by an extension of membership or by a levy on its present members? Shall the church popularize its regular services or undertake additional social activities? Shall the national revolutionary party support a program of military preparedness in its own country or advocate a policy of peace at all costs? Some members answer one way, some another—the interplay of divergent personal factors and divergent policies is very complex. The sense of solidarity may prevail, an adjustment may be reached, and a generally acceptable policy formed. But in the process acute differences may emerge sufficient to disrupt or even to end the life of the association.

The Type of Association and Internal Conflict. In conclusion, we may point out that if the association stands for a broad cultural interest or one strongly charged with emotional elements there is greater danger that difference will lead to schism. For here differences on matters of policy are apt to extend down into differences regarding the *implicit end* which the policy is meant to serve. The interest of a business firm is relatively simple. The end to which its policy must be adapted is accepted and understood without dispute. But it is otherwise with the interest of a church, of an artist group, or, in some cases, of a political party. Dissension over means may here reveal the inadequacy of the more basic agreement over ends. The end itself, at some level, is brought into the arena of conflict, and thus the solidarity of the organization may be shaken. When a church faces a declining membership it may be forced to raise the further question concerning its proper mission. When the business faces declining sales, its endeavor to restore profits raises no similar question regarding the appropriate definition of its quest. Such considerations help to explain the tendency to schism exhibited by churches which do not adhere strongly to authoritative interpretations, by left-wing parties generally, by artistic and other bodies united around some cultural conviction.

42 INSTITUTIONALIZATION *

BY LEOPOLD VON WIESE (1876–   )
UNIVERSITY OF KÖLN
AND HOWARD BECKER (1899–   )
UNIVERSITY OF WISCONSIN

INSTITUTIONALIZATION is essential to the upbuilding of plurality patterns; they may be said to become more complex and abstract in the same degree as they become institutionalized. It is by no means easy, however, to say what an institution is; many current definitions either beg the question or evade it. Cooley's statement is an example of question-begging:

"An institution is simply a definite and established phase of the public mind, not different in its ultimate nature from public opinion, though often seeming, on account of its permanence, and the visible customs and symbols in which it is clothed, to have a somewhat distinct and independent existence." [1]

This simply shifts the difficulty of explanation from "institution" to "public mind" and "public opinion," both of which are notoriously vague and ambiguous concepts. Moreover, there are many institutions which are difficult if not impossible to explain as outcomes of "public mind" of any kind; the connection assumed by Cooley arises largely from specifically American conditions or, more exactly, American conceptions of social conditions. In many past and present cultures, it is much easier to explain so-called "public mind" as an outcome of social institutions rather than the reverse. Sumner is a bit more definite:

* Reprinted by permission of the authors and of the publishers from Howard Becker, Systematic Sociology on the Basis of the Beziehungslehre and Gebildelehre of Leopold von Wiese (New York: John Wiley & Sons, Inc., 1932; republished 1950 by Norman Paul Press, Gary, Indiana).

[1] C. H. Cooley, Social Organization, p. 313.

"An institution consists of a concept (idea, notion, doctrine, interest) and a structure. The structure is a framework, or apparatus, or perhaps only a number of functionaries set to co-operate in prescribed ways at a certain conjuncture. The structure holds the concept and furnishes instrumentalities for bringing it into the world of facts and action in a way to serve the interests of men in society." [2]

Now, the implicit assumption underlying this formulation is undoubtedly correct, namely, that an institution is a component part of the total structure of a plurality pattern, and that the specific social function of the institution determines its own structure. Nevertheless, the definition is unacceptable because the term "concept" postulates an altogether too clear-cut and rational basis for institutions; modern social psychology has demonstrated beyond cavil the non-rational or even unconscious characteristics of many if not most institutions. If, however, we take "concept" to mean only the function or purpose which the *investigator* ascribes to the institution as a result of careful analysis of the behavior of its members, the above definition provides a good point of departure. In studying any given institution, it is necessary (1) to determine its underlying "concept," i.e., its function or purpose, and (2) to discover by what means this "concept" is realized in the sphere of social action. Of course, the investigator must usually learn a great deal about the structure of the institution before he can draw any valid conclusions concerning its function.

From the point of view of the present system, an institution may be defined as a network of relatively continuous or permanent interhuman processes and relationships initiating and maintaining connections between persons and groups within a plurality pattern for the purpose of preserving the latter or otherwise serving its interests.

Institutions may be either crescive (Sumner) or enacted. When they are crescive they develop out of customs (folkways, usages, conventions, common habits, etc.) and standards (mores, *Sitten*, codes of honor, rules of propriety, etc.). Such customs and standards are much less specifically directed toward the service of the plurality pattern than is the institution which develops from them. When institutions are enacted, they are products of relatively rational invention and intention attributable to one or more functionaries of the plurality pattern they serve; laws in the broadest sense of the term may be regarded as the clearest examples of enacted institutions.

[2] W. G. Sumner, *Folkways*, pp. 53–54.

A custom or standard becomes an institution when it is vouch-safed a greater degree of permanence, binding force, and union with the plurality pattern. Such institutionalization takes place when the erstwhile custom or standard fulfills a determinable function within the plurality pattern. Inasmuch as any custom or standard is from one point of view a network of human relationships, it is easy to see how the assumption of determinable function and the relative perma-nence thereby guaranteed shape it into an institution as above de-fined. Crescive institutions are, metaphorically speaking, "organic" outgrowths of customs and standards, and are usually more deeply rooted than enacted institutions. The latter are likely to endure only if they correspond to general social needs and the level of develop-ment attained by the plurality pattern—in other words, enacted in-stitutions must function as if they were direct outgrowths of customs or standards, as if they merely made existing usages more explicit and definite. Any institution must form an integral part of the struc-ture and life-process of the plurality pattern within which it func-tions, otherwise it is only a sham that does not contribute to the up-building of the plurality pattern. No matter how sweeping the legal fiat, institutions cannot be arbitrarily created; the greater number of enactments are still-births. It should also be noted that there are many customs that persist for a long time without taking over any de-terminable function that contributes to the upbuilding of the plural-ity pattern; the connection is relatively fortuitous and external. The use of force for the purpose of establishing enacted institutions is frequently fruitless, as the history of conquest shows. Only the most formal types of institution can be called into being by force, and for decades and centuries force is necessary to maintain them, whereas the more intimate relationships of the conquered group remain al-most untouched by the enactments of the conqueror (if the latter is so foolish as to attempt their regulation). British India affords a striking example of this; the really vital activities of Indian life go on in virtual independence of British rule, and efforts to alter those activities invariably provoke determined and successful resistance.

It is also advisable to discriminate between regulative and opera-tive institutions (following Ross' example). When they are regula-tive, a great deal of emphasis is placed on the norms which they in-corporate; they are social moulds or channels within which the be-havior of human beings "should" be confined, and in so far as they are effective, really *is* confined. Examples are furnished by marriage as an institution regulating the relationships of man and wife, the family as an institution regulating the relationships of parents and children, and property as an institution regulating control over economic goods. Further illustrations are afforded by ancestor-worship in China, the caste system in India, the blood-feud in Arabia, the duel among certain German students, and so on. Needless to say, not all customs become regulative institutions; they are often characteristic but not necessarily obligatory, as is shown by the donning and doffing of straw hats on certain dates, attendance at Spanish bull-fights, announcement of engagements, and wearing of mourning. When institutions are primarily operative, they are expected to render a definite service to the plurality pattern *in their institutional capacities;* normative guidance of personal behavior is quite secondary. Specific activities carried out in a socially acceptable form and with relatively constant social support characterize operative institutions. Social settlements, legal aid societies, immigrant protective leagues, and like organizations fall under this head.

The factor of coercion must be considered in relation to regulative and operative institutions, for it provides a further means of distinguishing between them. Regulative institutions do not always make use of *legal* coercion, but they emphasize norms so strongly that social coercion in the interests of the plurality pattern is always present; operative institutions also serve the plurality pattern, but their coercive function is subordinated to considerations of welfare, mutual aid, co-operation, etc.

Both regulative and operative institutions may be distinguished from mere customs by virtue of the fact that institutions tend to function for the purpose of preserving or otherwise serving the interests of the plurality pattern within which they are found, whereas customs may have no demonstrable connection with its interests. Hence it is possible for a network of relationships to be an operative or even regulative institution from the point of view of a particular plurality pattern because it serves the latter's interests, whereas, from the standpoint of another plurality pattern, it may be only a custom. For example, the theatre is an institution that furthers the aesthetic interests of that large body of persons making up the aesthetic plurality pattern or patterns within a given country, but so far as the political plurality pattern or state of that country is concerned, the theatre is only a place where a custom is practiced, for it does not serve the ends of the state. Similarly, the duel is not an institution from the standpoint of the state, but in earlier periods it was an operative institution in many circles, and among the officers of Continental armies it was a regulative institution with an elaborate set of norms, regulations, and restrictions. Again, the smoking of tobacco was an operative and sometimes a regulative institution among certain American Indian tribes, whereas in the modern world it is only a custom.

Such distinctions between custom and institution are of course more or less arbitrary; customs frequently develop into institutions; moreover, institutions often become relatively independent plurality patterns. A sharp line separating one from the other cannot be empirically drawn, but so long as the above distinctions are granted no more than ideal-typical validity they may be heuristically valuable. A common basis for all three is provided by the fact that they all represent configurations of interhuman processes and relationships; the concept of relation comprises them all.

If the number of persons whose interests are served by particular customs is large, and if these persons are influential and active, institutionalization sooner or later takes place. The customs then become so closely interwoven with social life that they may eventually be regarded as its characteristic, regular, and even necessary components. This tendency is often accelerated by introducing more plan and system into the social order. Certain persons become functionaries of the developing institution, and may be granted special privileges as a consequence. The custom has thereby been incorporated in a stable social structure insuring relative continuity; interruptions and accidents are eliminated so far as possible, and institutionalization is complete.

Emphasis must be laid on the fact that the total structure of social life is so complicated and interdependent that the distinction between institution and plurality pattern is very difficult to make, especially when the plurality pattern is an abstract collectivity. It is easy enough to say that the distinguishing characteristic of an institution is its subordination to the purposes of a larger structure comprising numerous institutions, but in actual practice the line is hard to draw. Many social structures that from the standpoint of a larger and more complex plurality pattern may justifiably be regarded as institutions, and hence as mere parts of an all-encompassing whole, may also be viewed as independent plurality patterns when taken in isolation. For example, the family is an institution of the state, nevertheless it is not only older and more deeply rooted biologically, but is also a relatively independent collectivity, able to perpetuate itself without state aid. In other words, a plurality pattern may have institutional functions within a larger structure and at the same time exist in its own right. All institutions that function efficiently tend to become more or less independent plurality patterns serving their own ends as well as the interests of larger bodies such as the state or the church; at present, industry and the press, among others, manifest this tendency. In spite of empirical difficulties in making distinctions, however, it seems advisable to retain the concepts of custom, institution, and plurality pattern as ideal-typical constructs; without their aid social phenomena would present only "a big booming buzzing confusion." Institutionalization is a constructive process, but like all processes of integration it is accompanied by complementary processes of differentiation. The danger of formalization and perversion is always present. A vital, plastic custom may become rigid and lifeless after institutionalization; an ornament, an amusement, or a recreation may become a regulative institution that is a scourge and a burden. The functionaries of the institution begin to play the master; blessings turn to curses. Nevertheless, there is no doubt that those who for any reason desire to render a plurality pattern more stable are well advised to institutionalize the customs that seem best adapted to cement social connections.

The material illustrative of the process of institutionalization is abundant, but only a very small proportion of its sub-processes can be noted here, and little or no comment is possible.

Institutionalization may be effected by *creating offices, establishing endowments or foundations, abrogating or setting aside customs opposed to institutional ends, recognizing seniority "rights," centralizing, decentralizing, defining and restricting powers,* and *conserving* elements or tendencies useful to the plurality pattern. The means by which institutionalization may be effected are exemplified by *appointment, christening, granting of titles, paying stipends or salaries, creating a police force,* and *putting community functions under national or municipal control.* Customs such as the *blood-feud* become tribal institutions that endure until other institutions displace them. In earlier periods, *ceremonial* was a very important means of institutionalization, as Spencer's discussion of ceremonial institutions plainly shows (in spite of its shortcomings in the light of present research). Standards are of course essential to most if not all upbuilding of plurality patterns; institutionalization and *standardization* are in many respects complementary. Many institutions adopt *symbols* in order to make it possible to conceive of them as self-existent entities. The influence of *taboo* has already been discussed in connection with domination and submission, but it is also an important means of institutionalization. Other sub-processes give some indication of the mental aspects of these remodelling and upbuilding processes. For example, *dogmatizing* and *legalizing* are means of impressing the idea of the institution upon the mind of its members, thus lending it stability. The *inauguration of political methods of control* makes quasi-states of many plurality patterns that previously were more or less non-institutional. *Patriarchy* and *gerontocracy* institutionalize parental and filial connections along authoritarian lines. *Tradition* may be used as a basis upon which to erect institutional structures, but almost wholly rational bases are sometimes utilized. Regulative institutions may at times rest content with *enforcement of rules* and thus leave the inner lives of their members unaffected, but by *providing ritual, sacrificing,* and otherwise stressing features that make more than a merely external appeal, the church and similar bodies secure far-reaching regulation.

43 NOTES ON INDUSTRIAL SOCIOLOGY *

BY REINHARD BENDIX (1916–   )
UNIVERSITY OF CALIFORNIA AT BERKELEY

THE studies of "rationalization" in industry have emphasized from the first, in contrast to the analyses of government administration, that it was important to consider the individual participant in the production process. For instance, historians concerned with the rise of the modern factory have stressed the many obstacles of individual working habits, the lack of accuracy and discipline, which stood in the way of this development. In the words of the Hammonds:

* Reprinted by permission of the author and of the editor from "Bureaucracy: The Problem and Its Setting," *American Sociological Review*, XII (1947), 493–507; excerpt taken from pp. 498–502.

"Scarcely any evil associated with the factory system was entirely a new evil in kind. In many domestic industries the hours were long, the pay was poor, the children worked from a tender age, there was overcrowding. . . . But the home worker at the worst . . . was in many respects his own master. He worked long hours, but they were his own hours; his wife and children worked, but they worked beside him, and there was no alien power over their lives. . . . The forces that ruled his fate were in a sense outside his daily life; they did not overshadow and envelop his home, his family, his movements and habits. . . .

"What the new order did in all these respects was to turn the discomforts of the life of the poor into a rigid system. . . . To all the evils from which the domestic worker had suffered, the Industrial Revolution added discipline, and the discipline of a power driven by a competition that seemed as inhuman as the machines that thundered in factory and shed." [1]

Clearly this process entailed untold suffering. But many of the historians from Marx to the Hammonds viewed this aspect of the industrial revolution primarily in a humanitarian manner. The fact tended to be overlooked that the suffering which occurred during the Industrial Revolution was the "instrument" by which the "human material" was gradually shaped into conformity with the requirements of machine production.[2]

This humanitarian concern with the "human factor" during the period of industrialization was a response to management's attitude towards the worker. Yet this attitude determined the organization of production. In writing of this problem as it appeared during the early 19th century, the Hammonds have shown by what reasoning the absolute supremacy of the entrepreneur was justified. It may suffice to quote only one of the arguments which were popular at the time:

"When there is too much labor in the market and wages are too low, do not combine to raise the wages; do not combine in the vain hope of compelling the employer to pay more for labor than there are funds for the maintenance of labor; but go out of the market. Leave the relations between wages and labor to equalize themselves.

[1] J. L. and Barbara Hammond, *The Town Laborer, 1760–1832* (London: Longmans, Green & Company, 1925), pp. 18–19.

[2] Contemporary illustrations of the importance of this factor may be found in John Scott, *Behind the Urals* (Boston: Houghton Mifflin, 1942) and Kuo-Heng Shih, *China Enters the Machine Age* (Cambridge: Harvard University Press, 1944).

You can never be permanently kept down in wages by the profits of capital; for if the profits of capital are too high, the competition of other capital immediately comes in to set the matter right." [3]

"It is easy to see," say the Hammonds by way of comment, "how this kind of reasoning produced the prevalent view of the capitalist as beneficent whatever the wages he paid or the conditions he imposed." [4] Yet, ironically these very practices of exploitation had the effect of decreasing rather than increasing industrial production. Indeed, "scientific management" began with the discovery that exploitation led to lower productive output.

"Many have long experienced in manufacturing operations the advantages of substantial, well-contrived, and well-executed machinery. Experience has also shown the difference of the results between mechanism which is neat, clean, well-arranged, and always in a high state of repair; and that which is allowed to be dirty, in disorder, . . . and much out of repair.

"If then, due care as to the state of inanimate machines can produce such beneficial results, what may not be expected if you devote equal attention to your vital machines, which are far more wonderfully constructed?"

And in answering the question which he had posed, Robert Owen indicated that it was *profitable* to consider the role of the "human factor" in the production process.

"I have expended much time and capital upon improvements of the living machinery; and it will soon appear that the time and money so expended in the manufactory of New Lanark, even while such improvements are in progress only, and but half of their beneficial effects attained, are now producing a return exceeding 50%, and will shortly create profits equal to cent per cent on the original capital expended in them." [5]

[3] Quoted in Hammond, *op. cit.*, p. 209.
[4] *Ibid.*
[5] Robert Owen, *The Forming of Character* (1813) quoted in L. Urwick and E. F. L. Brech, *The Making of Scientific Management* (London: Management Publication Trust, 1946), II, p. 57. The authors of this work ask: "if the principles of effective management were understood, why was it that hours of work were universally so long and conditions so poor? Why did Owen encounter such opposition in his fight for minimum standards laid down by law?" (*Ibid.*, p. 66). The answer does not simply lie in a reference to the forces of competition or the bigotry and ignorance of the employers, though both undoubtedly were of importance. As mentioned above, considerable importance should be attributed to the tradition of com-

From Owen's day to the recent development of "industrial sociology" it has been a recurrent theme, that proper and controlled attention to the worker's subjective role in the production process would be both humanitarian and practical. While Owen was a reformer and stressed the financial advantage for propagandistic reasons, later writers retained this appeal primarily because empirical studies showed the positive effect of improved personnel policies on individual output. Thus, the principle which Owen had formulated early in the 19th century has remained the same ever since. Frederick Taylor's statement of the same idea may serve as an illustration.

"The majority of men believe that the fundamental interests of employees and employers are necessarily antagonistic. Scientific management, on the contrary, has for its very foundation the firm conviction that the true interests of the two are one and the same; that prosperity of the employer cannot exist through a long term of years unless it is accompanied by prosperity for the employee, and vice versa; and that it is possible to give the workman what he most wants—high wages—and the employer what he wants—a low labor cost—for his manufacture."[6]

It should be remembered that Taylor confined himself to considerations of "human efficiency" and that he was concerned with substituting a rigorously planned working performance for the traditional, rule-of-thumb approach of each employee to his work. Taylor believed that his goals (as defined above) could be accomplished by detailed time and motion studies. But his writings show that he was aware of the many psychological problems which stood in the way of making his scheme of "task management" acceptable to the worker.

Taylor's successors have become increasingly concerned with these psychological problems inherent in the rationalization of the production process. They have continued the experimental testing of various factors which were either positively or negatively correlated with the output of the individual worker. Detailed experimentation in this field has indicated, however, that the factors constituting the external working conditions are neither singly nor in combination

pulsion, which the enforcement of a new work-discipline had initiated, because it was indispensable in machine-production.
[6] Frederick W. Taylor, *The Principles of Scientific Management* (New York: Harpers, 1919) p. 10.

responsible for the volume of output of the individual worker, as long as they are considered apart from the social and psychological effects of his status in the work group.[7]

The famous Hawthorne experiments[8] confirm this point. The controlled observation of small work groups over a number of years indicated that increased production on the whole seemed more closely related to the "morale" of the group than to any of the variables (e.g. differently spaced rest pauses, mid-morning meals, higher pay, variations in illumination, temperature, etc.) which were tested.[9] And this "morale" was related to the improved manner of supervision, the prestige position which members of the test group occupied, the increased attention which their individual problems, opinions and suggestions received, etc. This result of the experiments was regarded as a discovery for two reasons. For one, the history of the labor movement and of labor legislation had focussed attention on the attainment of minimal working conditions (in terms of hours, wages, safety devices, etc.). This made it appear plausible that these "conditions of work" were the causes of satisfaction. Secondly, management's tendency to think of the worker as the subordinate antagonist whose every demand was a challenge of managerial authority, made any concern with the causes of dissatisfaction unthinkable. Yet these experiments have done little more than confirm an old insight. Apparently Robert Owen was aware of the fact that the worker's satisfaction and full co-operation in the production process depended upon his recognition as a responsible human being and could not be obtained as long as he was treated as a cog in the production process. It seems equally clear that Karl Marx discerned the "human problem" of industrial civilization when he pointed out that the co-operation of laborers was not the result of their own efforts, but instead the work of an "alien power" over them.

"Laborers (under capitalism) cannot co-operate without being brought together: their assemblage in one place is a necessary condi-

[7] Elton Mayo, *The Human Problems of an Industrial Civilization* (Boston: Harvard University, Graduate School of Business Administration, 1946), pp. 1–54.

[8] In addition to the writings of Elton Mayo *cf.* especially F. J. Roethlisberger and W. J. Dickson, *Management and the Worker* (Cambridge: Harvard University Press, 1943) and T. N. Whitehead, *Leadership in a Free Society* (Cambridge: Harvard University Press, 1936) and the same author's *The Industrial Worker* (2 vols.; Cambridge: Harvard University Press, 1938).

[9] This statement disregards the relatively few cases in which personal preoccupation interfered with the workers' output. *Cf.* Mayo, *op. cit.*, pp. 101–112.

tion of their co-operation. . . . Being independent of each other, the laborers are *isolated persons,* who enter into relations with the capitalist, but not with one another. This co-operation begins only with the labor process, *but they have then ceased to belong to themselves.* On entering that process they become incorporated with capital." [10]

And somewhat further on in his analysis Marx speaks of the human consequences of this mediated co-operation of the workers.

"While simple co-operation leaves the mode of working by the individual unchanged, manufacture thoroughly revolutionizes it. . . . It converts the laborer into a crippled monstrosity, by forcing his detail dexterity at the expense of a world of productive capabilities and instincts. . . . The knowledge, the judgment and the will, which, though in ever so small a degree, are practised by the independent peasant and handicraftsman . . . —these faculties are now required only for the workshop as a whole. Intelligence in production expands in one direction, because it vanishes in many others. What is lost by the detail laborers, is concentrated in the capital that employs them. It is a result of the division of labor in manufactures, that the laborer is brought face to face with the intellectual potencies of the material process of production as the property of another, and as a ruling power." [11]

It is consistent with this statement to say that real human satisfaction is not to be found in the various improvements of working conditions, important though they are. It does not seem to go beyond these insights of nearly a century ago if Mr. Mayo states that the "many conflicting forces and attitudes," which are found in industrial relations

"center about . . . the work and the manner of its performance. Somehow or other, no effective relationship between the 'worker and his work' had been established; and since a community of interest at this point was lacking the group failed to establish an integrate activity and fell into a degree of discord which no one could understand or control. . . . If an individual cannot work with sufficient understanding of his work situation, then, unlike a machine, he can only work against opposition from himself." [12]

By what factors, then, is the development of "morale" and co-operation among workers hampered? As is well known, Marx did

[10] Karl Marx, *op. cit.,* pp. 361, 365. (My insert and italics.)
[11] *Ibid.,* pp. 396–397.
[12] Mayo, *op. cit.,* pp. 118–19.

not believe that it was possible to incorporate the worker's initiative, his pride and whole-hearted co-operation in a common task of production as long as he was subject to the necessities of an organization whose operation and purpose were planned and conducted without his participation. On the other hand, the various authors associated with the Industrial Research of the Harvard School of Business contend that *Management is in a position to create the conditions under which this "morale," this spirit of co-operation on the part of the workers, can flourish.*

> "Maintaining internal equilibrium within the social organization of the plant involves keeping the channels of communication free and clear so that orders are transmitted downward without distortion and so that relevant information regarding situations at the work level is transmitted upward without distortion to those levels at which it can be best made use of. This involves getting the bottom of the organization to understand the economic objectives of the top; it also means getting the top of the organization to understand the feelings and sentiments of the bottom." [13]

It is of interest to observe that the policy which is advocated here does not seem feasible in the light of the experimental evidence on which it is based.

The so-called Relay Assembly Test Group, to give but one example, (this group of five girls was carefully observed for a number of years) showed a great deal of co-operation with the experimenters and among themselves with the result that their level of output increased considerably. But this co-operation was due to the considered attention bestowed on the group (rather than to its external working conditions). Such attention would be incompatible with a large-scale production process.

> "To the investigators, it was essential that the workers give their full and whole-hearted co-operation to the experiment. . . . In order to bring this about, the investigators did everything in their power to secure the complete co-operation of their subjects *with the result that almost all the practices common to the shop were altered.*" [14]

Mr. Roethlisberger himself concludes, therefore, that under the working conditions of large-scale production it is impossible to pro-

---

[13] F. J. Roethlisberger, *Management and Morale* (Cambridge: Harvard University Press, 1944), pp. 192–93.
[14] *Ibid.*, p. 14. (My italics.)

vide a setting which promotes the kind of co-operation such as the experimental group showed.[15] Nevertheless, the experimenters proceeded to develop an interview program which was designed to free the production process from the various emotional difficulties and personal antagonisms that were found to lower the output of some of the workers under observation. But such interviews could not reproduce under ordinary working conditions what the experiment had achieved: to give each person pride in his work and in the successful performance of the group. The interviews, when practiced at large, could only succeed in eliminating from the production process the various personal factors, which had so far persistently retarded its further rationalization. On balance it proved to be more efficient to have the individual worker unburden his personal troubles to an interviewer, even if that cut down his time on the job; he was not a good worker while he worried about personal affairs, and he was likely to slow up his fellow-workers. Thus, it is not the co-operation of the workers which is increased, but some human "obstacle" to the further rationalization of the production process, which is eliminated.

I have tried to indicate in what manner the "human factor" in industrial organization has been analyzed. The basic shortcoming of these studies in industrial sociology lies in their insufficient awareness of the technological and institutional compulsions of large-scale organizations. Mayo, Roethlisberger, and others, have assumed that the production goals set by management furnish the only valid criteria for the interpretation and evaluation of industrial relations.[16] As a result they have found that workers are insufficiently co-operative, although they attribute this to the ills of our civilization.[17] But what appears as insufficient co-operation from the managerial point of view, may be evidence of co-operation nevertheless. It is found, for example, that workers tend to set social standards for the output of their group through informal understandings. Does this mean that they lack the spirit of co-operation, or that their spirit differs from that desired by the employer? Roethlisberger has stated that such behavior is evidence for the "lack of social function" in the job

[15] See also Whitehead, *Industrial Worker*, I, p. 254.

[16] *Cf.* Burleigh B. Gardner, *Human Relations in Industry* (Chicago: Richard D. Irwin, 1945), who defines the factory as "a coordinated system of activities directed to the production of goods" (p. 4).

[17] Elton Mayo, *The Social Problems of an Industrial Civilization* (Cambridge: Harvard University Press, 1945), chap. i. [*Cf.* A. G. Taylor, *Labor Problems and Labor Law* (New York: Prentice-Hall, 1950), pp. 297–299. — *Ed.*]

of the worker.[18] But can improved personnel policies restore to the worker that feeling of personal importance and integrity which the production process denies him? Is such a personnel policy even compatible with the organizational requirements of the production process? Mayo and others have stated that in our society "collaboration cannot be left to chance."[19] They believe that the suspicion, hostility and conflict which beset our industrial world, can be at least greatly alleviated if management sees its way towards improving employee relations. But they fail to ask how much the good "morale" of workers is worth in monetary terms, and they are indifferent to the question whether the process of production generates the very hostilities which interfere with its operation.[20]

44 THE INTER–INSTITUTIONAL BALANCE OF POWER IN WINDSOR, ONTARIO *

BY C. W. M. HART (1905–   )
UNIVERSITY OF WISCONSIN

WINDSOR is a city of something over 100,000 population. Because of its proximity to Detroit, many Canadians have already written it off as part of Canada and regard it as completely Americanized. This is a very superficial judgment. There are comparatively few important aspects of life in Windsor where the American influence is particularly strong and most of such influence is in trivial things which the tourist is apt to notice just because he is a tourist.

The industrial life of Windsor workers is dominated by the presence in the city of the Ford and Chrysler plants, together with a number of smaller auto-parts plants dependent upon the Big Two.

---

[18] Roethlisberger, *Management and Morale*, pp. 24–25.

[19] Elton Mayo's Foreword to Roethlisberger, *Ibid.*, p. xix.

[20] As a result industrial problems are almost exclusively treated as problems of defective communication. *Cf.* Gardner, *op. cit.*, passim.

* Reprinted by permission of the author and of the editor from "Industrial Relations Research and Social Theory," *The Canadian Journal of Economics and Political Science*, XV (1949), 53–73; excerpts taken from pp. 58–73.

The two big plants and practically all the small plants are organized in two Locals of the U.A.W.–Local 200, covering all Ford hourly-rated workers, and Local 195, which is an amalgamated local covering Chrysler and the parts plants. The membership of Local 200 is around 10,000; that of Local 195 is around 8,000. If we add to these two totals another two or three thousand workers organized in A. F. of L. craft unions, together with the local units of the railway brotherhoods, and a few C.C.L. unions other than U.A.W., we get a total of over 20,000 Windsor workers who are members of unions. If we allow the conservative average of one wife and one child to each union member and suppose that the additional children in larger families make up for the existence of bachelors, we may estimate that well over three-fifths of the population of Windsor consists of union members and union members' families, and two-thirds of that total are accounted for by the two U.A.W. locals. . . .

One further piece of information is necessary. Well over 40 per cent of Windsor people are Catholic in religion, this being by far the largest single religious group. The addition of the figures for Anglicans and United Church members fails to give a Protestant majority (as it does in most Ontario cities); to obtain a Protestant majority in Windsor it is necessary to add also the Presbyterians and the Baptists.

When we examine Windsor as a highly industrialized and highly unionized town, and direct our attention particularly to its community aspects, we get a very different impression of industrial society from that which is conveyed by the Mayo in-plant type of research study.[1] The worker as a bewildered and frustrated cog in the vast assembly-line type of plant is certainly there, and indeed in large numbers, but he is not quite so bewildered nor quite so frustrated as that literature would have us believe. Mayo's "disordered dust of individuals"[2] is very busy (in Windsor, at least), escaping from its disordered condition and reorganizing itself in very significant and effective ways through its unions; and, if one approaches the Windsor worker through his union activities rather than through his activities inside the plant, the overriding general impression one gets is that of an enormous amount of human energy, ambition, hard work, and intelligence seeking means of expression and, with many false starts and glaring errors, slowly finding and establishing con-

[1] See Elton Mayo, *The Social Problems of an Industrial Civilization* (Boston, 1947).—*Ed.*

[2] *Ibid.*, p. 9.—*Ed.*

structive and socially-satisfying outlets. Though it may sound strange, in view of the great body of literature upon the subject of trade unionism . . . and the long history of unions, one is almost forced to entertain the idea that it is still not definitely decided in our society what a trade union is or what it is supposed to do. Unions . . . are still, more or less hesitatingly, fumbling towards an acceptable equilibrium with the other and older institutions of the community.

Let us summarize some of the areas in Windsor where this "process of unionism finding itself" is most apparent.

(1) There is no community, worthy of that name, in the city of Windsor. There are only power groups, of which we can clearly define at least four, which are, to varying extent and on various issues, in a pretty constant state of competition and at times of open warfare. These four power groups are: (a) big business, as represented by Ford and Chrysler, (b) the Catholic Church, (c) the unions, (d) a somewhat miscellaneous group, which for the time being I shall call the local business group, though it could equally well be called the Chamber of Commerce group or "the people who have always run this town," or even "the best people." It is called here the local business group to distinguish it from the big business group which, as represented by Ford and Chrysler managements, has national and international interests rather than local ones.

Any analysis of Windsor as a town must be built around the shifting interrelationships of these four power groups. It will be noticed that no mention is made of a possible fifth group, the so-called general public. We omit any such group not, as might be the case in cities like Toronto or Vancouver, because, while there, it has no organization and is unable to make its presence felt; but because, in Windsor, it simply does not exist, even numerically. If we subtract from the total population of Windsor the unionists, the Catholics, the small business group and its satellites and hangers-on, and the various grades of supervisory and technical staff down to the rank of foreman at Ford and Chrysler, all of whom are included in one or more of the four groups mentioned, there is literally nobody left to make up the general public. In this respect Windsor and cities like it differ significantly from those bigger or less industrialized cities where the subtraction of these same elements or their equivalents would still leave a sizeable residue. In Windsor, it is the absence of any such fifth group that is largely responsible for the tensions and bitterness that are so noticeable in that town; there the conflicts between the four power groups are naked and overt, and not masked, as they are in bigger or less industrialized cities, by the presence of another mass of more or less neutral bystanders without any strong views on unions or labour.

Of course, it is obvious that membership in these four power groups overlaps. It is possible to be a good Catholic and a good unionist, or a good Catholic and a violent opponent of unions; it is even possible to be a member of the Chamber of Commerce yet support unions and be a member (though hardly an active member) of the C.C.F. But it is precisely because membership in, or support of, the different power groups is not mutually exclusive, and because many individuals are members or supporters of more than one of them, that competition between them is so sharp, and conflicting loyalties and inconsistent allegiances on the part of particular individuals so noticeable. The bitterness of the struggle is a function of the lack of clarity in the lines of membership.

(2) Among the four power groups, the union is the newest and, therefore, potentially the most expansionist. In an old town like Windsor, with roots going back to Cadillac and the days of the fur-traders, the spheres of influence of the other three, big business, the Catholic Church and the best people who have always run the town, are, by traditional usage and institutional squatters' rights, pretty well established. But into the nice, cozy, traditional alignment of forces and mutually respected spheres of activity the union is pushing and threatening to upset completely the hitherto accepted equilibrium. This would seem to be inevitable in any industrial town which has become so thoroughly unionized that there are virtually no more plants to organize. Union leaders can no more stand still than any other type of democratic leader; when they have got the town thoroughly organized and have obtained bargaining rights from most, or practically all, managements, they have to find other activities for the union to perform, and the U.A.W. leadership certainly, whatever may be the case with other unions, is finding such further fields of activity in an area which one hears increasingly described as "giving service to the membership." Service in such context does not (usually) refer either to plant organization or to wage-increase proposals, but to a quite different aspect of union activity, which I propose to call welfare-unionism as distinguished from wages-unionism. The word "service" here has the same connotations when used by a union

leader as it has when used by Chambers of Commerce, Rotary Club speakers, and the churches. In order to "give service" to the members, unions embark upon programmes or initiate activities that have little to do with wages and little indeed to do with economics, but which give a union local more and more the aspect of a social service institution. In so doing, of course, the union is expanding its activities into those preserves of "service" and "welfare" hitherto reserved for the churches, the best people, the Chamber of Commerce, and the various levels of government.

Four factors at least, and perhaps more, have combined to force union leaders increasingly into welfare-unionism. First, and underlying the others, is the general condition of the community, and especially the welfare services, in the typical medium-sized industrial city. With poor recreational facilities, comparatively poor education levels, heavy relief loads, poor housing and a high degree of tenancy, heavy indebtedness both public and private, high wages but also high living costs, Windsor exemplifies all that has ever been written about the blighting effects of industrialism upon town life. In the midst of such disorganizing factors, the individual needs help of all sorts and will go for it wherever it is provided. If the church and the state and the best people do not provide the facilities for help that the little man needs, he looks for it elsewhere, and he is increasingly finding it provided by the union hall.

Secondly, union executives, particularly at the local level, are forced into welfare-unionism by the simple elementary need of all elective officers—the need to get re-elected. Wage increases, strikes, and threats of strikes may be the occasions for the union getting headlines in the papers, but when the annual elections for union officers roll around, and it is important to remember that they are *annual* elections, it is not the loud speeches or the threats of strikes that will get an incumbent president and his "slate" the votes, it is "what the union has done for the membership during the year." And since, in times more normal than the present at least, this can hardly mean a wage-increase every year, it means in many years, possibly in all, the day-to-day fixing of individual troubles, free legal advice on how to cope with an eviction notice or the handling of a workmen's compensation problem, the backing of a note at the bank or the loan company, the intercession of the union with the police for a member's erring son, the arrangement of a needed hospital treatment; in many cases nothing more than sitting and listening to a member's troubles, patiently and in the best non-directive manner (though the union officer has never heard of the Hawthorne Counselling Plan nor of Freud). It is this constant and efficient attention to the day-to-day petty troubles of the membership,[3] and the "doing something" about those troubles that gets the executives of union locals re-elected and, of course, gives incumbent executive boards an enormous advantage over any challengers.

This factor, more than any other, is responsible for the continuing Communist control of many locals. The Communist officers remain in control election after election, not because the Communist locals are any better run than the others, nor because the Communists are any more welfare-minded than their right wing challengers, least of all because the membership vote for them *as Communists;* the main reason Communist executives get re-elected, in such a surprisingly high number of cases, is because they are already in, and having been in office for several years they have built up through their welfare activities such a backlog of goodwill and gratitude towards them, not as Communists but as individuals, that even the intervention of Walter Reuther himself cannot secure an election majority for their challengers. The advantage of the party in power over the outs, present at all levels of politics, is very greatly magnified by the conditions in which local union politics are, and have to be, carried on.

The third factor which seems causative in guiding or impelling union leaders into welfare-unionism is the relation of local officers to international officers. How important this factor is depends greatly upon the industry concerned, and the particular circumstances of the automobile industry have probably accentuated it in the U.A.W. The big locals in the U.A.W. tend to be locals in the plants of country-wide companies like General Motors, Chrysler, and Ford. Wage negotiations and collective bargaining for the membership of such plants take place on a company-wide basis. This, it will be remembered, was one of the big issues in the original General Motors sit-

---

[3] It is not going too far, I think, to suggest a very strong similarity between the "lift" which the Hawthorne workers got from being interviewed in the original interviewing programme at Hawthorne, and the "lift" which the obscure union member gets from bringing his petty but poignant problem to the union president or secretary-treasurer and hearing him get busy on the phone to the City Hall or the Rent Control Board or the agency involved. When he goes home to his family and to work next day, he says to his family and friends with a great deal of pride and restored morale: "the *union* is doing something about it." *Cf.* F. C. Roethlisberger and W. J. Dickson, *Management and the Worker* (Cambridge, Mass., 1939), p. 227.

down strikes of 1936–7, and one of the last points conceded by the company. General Motors held out almost until the end for individual-plant bargaining; the union clung to its demand for an agreement covering all General Motors plants and finally got such an agreement. This has become the pattern in the auto industry. It follows necessarily from it that, in the case of the Big Three car-makers, collective bargaining has to be carried on by union leaders attached to the international office (the headquarters staff, in other words), and the honour and glory of obtaining wage increases or the blame for failure to attain them go to those international-office men. The presidents of the locals in the plants of the Big Three are relegated to a comparatively minor role in the collective bargaining process.[4] The union leadership on such matters necessarily vests in the international men or, in Canada in particular, the regional director and his staff of international representatives. The precise nature of the relationship between international representatives and regional staffs on the one hand and the executive officers of locals on the other is still in process of being worked out in the U.A.W., and it may prove to be one of those organizational problems which remain indefinitely in an unsettled state. Ideally, one supposes, the relation of the union president to his regional director, or of the president of a General Motors local to the General Motors director, should be that of a parish priest to his bishop; in his own local (parish) he is the head man, but when he leaves his local for wider negotiations his role is to keep his mouth shut and support his regional director (bishop). But any such clear-cut and recognized relation as this is very far from being reached as yet. What is here suggested, however, is that in matters of wage-policy the international officers and their technical staff have to assume increasing responsibility and coverage, with the result that the local presidents and their executives, finding their area of action and leadership in matters of wage-policy disappearing, seek other fields for their energies, and undertake responsibility and initiate action in matters other than wage matters, and these inevitably lead into "welfare" matters.

The fourth factor that must be mentioned in this connexion is the character of U.A.W. union leaders themselves. Anybody acquainted

[4] The signing of the General Motors agreement in June, 1948, as illustrated in all the newspapers of the country demonstrates the difference in status. The international officers, coated, are seated at the table; the local presidents (including R. T. Leonard, formerly international vice-president, now president of his local) stand, coatless, in the background.

with the U.A.W. knows how fiercely and almost fanatically democratic it is. The tradition of rank-and-file control of all elected officers, whether local or international, is almost a fetish in this union
and has been so since its early days and the trouble it had in those
early days with its first president, Homer Martin. It results from
this strong tradition of democracy that any man who gets elected to
important office in the U.A.W. has to be primarily a skillful politician
rather than an orator, administrator, economist or negotiator of legal
agreements. Selekman regards this as the position of all union leaders: "The union leader . . . wins his position and then retains it
always as a political leader." [5] It is certainly true of the U.A.W.
leadership at all levels of the union hierarchy.

To say that a union leader is inherently and necessarily a good
politician implies no criticism of union leadership. Political skill contains as one of its main elements the ability to get along with other
people and to induce them to trust and follow a person who possesses
those qualities. Why our culture should not value such skill but
should rather regard it as *prima facie* evidence of hypocrisy and self-
seeking is quite outside the scope of this paper though it is worth
noting that most of the people, particularly in universities and newspapers, who consistently ridicule "the politician" have personalities
which make it unlikely that they could be elected even as dog-
catchers if they themselves ever ran for elective office.

The possession of this political ability is a fourth factor helping to
turn the interests of the local union leader away from wage unionism
to welfare unionism. With a sigh of relief he leaves technical and
wearisome negotiations with General Motors or Chrysler to the international representatives and turns to the personally much more
congenial task of "servicing" the membership of the local. In such
activities his political talents, his skills at getting along with people,
of improving the morale and gaining the trust of the little man, and
of knowing the right channels of communication with everybody in
town, are much more useful than they are at a bargaining table or
before a labour disputes tribunal.

We may sum up this aspect of unionism by saying that there are
within the union movement itself a number of factors—the desire of
elected officers to get re-elected, the need for increased division of
labour between local executives and international or regional officers, the necessarily political character of union leaders as people,

[5] Selekman, *Labor Relations and Human Relations,* p. 177.

company-wide bargaining leading to supra-local representation of the union at the bargaining table, and perhaps as a temporary but important factor the high wage-rates and employment-rates prevailing since the end of the war—all of which are potent in forcing local union leadership to explore new areas for union activity; and because of the *anomie* and community lacks of towns like Windsor such new areas for union expansion have been found very ready at hand in the "service" or welfare field.

(3) It does not require much thought to realize that the expansion of unions into the welfare field does *not* bring them into conflict with big business corporations. On the contrary, the better the local looks after the social and psychological needs of its membership, the better served are the interests of big business. This comes about in two ways. One is direct and obvious: if the social, recreational, and personal needs of the worker are well taken care of outside the plant, the happier, more contented, and hence more efficient the worker will be inside the plant. The wider and better-run the welfare activities of the union, the more efficient is the worker. Perhaps not the most important example in Windsor, but nonetheless an apt illustration, is provided by the recent opening of a bar with a club licence by Local 195 in the basement of the union hall. Here the union member can drink his beer in much more attractive surroundings and among much more congenial companions than in the usual deplorable atmosphere of an Ontario tavern (and Windsor contains some of the worst hellholes of that type in the province). Because of the restraints imposed by the presence of his fellow-workers, the average union member who uses the union bar is likely to drink less, enjoy himself more, and go to work in the morning in much better shape, than he did before the union got its licence. If from its Olympian heights, the Chrysler management have deigned to notice Local 195's bar, it should be pleased with it.

Of course, it is not altruism that prompted the Local 195 executive to instal beer in its basement. Part of their motivation undoubtedly was to increase their support with the rank and file by making the union hall more attractive to the members.[6] But their action in so doing illustrates the second and indirect way in which the incursions of unions into non-wage matters promote sentiments and bring about

---

[6] The anti-union forces in Windsor are so eager to distort any fact, in order to damage the unions, that I think it necessary to mention that the bar is closed during union meetings.

results which are desired by management. Not only do better union services promote more contented and happier workers, as in the case of the bar, but also the more the unions provide such services the greater becomes the stability and responsibility of unions. Spokesmen for management have long been demanding that unions should become more "responsible," by which they presumably mean more stable, more solid, more predictable, in a certain sense more "bourgeois." Such a result may well come about less through change in the unions' economic role than through change and expansion in the unions' social role. A union which is chiefly concerned with organizing, bargaining, and striking, is likely to have great difficulty in achieving responsibility; whereas a union which concerns itself with operating a bar, starting and managing co-operative stores, organizing educational classes, making short-term loans to indigent members, providing counselling services and free medical and legal services, publishing a union paper, and even (in one spectacular case) operating a charm school for members' wives, cannot help but develop a sense of responsibility, whether it wants to or not.[7]

In such ways, then, the unions, by taking care of some of the community's lacks, are to a noticeable extent rehabilitating the little man, the victim of the industrial system, and doing their share, or perhaps a great deal more than their share, to make him into a more efficient person. And by undertaking these wider responsibilities they are themselves becoming more responsible organizations with far too much at stake, in capital equipment among other things, to trifle lightly and irresponsibly with the continued welfare of the union. As this side of union affairs prospers and expands it may do much, much more than the counselling programmes of Hawthorne for example, to correct the sickness of the acquisitive society upon which Mayo and R. H. Tawney lay so much stress. It may also go far towards giving the union movement, and particularly the big locals, a stability, efficiency, and solidarity, and hence a discipline, which is presumably what management spokesmen are asking for in their recurrent complaints about "the unions' irresponsibility."

Viewed then, both from the point of view of their direct results upon the morale of the individual and their indirect results upon the union executives and union traditions, the welfare activities of unions must be judged as leading the union movement in a direction par-

[7] Cf. the varied activities of the Amalgamated Clothing Workers of America as extensively reported in *Life* for June 28, 1948.

allel at least to the interests of big business. Big business and big
locals may readily reach understanding along these lines. The recent
General Motors agreement of June 1, 1948, whereby the United
States company wrote a cost of living adjustment clause into its new
contract with the U.A.W., is possibly a very significant omen of the
type of understanding that is to come. It is an indication that big
companies like General Motors are ready to recognize living factors
outside the plant as relevant to discussions of wages. In this case they
have recognized only "economic" conditions as represented by the
cost of living, but this is an enormous step from the narrow economic
thinking of the General Motors of 1936. If today the General Motors
negotiators are willing to discuss amicably and reasonably the cost of
living with union leaders it seems a reasonable expectation that tomorrow may find them willing to discuss in similar spirit such
"social" problems as poor school systems or housing lacks or ineffi-
cient streetcar systems in the towns and cities in which they operate

(4) The expansion, then, of the union's role in the community
does not increase the area or intensity of conflict between the unions
and big business. On the contrary they seem likely to reach a wider
area of mutual accommodation. This accommodation and mutual
acceptance, amounting even to mutual respect, will probably come
easier in the case of the big locals and the unitary big-plant company
than between the international officers and the multi-plant company.
The relations in South Bend between the Studebaker Corporation
and Local 5 of the U.A.W. have recently been shown by Harbison
and Dubin [8] to have reached an advanced stage of mutual adjustment and respect. This study says nothing about the welfare activities of Local 5, nor does it tell us much about the community situation in South Bend, but it does indicate the possibility of understanding between a big local and a big company in a small city. The
authors add the significant comment that the Studebaker set-up is
not likely to set a pattern for other plants, by implication because
of the complications introduced by the multi-plant organization of
companies like General Motors and Chrysler and the diversity of
union control in cities like Detroit. Accordingly it would seem that,
potentially at least, South Bend and Windsor have a great deal more
in common than Windsor and Detroit, with South Bend indicating
the direction in which management-union relations may develop in

[8] Frederick H. Harbison and Robert Dubin, *Patterns of Union-Management Relations* (Chicago: Science Research Associates, 1947).

the future in Windsor. Furthermore, there seems clear evidence [9] that something like the same mutual respect and understanding as that at Studebaker is developing in Windsor between Ford of Canada and Local 200, though it must be added that there is little sign of anything similar in the present relations between Chrysler of Canada and Local 195.

The main reason why the expansion of the unions into welfare channels does not bring them into increased conflict with big business but has rather a reverse result, is that such expansion does not impinge upon the prerogatives or traditional activities of big business leaders. The owners or executives of the big-company plants are seldom local men, and, even when they are, they and their local managers are seldom active or interested in local issues or local affairs. The logics of the big plant executives are the logics of efficiency rather than the logics of power, especially local power; or perhaps it is rather that their needs for power and prestige are well cared for by the power they wield and the respect they command *within* the walls of the plant. The conflict which is provoked by the expansion of the unions' community role is a conflict which the forces which traditionally have "run the town," and those forces do not, usually, contain the big plant executives. In Windsor at least, while it may not be entirely clear who does run the town, it is perfectly clear that it is not the top management of Ford or Chrysler nor "stooges" for those managements. The extent of their indirect influence is almost impossible to determine. Of course, until social science develops a technique for measuring the "influence" of a man in a prestige position, there will always be those bigoted adherents of the theory that society is controlled by big business who will argue that any top executive is always there, a sinister figure, master-minding in the background, using the local politicians and Rotarians as his frontmen. Lacking any objective way of handling this difficult question one can only offer one's own opinion [10] which is that in Windsor, at least, the big automobile companies do their lobbying, if at all,

[9] This view and the evidence upon which it is based are discussed at length in *Report on Windsor* referred to above.

[10] Any experienced researcher will recognize that such an opinion is not dreamed up out of a clear sky but is the result of a great deal of informal probing both into what people in key positions say and abstain from saying; a great deal of weighing of incidents that happen and the reasons various people give as to why they happen, and the testing of various "hunches" to determine which one fits best all of the observable facts.

at the national capital and with the federal government, or through such bodies as the Canadian Manufacturers Association, and communicate scarcely at all with the local anti-union leadership. The groups who have always "run this town" and who find their control threatened by the rising strength and expanding activities of the big locals are distinct from "big business" and seem to be composed of the following elements in the population: (a) the Chamber of Commerce group, which includes the owners of locally-owned businesses and as an important section of these, the owners or managers of most of the parts—or supplier—plants, (b) the old families, (c) the churches, (d) the local politicians, (e) the local charitable interests, that is, the individuals who habitually and as of right sit on the boards of the Y.M.C.A., the Welfare Chest, the Boy Scouts, etc., (f) the "self-starters." Except for the last, these groups need no explanation; they are the same groups with the same backgrounds, drives, and values as are to be found in any other large town or smaller city in Ontario, the only difference being that in most Ontario towns the unions are not so strong and hence these groups do not feel their power to be so much threatened as they do in Windsor. The "self-starters" are an equally familiar group, but perhaps not under that name. They are the anti-labour individuals who always appear prominently in any strike-torn town and take the lead in anti-labour violence, urging the use of force to break the strike and identifying themselves fanatically with the interests of management. Since they are seldom members of any important management-group their motivation is a puzzle to everybody. Hence the name "self-starters," since nobody can understand what "makes them that way." [11]

These groups obviously overlap a great deal in membership and there is no space here to unravel their complicated interrelationships. But, considering them as a loosely organized but very powerful collection of overlapping groups, it is clear that it is they and their traditional roles in the town's power-structure that are threatened by the growing unions. People in trouble, in a town like Windsor, used to go to a clergyman or to a local politician or a local charitable body;

---

[11] In the original sit-down strike at Flint in January, 1937, when Governor Frank Murphy of Michigan was enquiring into the shooting at Fisher Plant No. 2, whereby fourteen sit-downers were wounded by gunfire, he was told by the local sheriff, "General Motors didn't want it, it was those small business men, those self-starters." Kraus, *The Many and the Few*, pp. 144–145.

now they go to the union. Such people used to repay their bene-
factors by such means as voting as the clergyman or politician or
charitable person wished, or appeared to wish; now they vote as the
union leader wishes. The increasing services provided by the union
lead to an increasing dependence upon, and loyalty to, the union,
and the union leaders hence assume increasing moral authority at
the expense of the older moral authorities. The trend is clear though
still in a very early stage of its development. The older moral authorities must either accommodate themselves to the unions by accepting some of their ideals and co-operating with them or fight
them tooth and nail long after Ford and Chrysler have stopped
fighting and, in the case of Ford at least, have begun working with
the unions. The Catholic Church gives every appearance of following the first course, of accepting and collaborating with unionism.
Forced to choose between voting Liberal as the traditional party of
the Church or voting C.C.F., as the unions are likely to urge, the
Catholic trade unionist in Windsor has in recent years followed the
unions' counsel to an extent, not sufficient indeed to make the election of the C.C.F. candidates certain, but nonetheless sufficient to
show the church authorities which way opinion is tending. As a
result, many observers of Windsor politics, of all parties, believe
the Church has been supporting the C.C.F. in Windsor elections in
recent years, and the voting figures are quite sufficient to show that
it has not been actively opposing it. Strong labour sympathy and
Christian Socialism are sufficiently strong among the Windsor Catholic clergy to make it very easy for any Catholic unionist who wants
to vote for the "political arm of labour" to do so with a clear conscience. In the provincial election of 1948 in Windsor, the Liberal
party, the traditional party of Windsor Catholicism and the dominant party in Windsor politics until the rise of the unions, ran a
very poor third, despite the appearance in the campaign of the federal minister of health in person. Furthermore, it was significant
that the only seat won by the C.C.F. was the seat with the strongest
tradition of Liberalism and the largest proportion of Catholics in its
population.

The Protestant churches, forced to choose between the Catholic-
union alliance and the "best people" are badly split and cannot be
neatly labelled in a short survey, except for the Anglicans, who in
Windsor, as elsewhere in Ontario, have always identified themselves
with "the best people," and, now that the latter feel their power and

prerogatives threatened, support them all the more strongly, even in certain instances fanatically.

The old type city-hall politician, if he wants to remain in office, has also been forced to accommodate himself to labour. Not even Windsor has yet reached the point where the labour vote can be swung in any one way or delivered by any one party or clique. Labour leaders in the town who have endeavoured to tie the union vote to any one political party have had their fingers badly burned, and their prestige as political fixers sadly tarnished. The present political situation in Windsor is in a state of flux that often approaches sheer confusion, and will presumably remain that way until certain wider issues in the Canadian political scene have been settled. But at the municipal level, while it is clear that nobody can be elected mayor unless he commands combined support from the unions, the Catholic Church, and the remnants of the old Liberal machine, it is equally clear that every municipal election brings nearer the day when the unions will have a permanent and secure majority on the city council, either of union men, or of men very responsive to union wishes.

Lastly, the small business man is threatened, or thinks he is, in two ways. One way is financially. The opening of a beverage room in the union hall of Local 195 was protested unsuccessfully by the local saloonkeepers; an application by Local 200 for a similar licence was rejected by the licence authority undoubtedly because of similar protests, though technical building and safety regulations can always be found to justify such rejection. The movement into co-operative stores, already well under way in Detroit and spreading into Windsor under U.A.W. auspices, is a potential threat to the turnovers of the small store keepers. Credit unions under the auspices of the locals are a threat to the volume of loan business of the banks and loan companies. And of course, if the habit of operating a union charm-school should spread, every beauty parlor operator in town would be storming the licence authority to prevent the unions providing such a service. The number of small business proprietors directly threatened in this way is small but it must grow with every expansion of the unions' activities. To have already stirred up the saloonkeepers, the grocers, the fuel merchants, and the beauty parlor operators is not a bad beginning towards consolidating the whole of the small business group in opposition to union-service activity.

The second and more important way, however, in which the small business group is threatened is in its moral rather than its financial role. The days when the saloonkeeper or the corner grocer were the only business men in a working-class neighbourhood and, as such, were sources of advice, sources of credit, and channels of communication between the humble factory worker and the higher ranks of the social and economic hierarchy, are going or gone in unionized towns, and to these groups the symbol of their diminishing prestige and capacity to have people dependent upon them is the rise of the union. Again we are confronted with institutional competition; the increase in prestige of the union has to be at the expense of other groups. The corner grocer and the neighbourhood tavernkeeper are affected by the same forces and in the same way as the clergy or the Y.M.C.A. Board of Directors, and with the same result; they must either compromise with the unions and become in effect "union-lovers," thereby becoming renegades in the eyes of the "best people" and the Chamber of Commerce, or, more easily, become fanatical anti-union "self-starters," denouncing all unions as communist and all union leaders as agitators and subversive influences.

Whatever group we select for intensive study we find the same pattern. The group most vociferous and violent in its opposition to unionism, whether it be the old families, the Chamber of Commerce, the local politicians, sections of the clergy, or the small business men, proves to be a group which is not threatened financially to any noticeable extent by union activity but which very obviously is threatened morally. Their shouts of hate and screams of rage at unionism and all its works are reflections not of a threat to their bank accounts but to their prestige and to the power symbols they have hitherto enjoyed. The humble factory worker now has his union and need no longer be subservient to the older prestige groups. He is not dependent, as he used to be, upon the corner grocer nor the local tavernkeeper, just as he is not dependent any longer upon the churches or the local Lady Bountifuls (of both sexes) or the local politicians. This shift of prestige evokes the violent hatred of those groups who are losing it for those (the union leaders) who are gaining it.

(5) There are two important corollaries of this analysis that need extensive discussion but which can only be mentioned very briefly in this paper. One is an internal problem of the unions which is a result of their increased welfare or service activities. It is the problem of obtaining suitable personnel to administer their complex, and in many cases, technical activities. The crux of this problem is the an-

nual union election. Although, as was pointed out above, an incumbent executive board enjoys an enormous advantage just because it is "in," nevertheless, the yearly vote is a great handicap to a union in building up any continuing body of competent technicians. A union which wishes to add to its staff technical specialists drawn from outside union ranks, can offer them only one year's security in the job, since, if the executive board which hired the technician is beaten in the next annual election, it is virtually certain that all its appointees will be fired by the incoming board, and new appointments made. For this reason, unions, whether local or regional offices, find it almost impossible to secure good technicians,—research men, welfare men, co-op men, and publicity men—from outside union ranks. Few competent people in these fields are likely to accept a union job on such insecure terms; hence the failure of labour unions, except in a few special cases, to build up, ғven in their present expansionist phase, any continuing solid body of top-notch specialists in the various specialized fields into which they seek to move.

There is, of course, another alternative, namely, to recruit the specialized personnel from within its own ranks. This is much more in line with the democratic traditions of the U.A.W. and the mildly chauvinistic thinking of unions generally, than the policy of paying big salaries to people recruited from outside union ranks. But it is difficult to find the right material in sufficient numbers. In Windsor, and almost certainly in other automobile centres, the average auto worker has not had a great deal of formal education and his background and experience do not fit him for technical or even administrative jobs. The process of selection whereby bright young men rise to notice in the locals is a process that accentuates aggressiveness, "proletarian glamour," and willingness to fight and suffer for the union, rather than qualities of personality fitted to research, teaching, or managerial jobs.

This will continue to be a chronic handicap of welfare unionism unless one of the two solutions is accepted as standard union practice. At present the U.A.W. seems unable to make up its collective mind between the two. It vacillates between hiring outsiders with technical training and selecting promising young men from union ranks and training them to do the jobs that need to be done in the locals. Neither policy is consistently followed. The result is the usual result of vacillation; the union reaps the weaknesses of both policies and the strengths of neither. Because of the insecurity of tenure, the people hired from outside union ranks tend to be rather inferior practitioners of whatever skill the job requires; the men selected from within union ranks might do a first-rate job if they were given first-rate training. They are not being given such training, partly because the making of specialists out of good union members is contrary to the highly-valued democratic traditions of the U.A.W., partly, I think, because of a failure to realize how much training is needed by a man who has never finished high school, to make him into a good researcher or counsellor or publicity or educational man, or even into a negotiator or office executive, as competent as those management is able to hire and is in the habit of hiring.

(6) The second corollary is so obvious as to need no elaboration. As labour, through its increased welfare activities, becomes more community-conscious, it becomes necessarily a political power in the union towns, and as such it seeks to make its desires heeded at the city hall. It is thus in the position of seeking to control the state, at the local level, in the interests of labour. It is difficult to see how or why any such movement can stop with the city hall. Many of the social or community problems with which labour is now concerned are incapable of solution at the municipal level. The same factors which, in the Windsors of the country, are forcing local unions to make more and more demands upon the municipal governments, and to use union political action to obtain them, must increasingly operate on a wider front and force labour to challenge the older power groups and the older political parties on the wider battlegrounds of the province and of the nation. The final end to labour's expansion into welfare fields has to be a Labour party, in effect, if not in name, operating at all levels of government. Walter Reuther has made no secret of his belief that this is inevitable in the United States, and from the situation in Windsor, it seems clear that such a result is being forced upon the unions by the logic of circumstances and owes little or nothing to the individual whims or preferences of particular labour leaders.[12]

In the foregoing pages we have selected a few aspects of Windsor to illustrate the general situation. The rise of the trade unions in Windsor and their institutional expansionism constitute an instructive case study in the characteristics of social institutions. As Professor Tannenbaum has said:

[12] Such a trend is much further developed in Canada than in the United States, because, of course, of the political immaturity of the latter country.

It is a characteristic of a social institution to seek to encompass the whole life of man. The family, the church and the state have at different times encompassed the individual from the cradle to the grave and prescribed his spiritual as well as his material destiny. So any new institution coming into existence must seek to embrace all of the life of man . . . hence the new institutions compete with the old, not merely for [man's] loyalty, but also for the exercise of the innumerable responsibilities and functions, and the satisfaction of the innumerable needs and aspirations that the life of man generates in a living world. The difficulty lies in the fact that the field, though complex, is limited, and that whatever one institution performs, is at the expense of another institution. . . . Thus institutions, all at the service of man, are competitive with each other and the conflict between them is in fact irremediable. Institutional friction and instability are therefore the normal state of society and the hope of peace and quietude between institutions is an idle dream. Between the institutions the conflict is moral, psychological and political for the guidance and governance of the whole man.[13]

The applicability of this type of theory to the Windsor situation, exemplifying as Windsor does the moral, psychological, and political struggle between the new institution, the unions, and the older institutions for the "guidance and governance of the whole man," needs little argument.

What then does all this tell us about the relation of industrial relations research to social theory? Basically and briefly there are three main conclusions that may be drawn.

(a) In attacking the older economic view of labour as a commodity and insisting that the narrow psychological basis of Ricardo and classical economics was a poor basis for understanding labour problems, Elton Mayo is essentially right. Any commodity which can expand to become an institution and to challenge the state, the family, the church and the existing power groups in industrial towns is hardly capable of being fitted into commodity theory.

(b) In initiating in-plant research and drawing the main conclusion from such research that industrial man was a poor, lost soul, whose main concern, even when sweating on the assembly line, was not with wages but with finding a more satisfactory social life for himself, and that therefore the theories of sociologists like Durkheim and Radcliffe-Brown were much more applicable to any analy-

[13] Frank Tannenbaum, "The Balance of Power in Society," *Political Science Quarterly*, LXI, No. 4, (December, 1946).

sis of contemporary industrial society than the theories of Ricardo or John Stuart Mill, Mayo is on equally sound ground, though he weakens his sociological case considerably by interlarding his analysis with far too much of the individualistic psychology of Freud, and hence tends to become preoccupied with individual disorganization and reorganization, rather than with social disorganization and reorganization.

(c) Most importantly, Mayo's approach leaves his work open to misrepresentation not only by his opponents but even by the more management-oriented of his supporters. Since all the in-plant research approaches the worker through his activities and preoccupations *upon the job,* it gives little or no indication of the importance of large, strong, well-run unions and their function in reorganizing the victim of the soulless assembly-line plant, and giving him back his self-respect and rescuing him from *anomie.* Because Mayo and his followers pay so little attention to unions as social institutions, it is possible for some at least of the strongest supporters of industrial-relations research to write as if the reorganization of the worker and of the industrial system could be achieved only by managerial action. In Mayo's latest book, there is a painfully clear example of such thinking in the foreword—a very eulogistic one—written by the former dean of the Harvard School of Business, Wallace B. Donham.

> Mayo gives us instances [says Dean Donham] where industrial administrators have succeeded in making factory groups so stable, . . . that men in the groups explicitly recognized that the factory had become for them the stabilizing force around which they had developed satisfying lives. This accomplishment was achieved in spite of technological changes within the plant and social chaos in the community outside. . . . Thus Mayo shows us . . . that it is within the power of industry to create within industry itself a partially effective substitute for the old stabilizing effect of the neighbourhood. Given stable employment, it might make of industry (as of the small town during most of our national life), a socially satisfying way of life as well as a way of making a living.[14]

This example illustrates very clearly the type of conclusion that may be drawn from the in-plant type of research. The small town or the old neighbourhood used to be a stabilizing force in human relations but it has gone forever; the modern industrial community is

[14] Mayo, *The Social Problems of an Industrial Civilization,* Foreword, pp. viii–ix.

not a community at all, it is merely a social chaos. The only alternative available, the obvious substitute, is industry, nice big beautiful industry. Through counselling programmes, combing the psyche of the worker, better personnel-selection programmes, applied anthropology, and the rest, the beautiful factory will . . . replace the beautiful but long-lost small town where we all used to be so happy.

Dean Donham's error clearly lies in thinking of this as *the only* alternative. This is a theoretical error that springs directly from the empirical error of neglecting to study unions. Because unions are mentioned so rarely in the factual studies of plant situations, their theoretical significance in contemporary industrial society is ignored. What the present paper has endeavoured to point out is that there is another road leading out of the *anomie* and the social chaos of industrial society, and one which is not merely theoretically possible but is already in use in highly industrialized towns like Windsor. Instead of going inside Dean Donham's beautiful plants to find the more satisfactory and stabilized life, the worker, or at least the auto worker, has gone into the union hall. There, within his union, he is finding his own ways of building a more satisfying social life; and when he looks out at the social chaos that is Windsor, he does not run for help into the Ford plant or the Chrysler plant, rather he calls upon his union to undertake the job of cleaning up that social chaos and rebuilding the community along more satisfying lines. "Labour," the commodity of Ricardo, has been changed by the work of Mayo and his associates into "the worker," a disordered dust of slightly psychopathic individuals; what the Windsor evidence indicates is that the psychopathic phase, if it ever existed, is about ended, and that "labour" or "the worker" has now become "the union," a new and expanding social institution, and a social reform institution into the bargain. It would appear obvious then, that in addition to economic studies of labour, such as the older literature provides, and the psychological studies of the worker which the Mayo school has given us, we are badly in need of empirical data upon the sociology of labour unions and their place in the industrial community. The central problem of industrial society appears to be the impact of the new institutions upon the older equilibrium of institutional forces. The chief conclusion . . . may be summed up by saying that if there is a new field of social research called industrial sociology, it is high time workers in that field discovered the union and explored its role—still in the process of being formulated—in the community.

45 BUSINESS AS A SYSTEM OF ORGANIZED POWER *

BY ROBERT STAUGHTON LYND (1892–   )
COLUMBIA UNIVERSITY

THE characteristic thing about democracy is its diffusion of power among the people. That men have recurrently had to have recourse to revolutions in order to assert such a pattern of power attests the inveterate presence within society of a contrary tendency. Power is no less "political" for being labeled "economic" power; for politics is but the science of "who gets what, when, and how." Alexander Hamilton advocated and Jefferson opposed the effect of clotted economic power to substitute concentrated minority class power for diffused power. Lincoln referred to this same tendency when he wrote in 1860, "Soberly, it is now no child's play to save the principles of Jefferson from total overthrow in this nation"; and he went on to speak of "the miners and sappers of returning despotism" engaged in undercutting democracy. The preponderant weight of economic power in the Constitutional Convention, while conceding the outward forms of political democracy, went on at once to curb the exercise of the very power it had just granted; it crippled the force of democratic power at the source by parceling up this power by a marvelously dexterous system of barriers to its expression. Thus political equality under the ballot was granted on the unstated but factually double-locked assumption that the people must refrain from seeking the extension of that equality to the economic sphere. In short, the attempted harmonious marriage of democracy to capitalism doomed genuinely popular control from the start. And all down through our national life the continuance of the union has depended upon the unstated condition that the dominant member, capital, continue to provide returns to all elements in democratic society sufficient to disguise the underlying conflict in interests. A crisis within the economic relations of capitalism was bound to precipitate a crisis in the democratic political system.

Democracy in the era of economic liberalism has viewed power

* Reprinted by permission of the author and of the publisher from Lynd's "Foreword" to Robert A. Brady, *Business as a System of Power* (New York: Columbia University Press, 1943), pp. vii–xviii; excerpts from pp. viii–xvi reprinted.

as a thing to be feared, rather than used; and this disposition, coupled with the checks on democratic action written into the Constitution, has prompted American democracy to state the problem of power negatively. It has been casual, to the point of recklessness, about the positive development of its own authority. Formally, democracy has held all the aces. But actually, as Laski has pointed out, "The disproportion in America between the actual economic control and the formal political power is almost fantastic." Despite intermittent guerilla warfare between state power and private economic power through all our national life, democracy has slurred over the challenge to its very existence inherent in growing economic power. This has been due to a number of factors. (1) The fact that the issue between the two types of power has been so heavily cloaked under the sectional issue between the agrarian and the Eastern industrial states has diverted attention from the fact that capitalist economic power constitutes a direct, continuous, and fundamental threat to the whole structure of democratic authority everywhere and always. (2) The appearance of the Industrial Revolution simultaneously with political democracy distracted men's attention from the perennially unfinished task of building democracy. Equipped with a new and marvelously growing technology and with a raw continent beckoning to be exploited, Americans turned their attention all down through the nineteenth century to the grand adventure of getting rich. Democracy was taken for granted as substantially achieved, or at most requiring only to be defended. And a naïve and dangerous popular faith has grown, notably since the Civil War, that democracy and capitalist enterprise are two aspects of the same thing, so that the progress manifestly occurring in industry must also be happening in the democratic political system. Since democracy itself thus failed to throw constantly new goals ahead to catch the imagination and to evoke the energy of its citizens, men thus deprived of anything bigger to work for have in the main vindicated the cynical view that they are motivated only by selfish personal interests. Under such a distorted view of democracy, in which the state and society are nothing and the individual everything, democracy has become increasingly identified with the protection of one's personal affairs; and this has steadily sapped its vitality. (3) Because this "American way" has worked so seemingly opulently, and because of man's need in the rough and tumble of an increasingly insecure world to feel immutable security somehow back of him, American citizens, preoccupied with everything but the affairs of democracy, have increasingly imputed to the Constitution, the central symbol of American democracy, an extravagant finality. If this great and mysterious It were but defended, democracy remained unchallenged.

In such an environment, democracy has been largely tolerant of the businessman, for the most part encouraging him with a lavish hand; for upon his restless enterprise the public welfare was conceived to rest. The "trust busting" of the turn of the century was a protest against what seemed to be excesses in an otherwise normal system, not a protest against the system itself. Even in recent decades, as business has grown in power until it has become a jostling giant, democracy has largely failed to recognize its political significance. The world was large and its wealth seemingly unlimited, and if business was growing bigger and more noisily insistent, this was viewed as but a surface manifestation of rugged growth. Down to the First World War abroad, and until 1929 in the United States, what businessmen did was regarded as primarily their own business. Since the fruit of their activities slopped over in taxes, wages, and dividends, it was manifestly contributing to general welfare.

But this nominal division of powers could not be maintained within the structure of capitalist nationalism. As industrialization has spread over the world and competition has increased, the reciprocal relation between state power and economic power has become more apparent. The fundamental import of what has been happening at a quickening tempo since the Russian Revolution of 1917 is the abandonment of the liberal fiction of the separateness of these two kinds of power. Organized business enterprise is less and less willing to tolerate checks on its activities by the state; more and more it needs the state as active ally; and the national state, in turn, having delivered itself over by accepting the definition of its welfare as synonymous with the welfare of its business system, needs increasingly the utmost of aggressive efficiency from its businessmen. Business is in politics and the state is in business. The state political apparatus can tolerate only the most efficient management of the economic system, since it depends directly upon the latter for national power in foreign relations; whereas the economy must have the political power to extend control, as the Nazis have demonstrated, to the regulation of the social sphere, "not to gratify lower-class maudlinness or rapacity but to secure national concord and efficiency" as an essential aid to foreign economic competition. The result is an unmistakable trend toward the monolithic power structure of the totalitarian state.

And the public does not know what to do about this merging of powers up aloft over its head. As business has organized and has begun to state cogently and lavishly the case for its version of such an "ordered society," the popular challenge expressed earlier in the campaign to curb bigness by governmental action has become confused and blunted. Big business has carefully disseminated to the little man at the grass roots enthusiasm and pride as an American in the superefficiency of the marvelous assembly lines and other paraphernalia of giant technology that produces his automobiles and other daily conveniences. The little man is puzzled, hypnotized into inaction: if he is not to oppose *bigness* itself, the bigness of Henry Ford, Du Pont, and the other great corporations that makes these characteristically American things possible, what *is* he to oppose about big business? The technique of dazzling, confusing, and dividing the opposition, used by Hitler, has been skillfully practiced by the propagandists for big business.

The rapidly spreading web of interindustry organization of this business power is the immediate focus of Brady's book. We live in an era in which only organization counts; values and causes with unorganized or only vaguely organized backing were never so impotent. The rapidity of current change creates the need for quick decisions, which puts the organized minority that knows what it wants at a thumping advantage over the scattered and wistful majority. In fact, it is able, as the Nazis have demonstrated, to exploit majority confusions ruthlessly in the name of majority values to minority ends.

One of the most striking conclusions from Brady's book concerns the similarity in type and function of the organization of business interests from nation to nation, despite seemingly widely dissimilar national backgrounds. This is due primarily to the inner common tendencies within capitalist-controlled technology wherever it operates. But it is also due in part to the fact that men operating across the world from each other learn organizational and other tricks of their trade as rapidly as these appear. Major changes in the way men live and work together under industrial conditions no longer happen in one industry or one country and then spread at a pace to be measured in decades or generations. Inventions have shrunk physical space and organization has diminished social space.

World competition sees to it that a profitable technical or organizational device runs around the world of organized interest before common folk in the country of origin are generally aware that it has been developed.

Social organization around functional concerns is normal to human beings. Western liberalism, imputing freedom and rationality to the individual, washed its hands of the problem of securing positive organization; it proceeded on the assumption that, wherever organization was socially desirable, men would recognize the need and forthwith organize themselves. Such a theory not only misread human nature but it failed to take account of the momentum developed within such a cultural complex as machine technology owned and exploited within a legally buttressed system of private property rights. Liberal democracy has never dared face the fact that industrial capitalism is an intensely coercive form of organization of society that cumulatively constrains men and all of their institutions to work the will of the minority who hold and wield economic power; and that this relentless warping of men's lives and forms of association becomes less and less the result of voluntary decisions by "bad" or "good" men and more and more an impersonal web of coercions dictated by the need to keep "the system" running. These coercions cumulate themselves to ends that even the organizing leaders of big business may fail to foresee, as step by step they grapple with the next immediate issue, and the next, and the next. Fantastic as it may sound, this course may end by the business leaders of the United States coming to feel, in the welter of their hurrying perplexities, that survival depends on precisely the kind of thing Germany's big business wants: the liquidation of labor and other popular dissent at home, and a "peace" more vindicative than the Versailles Treaty, that will seek to stabilize an Anglo-American feudal monopoly control over the entire world.

Liberal democracy likewise never solved the problem of bigness; but it alternately fought and condoned it in a confusion of inconsistent policies. A cultural system drenched with the artisan spirit of small enterprise found difficulty in accepting the facts that modern machinery demands integration and that productive enterprise, released from making a pair of shoes for a known local customer and set to making standard goods for an impersonal and theoretically unlimited "market," likewise demands organization. Hence the recurrent efforts to curb bigness. But both bigness and monopoly are normal antecedents to the stage of planned provision for the needs of society which we are now entering, and there is no longer any point in attacking either. The only relevant questions today are: Who controls these productive facilities, and to what ends? and How effectively are they organized to achieve these ends? Or, stated in another way: Will democratic political power absorb and use economic resources, bigness and all, to serve its ends, or will big economic power take over state power?

The modern phase of business as a system of organized power began with the spread of the corporate organization of industry after the 1860's. The world of 1870 did not speculate much about the grip which corporate business was to have on the lives of all of us a half-century later. Corporate organization, like the monopolies it made possible, was viewed as the exception, unadapted to general business. The precise significance of Brady's book is that he takes this same organizational tendency within industrial society—now become the rule rather than the exception and moved along to its contemporary stage of organized inter-monopoly control—and shows us where the logic of such a centrally organized system of power is carrying us. For synchronized monopoly directed by a peak all-industry strategy board is but corporate business come of age. The difference between the early and the mature stages is that, whereas corporate organization completed the taking of the instruments of production out of the hands of the laborer and strengthened economic power in its challenge to democratic political power, the mature stage Brady describes is moving on to wrest even the formal political means of curbing economic power from the hands of the citizens of democracy. Corporate organization pocketed production; its giant offspring is pocketing the nation, including the entire lives of its citizens. And organized business is extending this anti-democratic web of power in the name of the people's own values, with billboards proclaiming "What's Good for Industry Is Good for Your Family," and deftly selling itself to a harassed people as "trustees," "guardians," "the people's managers" of the public interest.

The large identities in problem and in organizational form to meet these problems in nation after nation suggest with startling emphasis that we in the United States are caught in the same major coercions that industrial capitalist nations everywhere face. We, too, have no choice as to whether economic and state power shall be merged; for there will be no survival for nations that seek to perpetuate the economic wastes and frictions and the social anarchy entailed in the operation of state power and economic power as rivals. The sheer fact of the emergence of the phenomenon of effectively planned nations has, because of the logic of organization inherent in modern technology, outmoded at a stroke the old system under which all our American national life has been lived. In the United States, the present stage of organized, centralized business power, already reaching out in control of schools, media of communication, public opinion, and government itself, provides more than a broad hint of the direction events will take, if present tendencies remain unchecked. . . .

Born as a nation coincidentally with the upsurge of the Industrial Revolution, situated in a rich continent which we have built up with the bodies of cheap foreign labor, protected by the accident of location during the years of our fumbling growth, we have through all our national life been borne forward by a favoring tail wind. This past we view, quite characteristically, not as a stroke of luck but as the vindication of the superior rightness of "the American way"; and this makes for complacency. Growing out of this is our blindness to any way of conceiving our national future other than in terms of the simple extension of our expansive past. Our national naïveté about organization is disastrous in the present crisis. We are called "a nation of joiners," but the individual still holds the focus of our national imagination. With all the flotsam and jetsam of our "joining," we have little popular belief in or experience of the hard-bitten type of relentless organization for power ends; and where we see it, for instance, in the Tammany type of politics, we deplore it even as we condone it as a special case and a somehow necessary evil. Of all the Western industrial nations, we are the least class-stratified psychologically and the only one without an active labor party or its equivalent in our national political life. And, again, this is not because "the American way" is fundamentally different, but primarily because the American ideology as regards capitalism is less sophisticated than is that of any other Western nation.

Thus our traditions conspire to make us unable to read the meanings behind the organization Brady describes. We are opaque to the political import of this massing of business power, and we still insist on regarding it as primarily a concern only of the businessmen. Meanwhile, the lawyers with their convenient conception of the role of the law, the public-relations men, the press, and all the other pliant agents of organized business go busily about on cat feet as they spread the net and tighten the noose for those so abundantly able to make it "worth their while." Burnham's plausible thesis of the "managerial revolution" has been seized upon by business, and a powerful medium like *Fortune* proclaims itself in its new editorial policy as the organ "for the managers of America." But behind the fiction of the "manager class" so conveniently sterilized from the taint of special interest stands the same old power. "The voice is Jacob's voice, but the hands are the hands of Esau."

46 RELIGIOUS INSTITUTIONS *

BY J. O. HERTZLER (1895–   )
UNIVERSITY OF NEBRASKA

DUE to the varied, complex, and protean nature of religion, no interpretation of it in either its individual or its social aspects will meet with universal acceptance. The particular cultist or religious professional can be very explicit about what religion is, or about what passes for religion with him, but many others will not accept his definition, and will disagree with him as to what must be included as essential or rejected as contrary or unimportant. "Religion" for one person or group may be irreligion for others. Yet everywhere religion is a great human reality—a fact both of the individual consciousness and of the institutional order.

THE NATURE OF RELIGION

Religion is a spontaneously appearing, perennial, and universal attribute of man. Its beginning is unknown. Among almost all peoples and in all times and places there are aspects of individual consciousness and poignant human experiences on the one hand, and social quests and dominant expressional and regulatory features of the institutional system on the other, which are denominated as specifically religious. From earliest times, as a French writer has said, man has been "incurably religious."

* Reprinted by permission of the author and of the publisher from *The Annals of the American Academy of Political and Social Science*, 256 (March, 1948), 1–13.

A popular book on religion some years back opened with the dramatic statement: "In the beginning there was fear; and fear was in the heart of man; and fear controlled man."[1] Religion seemingly grows out of the fact that man lives in an atmosphere of uncertainty, insecurity, and incompletion. He is concerned about the unknowns and inexplicables about him. The element of chance, here and hereafter, everlastingly must be contended with. Man is awed and dismayed by the enormity, the stupendous forces and inexorable processes, the timelessness, of the universe. He feels himself in the presence of something which in its complexity, its power, and its mystery passes comprehension. As he faces the more or less recurrent crises of life—the holocausts of nature, war and revolt, accident, pestilence, and sickness, personal defeat and humiliation, the nature of life, the mystery of death, the enigma of the hereafter—he wonders about the security of himself and his group, about the continuity of himself. There are the disillusionments and tribulations as he associates with his fellow men, as well as the urgent social "needs" that seem to be beyond his satisfaction or control. There is often a feeling of not living a sufficiently full and good life.

Man has the conception of a supernatural, extrahuman Something, which is the cause and manipulator of forces or powers at work in the universe. He feels that he is dependent upon this power or powers, and that they mightily affect his present well-being; often, also, his ultimate destiny.

Religion is one phase of man's cultural system—a body of attitudes, ideas, and techniques—whereby he explains and adjusts himself to the unknown, the mysterious, and the mighty. By means of the various elements of religion he reaches out beyond the mundane—the material, the social, the readily knowable and observable, the relative, the temporary, the things and affairs more or less within his natural means of control—and tries to achieve a harmonious relationship with this power.

Religion and Magic. This effort raises the distinction between religion and its universal and seemingly inseparable complement, magic. Both relate to the mysterious power. Strictly, magic looks upon the universe as mechanistic and passive. There is in the universe mystical force or mana which is independent of human limitations. By the use of proper procedures one can exert power over this

[1] Lewis Browne, *This Believing World* (New York: The Macmillan Company, 1939), p. 27.

mysterious force and thwart it if circumstances so indicate; or, one can appropriate the mana and compel it to serve one's own human ends. Magic is a technique for controlling the unknown cause to produce a desired effect. The process is of a manipulative nature and is practically automatic. Magic is, in a sense, the predecessor and ancestor of science.

Religion, on the other hand, personalizes the supernatural power or powers, and regards them as voluntary agents. It is a technique for communicating with them and establishing friendly relations with them. Religion involves worship and prayer; it implies devotion and allegiance; it is a matter of emotion and moral attitude.

In spite of the distinction just drawn, the difference is one of degree rather than of kind; the occult and personalized aspects of the supernatural cannot be separated. Religion has never entirely displaced magic. Magical practices still persist even in the so-called "higher" religions to this day.

Belief and Faith. Basically, religion consists of a set of mighty hypotheses and postulates which we know as beliefs. These are the products of the consciousness of individuals and groups. Most men believe in these unseen forces in the universe, which they usually personify, since they cannot communicate with an abstraction. They believe that these beings pertinently affect the present individual and social welfare and the eternal destiny of mankind. They believe that various individual and social practices and other cultural vehicles will effect communication with and adaptation to these powers. Occasionally a body of ideas which avoids the supernatural passes as religious and is a matter of belief; e.g., the sacredness of man's relationship to his fellow men.

A given group's strongly held beliefs are invariably intertwined with value judgments regarding the supernatural or the sacred. These value judgments combined with the basic beliefs constitute a faith. Faith involves ideals and objectives and aspirations. It is "the substance of things hoped for, the evidence of things not seen" (Heb. 11:1). It has dynamic quality; it gives men strength "to move mountains." To have faith is to be faithful; that is, to hold fast to the values and their implications, to cherish the object or objects of valuation as something good, to translate the values and ideals into thought and action, and often to propagate them. Obviously, religion in its very nature is a matter of many and diverse beliefs and faiths.

INSTITUTIONALIZATION

From earliest times, the basic, engrossing, and more or less continuous human wants and social needs and interests of mankind have been socially satisfied by means of rather complex and durable cultural devices which we speak of as social institutions. These are standardized, accepted, and usually enforced systems of social behavior. They order, regulate, and correlate the activities and relationships of all individuals and subgroups of the culture area as they carry on the operations necessary to satisfy the wants and needs. By means of them human beings, in the different segments of human life, live in a co-operative, disciplined, and predictable manner.

Institutions reflect the physical backgrounds and the general culture of the area of which they are a part; they serve as important carriers of culture elements. They are the products both of long, spontaneous development and of deliberate contrivance. They invariably function as social conservators. The problem with most of them is to keep them flexible and abreast of the times in both their functioning and their structure.

From earliest known times, religion has assumed institutionalized forms. Apparently it must do certain things for individuals and communities, and it cannot exist without social expression and social organization. Even in the most highly personalized religion, in the fleeting cults, and in the modern secularized forms, there is noticeable, however veiled, the influence of institutionalization. Newly originated religions cannot outlast a single generation without taking on institutional forms. Religious systems the world over, though varying greatly as to specific factors, functions, and features, all conform to the general pattern of institutions.

Religious institutions, especially those of the higher cultures, will be briefly discussed with respect to (1) their typical structural features and (2) the main individual and social functions they perform.

STRUCTURAL FEATURES

Most institutions, regardless of the pivotal social systems of which they are functioning parts, are made up of an array of constituent elements or "type parts." These elements are both of an abstract and a tangible nature. Significant are the conceptual and the ideological features, the fairly uniform attitudes and their overt expressions, the habits which cause the individuals and groups to *act* institutionally, the codes and other normative rules, the personnel elements (members and functionaries), and the sentiment-charged symbols, the physical structures, and the utilitarian paraphernalia.[2] Counterparts of these are found in religious institutions.

Theologies and Creeds. Most religions have their bodies of ideas, beliefs, doctrines, dogmas, articles of faith, ideals, and ideologies rationalized and systematized in the form of theologies and creeds; occasionally also in mythologies. These are the reasoned interpretations [3] of the religious experience of the particular group; they give the religious views stability, consistency, and order; invariably they are authoritatively established. Some are much more elaborate, systematic, and well rationalized than others.

The theologies of different religious groups differ and conflict because of the variant interpretations of their religious experiences and their world views. For the individual of the particular religious group, however, the theology brings clarity, order, and durability into his religious experience; for the group, it makes possible unity of belief and the social transmission of the religious conceptions.

Codes. The conduct supposedly required by the supernatural power both among men and toward him, if rapport with him and his followers is to be had, is stated rather specifically in commandments, lists of taboos, bodies of law, moral codes, books of "discipline," and so on. These define religiously satisfactory or essential behavior, or they prohibit undesirable or dangerous behavior. These formalizations of conduct are closely related to the next element.

Practices and Techniques. Most religions have their complexes of standardized practices and techniques which function as a means of communicating with the Supernatural, of expressing awe and obedience, reverence and homage, of appeal, of appeasing and propitiating, of securing emotional unity among their own members, of increasing the intensity of their religious feeling, and frequently of propagating their faith. As Wach points out, these are the *practical* expressions of religious experience, as distinct from the intellectual; they are religiously inspired acts.[4] Almost universal forms are sacrifices, sacred music, drama, dances or other rhythmic or united responses or performances, hymns and chants, invocations and bene-

[2] *Cf.* J. O. Hertzler, *Social Institutions* (Lincoln: University of Nebraska Press, 1946), pp. 1–66.

[3] "The *content* of the intellectual expression of religious experience . . ." J. Wach, *Sociology of Religion* (Chicago: University of Chicago Press, 1944), p. 23.

[4] *Ibid.*, p. 2⁵.

dictions, rituals, liturgies, ceremonials, and above all prayer, both private and group.

Among almost all religious groups, whether large or small, whether hierarchically organized or taking the form of a "local congregation," the greater proportion of these techniques, in one form or degree of formalization or another, constitute a set of established patterns of worship. The widespread practices of instructing, indoctrinating, and proselyting may also be placed in this general category of institutional elements.

Organized Groups. Among the most obvious features of religious institutions are the associations or organizations of human beings. These consist of persons with similar religious attitudes and interests and holding to a common body of beliefs, values, and objectives. As a group they feel that their massed agreement regarding their beliefs and practices makes these not only the most efficacious but often the sole means of salvation. Religious bodies are face to face only in their local manifestations; mainly they consist of persons and groups scattered over wide areas, even globally, and bound together by an effective system of intercommunication.

The personnel of most religious associations can be divided into laity and priesthood or clergy. The laity are the great mass of cooperating, rank-and-file devotees of a common faith—the element for which all aspects of religion exist in the last analysis. The priesthood or clergy are the specialized functionaries, usually with some degree of hierarchical organization. They are presumed to have exceptional insight into and influence with the unseen Power because of their charismata, and hence serve as special intermediaries between the laity and this Power. They are the expert class that is specially versed and certificated in doctrine and that provides and teaches the special knowledge and interpretation; they perform special acts of intercession and worship; they are empowered to receive confession, arrange forgiveness, and fix penance; they usually advise on numerous matters and provide various social and spiritual services; and in most religious organizations they perform a host of administrative functions relating to the mere mundane operation of the institutional machinery.

Symbols and Physical Equipment. Almost all religions have their emotion-charged and emotion-eliciting symbols such as the cross or crescent, statuary, images, and other sacred art objects. All have their special material equipment and paraphernalia for conducting their worship and for carrying on their multiple organizational activities. Notable are extensive properties such as shrines, temples, tabernacles, church buildings, abbeys, cathedrals, and so on, equipped with altars, baptismal fonts, organs, pulpits, parish halls, office equipment, not to mention such special and occasional additions nowadays in the United States as steam tables, gymnasia, and bowling alleys.

The churches are the particular though varied form which religious institutionalization takes among the Christian peoples of Western civilization. The church, however, has its counterpart in some degree in all religious systems. A particular church consists of a body of believers with the same faith. It has its special body of doctrine and appropriate organizational form; it canalizes religious behavior, and does much educating and some disciplining. Churches will be discussed as to special institutional characteristics, contemporary trends, and problems in several other articles in this volume.

SOME MAJOR FUNCTIONS

The real justification of a social institution or anything else that *is,* is its functioning—the satisfying experiences it offers, the services it renders for human fulfillment and social well-being. This applies also to religious institutions; otherwise religion could not be regarded as a good thing. Religion has significance in both the individual or inner and the collectivist, community, or social aspects of human life. Without attempting even the barest inventory, several of the most significant historical functions of the religions of the higher cultures will be briefly set forth.

Facilitate Religious Experience.   In the last analysis, religions are the means of inducing, formulating, expressing, enhancing, implementing, and perpetuating man's deepest experience, the religious. This is religion's primary raison d'être. Man is first religious; the instrumentalities follow. Religion is a condition within.

There is nothing mysterious about religious experience; it is as normal, natural, and inevitable, with man the special kind of creature he is, as experience of satisfaction with respect to nutrition and reproduction. In common with other types of human experience, it seeks the satisfaction of *needs* of great pertinence. The significant things in it, at the higher religious levels, are the inner emotional, mental, and spiritual occurrences which fill the pressing human needs of self-preservation, self-pacification, and self-completion.

What are some of the more important experiences in the so-called higher religions? These will be found to be mutually exclusive.

The chief experience is the sensing of communion with the supernatural power. In the higher religions this involves also a harmonious relationship.[5] As John Fiske put it, man refuses to be psychologically alone in the universe. He wants the feeling that he has something outside and beyond himself and his kind to go to. Prayer in its higher forms is a reverential and usually serene conversation with the Divine, whatever its form is conceived to be. Worship is the various ways in which man expresses awe, respect, gratitude, and allegiance. Prayer and worship epitomize *sacred* experience.

Related to this is the feeling of men that they are relatively secure in an ordered, dependable universe. Man has the experience of being helpfully allied with what he cannot fully understand; he is a co-ordinate part of all energy and being and movement. The universe is a safe and permanent home.

Many of the religions also satisfy for many the need of being linked up with the ultimate and eternal. Death is not permanent defeat and disappearance; man has a "second chance." He is not lost in the abyss of endless time; he has endless being. He experiences a commanding release from materiality, temporalness, finiteness; he believes that he will achieve infinite and eternal completion.

Religion at its best also offers the experience of spiritual fulfillment by inviting man into the highest realm of the spirit. As John Burroughs put it in *Accepting the Universe*, "Religion is a spiritual flowering, and the man who has it not is like a plant that never blooms." It summates, epitomizes, relates, and conserves all the highest ideals and values—ethical, aesthetic, and religious—of man found in his culture.

There is also the possibility among higher religions of experiencing consistent meaning in life and enjoying guidance and expansiveness. The kind of religious experience that most moderns seek not only provides, clarifies, and relates human yearnings, values, ideals, and purposes; it also provides facilities and incitements for the development of personality, sociality, and creativeness. Under the religious impulse, whether theistic or humanistic, men have joy in living; life

---

[5] "The central fact of the higher religious experience is communion and union with the deity, and the roots of this conception are found in all the religious ideas and usages that have been formulated and practiced in human history." C. H. Toy, *Introduction to the History of Religions* (Cambridge: Harvard University Press, 1924), p. 9.

leads somewhere. Religion at its best is out in front, ever beckoning and leading on, and, as Lippmann put it, "mobilizing all man's scattered energies in one triumphant sense of his own infinite importance."[6]

In addition to these functions within man, there have always been the outer, social functions. The two have never been separable.

Promote Social Solidarity. Religion and social life have a peculiarly intimate connection. Religion integrates. Some of the oldest, most persistent, and most cohesive forms of social grouping have grown out of religion. A common faith or set of ultimate value judgments, common sentiments, a common worship as well as other common experiences, and an inclusive organization have been potent factors in knitting together in one solidary and co-operating body a number—often a very large number—of believers. These groups have varied widely from mere families, primitive totemic groups, and small modern cults and sects to the memberships of great, widely dispersed world religions.

Durkheim's famous viewpoint is pertinent here, namely, that every "society" is characterized to a certain degree by the possession of a common "religion," for religion is essentially a system of common values, and without these there can be no society.[7] In fact, Durkheim defines religion as ". . . a unified system of beliefs and practices relative to sacred things . . . beliefs and practices which unite into one single moral community . . . all those who adhere to them."[8] His view is that every religion pertains to a community, and, conversely, every community is in one aspect a religious unit.[9]

At any given time most of mankind is divided into vast, more or less integrated groups based upon somewhat unique but uniform religious beliefs. Within these groups there is considerable unity; between them there is, with occasional highly advertised exceptions, competition, even sharp antagonism.

Most of the religious groups function as rallying points. Since religion is a matter of belief and faith, there is latent a lurking doubt among many of the members as to whether the beliefs are right. But

---

[6] W. Lippmann, *A Preface to Morals* (New York: The Macmillan Company, 1929), p. 50.

[7] E. Durkheim, *Elementary Forms of the Religious Life* (translated by J. W. Swain; New York: The Macmillan Company, 1915).

[8] *Ibid.*, p. 47.

[9] *Cf.* especially T. Parsons, *Structure of Social Action* (New York: McGraw-Hill Book Company, 1937), chap. xi.

if many thousands or millions believe so, the individual is sustained and assured. This same situation, in part at least, leads to proselyting, in that this augments the group, as well as being a means of sharing "a pearl of rare price" with an ever larger fellowship.

The integrating function of religion, for good or ill, has often supported or been identified with other groupings—political, nationality, class, racial, sociability, even economic.

At the same time, religious institutions have aided in amplifying social structure, in creating diversity of social groups, and in the specialization of functions and classes.

Elevate Social Standards. Most of the advanced religions tend to incorporate the major social values and ideals of the group—the great goals of social conduct which have grown out of group experience. Such magnificent and beneficent conceptions as the Golden Ages, past or future, with the attendant principles of attainment, the Golden or Silver Rules, love as a universal social agent, service of fellow men as an obligation, the high aesthetic and ethical principles related to beauty, goodness, and justice, the "superior man," the "noble path," the brotherhood of man, and the Good Community, here or elsewhere, have invariably stemmed from or been incorporated with religions. Religion has thus functioned as a great social lighthouse.

Through its peculiar sanctions religion has been able to give these values and ideals an emotional drive that has made them socializing *agents* as well. The socially approved values have been impressed upon individuals and groups through creeds and codes and rituals; behavior consistent with them has been greatly stimulated, energized, and more readily enforced. Much maladjustment has been avoided, and much constructive social behavior has been facilitated. As part of religious systems, these great survival values have also been conserved and a continuity has been given to them.

Agent of Social Control. Religion not only integrates and socializes; it also carries on a related function in most social systems, namely, that of social control. It is a form of social control used by the group to constrain the individual through supernatural power to conform his beliefs and actions to those of his group. Religion aids custom and law in making anything right or wrong.

It is especially significant to note the widespread use of religious sanctions to support the ethical codes and moral practices among many peoples. Strictly speaking, ethical systems consist of the systematized and more or less permanent ideas of right and wrong, or good and bad, in conduct among a people, along with the accompanying principles, customs, and codes. They set up the required, approved, and forbidden areas of behavior. They exist because men *must* behave in certain ways among their fellows; their objectives are purely temporal, social, and utilitarian; they grow out of long-time, everyday experience. Every new ethical rule springs from the necessity of providing for some new social situation.

Almost everywhere, however, these purely temporal social requirements, as prescribed by custom or stated in commandments and legal codes, have been placed under the irrefutable and inexorable jurisdiction of the omnipresent, omniscient, and omnipotent gods. The scheme of supernatural rewards and punishments has been marshaled to support the mundane codes, the codes thus having an efficacy that no mere social imagination or desire for group welfare could provide.

Influence Other Institutions. Religion has also functioned as a tremendous engine of vindication, enforcement, and sanction of various other institutions. In some instances religious organizations have actually inaugurated social activities in fields not strictly religious.

For thousands of years of man's career, religion has exerted a vast influence over economic and political life. The gods had to be placated if man was to be successful in his economic activities; government and law were based on or allied with divine dictates. Both the economic and the political systems received their validity from on high. Today religion is still called upon to support rulers, contracts, forms of property, oaths, and other legal procedures. Divine blessing is still invoked in behalf of governmental agents and enterprises.

Until a century or so ago most education was under religious auspices and much of it was primarily for the transmission of beliefs and religious usages. Some religious organizations still provide much education, secular and sacred, and try to manipulate public education. Religion has set its stamp on sex practices, marriage, and the family.

Much of the recreation of the past related to religious festivals, assemblies, and holidays; today religious organizations try to provide recreation of a certain moral quality. Until recently much art was used to glorify the gods, illuminate religious experience and teach religious lessons; religion still seeks to safeguard the aesthetic productions from immoral influences. Through most of history, charitable, or what we now deem social work, activities have been carried on under religious auspices.

Other influences might be mentioned. Religion has been the actual mother of some, now secular, institutions; the foster mother of many.

A Therapeutic Agent. This is a much emphasized function to which only the barest attention can be given. The various religious experiences and practices have tended to secure extrahuman or superhuman aid in the ills of life; they have had, and for many do still have, much therapeutic value. One of the primary objectives of religion is to answer questions; it never raises them. Individual weaknesses, feelings of insecurity, disbelief and doubt, are lost in the common strength and unity of the religious fellowship. The sense of cosmic peace frees many a person from a host of harassing and distracting fears, frustrations, and anxieties.

The belief in immortality, where held, functions as a redress for the ills and disappointments here and now. The tensions accompanying a repressive consciousness of wrongdoing or "sinning" or some tormenting secret are relieved for the less self-contained and self-sufficient by confession, repentance, and penance. The feeling of individual inferiority growing out of various social situations or individual deficiencies or failures is compensated for by communion in worship or prayer with a friendly but all-victorious Father-God, as well as by sympathetic fellowship with others who share this faith, and by opportunities in religious acts for giving vent to emotions and energy.

Religion is especially important in times of travail, tragedy, and crisis. When natural holocausts—flood, drought, pestilence, earthquake—rage; when men are suffering from man-made catastrophe —war, revolution, economic depression—religion gives them, individually and in groups, great solace. When life on earth appears chaotic, and when great harm and suffering must be endured, men have not infrequently found a refuge in "the everlasting arms." The gods have alleviated much fear and saved men from much more. The great crisic transitions of life—birth, puberty, marriage, death— are also sacramentalized by religion, thus relieving all concerned from much strain in adjusting themselves to the stupendous changes.

A recent study as to why Americans are religious is replete with such phrases as: "provides help in times of stress"; "gives sense of security"; "furnishes moral support"; "gives me courage"; "brings comfort"; "gives strength"; "gives peace"; "brings contentment"; "makes me unafraid to die"; "gives assurance"; "makes me self-confident"; and so on.[10]

SOME SOCIOLOGICAL ASPECTS

There are certain features of religion in its recurrent manifestations in human societies which have considerable sociological pertinence. No effort will be made to give an exhaustive array, but only to present concisely certain social scientific observations regarding the institutional character of religion.

Reflect Cultural Level. The various elements of religious institutions throughout history, like those of other institutions, have been essentially earthly, man-made, and human administered.[11] Of course, man did not devise the universe or produce whatever unseen powers there be, but all the interpretations of these modes of adjustment to them are man's.

Everywhere religion is the product of mental and social processes, along with science, philosophy, art, and ethics; everywhere it is a product of group collaboration, a complex engendered by members of a given society under given circumstances. Diversities are explained by all of the influences—physical, intellectual, cultural, historical, and social—which affect individual and group life. From its very nature, religion has been a great variable taking many particular forms both as between and within different peoples, regions, and eras.

It is in such an examination as this that the sociology of religion and the sociology of knowledge meet. As Toy has so well pointed out, the external history of religion is the history of the processes by which religious sentiments, ideas, activities, and organizations have attached themselves to the various conceptions formed by man's observation, reflection, and experience. When intellectual reactions are bottomed in a low or rudimentary culture, religion is crude; when culture is chaotic, the religion will be also; the more substantial the cultural background and the more extensive the cultural horizons, the higher the plane of thought, the more expansive the religious ideas and viewpoints.

[10] C. S. Braden, "Why People Are Religious—A Study in Religious Motivation," *Journal of Bible and Religion*, XV (January, 1947), 38–45.

[11] Note the apt phrase of E. S. Ames: ". . . from the first religion has been borne in earthen vessels . . ." *Religion* (New York: Henry Holt & Company, 1929), p. 275.

The very nature of the gods is a case in point. They reflect and embody man's concepts of both the mundane and the extrahuman powers that are operative. They are rationalizations of man's conceptions of himself; they have rational human qualities and human modes of procedure, and are human beings in all except power. At a low intellectual and cultural level and in a circumscribed environment, they are crude, local, and often malevolent ghosts or spirits. As conceptions of human personality, the dignity of man, and man's other ethical views have been elevated, the gods have improved in moral qualities.

The jurisdiction and sphere of the gods has reflected man's grasp of community and his systems of physical science. A "universal" religion rests on a conception of universal cultural diffusion. When, finally, the conception is reached that all nature is governed by natural law, the theistic view assumes that the deity works through scientifically established natural means.

Similarly, ritual has quite consistently been the religious application of the code of social manners; the abode of the soul has changed with the knowledge of the universe. The methods of establishing friendly relations with supernatural powers have been the same as those employed to approach human rulers, namely, by gifts, petitions, messengers or intermediaries, and tributes.[12]

In general, the religion reflects the whole background and make-up of a people. For example, in the United States, religion in its various "Christian" manifestations reflects different secular groups, interests, and needs; philosophic currents; economic and political conditions; class structure; the multiplicity of the cultures developed by the stocks and varieties of people who make up the population; historical situations such as frontier life, the Civil War, immigration, industrialization, urbanization, and technology.

Reflect Social Structure. Similarly, religion in its areal and group scope has ranged from the clan or tribal area, through the city-state, the state, the nation, the race, and finally in some instances has effected a fusion of all mankind, depending upon the prevailing concept of human interrelationships. In its organization it has reflected the general social, including specifically the political, organization.[13]

---

[12] Toy, *op. cit.*, pp. 8–9, 265–66, 307–9, 450–65, 478–79, 484.

[13] "In France, for instance, there is still a bishop, as a rule, wherever there was a Roman municipality, and an archbishop wherever there was a provincial capitol." J. M. Robertson, *A Short History of Christianity* (London: Watts, 1902), p. 209.

Religion has always, of necessity, organized itself in accord with the general structure of social systems.[14]

Religion has always been dependent upon changing human experience, and it has always been appropriating useful ideas and methods from other departments of life. It is not something apart.

Relation to Change. As a strategy for self-preservation and spiritual security and as a medium of social adjustment, religion shifts as all else does—though belatedly, as we will note below. Even during those periods when religious institutions dominated all others, they changed. When religious organization loses its supremacy among institutions, this accommodative tendency is much more readily observed. For example, as physical and biological science has advanced in the last century, man's conception and grasp of the "natural" have greatly modified his interpretation of and dependence upon the "supernatural"; and as social science and his social consciousness have developed, the relative emphasis upon "God" and "man" has been modified. As men have gained confidence in their accumulating knowledge and their demonstrated ability to manipulate nature and themselves, they have felt more secure; they have worried less both about this world *and about the next*. Both naturalism and humanism have affected religion mightily. It has become less God-centered, more man-centered; less passive, more creative; but also less sacred, more secular.

While religion does accommodate itself to intellectual and social change, this adjustment is tardy and subject to much resistance. All institutions, as products of the past, as bulwarks against chaotic social relationships, and as highly organized social instrumentalities, tend to develop inflexibility in their functioning and fail to keep abreast of the needs of the times. However, these tendencies seem to be greater in organized religion than in most other institutional fields. There is so much of the "dead hand" in theology, ritual, and the forms of organization. Why?

Because the major preoccupation of religious institutions is with the unknown and mysterious, and they rest upon belief and faith, they cannot be checked so readily by normal procedures of perception, understanding, and investigation. The doctrine is derived from revelation and authority, hence is strongly authoritarian, even infallible, in character. After the doctrine has been systematized, the rules of faith established, and the forms of worship fixed, then any devia-

[14] Toy, *op. cit.*, pp. 7, 405, 465, 481, 538.

tions and opinions at variance with the officially accepted teachings are classed as heresy.[15] Not only is experimentalism not encouraged, it is looked upon with suspicion. Religious organizations, as organizations, are at least as likely as others to develop precedents, to routinize activities, and to acquire a momentum which gives them a holdover power in many of their operations after these have ceased to have pertinence and timeliness. Finally, more than in any other institutional system, religious institutions have a protected position and claim to have a unique finality. The matter is summarized in a phrase by MacIver: "Revelation stands in the way of revaluation." [16]

In concluding the last three sections, it may be pointed out that the solution is not deinstitutionalization, for the essential contributions of institutionalization outweigh its evils. To conceive of a noninstitutionalized religion is sociologically infantile. The big task is institutional reconstruction. Since religious agencies of all kinds are made by man, they must be and can be continually remade. If men are to meet their spiritual needs in an ever more rapidly changing world, religion must be redefined, clarified, reorganized, and subjected to much thoughtful experimentation.

Religious Institutions as Determiners. The significance of continual reconstruction of religious institutions is underscored when we examine ever so briefly their influence as determiners of individual belief and behavior. The forces of organized religion are for most men really the determiners of the kind and quality of their religious life. Even in an age of widespread education and of freedom of thought, most people feel incompetent to think out seriously for themselves a satisfying religious philosophy. They lack the philosophic capacity, the intellectual training, and the spiritual audacity. They accept the ready-made beliefs and routines of some organized religious group, frequently that of their parents or their immediate culture group. Even if they break away from their particular group they are very likely to accept, again at second hand, the views of some other group. Relatively few persons "go it alone" . . .

This means also, of course, that the peculiar religious needs of many individuals are not satisfactorily met. Many people object to accepting faith like the multiplication table. Hence, most faiths are accepted today with considerable mental reservation by at least a portion of the population.

[15] *Cf.* Wach, *op. cit.,* p. 142.
[16] R. M. MacIver, *Society* (New York: Farrar and Rinehart, 1937), p. 319.

Overinstitutionalization. Organized religions tend to become overorganized, from the very fact of their organization as "going concerns" and the resulting emphasis on their structural aspects, the fact that they are used for control purposes, that they are established and autonomous. They become ends in themselves rather than means. The real end is lost sight of. There is an overemphasis on machinery, fixed and standardized forms and creeds and theologies, and even souls that fit into a special pattern. The personnel, both professional and lay, drift into a more or less perfunctory and mechanical way of acting. Religious experience and expression are then easily confused with theology and ritual, "sacred" aesthetics, ceremonies, minor and very temporary details—even check-writing and attending church-promoted clubs. The organization is likely to pose and exaggerate. This also makes for intolerance and artificiality.

The most sinister fact, though, is that it is easier to administer the affairs of an organization than it is to keep creeds flexible, codes of conduct clear and uncompromised, and the life of the spirit immanent. Historically this has meant either the eventual disappearance of the particular religious organization or, more commonly, reform or schism, especially in the form of new sects and cults.

DECLINE OF INSTITUTIONALIZED RELIGION IN THE UNITED STATES

Among primitive peoples, in most ancient civilizations, in medieval Europe, and in certain portions of the modern world, the prevailing religion has exercised quite uniform control over the entire population of a political, ethnic, or culture area. It was a uniform, universal, and unavoidable social compulsive. But in the Western world increasingly, and especially in the United States, religion has undergone a series of changes which have mightily diminished its institutional sway.

Lack of space prevents more than mention of these changes. Frequently emphasized are: the voluntary nature of participation as against automatic or compulsory membership in other eras and areas, with the attendant loss of enforcement power, especially the enforcement which the state gives various institutions; the encroachment of science upon the realm of the unknown and supernatural, and less preoccupation with the mysteries of life; the divided loyalties and divided organizational support due to the multiplication of diverse and even competitive denominations, sects, and cults, and the consequent confusion of beliefs; the fact that in the United States no more than half the total population admit membership in these various organized groups; the loss of an array of social services to or a losing competition with a host of nonreligious agencies, especially semipublic organizations and the modern "service" state, and the pressure to support these latter, for example, as community chest contributors and taxpayers; the secularization of thought generally as against the theocentric thinking of medieval society, for example, and the accommodation of both laity and clergy to these secular currents; and the loss of much of the prophetic, proselyting, and reformist power of religion.[17]

Organized religion has become a purely voluntary, semiprivate affair; its jurisdiction, for better or worse, is divided, and its power to standardize behavior and exercise social control, either for individuals or for groups, has diminished as that of various other institutions has been augmented; its influence has evaporated from one department of life after another. On the basis of the more common criteria of an institution, some social scientists are inclined to raise the issue as to whether it can properly be designated today as an institution.[18] At any rate, religious institutions have lost their centrality; they "speak with a divided voice."

WHAT NEXT?

The solution of this situation is not a state church with automatic membership and nation-wide hegemony, not an abandonment of freedom of thought and freedom of worship, not any relaxation of tolerance and catholicity of religious thinking and acting. Walking backward is not a way out. However, one of the most luminous texts in the book of life is: "Above all religions is religion." What *is* the next phase of organized religion in the United States?

[17] "The Western community is a secular community in which religion is tolerated, but no longer gives the regulative principles for every kind of human activity." A. H. Hourani, *Syria and Lebanon* (London and New York: Oxford University Press, 1946), p. 81.

[18] Cf. R. C. Angell, *The Integration of American Society* (New York: McGraw-Hill Book Company, 1941), p. 159.

SECTION NINE
Sociology in Social Policy

47 CAN SCIENCE SOLVE SOCIAL PROBLEMS? *

BY GEORGE A. LUNDBERG (1895–   )
UNIVERSITY OF WASHINGTON

A<small>LTHOUGH</small> I think it is unquestionably true that the social sciences have made, during the present century, more actual progress than in all preceding history, it would be absurd to pretend that this progress is, as yet, reflected to any great extent in our management of social affairs. Scientific information of a more or less reliable character is more widely diffused than ever before, but the scientific mode of thought has obviously made very little headway. Practically no one approaches the major social problems of the day in a spirit of disinterested scientific study. The idea that these problems are to be solved, if at all, by the use of instruments of precision in hands that do not shake with fear, with anger, or even with love,[1] does not seem to have occurred even to many people who pass for social scientists. They have joined the journalist and the soapbox crusader in the hue and cry of the mob. Their supposedly scholarly works bristle with assessments of praise and blame, personalities and verbal exorcisms which have no place whatever in the scientific universe of discourse. Not only do these angry men pass in the public eye as great social scientists of the day, but they not infrequently presume to patronize honest scientists who stay with their proper tasks of building a science and the instruments by means of which any difficult problems are to be solved.

But behind this fog, this dust storm of books about the inside of various political movements, the private life and morals of its leaders, and the treatises on democracy, substantial work is going on. Men are patiently accumulating data about human behavior in a form which in the fullness of time will permit a type of generalization which has never before been possible. Some are engaged in the undramatic but fundamental work, basic to all science, of classifying the

---

* Reprinted by permission of the author and of the publisher from chap. ii of *Can Science Save Us?* (New York: Longmans, Green and Company, 1947), pp. 21–34.

[1] *Cf.* R. L. Duffus, *Harper's,* December, 1934.

multitudes of human groups and behavior patterns as a first step toward the formulation of generalizations regarding them. Still others are pioneering in the construction of actuarial and other tables from which may be predicted not only the prevalence of births, deaths, marriages, and divorces, but also the probable relative degrees of happiness in marriage, the probable success or failure of probation and parole, and many other equally "human" eventualities. A wealth of valuable information and generalizations have already been developed about the social characteristics and behavior of populations, such as the distribution of wealth, occupations, mobility, intelligence, and the various conditions with which these characteristics vary. Important instruments have been invented in recent years for measuring opinion, status, social participation, and many phenomena of communication and interpersonal relations.

Indeed, the invention and perfection of instruments for the more accurate and precise observation and recording of social phenomena must be regarded as among the most important developments in the social sciences. It is easy to point to the flaws in these instruments as it was easy to point to the flaws in the early microscopes and telescopes. But, without these beginnings and the patient centuries of undramatic labor, sciences like bacteriology could not have appeared at all.

Finally, there are those, and they may be the most important of all, who are experimenting with and inventing new systems of symbolic representation of phenomena. New adaptations of mathematics by which otherwise hopeless complexities can be comprehended are quite fundamental but do not lend themselves to popular display. The work of Leibnitz, Faraday, and Hertz was not the popular science of their day. Yet it is by virtue of their strange calculations with strange symbols that men today fly and broadcast their speech around the earth. This should be remembered by "writers" and others who complain that social scientists are adopting "jargon" and "esoteric" symbols which go beyond the vocabulary of the current "best-seller."

If I deal primarily with these more obscure and undramatic labors of social scientists, it is because I regard them as more important in the long run than the conspicuous contemporary achievements which are common knowledge. I do not overlook or underestimate these more obvious and demonstrable achievements. The transition in our time to more humane treatment of children, the poor, and the unfortunate, by more enlightened education, social work, and penology must in large measure be attributed to the expanding sciences of psychology and sociology. I know, of course, that whenever a war or a depression occurs journalists and preachers point to the impotence of economists and political scientists either to predict or prevent these disasters. The fact is that the course of events following World War I, down to and including the present, was predicted with great accuracy by large numbers of social scientists. That nothing was done about it is not the special responsibility of social scientists. "Doing something about it" is the common responsibility of all members of a community, including scientists, and especially of those who specialize in mass education, mass leadership, and practical programs.

It is not my main purpose to review the past and present achievements of the social sciences. . . . I am here concerned primarily with the probable future of the social sciences. Even if I should admit that social scientists are today merely chipping flint in the Stone Age of their science, I do not see that we have any choice but to follow the rough road that other sciences have traveled. The attainment of comparable success may seem remote, and the labors involved may seem staggering. But is the prospect really unreasonably remote? Suppose that someone four hundred years ago had delivered an address on the future of the physical sciences and suppose that he had envisioned only a small fraction of their present achievements. What would have been the reaction of even a sophisticated audience to predictions of men flying and speaking across oceans, seeing undreamed-of worlds, both through microscopes and telescopes, and the almost incredible feats of modern engineering and surgery? Nothing I have suggested, I think, in the way of mature social science with comparable practical application seems as improbable as would the story of our prophetic physicist of four hundred or even one hundred years ago. . . .

We have hitherto lacked boldness and an adequate vision of the true task of social science. Research in this field is today for the most part a quest for superficial remedies, for commercial guidance, and for historical and contemporary "human interest" stories. Everybody recognizes the importance of bookkeeping, census taking, studying the condition of the Negro population, and predicting the number of girdles that will be purchased in department stores a year from now. But there are types of research the immediate practical uses of which are not so obvious, yet which are essential to scientific development.

Shall we or shall we not assume that we can formulate laws of human behavior which are comparable to the laws of gravity, thermodynamics, and bacteriology? These latter laws do not of themselves create engineering wonders or cure disease. Nevertheless they constitute knowledge of a kind which is indispensable. The present argument is obviously handicapped in its most crucial respect, namely, its inability, in the space here available, to exhibit laws of social behavior comparable to the physical laws mentioned. Yet we have made considerable progress in this direction.

Finally, we come to what is regarded by many people, including scientists, as the most fundamental difference of all between the physical and the social sciences. "To understand and describe a system involving values," says Huxley, "is impossible without some judgment of values." "Values," he goes on to say, "are deliberately excluded from the purview of natural science."

It would be difficult to find a better example of confused thinking than that offered by current discussions of "values" and their supposed incompatibility with science. A principal cause of the confusion is a semantic error which is extremely common in the social sciences. In this case, it consists in converting the verb "valuating," meaning any discriminatory or selective behavior, into a noun called "values." We then go hunting for the *things* denoted by this noun. But there are no such things. There are only the valuating *activities* we started with. What was said above about motives applies with equal force to values. They are clearly inferences from behavior. That is, we say a thing *has* value or *is* a value when people behave toward it so as to retain or increase their possession of it. It may be economic goods and services, political office, a mate, graduation, prestige, a clear conscience, or anything you please. Since valuations or values are empirically observable patterns of behavior, they may be studied as such, by the same general techniques we use to study other behavior.

As a matter of fact, everybody is more or less regularly engaged in such study of other people's values. It is quite essential to any kind of satisfactory living in any community. We try to find out as soon as possible what the values of our neighbors are. How do we find out? We observe their behavior, including their verbal behavior. We listen to what other people say about them, we notice what they spend their money for, how they vote, whether they go to church, and a hundred other things. On a more formal and scientific level, opinion polls on men and issues are taken to reflect the values of large groups. Economists, of course, have been studying for years certain kinds of evaluations of men through the medium of prices.

There appears to be no reason why values should not be studied as objectively as any other phenomena, for they are an inseparable part of behavior. The conditions under which certain values arise, i.e., the conditions under which certain kinds of valuating behavior take place, and the effects of "the existence of certain values" (as we say) in given situations are precisely what the social sciences must study and what they are studying. These values or valuating behaviors, like all other behavior, are to be observed, classified, interpreted, and generalized by the accepted techniques of scientific procedure.

Why, then, is the value problem considered unique and insurmountable in the social sciences?

The main reason seems to be that social scientists, like other people, often have strong feelings about religion, art, politics, and economics. That is, they have their likes and dislikes in these matters as they have in wine, women, and song. As a result of these preferences, both physical and social scientists frequently join other citizens to form pressure groups to advance the things they favor, including their own economic or professional advancement, Labor, Capital, Democracy, the True Church, or what not. To do so is the right of every citizen, and there is no canon of science or of civil law which requires scientists to abjure the rights which are enjoyed by all other members of a community.

The confusion about values seems to have arisen because both scientists and the public have frequently assumed that, when scientists engage in ordinary pressure-group activity, that activity somehow becomes science or scientific activity. This is a most mischievous fallacy. It is not surprising, perhaps, that the public should be confused on this point, because it may not always be clear when a scientist is expressing a scientific conclusion and when he is expressing a personal preference. But it is unpardonable for scientists themselves to be confused about what they know and say in their capacity as scientists and what they favor in religion, morals, and public policy. To pose as disinterested scientists announcing scientific conclusions when in fact they are merely expressing personal preferences is simple fraud, no matter how laudable or socially desirable may be the scientists' "motives" and objectives.

But is it possible for a person to play two or more distinct roles, such as scientist and citizen, without confusing the two? The answer is that it is being done every day. It is the most obvious commonplace that the actress who plays Juliet in the afternoon and Lady Macbeth at night does not allow her moral or other preference for one of these roles to influence her performance of the other. In any event, her competence is measured by her ability to play each role convincingly. During the same day she may also be expected to fulfill the roles of wife, mother, etc. Likewise, the chemist who vigorously campaigns against the use of certain gases in war obviously cannot allow that attitude to influence in the slightest degree the methods of producing or analyzing these gases. Science, as such, is nonmoral. There is nothing in scientific work, as such, which dictates to what ends the products of science shall be used.

In short, it is not true that "to understand and describe a system involving values is impossible without some judgment of values." I can certainly report and understand the bald fact that a certain tribe kills its aged and eats them, without saying one word about the goodness or badness of that practice according to my own standards, or allowing these standards of mine to prevent me from giving an accurate report of the facts mentioned. The only value judgments which any properly trained scientist makes about his data are judgments regarding their relevance to his problem, the weight to be assigned to each aspect, and the general interpretation to be made of the observed events. These are problems which no scientist can escape, and they are not at all unique or insuperable in the social sciences.

Have scientists, then, no special function or obligation in determining the ends for which scientific knowledge is to be used? As scientists, *it is their business to determine reliably the immediate and remote costs and consequences of alternate possible courses of action,* and to make these known to the public. Scientists may then *in their capacity as citizens* join with others in advocating one alternative rather than another, as they prefer.

To the extent that their reputation and prestige is great, and to the extent that their tastes are shared by the masses of men, scientists will, of course, be influential in causing others to accept the goals the scientists recommend. In this sense, social science will doubtless become, as physical science already is, an important influence in determining the wants of men. That is, as a result of scientific knowledge, men will not want impossible or mutually exclusive things.

They will not seek to increase foreign trade and at the same time establish more comprehensive and higher tariffs. They will not seek to reduce crime but at the same time maintain a crime-promoting penal system. They will not destroy the productive power of a nation and still expect it to be peaceful, prosperous, and democratic. They will not expect a world organization to be conjured into existence by semantically deranged "statesmen," before the necessary preceding integration of the constituent units has been achieved.

The development of the social sciences and the diffusion of scientific knowledge will doubtless greatly influence in the above ways the wants, wishes, and choices of men. But there is still an important difference between a statement of fact and the dictation of conduct. It is one thing for a physician to tell a patient: "Unless you undergo this operation, which will cost so much in time, money, and pain, you will probably die in one month." It is another matter to say: "Science, for which I am an accredited spokesman, says you shall undergo this operation." Any scientist who pretends that science authorizes him to make the latter statement is a fraud and a menace. Dictation of this type has not accompanied the rise of physical science and it need not result from the full maturity of the social sciences. This needs to be kept in mind especially in these days of much worry about brain trusts and whether, with the development of atomic fission, scientists must become a priestly class dictating all public policy.

The misunderstanding regarding the relation of scientists to practical affairs is so widespread and mischievous as to warrant further emphasis. The *application* of scientific knowledge obviously involves value judgments of some sort. This problem is equally present in the other sciences. After we know how to produce dynamite and what it will do, there remains the question: Shall we drop it from airplanes to destroy cathedrals and cities, or shall we use it to build roads through the mountains? After we know the effects of certain drugs and gases, the question still remains: Shall we use them to alleviate pain and prevent disease, or shall we use them to destroy helpless and harmless populations? There is certainly nothing in the well-developed sciences of chemistry or physics which answers these questions. Neither is it the business of the social sciences to answer (except *conditionally,* as we have seen) the question of what form of government we should have, what our treatment of other races should be, whether we should tolerate or persecute certain religious groups, whether and to what degree civil liberties should be maintained, and a multitude of other questions which agitate us. What, then, are social scientists for and what should they be able to do?

Broadly speaking, it is the business of social scientists to be able to predict with high probability the social weather, just as meteorologists predict sunshine and storm. More specifically, social scientists should be able to say what is likely to happen socially under stated conditions. A competent economist or political scientist should be able to devise, for example, a tax program for a given country which will yield with high probability a certain revenue and which will fall in whatever desired degrees upon each of the income groups of the area concerned. Social scientists should be able to state also what will be the effect of the application of this program upon income, investments, consumption, production, and the outcome of the next election. Having devised such a tax program and clearly specified what it will do, it is not the business of the social scientists any more than it is the business of any other citizens to secure the adoption or defeat of such a program. In the same way, competent sociologists, educators, or psychologists should be able to advise a parent as to the most convenient way of converting a son into an Al Capone or into an approved citizen, according to what is desired.

My point is that no science tells us *what to do* with the knowledge that constitutes the science. Science only provides a car and a chauffeur for us. It does not directly, as science, tell us where to drive. The car and the chauffeur will take us into the ditch, over the precipice, against a stone wall, or into the highlands of age-long human aspirations with equal efficiency. If we agree as to where we want to go and tell the driver our goal, he should be able to take us there by any one of a number of possible routes the costs and conditions of each of which the scientist should be able to explain to us. When these alternatives have been made clear, it is also a proper function of the scientist to devise the quickest and most reliable instrument for detecting the wishes of his passengers. But, except in his capacity as one of the passengers, the scientist who serves as navigator and chauffeur has no scientific privilege or duty to tell the rest of the passengers what they *should* want. There is nothing in either physical or social science which answers this question. Confusion on this point is, I think, the main reason for the common delusion that the social sciences, at least, must make value judgments of this kind.

But it does follow, as we have seen, that science, by virtue of its true function, as outlined above, may be of the utmost importance in helping people to decide intelligently what they want. We shall return to this subject in the concluding chapter. In the meantime, it may be noted that the broad general wants of people are perhaps everywhere highly uniform. They want, for example, a certain amount of physical and social security and some fun. It is disagreement over the means toward these ends, as represented by fantastic ideologies, that results in conflict and chaos. I have pointed out that, in proportion as a science is well developed, it can describe with accuracy *the consequences* of a variety of widely disparate programs of action. These consequences, if reliably predicted, are bound strongly to influence what people will want. But it remains a fact that science, in the sense of a predicter of consequences, is only *one* of the numerous influences that determine an individual's wants and his consequent behavior. Science and scientists are still the servants, not the masters, of mankind. Accordingly, those scientists who contend that they can scientifically determine not only the means but the ends of social policy should be exposed as scientific fakers as well as would-be dictators. Yet this is the very group which professes to be concerned about the democratic implications of the position I am here defending!

Finally, this view seems to some people to do away with what they call "the moral basis of society." Obviously, it does nothing of the sort. The question is not about the moral basis of society but about the social basis of morals. We merely advocate a scientific basis for morality. Presumably, all will agree that morals exist for man, not man for morals. Morals are those rules of conduct which man thinks have been to his advantage through the ages. Why should we then not all agree that we want the most authentic possible appraisal of that subject?

There appears, then, to be no reason why the methods of science cannot solve social problems. Neither should we expect more from social than from physical science. As *science,* both physical and social sciences have a common function, namely, to answer scientific questions. These answers will always be of an impersonal, conditional type: "*If* the temperature falls to $32°$ F., *then* water (H_2O) will freeze." "*If* a certain type of tax is adopted, *then* certain types of industrial activity will decrease." Neither of these statements carries any implications as to whether or how the knowledge should be used. Far from being a weakness, this characteristic of scientific knowledge is its greatest strength. The wants of men will change with changing conditions through the ages. The value of scientific knowledge lies precisely in this impersonal, neutral, general validity for whatever purposes man desires to use it.

For this reason, those scientists and others who try to identify science with some particular social program, sect, or party must be regarded as the most dangerous enemies of science. They are more dangerous than its avowed enemies, because the defenders of "democratic," "communist," "religious," or "moral" science pose as defenders of science and carry on their agitation in the name of lofty social sentiments. That this group is confused rather than malicious is evident from their proposal that scientists should take an oath not to engage in scientific activity which may be "destructive" or contrary to "toleration," "justice," etc. The absurdity of the proposal is readily apparent, if we consider any actual scientific work. No scientist can foresee all the uses to which his work may be put, and in any event it is a commonplace that the *same* drug may be used to cure or to kill people. It may be granted that preposterous proposals of this kind are a temporary hysterical phenomenon superinduced by such dramatic developments as the atomic bomb. It may be granted that the agitators are motivated by lofty social sentiments. Unfortunately, the same has been said for prominent proponents of the Inquisition.

The uses to which scientific or other knowledge is to be put have always been and will continue to be a legitimate concern of men. Science, as we have noted, can be valuable in helping men to decide that question. . . . Our warning here has been directed against attempts to corrupt scientific methods and results by allowing them to be influenced by the temporary, provincial, ethnocentric preferences of particular scientists or pressure groups.

48 SUBSIDIES FOR SOCIOLOGICAL RESEARCH *

BY ALFRED MCCLUNG LEE (1906–   )

BROOKLYN COLLEGE

O PINION and attitude studies have become a sizable element in industrial, distributive, and political planning in the United States.

Industrialists have learned that "attitudes" have something to do with personnel morale, efficiency, and productivity and with the ways in which present and potential employees are likely to react in crisis situations.

Consumer acceptance tests have helped distributors of items packaged and advertised for retail sale to select more effective labels, cartons, and advertisements.

The relative accuracy of poll predictions of elections gave politicians and business men some respect for poll reports of all sorts prior to the failure of the commercial pollsters to predict correctly the November 2, 1948 Federal election results, but this setback only temporarily placed these efforts in a more accurate perspective. Public relations counselors, who once proved their worth to clients with bulging scrapbooks, have subsidized a wide range of surveys and polls—all "scientifically" certified [1]—in order to prove their claims to the manipulation and modification of social opinion and action.

And as opinion and attitude studies have thus grown in commercial importance, they have begun to absorb more and more of the energies of leading social science departments in our colleges and universities and to occasion the establishment of related academic institutes and bureaus of social research. For the first time, Ph.D.'s in sociology and social psychology face opportunities within their chosen profession for commercial as well as teaching, research, and occasional civic positions.

---

* Reprinted by permission of the editor in an adapted form from "Sociological Theory in Public Opinion and Attitude Studies," *American Sociological Review*, XII (1947), 312–323; pp. 312–314 used.

[1] See the author's "Implementation of Opinion Survey Standards," *Public Opinion Quarterly*, XIII (1949–50), 645–652.

Academic sociologists until recently devoted their research efforts chiefly to experimental surveys and field investigations, to comparative studies of field reports and social theories, to analyses of institutional and life-history records, and to methodological experiments in the processing of data. In thousands of such projects, sociologists and their students used gradually improved survey and other research techniques, cross-cultural materials, life-history data on a wide range of types, and documentary records to develop the beginnings of a broad science of sociology. But as a result of the recent mushrooming of commercial opportunities and subsidies, even sociology departments which were once dedicated to analyses of obscure contentions in the history of social theory have now purchased tabulating and calculating machines, and they are diverting the labors of their students from libraries to "laboratory work."

Sociologists who had felt some community and administrative pressure as a result of their diagnoses of crime, sex, housing, and race problems are now finding their usefulness appreciated by corporations and trade associations which underwrite their opinion and attitude surveys under conditions alleged to protect the freedom, objectivity, and general academic respectability of the researchers. Even cultural anthropologists are learning that a battery of interviewers armed with schedules can furnish the raw materials for orderly columns of figures in "applied anthropology" which can compete in professional prestige with a cross-cultural survey or a field report on the people of Erewhon, and they are sometimes more easily financed.

Editors and engineers started something with their old-time straw ballots and personnel efficiency studies that has expanded and matured into the modern and closely related techniques of election prediction, consumer acceptance testing, employee personality and morale analysis, and public opinion measurement.[2] Editors and engineers continue to admire the offspring of their techniques, but the techniques are now controlled by social scientists. Under such headings as public opinion polling, industrial sociology, market research, social psychology, and human engineering, the magic of these techniques is bringing research funds to social psychologists and psychological sociologists that exceed anything before tapped by these specialists.

---

[2] See Claude E. Robinson, *Straw Votes* (New York: Columbia University Press, 1932); Elton Mayo, *The Human Problems of an Industrial Civilization* (New York: The Macmillan Company, 1933).

Attitude and opinion studies are thus obtaining for sociologists the kind of commercial sponsorship and opportunities that opened up for chemists forty years and more ago and to psychologists following World War I. As a part of this development, sociologists are adapting to their purposes a system introduced to chemists of the United States in 1906–07 by the late Professor Robert Kennedy Duncan of the University of Kansas, the industrial fellowship system which Duncan helped to enshrine in 1913 in Mellon Institute of Industrial Research at the University of Pittsburgh.[3] This arrangement involved the private subsidization of research by commercial interests in order to bring practical problems into an academic environment for study and possible solution with any research products assigned in advance to the donor of the subsidy. Duncan[4] believed that, in industry, "the really important problems can only be solved by the rendering of aid from outside—by men attacking the problem with a perfectly open mind and armed with a wide range of new facts apparently unrelated but potentially applicable." He contended that his fellowship system facilitated this type of contribution to industry and hence to society. He claimed that the system "affords a young man every incentive to lay his hands on the vast body of correlated knowledge called Science, and to make it subserve the practical needs of the human race."

Duncan's system did many of the things he claimed for it within the narrow confines of a physical science unaware or smugly ignorant of its social and societal consequences. But many of the problems that Duncan thought he had solved remain to plague sociologists who attempt to work out variants of his scheme as steps toward their new professional and commercial objectives. A "perfectly open mind" in physical or even biological science is one thing, especially when the donor controls any patents or other products and thus can keep disturbing gadgets or principles out of harm's way.[5] A "perfectly open mind" in sociology is at least as valuable to society as is its equivalent in physical science, but it is a much more difficult accomplishment even under ideal conditions and especially when the

---

[3] E. R. Weidlein and W. A. Hamor, *Glances at Industrial Research* (New York: Reinhold Publishing Company, 1936), chap. 2.

[4] R. K. Duncan, *The Chemistry of Commerce* (New York: Harper & Brothers, 1907), pp. 248–249, 256.

[5] For an analysis of interest factors and the social science researcher, see the author's "Interest Criteria in Propaganda Analysis," *American Sociological Review*, X (1945), 282–288.

situation is complicated by the fact of a donor's grant renewal always around the corner. At the least, it requires a patient, understanding, or deceased donor.

It is not so long (1934) since the Federal Trade Commission [6] reported how the electric and gas utility companies and trade associations used just such "endowments for research, scholarships and fellowships" to obtain "influence with school men." Some professors "were paid to make studies or to write articles. Direct money payments, some quite large, were made to many educational institutions, including several of the leading universities." This was then regarded as disreputable. Professors and other teachers, it was contended, should serve broad public interests rather than the private special interests which subsidized them. Such subsidies are today much more common than they were in 1934. To say, however, that sociologists and social psychologists are less subject to bias toward the sources of their research grants than engineering and economics professors would smack of professional chauvinism.

If research subsidies and job possibilities for graduates came from a wide enough range of organizations, the danger of special-interest subsidies for research would lie chiefly in the further de-emphasis of basic research projects. If unions, professional societies, majority and minority political parties, and governmental and civic agencies as well as industrial, distributive, and financial interests were all to share adequately in the subsidization of sociological research, such subsidies would motivate sociologists towards special managerial technologies rather than towards the development of a well-rounded scientific sociology to advance human understanding and to serve broad social goals. Fortunately, sociology—like other academic disciplines—attracts to it many who refuse to permit themselves to be diverted from the service of humanity through the curious investigation of their chosen subject-matter.

To the extent that the system of special-interest subsidies for research becomes imbedded in academic departments of sociology, commercial incentives will replace teaching and academic research objectives for student majors. The orientation of future teachers, researchers, and textbook writers may thus be expected to veer toward emphases upon data and theories useful primarily in managerial

---

[6] *Efforts by Associations and Agencies of Electric and Gas Utilities to Influence Public Opinion* (70th Congress, 1st Session, Senate Document 92 Part 71A) (Washington: Government Printing Office, 1934), pp. 173, 393.

manipulations and only secondarily, if at all, in the development of a
scientific sociology of service broadly to mankind—to the manipulated as well as to the manipulators.

49   THE ASSAULT ON SOCIAL SCIENCE *

BY GEORGE SIMPSON (1908–   )
THE COLLEGE OF THE CITY OF NEW YORK

THE behaviorist, neo-positivist school of sociology in America, with
its emphasis upon mathematical symbolization, has gained many
cohorts during the last quarter of a century, but it is only latterly that
it has found a champion to present its tenets systematically and in
full panoply. If in this paper we direct ourselves almost exclusively to
one representative of this school which has so many followers, it is
because his presentation of its case is both most recent and most
thorough. Indeed, it should be a source of deep gratification that the
position of this school of thought has finally been placed upon a full
canvas, and been offered for popular showing. Only thus could both
its merits and demerits be made obvious.

For two decades, in a series of publications long and short, Professor George Lundberg, erstwhile president of the American Sociological Society, has carried on a campaign for scientific method in the
social sciences, and particularly sociology. The kind of world Lundberg wants is one in which the social scientist will be accepted as the
final authority in informing men of how they can achieve the goals
they set for themselves without himself approving or disapproving
of these goals. We have attempted to show that science, as the most
effective instrument of achieving *whatever* goals we may pursue,
should be welcomed by all men, however they may disagree on questions of final causation, the origin or the final destiny of man." This
campaign has now become so distinct to Lundberg that the delinea-
ments can be stated in epigram and aphorism, simple enough to convey his meaning even unto the scientifically untutored. In his latest
presentation, *Can Science Save Us?*, he has made a case which the

* Reprinted by permission of the author and of the editor from *American Sociological Review*, XIV (1949), 303–310.
[1] *Can Science Save Us?*, p. 97.

layman and the beginner can understand and which is obviously the completion of a long struggle in the direction of a systematic position.

Properly to appraise where Lundberg and his followers stand, it is necessary to discuss certain major issues with which he deals. These issues have been raised in *Foundations of Sociology; Can Science Save Us?* and in an oblique sort of way in *Social Research*. The issues are as follows:

1. The nature of science.
2. Social research and social problems.
3. The training of social scientists.
4. Imputation of motives.
5. Values, social science, and the "good society."

We shall here follow the procedure of stating *seriatim* Lundberg's position on each issue with accompanying analysis and criticism.

1. **The Nature of Science.** To Lundberg science is "a technic of adjustment." It is the "accepted point of reference" for the achievement of "adjustment" which, he tells us, is "a word used to describe the situation under which the activities of an organism come to rest or equilibrium." The organism comes to rest or equilibrium when its tensions or imbalances are released.[2]

Here Lundberg's discourse appears to be a confusion of the logic of science with the psychological satisfaction which scientific explanation gives to the individual. If science achieves adjustment for the individual why does Lundberg feel it necessary to convert men to what will get them in equilibrium and what is to him "in our time and for some centuries to come, for better or for worse . . . to an increasing degree the accepted point of reference with respect to which the validity (Truth) of all knowledge is gauged."?[3] Men apparently are not yet ready to accept this "form of adjustment" as the way to ease their tensions and achieve satisfaction through getting the organism into adjustment with their environment. But that is because science as the corpus and method of solutions to human problems is upsetting to the adjustments which men have made to their environment. For science is not a form of adjustment, but a critique of the human adjustments that have been made. The life of reason epitomized in its highest form by science is for Lundberg nothing more than an extension of biological adjustment. But if irrationality can adjust men to their "problems," why should they turn

[2] *Foundations of Sociology*, p. 5.
[3] *Can Science Save Us?*, p. 36.

to science? Men resist scientific method because the human *organism* prefers to remain in equilibrium (adjustment for Lundberg) and not to overcome illusions. To give up the adjustments he has made, in return for science, man must become the critic of the adjustment process itself. The process is not self-critical; only reason arising above the inherent irrationality of the adjustment process can achieve that state where man is willing to accept the presence of folly as his own worst enemy. Murphy [4] has stated: "To open one's eyes and see what is there to be seen, honestly, accurately and without the bias of preconception, prejudice or tradition, is an intellectual, and not merely a physiological achievement." To confuse the activity by which man triumphs over "adjustment" with adjustment itself is like identifying medicine with disease itself. Lundberg appears to conceive of the continuum of evolution as involving no qualitative discretion in the differentiation of species. Logic becomes a form of behaviorism and science the handmaiden of biology.

   2. **Social Research and Social Problems.** Lundberg cites as examples of good scientific work in sociology and the social sciences a piece of research by Stuart C. Dodd and one by Samuel A. Stouffer. "Under the auspices of Allied Force Headquarters, Stuart C. Dodd developed a polling organization for determining in the invaded areas facts regarding the behavior and conditions of life as well as opinion regarding such subjects as public security, crime and the mores governing its control, the people's satisfaction with governing officials, attitudes toward cobelligerency, status of shelter and clothing, food supply and distribution, etc." It was used in Sicily. "A survey indicated that very few people had received their sugar ration for five months. Thereupon the local officials were confronted with these facts and were told to get busy. A follow-up survey in a week showed the situation greatly improved and in two weeks practically corrected. Here we have a public which for the first time in years finds itself consulted on such matters and then observes that its complaints actually bring results. Experience of this kind probably goes farther than any propaganda for democracy that could be invented."[5]

   The other piece of research which Lundberg looks on with favor —that by Stouffer—appeared some years ago in the *American Sociological Review*. Stouffer studied the mobility habits of an urban population and arrived at the following generalization: "The number of

[4] Arthur E. Murphy, *The Uses of Reason*, p. 34.
[5] *Can Science Save Us?*, pp. 38–9.

persons going a given distance is directly proportional to the number
of opportunities at that distance and inversely proportional to the
number of intervening opportunities." [6]

Such individual pieces of research Lundberg feels will ultimately
add up to a significant body of verified knowledge, and form a corpus of instruments for further research. "Men are patiently accumulating data about human behavior in a form which in the fullness of
time will permit a type of generalization which has never before
been possible. . . . Important instruments have been invented in recent years for measuring opinion, status, social participation, and
many phenomena of communication and interpersonal relations. Indeed, the invention and perfection of instruments for the more accurate and precise observation and recording of social phenomena must
be regarded as among the most important developments in the social
sciences." [7]

Lundberg's two instances of what he calls "basic scientific work"
are apt to appear as trivia to the layman, who, Lundberg says, should
learn to turn to the social scientist if he wants workable answers. A
look at the present situation in Sicily and Italy which confronts this
nation would show Lundberg that Dodd's investigation is a typical
example of trying to take care of minutiae in the belief that policy
will take care of itself. When the invasion of Europe began—as it
did in Italy—some social scientists were convinced that a test of what
kind of world we were going to get out of the war was in the offing.
It was demanded that no traffic be had with Italian Fascists and that
the common people of Italy be called upon to revolt, and that American money and men be thrown into a program of establishing democratic institutions there. It was pointed out that, failing this, civil war
might be imminent and the Communist alternative might shape up
as a possibility. One hypothesis that might have been prosecuted
was the effect that putting a Fascist general like Badoglio in power
would have upon the Italian masses and on the growth of communism. Was the malfunctioning of the rationing system which Dodd
investigated a part of the collapse of the Italian political system or
did it just malfunction in a vacuum? Apparently social research accepts the creation of the general problem with social piety and then
investigates the sugar rationing system on the assumption that we
must accumulate many thises and thats in order to gain respect for

[6] *Op. cit.,* pp. 40–41.
[7] *Op. cit.,* pp. 22–3.

the social scientist sufficient for him to be recognized as the arbiter of disputes and problems plaguing mankind. Until that happens, according to Lundberg, "The nations doubtless will continue to rage and the people to imagine vain things."[8] Meanwhile, in the catacombs social scientists will painstakingly with slide-rule and frequency-table be investigating why nations rage and people imagine vain things; and when rage has subsided and vanity been overcome, the social scientist will emerge from his lair, chart in hand, to announce that if he had been listened to, rage would have been abolished and vanity relieved.

In the case of the law which Stouffer arrived at concerning the mobility-habits of an urban population, it is difficult to see how this differs from the simple declarative statement that people migrate until they find what they want. Stouffer studied numbers of cases of movement, showed that people did not go any further after they found what they were looking for, but did go further if they did not find what they were looking for, on the way. Mobility in urban areas offers a magnificent opportunity for studying the "rootless" character of American culture. Or to postulate the hypothesis of Robert S. Lynd:[9] "Since urban living operates seriously at present to confuse and to devitalize our culture, science needs to discover ways to knit these loose population masses into living communities of interest, before this degenerating tendency renders the culture impotent." To apply Lynd's more general hypothesis to the problem which Stouffer was facing, it would be asked, Is mobility a search for opportunities or is it a sign of psychic restlessness, a searching for the evanescent new in a culture which permits little spontaneous expression on the part of its members?

How does it happen that American culture in the form of the social sciences sets such great store by research like Dodd's and Stouffer's? All sociological inquiry would seem to be concerned with illuminating the structure and functioning of social relationships (human behavior oriented towards other individuals) in cultures. It is not necessarily concerned with helping a given type of structure or set of functions to keep going or strengthen its position relative to other structures or functions. That is, sociological research is not synonymous with "administrative research" or, *a fortiori*, with "market research." To do better what is already being done or to sell

[8] *Op. cit.*, p. 115.
[9] R. S. Lynd, *Knowledge for What?*, p. 244.

more goods or satisfy more consumers with the same goods does not add one iota to our understanding of the why and wherefore of modern administrative processes or modern conditions in the market. It does not tell us what kind of behavior our culture sets store by, nor hold this kind of behavior up to the ideals being professed as the intellectual and moral guides of behavior—the values to which we swear allegiance.

3. The Training of Social Scientists. The basic integrating principle in education and particularly in the education of social scientists is, for Lundberg, "an understanding of the nature of scientific method as applied to human affairs." [10] The humanities will be relegated to the status of aids to science and art. Contemporary science, he says, is simply the residue of the groping of all the ages. [11] Most of the "classics" will be relegated to the history of error; what we really need is "more and better classics regarding human behavior." [12] The training of social scientists will involve substituting for the language of folklore refined mathematical symbols. "Geometric, arithmetic, and algebraic ways of expressing relationships usually come with the maturity of every science. . . . The more intricate and variable is the situation we wish to describe the more dependent we become upon mathematical systems of symbolization. Sociology has for some time felt this need. . . . More recently much work has been done in the development of measuring instruments adapted to societal phenomena hitherto unmetricized. With the rapid developments in this field, the time is ripe for the systematization of the whole field of general sociology in quantitative symbols which, however unique the subject-matter to which they refer and however unmetricized as yet some of these phenomena may be, can nevertheless be manipulated according to the already established and tested rules of mathematics." [13]

Mathematical symbols and statistical techniques appear to be the criteria of the scientific to Lundberg. But to attack those problems most adaptable to certain techniques available is to cut the problem down to the size of the techniques, instead of lifting the techniques up to the size of the problem. There can be no sensible dispute concerning the great worth of advanced statistical methods properly ap-

[10] *Can Science Save Us?*, chap. iv.
[11] *Op. cit.*, chap. iv.
[12] *Op. cit.*, p. 75.
[13] *Foundations of Sociology*, pp. 122–3.

plied. But proper application has to do with their pertinence to the problem under investigation. To decide upon pertinence by establishing the fitness of the problem to be handled in terms of the techniques available is to put the cart before the horse. Instruments are one thing; the calibre of the problems posed is quite another, and if we are to be the slave of our instruments we may never get fundamental problems solved or we may become involved in minutiae which we hope will add up at some millennial date. We reach a kind of statistical metaphysics where the nature of the problem has been shrouded in the obscurity of the symbols by which alone it is permitted to be prosecuted.

This transformation of social science from a field of knowledge into a bundle of research-techniques is strictly in conformity with the structuring of behavior along procedural lines in all parts of American culture. The way you go about things becomes far more important than what you go about. A new occupational group—administrators and administrative-researchers—has grown up, who for a consideration will find out for all people how they can accomplish whatever it is they wish to accomplish. The aim is to turn out an organized professional group of public-opinion pollers, market-researchers, interviewers, and enumerators, who will aid men to solve the problems of the culture within the ambit of the mechanisms existent. It is highly noteworthy that the kind of problems dealt with by this school of thought is considered quite innocuous by the administratively and economically affluent. Can it be that these techniques are inherently bulwarks of a *status quo?* Or is it that addiction to this point of view is itself a social ideology, having as its concealed major premise that any society that will let social research be carried on in this fashion is worth defending as already being properly organized? Lundberg is much encouraged because physical scientists, large corporations, and other groups are becoming enamored of the uses of social science.[14] The more they look with favor upon the kind of problems this approach deals with, the more satisfied Lundberg is that all is going well with social science. It has not yet struck him that these groups are enraptured with his viewpoint and the sort of problems it can handle, precisely because it is so narrow that it asks only questions they want answered—or asked.

[14] *Can Science Save Us?*, p. 55.

Lundberg is very much concerned about the misguiding of "students into historical and philosophical blind alleys instead of providing them with the technical equipment upon which all modern science relies for verification of its theories." [15] These blind alleys can, however, never be as blind as the insistence that our society be construed as structured in such a way as to be capable of statistical manipulation by handling only such data as conform to the canons of such manipulation. One does not gain comprehension by torturing data into preconceived symbolism. That social research does honor to this approach is less a reflection upon it than upon the culture which allows it to flourish as the finest growth of scientific achievement. Our culture in the higher sociological learning has become a technicians' utopia, and thus comes to reflect the high technological achievements of our society despite the low estate of our ability to handle the human adjustments to this technology in terms of the democratic ideals professed.

4. Imputation of Motives.   On this basic problem, Lundberg tells us in one book that "human motives are anything but immune to scientific investigation." [16] In another book, he writes: "We no longer find it helpful to bother with the motives of tornadoes, bacteria, or even of the higher animals, except man. . . . In the social sciences it is felt we must go 'farther'. . . . It does not follow that we should engage in a futile search in nature for entities to correspond to these animistic words that happen to be part of our vocabulary. When the interaction of the observable components of a situation has been described scientifically, purpose and motive have also been described, and all scientific 'purposes' have been served." [17] According to Lundberg men impute motives to events according to their predilections. "The same event may be attributed to economic motives, the Oedipus complex, or the conjunction of the planets, according to whether one is an economic determinist, a Freudian, or an astrologer." [18]

For psychoanalysis Lundberg appears to have little use until its terminology can be translated into terms of behavioristic and operational psychology. [19] "To a scientist, the motives of a stone rolling downhill or of a boy murdering his father are simply the full set of circumstances resulting in either event. These conditions are equally

---

[15] *Foundations of Sociology*, p. 123.
[16] *Can Science Save Us?*, p. 19.
[17] *Foundations of Sociology*, p. 222.
[18] *Can Science Save Us?*, p. 19.
[19] *Foundations of Sociology*, p. 285.

subject to scientific investigation in both cases." [20] He accepts the "cures or satisfaction afforded such [psychoanalytic] patients and practitioners of psychoanalysis" and does not question them "any more than I question the therapeutic value of the Catholic confessional, Christian Science, or the Grotto at Lourdes." [21] He believes that psychoanalytic interpretation "consists apparently of injecting 'motives' and 'goals' into the situation. From my point of view, motives and goals can be inferred only from behavior." [22]

Lundberg's remarks on psychoanalysis are most revealing of his stand here. He is steadfast in his refusal to acknowledge that behavior takes place on an "unconscious" level and that overt behavior is not necessarily an index of what is happening to make the individual act the way he does. With such concepts as frustration, anxiety, rationalization, projection, ambivalence, and catharsis he will have no traffic, since he cannot subsume them under what he thinks are conventionally accepted scientific methods. He has decided what he is going to permit to be called scientific, and it does not seem to matter what we have learned about the depths of human motivation and the structure of personality after half a century of clinical investigation. Whatever does not fit his impoverished categories of "attraction-repulsion," "interaction," and "co-operation, competition, conflict," is banished from social science. By shrouding relationships in a new behavioristic jargon he is sure he will be able to attack problems which he does not permit himself to recognize. And Lundberg has on his side the fact that he has already made it clear that it will take years, perhaps centuries, before all of these behavioristic concepts will be sufficiently investigated in all their presumed richness and variety. Human emotions which go deep into the life-history of the individual are reckoned away by stimulus-response, attraction-repulsion, association-dissociation, and other superficial terminology. Sociology and social psychology become sciences by thinking away all problems and approaches which do not fit into the preconceived methodology, which has been uncritically borrowed from other sciences. Lundberg (and it must be remembered that he is here throughout considered typical of many others) appears ready to charge that psychoanalysis invented what it perhaps unfortunately calls the Oedipus-motive. He seems unwilling to admit that it was first forced

[20] *Can Science Save Us?*, p. 19.
[21] *Foundations of Sociology*, p. 284.
[22] *Op. cit.*, p. 286.

upon Freud by the incidence of cases. He appears to be implying that these fundamental principles of human motive-analysis were somehow guessed at or fabricated out of whole cloth. It may be acknowledged that psychoanalysis has been lax in making statistical computations of its cases without thereby invalidating its principles of interpretation of behavior.

5. **Values, Social Science, and the "Good Society."**   On values and valuation, Lundberg writes: "Since valuations or values are empirically observable patterns of behavior, they may be studied as such, by the same general techniques we use to study other behavior." [23] And "the only value judgments which any properly trained scientist makes about his data are judgments regarding their relevance to his problem, the weight to be assigned to each aspect, and the general interpretation to be made of the observed events." [24] Science, he says, cannot be identified with any social program, religious sect, or political party. He writes: "The favorite cliché is that 'science can flourish only in freedom.' It is a beautiful phrase, but unfortunately it flagrantly begs the question. The question is, under what conditions will the kind of freedom science needs be provided?" [25] And he concludes that "the services of *real* social scientists would be as indispensable to Fascists as to Communists and Democrats, just as are the services of physicists and physicians." [26] As for himself, he is a democrat, but he writes: "My attachment to democracy may be, in fact, of *scientific* significance chiefly as indicating my unfitness to live in a changing world." [27] He is so partial to democracy "with all its absurdities, that I would find some current alternatives quite intolerable, and that I may even find it worth-while to go to any length in defense of democracy of the type to which I am accustomed." [28]

"In short," Lundberg concludes, "we merely obey here the ancient injunction to render unto Caesar the things that belong to Caesar. The more general form of that adage is this: Render unto science the things that belong to science and to metaphysics the things that belong to metaphysics." [29] Finally, "it comes down, then, to this:

[23] *Can Science Save Us?*, p. 26.
[24] *Op. cit.*, pp. 28–9.
[25] *Op. cit.*, p. 45.
[26] *Op. cit.*, p. 48.
[27] *Op. cit.*, p. 46.
[28] *Op. cit.*, p. 46.
[29] *Op. cit.*, p. 97.

Shall we put our faith in science or in something else?"[30] And, "If we do not place our faith in social science, to what shall we look for social salvation?"[31]

Lundberg appears to be eminently correct in denying that the social scientist must inject his own values into a study of a social problem, whether in a primitive society or in modern American culture. And the scientist, as citizen, Lundberg claims, has no "pull" with the higher powers which gives him the authority to tell men what to do. But he moves from this position to one where he finds that there is no social environment in which social science flourishes more than in any other. Science may be the handmaiden of Communism, Fascism, democracy, technocracy, or what have you?

But science is also a social phenomenon, and it carries values with it, despite Lundberg's protestations: that is, the assurance of opportunity to discover the truth whatever it is, the assurance that men are permitted to lead the life of reason and science, that opportunity for individual development be open to all on the proven ground that intellectual ability is found spread throughout the population regardless of family, birth, race, creed, and color. For Lundberg, a *real* physician would have no compunction about being employed in Buchenwald and a *real* physicist would see nothing wrong with banning Jews from physical science. And a *real* social scientist would have no compunction about working for Herr Goebbels on how to conceal from the people the actual basis of political power behind a mélange of lies and appeals to brutality. And everybody knows that the Russians permit free and open investigation into the effect of governmental bureaucracy upon the freedom of learning and the structuring of personality.

If social scientists ask only the questions that those in power permit them to ask, then of course Lundberg is correct. But the problems which social science faces are not set, scientifically, by what those in power want answered or will permit to be answered. Does Lundberg think that it makes no difference to social scientists what type of society they live in, since the kind of questions they ask and answer can serve to make them *personae gratae* under any system? He writes: "I have emphasized that physical scientists are indispensable to any political regime. Social scientists might well work toward a corresponding status. Already some of them have achieved

[30] *Op. cit.*, p. 114.
[31] *Op. cit.*, p. 104.

it to a degree. Qualified social statisticians have not been and will not be disturbed greatly in their function by any political party as long as they confine themselves to their specialty. Their skill consists in the ability to draw relatively valid, unbiased, and demonstrable conclusions from societal data. *That* technique is the same, regardless of social objectives. No regime can get along without this technology." [32] But technology is a servant of the kind of hypotheses that are being prosecuted, and of course if no challenging hypotheses—calling into question the ability of social structures to achieve aims agreed upon—are set up, nobody would wish to disturb the sleeping dogs. This, to mix the metaphor, is a new, streamlined version of the ivory-tower.

It is revealing to note under what auspices Lundberg expects social science to advance. "Shall we put our faith in science or in something else? . . . This is the question which ultimately must be answered by everyone, but first by scientists themselves, by legislatures, by the Foundations, and by individuals who endow and finance research and education. If it is answered in the affirmative, then social research institutions will make their appearance, which will rank with Massachusetts and California Institutes of Technology, Mellon Institute, the research laboratories of Bell Telephone, General Electric and General Motors, not to mention some two thousand others. For some time the sponsors of these enterprises devoted to physical research have been wondering if the solution to social problems does not lie in the same direction. When they undertake to support social research as generously as they have supported physical research, they will obtain comparable results." [33]

In truth, Lundberg does not seem to understand science as an intellectual pursuit, and certainly not as the highest achievement of human reason, particularly since human reason turns out to be a form of adjustment, just like any other. His view of science suffers from compounded ambiguity. He does not understand that science can be considered in three frames of reference: (1) the accumulated knowledge we have of segments of the universe, natural, human, and social; (2) the only method of arriving at true propositions; and (3) a collective enterprise entered upon by groups of individuals. As the third it carries no ethics with it for Lundberg. But surely he cannot fail to admit that science is the sworn enemy of human prejudice,

[32] *Op. cit.*, p. 48.
[33] *Op. cit.*, pp. 114–5.

intolerance, superstition, and all other methods alternative to the discovery of truth. Science as a sociological phenomenon is a morality; as well as being a method of inquiry as a logical and methodological phenomenon, and a statement of our accumulated knowledge as an epistemological phenomenon.

Lundberg's approach gives all groups in society the right to claim scientific sanction for their behavior in the name of the instrumentality of science. Anybody can be shown how to achieve anything; and instead of a code of ethics strictly derivative from the practice of the calling of a scientist, we have a lavishly elaborated anarchy of tastes and viewpoints all capable of operating with the findings of science even if they violate all the canons of its ethics. This serves as a very handy apologia for all kinds of useless research being done today all over the country, and it places the sociologist on such a sanctimonious, impersonal level that his every conclusion is above suspicion of being prejudiced or ill-intentioned. The sociologist appears as a disinterested spectator from Mars, able to point out to men their foibles and follies, himself above the strife and ready to serve all confused human beings of whatever race, creed, and previous and present condition of servitude—or political belief.

Lundberg fails to appreciate what scientific endeavors do to men. For men to accept scientific solutions to problems posed by the social sciences requires that men have learned to set store by rationality, that "appeals to reason" will be heeded. In turn, of course, it means that society be so structured that men of science can investigate social problems without fear of persecution, and that there be some power-instrumentality whereby they may work for the application of such solutions. But this involves the social scientist in (1) a set of values as to what kind of society this is; and (2) the necessity for defending that society as the good society. Such a society is what we mean by democracy. Democracy is a structuring of society so as to achieve and apply, as far as possible, the rational findings of social science to the problems posed to men. It is a process of achieving a rational society, and the instrument of achievement is science. Wherever the findings of science are not applied, democracy is retarded. To the degree that men can nevertheless urge such solution, to that degree democracy is still possible.

Highly questionable is Lundberg's view that social science is in a very undeveloped state. It is, however, most amazing how much we know about the structure and functioning of social relationships in different cultures, including our own. What is more amazing is how little we do with our knowledge. It is puzzling that he, at this stage of scientific knowledge, should contend that the reason the findings of social science are not listened to is that we know so little scientifically about social problems. The findings of social science are not heeded because society is not rationally structured. That society is not rationally structured is demonstrated when social scientists think that the way to advance social science is to surrender its birthright as the analyst and critic of social structures and to gather unto themselves little jobs for corporations, fund-raising associations, magazines interested in market-research, and other oddments of American culture. This hired-man status of the social scientist itself reflects the non-rational values of our culture.

Reason involves an acceptance of those values inherent in science as a social calling—of tolerance, equality of opportunity, freedom of discussion and press and assembly, and of cooperation. The divorce of science and values is a divorce of science as the method of arriving at, and as a corpus of, valid propositions, and science as an activity which involves a structuring of social relationships and an interdependence of function in a joint, collective undertaking. In the former, science is seen as a study of objects; in the latter, it is seen as the unity of subject and object. To assume that scientific self-consciousness (man's consciousness of himself as rational or capable of rationality in spheres where he has not yet reached valid propositions) and science as a body of knowledge and a method of inquiry are bifurcated is to fall foul of the pluralistic fallacy that since man participates in our society in many groups therefore he himself is not a unity. It is the divorce of reason from its highest manifestation. It is bad enough when natural scientists come to believe that there is no necessary connection between their vocations and their values; but here comes a social scientist to announce to the natural scientists that they are right in assuming this bifurcation, and that man lives many lives in a pluralistic society. This invitation to irrationality is of course very seductive since it requires that reason not be pushed too far.

It is altogether likely that the position represented by Lundberg will result not in the furthering of social science, but in revealing to men how muddled and confused, how deceptive and laden with false promises, and how far removed from their basic problems is this approach which has captured large segments of American social science by technical *coup d'état* and by selling its wares to all comers. It is to be hoped that being all things to all men is only a temporary avocation of social science in America.

* The social auspices under which scientific endeavors operate are themselves representative of a prevalent morality. Science is organized through that social process that accords with conventional morality. Truth is being discovered to enhance the acquisitive aggregations which subsidize it. There is a taint of the promiscuous and mischievous about an investigation which has not taken place under proper supervision.

The ideology which serves to explain, defend, and buttress this conception of the instrumentality of science is now fairly complete, with its acceptance by the social sciences. Governments are being peopled with scientists, particularly social scientists, who have no part in what is called "policy." This "policy" is set on what are called the "highest levels" which means by politicians who represent interest-groups. The technicians in their turn have as their bounden duty the discovery of ways and means of making policy work. Some government bureaus even refer to themselves as "figure factories," organizations to tabulate statistics for policy-makers.

Against such preponderance of social force, science learns its place. The smirking of scientists, particularly social scientists, at the distortion of their findings in behalf of "policy" is a defense-mechanism, which, if broken through, would reveal the resentment they feel at their own surrender of rational morality to whatever powers that be. Or else allegiance to truth is viewed as an occupational luxury which is out of place in a practical world.

* These concluding paragraphs reprinted by permission of the author and of the editor from George Simpson, "The Scientist—Technician or Moralist?," *Philosophy of Science,* XVII (1950), 95–108; pp. 98–99 reprinted.

50 SOCIAL PLANNING AND SOCIAL ORGANIZATION *

BY SVEND RIEMER (1905–   )
UNIVERSITY OF WISCONSIN

SOCIAL planning today permeates the life of the country. This is not a war phenomenon only. The roots of social planning, as a matter of fact, reach far back into the very beginnings of the industrialization process.[1] To be sure, social order is based today primarily upon a system of free competition and the market as an organizing principle; but we are confronted—to say the least—with a maze of "unorthodox" procedures in the economic and the social field. As a rule, all elements of social planning are looked upon as a series of temporary adjustments to abnormal disturbances, such as war or economic depression. These measures, however, have gained sufficient prominence to warrant a systematic analysis.[2]

Unfortunately, the discussion of social planning has proceeded under a handicap. It has been customary to identify social planning with either "scientific prediction"[3] or "bureaucratic" procedures.[4] The result has been—at best—an unnecessary duplication of terminology and—at worst—an ideologically tinted confusion of issues.

Social planning is characterized by three criteria. These criteria are substantially related to each other, but it seems difficult, at present,

---

* Reprinted by permission of the author and of the editor from *The American Journal of Sociology*, LII (1946–47), 508–516.

[1] "To plan or not to plan is no real issue. Planning even of economic affairs has existed at all levels of our national life, both public and private, since the beginning of our history" (Charles E. Merriam, "The Possibilities of Planning," *American Journal of Sociology*, XLIX [March, 1944], 397).

[2] A somewhat different attempt to define social planning is presented by Arthur Lewis Wood in "The Structure of Social Planning," *Social Forces*, XXII (May, 1944), 308 ff. The author relates the problems of planning to the traditional means-ends discussions and elaborates on problems of control. He offers a comprehensive bibliography on the theoretical discussion of social planning.

[3] Leonard Doob, *Plans of Men* (New Haven: Yale University Press, 1944); Talcott Parsons, *The Structure of Social Action* (New York and London: McGraw-Hill Book Co., 1937), particularly, chap. ii, "The Unit of Action Systems," pp. 43–51; Pitirim A. Sorokin, "Is Accurate Social Planning Possible?" *American Sociological Review*, I (February, 1936), 12–25.

[4] Friedrich A. Hayek, *The Road to Serfdom* (Chicago: University of Chicago Press, 1944).

to subsume them under one general principle. They constitute three different aspects of one and the same syndrome: (1) Social planning is concerned with the concrete detail of its subject matter. (2) Social planning co-ordinates diversified technical skills and professional training. (3) Social planning calls for the proclamation and specification of values.[5]

1. That social planning is concerned with the concrete detail of its objective may not seem, at first glance, to deserve any special attention. All science is preoccupied even with the minor details in its field of observation. But every particular scientific approach is limited, also, by the frame of reference to which it is committed. All details may be of relevance, but some of them are relevant simply as data of which cognizance must be taken, while others enter into that system of functional relationships which a given frame of reference tries to investigate. Scientific endeavors directed at the mastery of man's environment are limited in that they focus attention upon particular sets of cause and effect relationships. Economic or political or technological conditions are elucidated one by one. Predictions are made with only isolated factors in mind. The penetration of the future is limited to one particular aspect only.

In social planning the emphasis is on the projection of a concrete master-plan into the future. To be sure, the penetration of the full detail of all causal cross-relations involved in the planning process will appear as a task ad infinitum. In any planning report on housing, on neighborhood development, or on the exploitation of the natural and human resources of an area, it will never be possible to obtain complete photographic fidelity. Yet the challenge is ever present to extend the investigation into further angles of the situation at hand. The planning task is never fulfilled. The conclusions are never as final as those obtained in scientific investigations which set their own limitations in the definition of their problems. There is no distinction in planning between relevant and irrelevant facts; there is only a distinction between conditions of first, second, and third im-

[5] Our theoretical statement coincides surprisingly well with the following discussion of "three distinct phases" in practical planning activities: "The process of planning involves three distinct phases. The first task of state planning is to obtain an estimate of the situation and the tendencies. . . . The second phase of planning, which must proceed simultaneously with the third, is the formulation of a plan for dealing with the problem. . . . Finally, the process of State planning involves the correlation of plans of individual State departments" (*The Future State Planning* [a report to the Advisory Committee by the State Planning Review Group, National Resources Committee, Washington, D. C., 1938], p. 11).

portance; a distinction which unavoidably implies value judgments.[6]

2. Social planning is predicated upon the co-ordination of technical skills and professional training. The need for such co-operation follows from the above definition of the planning task. No isolated problem is abstracted in social planning to be dealt with successfully by either architect or engineer, land economist or sociologist. Ideally, all skills have to be invested, all viewpoints have to be brought to bear upon the masterplan that is projected into the future.

To be sure, city plans have been laid out with only the interests of the architect in mind. Resettlement programs have been carried through under the guidance of the agricultural economist only. As our definition would have it, such measures fall short of the challenge offered in social planning. They represent applied science and do not accept social planning as a comprehensive principle of social organization.

Not only are all scientific disciplines and fields of technological knowledge challenged to make their unique contribution to any planning task. Practical needs will frequently emphasize or stimulate the creation of new borderline sciences. In the organization of planning projects the new function of the "co-ordinator" originates to meet the need for arbitration and the well-balanced mobilization of different scientific contributions.[7]

3. The most definite break with traditions in the field of social organization and scientific inquiry is indicated by the third criterion. Planning problems do not find their solution by the assignment of efficient means to the obtainment of a set goal. Upon the planning expert rests the responsibility of defining a system of values worth

[6] The emphasis upon "social significance" in the process of problem selection has been stressed by various authors such as Gunnar Myrdal, Robert Lynd, and Karl Mannheim. See Karl Mannheim's *Diagnosis of Our Time* (New York: Oxford University Press, 1944), p. 73. "It was exactly this kind of neutralization which brought about a mental climate which from the very outset discouraged every attempt to make a distinction between essential and non-essential issues. The academic mind was proud of paying the greatest possible attention to trifles and ridiculing those who wanted first things to come first." For a different opinion see the writings of George Lundberg, e.g.: "The Growth of Scientific Method," *American Journal of Sociology*, L (May, 1945), 502–13.

[7] For a good discussion of the sociologist's part in a co-operative planning project see Carl C. Taylor, "The Sociologist's Part in Planning the Columbia Basin," *American Sociological Review*, II (June, 1946), 323.

Prerequisites for efficient team work with other professionals in the social sciences were stated in the discussion of the above-mentioned paper by Marion Clawson, Bureau of Agricultural Economics, *ibid.*, p. 332.

striving for. This necessity is frequently obscured by the delegation of power to the social planner in terms of truisms. He is called upon to plan for the "welfare of the community," but it is left to him to specify such general statements in terms of tangible objectives that can serve as a guide for concerted community action.[8]

It has been noted by various authors that the means-ends discussion receives an unusual twist in the consideration of planning problems.[9] The attempt has been made—by Robert Lynd, for example—to settle the matter by proclaiming once and for all a set of social values that are sufficiently general to be accepted by everybody.[10] Unfortunately, this miracle can never be performed without the introduction of a considerable amount of word-magic. Contradictory values, such as the desire for the "realization of personal powers" and the craving for "physical and psychological security," stand side by side as goals to be obtained by a well-guided process of social planning. Political opinions will not clash on this level of abstraction. They will clash, however, when it comes to a specification of these values, when their relative importance will be weighed and when various instrumentalities are recommended for the *fulfilment of these basic desires*.[11]

We run into a somewhat different confusion of issues wherever the controversy of "planning versus fredom" raises its ugly head.

---

[8] Note the unavoidable vagueness in the formulation of comprehensive planning goals by the National Resources Planning Board:

"I. The fullest possible development of the human personality, in relation to the common good, in a framework of freedoms and rights, of justice, liberty, equality, and the consent of the governed.

"II. The fullest possible development of the productive potential of all of our resources, material and human, with full employment, continuity of income, equal access to minimum security and living standards, and a balance between economic stability and social adventure.

"III. An effective jural order of the world outlawing violence and imperialism, old or new fashioned, in international relations; and permitting and energizing the fullest development of resources and rights everywhere. . . ."

It is the official purpose of the T.V.A. to "foster an orderly and proper physical, economic, and social development of the area." Although there are further specifications about the functions of this government corporation, the planning officials are operating within a wide framework of responsibilities and are challenged to use their initiative.

[9] *Cf.* Gunnar Myrdal, *An American Dilemma* (New York: Harper & Bros., 1944), II, App. II, "A Methodological Note on Facts and Valuations in Social Science."

[10] *Cf.* Robert Lynd, *Knowledge for What?* (Princeton: Princeton University Press, 1939).

[11] The notion that the formulation of values and the specification of values should be looked upon as part of the planning process itself seems to be supported by the well-recognized need to "keep planning flexible" and not firmly attached to pre-

The all-out opponents of social planning usually gain their point by a proper definition of the planning process which entails restriction and the usurpation of dictatorial powers by an uncontrolled bureaucracy.[12] The promoters of social planning, on the other hand, do not refrain either from ideological hypostatizations. Aware of the need for a definition of planning ends and purposes, they gain their point by phrasing the general planning objectives in such a manner as to take the wind out of the sails of their opponents. They advocate "planning for freedom," a scarcely objectionable but not very articulate undertaking.[13]

Under the circumstances, we may do well to avoid the futile attempt of committing ourselves, once and for all, to a series of planning objectives of general validity. It seems called for, rather, to make the proclamation of ends and their specification in terms of tangible objectives and the choice of adequate social and technological instrumentalities part of the planning process itself. This does not do in-

---

established goals. *Cf.*, e.g., Neal C. Gross, "A Post Mortem on County Planning," *Journal of Farm Economics*, XXV (August, 1943), 645. The author introduces a distinction between "planning" and "design." Design is rigid while planning has to remain flexible.

[12] The problem involved in the usurpation of power by a bureaucratic system that becomes an end in itself was discussed by Reinhard Bendix, "Bureaucracy and the Problem of Power," *Public Administration Review,* summer, 1945, pp. 194–209.

[13] *Cf.* Mannheim, *op. cit.*, p. 7: "We shall have to make a distinction between planning for uniformity and planning for freedom and variety. In both cases coordination plays a great role, coordination of the means of social techniques such as education, propaganda, administration, etc.; but there is a difference between coordination in the spirit of monotony and coordination in the spirit of variety." And p. 20: "But there must be something, a third way, between totalitarian regimentation, on the one hand, and the complete disintegration of the value system at the stage of laisser-faire on the other, what I call the democratic pattern of planning for freedom. It consists essentially in the reverse of a dictatorial imposition of external controls. Its method is either to find new ways to free the genuine and spontaneous social controls from the disintegrating effects of mass society, or else to invent new techniques which perform the function of democratic self-regulation on a higher plane of awareness and purposeful organization."

Cf. also Merriam, *op. cit.*, p. 404: "The fear that planning will interfere with the development of free industrial society is groundless. The very purpose of planning is to release human abilities, to broaden the field of opportunity, and to enlarge human liberty. We plan primarily for freedom; the ways and means and instruments are secondary to the main purpose. The right kind of planning—democratic planning, is a guaranty of liberty and the only real assurance in our times that men can be free to make a wide range of choices."

For a discussion of the complicated relationship between freedom and planning see Hans Speier, "Freedom and Social Planning," *American Journal of Sociology,* XLII (January, 1937), 463–83. See also Barbara Wootton's reply to Hayek, *Freedom under Planning* (Chapel Hill, N. C.: University of North Carolina Press, 1945).

justice to those phenomena with which we are concerned. The objectives of planning are seldom strictly defined as the process gets under way. Thereby, as a matter of fact, social planning is distinguished from other processes of bureaucratic execution.

If the determination of values is made part of the planning process itself, it will be impossible for the planning promoter to ask for the blessings of the community with only his ulterior motives and his professional integrity in mind. We are challenged to continuous criticism and to constructive participation if we know that in social planning the specified ends as well as the means should be the object of consideration. There is a guaranty in this conception of social planning that we shall remain aware of the necessity of allocating initiative and of arbitrating policies in addition to the use of expert skills and scientific discoveries.

Our definition of social planning may be as good as any other, but it is not necessarily better unless it does focus our attention on some essential features in the general trend of change in our social order. Let us examine, first, how our definition fits into the discussion of basic economic institutions.

Modern economic enterprise originates at the beginning of the Industrial Revolution as a new principle of social organization. Within the market economy of the nineteenth century the speculative adjustment to price and cost constellations determined economic success as well as prestige, impoverishment as well as the loss of social status both of individuals and of whole social strata of an extremely mobile society. In the very core of this institution, however, we are confronted with a paradox that was sooner or later to crush its limitations.[14]

Private economic enterprise is based on the assumption of free competition and automatic adjustment to a given system of prices, while—at the same time—a break with these basic assumptions is economically rewarded. Monopolistic operations are of the same date as the plea for free economic competition. The monopoly, though, is only the most blatant self-contradiction of our market economy. From early days the calculations of the entrepreneur penetrated beyond the fringes of his own institution and the abstract price system.

---

[14] The paradoxical character of the price-and-profit system was discussed by Henry Pratt Fairchild in "Free Enterprise and Full Employment," *American Sociological Review*, XI (June, 1946), 271 ff. See also earlier publications by the same author.

He "planned" his productive activities—we may say—into the dynamic changes of supply-and-demand constellations. He built his speculations into the future. Contrary to the assumptions of orthodox economic theory, the dimension of time enters into the picture. We are confronted with a speculative interaction of entrepreneurs who orientate themselves at the anticipation of future trends of production and consumers' demand.

Thus, a considerable amount of actual planning has been part of our economic system since the first days of the Industrial Revolution. This was true, however, in a limited sense of the word only. *It was planning for profit.* The concrete ends of economic pursuit were left outside of consideration, and behavior was guided by the abstract mechanism of the price system. In this "adjustive" market economy the full possibilities of social planning could never be realized.

In spite of close statistical familiarity with the periodic business cycles of the nineteenth century they have never been mastered in practice to the extent of a reliable prediction of the economic crisis. The many independent agents remained ensnared in a vicious problem of prediction that approaches the famous riddle of Achilles and the turtle. When, on the basis of previous experience, the individual entrepreneurs foresaw the approaching crisis and acted accordingly, their very foresight represented in itself a change in the prevailing institutional conditions. With observer and agent identical, prediction changed the facts upon which it was founded and, thus, always limped a step behind the economic reality of the day. This type of economic planning was bound to defeat its own ends.

Later economic theory—pushing forward into the realm of a "dynamic equilibrium"—is concerned with the logical organization of a maze of producers' and consumers' propensities. The effects of alternate reactions to innumerable possible changes in the supply situation, in the price level, etc., are followed through at the hand of more or less intricate equations which are all reducible to one assumption based upon the institution of market exchange, namely, that price times quantity of one commodity will equal price times quantity of any other commodity against which it is exchanged on the market. "Economic planning," here, consists of more and more refined calculations of consumer and producer relations to the market situation and attempts to manipulate these reactions from central key positions.

This is obviously not social planning in terms of the above-mentioned criteria. Prediction proceeds on a high level of abstraction. The production process is influenced not by detailed corrections in the supply-and-demand situation of specific goods but in a general manner through manipulations of the price level. The effects of such general stimulation are not controlled in their quantitative extent. Planning is deficient inasmuch as it is not concerned with the qualitative aspect of functionally interrelated goods and services. The institutional mechanism available for the control of the productive process is not adequate to cope with the problem of disproportionate industrial expansion.

This inadequate perspective upon the national production process is reflected in the wage dispute between the two large interest groups in our economic system. On a high level of abstraction both parties arrive at contradictory recommendations for economic policies. These theoretical justifications for either wage increase or reduction are unqualified and absolute. They cannot be appeased or compromised.

Wages are viewed as a cost factor, on the one hand, and as purchasing power, on the other. Their negative influence upon the profit incentive is emphasized by one group, their stimulating influence upon the market for consumer goods by the other. Who is right? The answer depends upon a detailed quantitative analysis. Both ways of reasoning contain an element of truth. A valid judgment of the situation, however, cannot be offered on this level of abstraction. The two effects are likely to counteract each other. The exact consequences can be predicted only on the basis of statistical analysis of any concrete situation. The conclusion can never be absolute but must be relative to specific circumstances and limited in the extent of recommended measures.

The violent political, social, and economic upheavals of recent decades in the non-democratic countries have thrown an interesting light upon the above-mentioned issue. Both Russia and Germany restricted the standard of living and diverted productive capacity that might have been available for immediate consumption toward armaments and—in Russia—toward an industrialization process of unprecedented scope. The problem of investment versus immediate consumption has been made an issue of conscious planning with the industrial, economic, and political future of the nation in mind. In the democratic countries the outcome has been more or less left to the push and pull of forces which cater to the immediate advantages of the two pressure groups involved.

In an era of widening national ambitions and power politics, in the era of the atomic bomb during which bids may well be made for world supremacy, such procedures seem rather obsolete. They were at the bottom of the great democracies' failure to stem at an early date the tide of political expansion by those countries where the dictator had his hand at the switchboard of large-scale industrial policies. In the future we may want to institute procedures which throw these basic issues open to democratic arbitration and conscious direction.

With our approach to the problem of planning, then, we have gained insight into the essentials of a thoroughgoing process of economic reorganization. We observe the gradual abandonment of an institutional setup in which small units were co-ordinated on the basis of abstract and automatic market orientation, in which economics appear as a specialized sphere of activities removed from technology and other instrumentalities in the productive process, and, furthermore, in which the consideration of values and of the final goals of production is beyond the perspective of any participant in the economic life of the community. Our criteria of social planning furnish a tentative conceptualization of the general trend of change in our economic institutions.

There are other significant and timely problems in the social sciences which become visible and amenable to an integrated approach by the use of our definition of social planning. Sociological or socio-psychological interpretations of our present social order tend to make use of two stereotypes, arranged in the dichotomy of the modern "entrepreneur," on the one hand, and the "bureaucrat," on the other. The two types are placed in juxtaposition: the entrepreneur being endowed with the qualities of inventiveness, initiative, and a speculative grasp into the future; the bureaucrat, best exemplified in the civil-service employee, characterized by reliability and careful precision in the execution of performances according to administrative rules or office regulations. Max Weber's classic formulations of the problem are sufficiently well known not to need further elaboration.[15]

It will seem, however, that recent changes in our social institutions

[15] Now available in translation: H. H. Gerth and C. Wright Mills, *From Max Weber* (New York: Oxford University Press, 1946), pp. 77–159, and 196–245. See also Robert K. Merton, "Bureaucratic Structure and Personality," *Social Forces*, XVIII (May, 1940), 560 ff.

have placed a penetrating discussion of their implications beyond the reach of this traditional pair of concepts. Bureaucracy has moved into the large, modern, economic enterprise, and an increasing degree of responsibility for initiative is delegated to various branches of executive government. There arises, on the scene of administrative action, the somewhat enigmatic figure of the government "expert" who makes contributions on the basis of his skills or his professional proficiency as either engineer or architect, city-planner or economist, statistician or sociologist. In many instances the function of the expert is fairly well covered by the stereotype of the "bureaucrat" who applies specific techniques to the obtainment of well-defined ends. With the extension of administrative action, however, in the fields of welfare and rehabilitation, of city-planning and rural conservation, etc., the function of the "expert" is by no means exhausted in the execution of routine jobs. He is charged to assume initiative. It is his task to propose new measures to the local or federal legislatures. He experiments with various methods and undertakes surveys in order to be able to define more specifically the needs of the community.

Nor does the modern expert confine himself to a clearly staked-out field of professional competency.[16] In the pursuit of his duties he finds it necessary to overstep the border lines of his discipline. The very nature of his task will demand the co-operation with experts of different competency. His achievements will be measured, together with those of other experts, in the rather complex realm of general community welfare. His achievements, thus, will preclude precise measurement because of the multitude of cause-and-effect relationships that are entangled in the process of social planning.

Undoubtedly, the function of the "expert" needs further investigation and theoretical clarification. It might be possible to labor in this field of analysis with the traditional dichotomy of "entrepreneur" and "bureaucrat." As ideal types, these two concepts are not required to reflect reality as is but may be used in its interpretation, indicating the degree to which the characteristics of either are present in various positions of government or economic enterprise. There occurs, how-

[16] With regard to the relationship between academic social science and social planning cf. Robert K. Merton, "The Role of the Intellectual in Public Bureaucracy," Social Forces, XXIII (May, 1945), 405 ff.; Florian Znaniecki, The Social Role of the Man of Knowledge (New York: Columbia University Press, 1940); Lynd, op. cit.; Myrdal, op. cit., App. II, 1035–65; Reinhard Bendix, "Social Science and Social Action in Historical Perspective," Ethics, LVI (April, 1946), 208 ff.

ever, in the history of all sciences, the moment at which a basic theoretical framework needs so much patching-up by various supplementary theories and conceptual constructions to deal with the problems of the day that a more fundamental reconsideration of the underlying theoretical approach may be called for. Our attention is called to the function of social planning and the need for its conceptualization.

The political scientist, today, is well aware that the theory of checks and balances or the classical conception of the separation of powers require many qualifications and additional comment if applied to contemporary government. Judiciary, legislature, and executive are by no means so clearly segregated as intended by a constitution that dates back to the early days of industrialization.

The interpretation of the Constitution itself by the Supreme Court is clearly recognized as being more than exegesis of inherent intentions. There is sufficient incongruity between an era that did not know of large holding companies or organized labor and our present problems to place an actually policy-making responsibility in the hands of the Supreme Court. Needless to say, this was not contemplated in its original conception.

The legislator, on the other hand, is restricted in his free personal initiative by party loyalties, by the consideration of pressure groups, by the contemplation of letters received from his constituency, and by the observation of the results from recent opinion polls. Committee work forces the legislator to tasks of research, interviewing, statistical analysis, and social investigation that require expert competency in addition to leadership abilities in the formation of political opinions. Bureaucratic and expert functions are strangely intermingled. The task of supplying legislative initiative is far too complex to be conceived in a clear-cut separation from executive operations.

Another incisive change in our political traditions stems from the growing need for the assumption of initiative on the part of executive government. There is a wide range of opinions on this issue. There are those who hold that even the modern planning expert is functioning within a given order, while the legislature determines direction and extent of actual building or engineering activities, and there are those who curse about "red tape" and whisper about a managerial revolution.

There can be no doubt that an increasing number of government executives are burdened by far-flung responsibilities that are by no means circumscribed in detail. The executive finds himself frequently in the position of the professional city-manager who is asked—with the general welfare of the community in mind—to carry to the citizenry ideas about organizational and technical improvements and, furthermore, to challenge them to concerted action in new fields of endeavor where lack of planning and co-operation incurs waste of human and natural resources or causes phenomena of social disorganization.

This type of "initiative" differs from the function originally assigned to the government executive. The transition is gradual enough, to be sure, to allow for various interpretations. The modern expert and planning official acts on the basis of delegated authority. But the authority rendered often leaves a great amount of freedom to specify the ways and means by which to achieve "community welfare" and to give him the chance to proceed at his own discretion between reappointment periods. The problem arises how to rearrange the checks and balances of democratic government within an institutional setting that differs widely from the clear functional division of authority in the past. The ties between the expert and the people have to be reconsidered on a new basis.[17]

The increasing interest in opinion polls in recent years is not a chance occurrence. There is growing need for instruments that permit the expert to unburden himself of some of his responsibility and to reassure him of contact with the people for whom—in the last analysis—he is planning the layout of the urban fringe and for whom he is planning family homes and neighborhoods and highways and park developments.[18] To what extent such measures will become the standing equipment of the government expert in the future is hard to predict. Polling institutions, as we know, are already established in various branches of military and civilian government.[19] Undoubt-

---

[17] The need for motivation in favor of planning is stressed by Robert S. Lynd in "The Implications of Economic Planning for Sociology," *American Sociological Review*, IX (February, 1944), 14–20.

[18] The need of agreement between the planning expert and the population for which the plans are made is stressed by Bushrod W. Allin in "Is Planning Compatible with Democracy?" in the *American Journal of Sociology*, LVII (January, 1937), 510 ff. His illustrations are taken from the work of the Agricultural Adjustment Administration.

[19] For the use of public-opinion research in connection with practical planning purposes cf. *Public Opinion on the City's Budget Planning* (Kansas City, Mo.: Civic Research Institute, 1943). The report is prepared by Don Cahalan, staff opinion research specialist. From the Introduction: "The Institute feels that the *whole* people

edly, the function of initiative and social as well as political leadership will have to be allocated with greater care than heretofore. If the determination of values and their specification is part and parcel of all planning activities, then the theory of the "separation of powers" is, indeed, ready for overhauling and adaptation to modern conditions.

How are we going to plan for the planner? How are we going to adapt our university education to the training of experts able to cope with the exigencies of social and economic planning activities? [20] The crisis of our academic institutions is, as far as I can see, closely related to new demands that arise in an era of planning.

It has been customary to view the crisis of modern university education as the result of an excess of specialization. Various compromises are weighed today between the contradictory needs for professional training and for general intellectual orientation.[21] It seems more adequate, however, to place the controversy at a somewhat different angle.

We are faced today by two principles of departmental organization in our universities, one that is concerned with the separation of different disciplines of thought following the tradition of scientific problem isolation, the other concerned with different fields of observation and fields of practical activities in which the co-operation of different disciplines of thought may be called for. We are in the midst of many makeshift adjustments to either point of view. There are departments of economics and sociology and political science, but there are also departments of education and journalism and housing and social planning, all staffed with sociologists and economists and political scientists in somewhat embarrassing duplication.

The crisis, thus, is placed right in the midst of the field of profes-

---

should take more voice in the decisions—it believes that it is in the public interest to draw the people and the city government together in a discussion of war-time problems. For this reason the Institute conducted a city-wide opinion survey to 'bring the mountain to Mohamet': the people of Kansas City to their government."

[20] *Cf.* John M. Gaus, "Planning for the Education of Planners," *Journal of Land and Public Utility Economics,* XXI, 307 ff. The article is accompanied by reports on planning curriculums at California, Harvard, Massachusetts Institute of Technology, McGill, North Carolina, Syracuse, and the University of Wisconsin. See also Karl Mannheim, *Man and Society in a Time of Transition* (New York: Harcourt, Brace & Co., 1940), p. 74, and Wootton, *op. cit.,* pp. 158 ff.

[21] The importance of "general education" was stressed in the well-known report of the Harvard Committee. See *General Education in a Free Society* (Cambridge: Harvard University Press, 1945).

sional training as such. The days are gone when the wearer of the old school tie took a degree in classics at Oxford and proceeded to a business position in downtown London. The problem is how adequately to equip the student for performances which—by the very nature of our social organization—will run across the border lines of various scientific disciplines of thought. Perhaps the future will discriminate between integrated professional training, on the one hand, and the need for specialized scientific research, on the other. Perhaps we are making it unnecessarily hard for the student today by leaving it to him to pick a good combination salad from our course offerings and permitting him to struggle with the rather difficult task of integrating stray information into the working tools that will make him useful to the community and furnish him with an income.

It is the challenge of social planning, again, that invites us to consider the need for interdisciplinary co-operation. It is the responsibility involved in social planning, furthermore, that forces us to give more attention to the underlying assumptions and the traditionally accepted values upon which, in the various social sciences, we tacitly agree, to which we cling with a certain amount of inertia, and upon which we build our argument and our conclusions.